McGraw Hill create

D1297984

Course Introduction to Religion

Course Number **REL 103**

Religious Readings

Michael Mckenzie

Keuka College

The McGraw-Hill Companies

McGraw Hill create

http://create.mcgraw-hill.com

ISBN-10: 1121774113 ISBN-13: 9781121774117

Contents

Afterlife

H: 17-18
B: 82-83, 111-112
Africa: 129-132, 133-134
J: 207-208
C: 260-262

Credits

Religions of the East -- Hinduism

Hinduism

INTRODUCTION

Contemporary Hindus commonly refer to their religion as "universal truth" *(sanātana-dharma),* implying that it is a meta-tradition that is able to embrace the truths of all other systems of thought while transcending them through its expansive capacity to embrace truth in multiple manifestations. Hinduism is the dominant religious tradition of the Indian subcontinent, and currently over 700 million people consider themselves Hindus.

Hinduism is, however, a difficult tradition to define. Its dominant feature is diversity, and its adherents are not required to accept any doctrine or set of doctrines, to perform any particular practices, or to accept any text or system as uniquely authoritative. Many Hindus, for example, are monotheists and believe that there is only one God, despite the proliferation of gods in Hinduism. They assert that God has many manifestations and that God may appear differently to different people and different cultures.

Other Hindus are polytheists who believe that the various gods they worship are distinct entities, while pantheistic Hindus perceive the divine in the world around them, as a principle that manifests in natural phenomena, particular places, flora and fauna, or other humans. Some Hindus consider themselves to be agnostic, contending that God is in principle unknown and unknowable. Other Hindus are atheists who do not believe in the existence of any gods; this position does not lead to their excommunication by their fellow Hindus. Even more confusing, in daily practice it is common to see one person or community sequentially manifesting combinations of these attitudes in different circumstances.

Hinduism has a plethora of doctrines and systems, but no collection of tenets constitutes a universally binding Hindu creed, nor is there any core belief that is so fundamental that it would be accepted by all Hindus. Hinduism has produced a vast collection of sacred texts, but no one text has the authority of the Christian Bible, the Jewish Torah, or the Muslim Qur'an. Perhaps the most widely revered sacred texts are the Vedas ("Wisdom Texts"), most of which were written over 2,000 years ago. But despite their generally accepted authoritativeness, few Hindus today are even able to read them, and the *brahmins* (priests) whose sacred task is to memorize and recite them generally are unable to explain what they mean.

In searching for a way to define the boundaries of Hinduism, the term *Hindu* may provide some help. It was originally coined by Persians who used it to refer to the people they encountered in northern India. Thus, the term *Hindu* referred to the inhabitants of a geographical area, and in later centuries it was adopted by people of India who identified themselves with the dominant religious tradition of the subcontinent.

Contemporary Hinduism is still delimited more by geography than by belief or practice: A Hindu is someone who lives on the Indian subcontinent or is descended from people of the region, who considers himself or herself a Hindu, and who is accepted as such by other Hindus. There are no distinctive doctrines whose acceptance would serve as a litmus test of orthodoxy, no ecclesiastical authority that is able to declare some to be Hindus in good standing or label others heretics, and no ceremony whose performance would serve as a definitive rite of passage into the tradition. There is no founder of the tradition, and no dominant system of theology or single moral code.

Contemporary Hinduism embraces groups whose respective faiths and practices have virtually nothing in common with one another. This is not to say, however, that Hinduism lacks distinctive doctrines, practices, or scriptures; in fact, the opposite is the case. Hinduism has developed a plethora of philosophical schools, rituals, and sacred texts, and its adherents commonly assert a belief in a shared heritage, historical continuity, and family relationships among the multiple manifestations of their tradition. The selections given below represent only a small sampling of the vast corpus of Hindu religious literature. In addition, it should be noted that this literature represents only a tiny part of the Hindu tradition and primarily reflects the views and practices of a small intellectual elite. The vast majority of Hindus have been—and continue to be—primarily illiterate agricultural workers with little if any knowledge of the sacred scriptures. Their practices generally are derived from local cults and beliefs that may have little in common with the religion and philosophy of the authors of the scriptures. Furthermore, these texts do not form a coherent system but instead are as diverse as Hinduism itself. They were written over the course of millennia and reflect shifting paradigms and divergent political, religious, and social agendas, geographical differences, and varying ideas about how people should worship, think, live, and interact.

History of Hinduism and Hindu Scriptures

Hinduism can be compared to a complex symphony in which new themes are introduced as the piece develops, while old ones continue to be woven into its texture. Nothing is ever truly lost, and elements of the distant past may return to prominence at unexpected times, though often in forms that are altered in accordance with the intellectual and religious currents of a particular time and place. The scriptures of Hinduism reflect its diversity and its complex history. They include ancient hymns to anthropomorphic gods and liturgical texts detailing how priests should prepare sacrifices, mystical texts that speculate on the nature of ultimate reality, devotional literature in praise of a variety of deities, philosophical texts of great subtlety and insight, and combinations of these and related themes.

The earliest stratum of Indian sacred literature accessible today is found in the Vedas, which evolved into their present form between 1400 and 400 B.C.E. The earliest of these were codified around 1300 B.C.E. by people who referred to themselves as Āryans, meaning "noble" or "wise." They referred to other residents of northern India as "slaves" *(dāsa* or *dasyu),* but the actual relations between these groups is unclear.

The Vedas are referred to by Hindus as "revelation" (*śruti;* literally, "what is heard"), in contrast to other scriptures referred to as "tradition" (*smṛti;* literally, "what is remembered"). Both classes are regarded as canonical, but the latter is not considered to have the same level of authoritativeness as the Vedas. According to tradition, the Vedas are not the product of human composition *(apauruṣeya)* but are a part of the very fabric of reality. They were directly perceived by "seers" *(ṛṣi),* whose mystical contemplations—aided by ingestion of an intoxicating beverage called *soma*—enabled them to intuit primordial sounds reverberating throughout the universe and render them into human language as the books of the Vedas.

There are four Vedas: (1) the *Ṛg Veda,* so named because it is composed of stanzas *(ṛk);* (2) the *Sāma Veda* (composed mostly of hymns taken from the *Ṛg Veda* and set to various melodies, or *sāman*); (3) the *Yajur Veda* (composed of *yajus,* selected ritual prayers, mostly taken from the *Ṛg Veda*); and (4) the *Atharva Veda* (a collection of ritual texts named after the sage Atharvan). The Vedas contain several primary types of literature: (1) chants or hymns *(saṃhitā),* generally directed toward the gods *(deva)* of the Vedic pantheon; (2) ritual texts *(brāhmaṇa),* which detail the sacrifices performed by brahmins; and (3) mystical texts concerned with the quest for ultimate truth *(āraṇyakas* and *upaniṣads).*

Indo-Āryan Religion and Society

The origins of the Indo-Āryans are a matter of considerable controversy among scholars. Early European Indologists, basing their analysis on obscure passages in Vedic texts, speculated that the Āryans were invaders from central Europe who entered the subcontinent, where they encountered indigenous inhabitants (commonly referred to as Dravidians) and conquered them with superior military technology. In recent years most of these assumptions have been debunked, and a consensus has developed that there is no real evidence to support the "Āryan invasion" theory.

It now appears that the Indo-Āryans may have been indigenous to the subcontinent and that they distinguished themselves from other peoples as the holders of the sacred Vedic scriptures and performers of Vedic rituals. Archaeological evidence from Dravidian cities in the Indus Valley region suggests that the inhabitants attained a high degree of social development, although their society probably was in decline by 1300 B.C.E. Little is known with any certainty about their civilization, but there appears to have been interaction between them and the Indo-Āryans, which may have led to cross-cultural influences.

From an early period, as indicated in their sacred texts, the Indo-Āryans and their descendants propounded the idea that human society ideally should be stratified, with each social class having clearly defined functions and duties. At the top of the hierarchy were the brahmins, or priestly class, whose sacred duty was to perform sacrifices to the gods described in the Vedas. Many of these gods were personifications of natural phenomena, such as the sun, moon, wind, and so forth. Many gods were believed to have dominion over a particular natural force or phenomenon, and the rituals of the Vedas were commonly directed either to one god or to a small group of gods who were considered to have the ability to affect a particular sphere of divine provenance.

The role of the priests was central in this system: They were expected to remain ritually pure and to preserve the sacred texts, along with the lore of priestcraft. Their social function prevented them from engaging in manual labor, trade, agriculture, or other nonpriestly occupations that were considered polluting. In exceptional circumstances occasioned by special need, they were allowed to earn a living by other means, but ideally their lives should be devoted to study of the sacred Vedas and performance of Vedic rituals. This was crucial to the maintenance of the system of "upholding the world" *(loka-saṃgraha)*, a core concern of Vedic religion.

In this system, the brahmins performed a pivotal function in offering sacrifices to the gods. The sacrifices generally were transmuted into smoke through the agency of Agni, god of fire (who is manifested in the ritual fire, as well as in other forms of combustion). Smoke converted the material of the sacrifice into a subtle essence suitable for the gods' consumption, and the process required that the brahmins remain ritually pure, because any pollution they acquired was passed on to their sacrifices. The gods would naturally be insulted if offered unclean food and would respond by denying those requests the brahmins made on behalf of the sponsors of the sacrifices.

The Vedic system was based on a symbiosis of gods and humans: The gods required the sacrificial offerings, and humans needed the gods to use their supernatural powers to maintain cosmic order *(ṛta)*. The system assumed that humans only prosper in a stable and ordered cosmos, an idea reflected in the story of the slaying of the demon Vṛtra ("Obstructer") by Indra, the king of the gods in the Vedas. Demons thrive in chaos, and at the beginning of time Vṛtra rules over a chaotic cosmos until Indra, after a mighty battle, slays him and thereby makes it possible for the gods to establish order.

This primordial battle reflects the crucial role played by the gods in establishing and maintaining cosmic law. The concerns of Vedic literature are primarily practical and this-worldly. They focus on particular pragmatic goals, such as bountiful crops, fertility, peace, stability, wealth, and so forth. The results of the sacrifices are believed to accrue in the present life, and although a world of the dead is mentioned, it does not play a major role in the early Vedic tradition.

The Upaniṣads and Yoga

The focus shifts in the later Vedic period, in which texts of speculative philosophy and mysticism begin to appear. Referred to as Āraṇyakas and Upaniṣads, they were written by sages who often expressed dissatisfaction with the ritualism and this-worldly focus of the early Vedic texts. Their authors sought the ultimate power behind the sacrifices, the force that gives rise to gods, humans, and all the other phenomena of the universe. They found this by a process of inward-looking meditation that sought an unchanging essence beyond the transient phenomena of existence. The present life was no longer viewed as the beginning and end of one's existence; rather, living beings were said to be reborn in successive lives in accordance with their actions *(karma)*. The actions of the present were said to result in opposite and equal reactions in the future, and one's present life was said to be a result of the karma accrued in the past. The cycle of existence *(saṃsāra)* was said by the sages of the Upaniṣads to be beginningless, but it may be ended. It is perpetuated by a basic misunderstanding of the true nature of reality (*avidyā,* or "ignorance"), but one may escape it by attaining correct understanding of truth, which is found only by people who shift their attention from external things to find the truly real.

By following the path of wisdom that correctly discriminates the real from the unreal, the truly important from the merely pleasant, and the changeless from the transitory, the sage eventually discovers that within everyone is an eternal, unchanging essence, an immortal soul referred to as the "self" (ātman). The Upaniṣads declare that this essence alone survives death and that it has been reborn countless times in an infinite variety of different bodies, while itself remaining unchanged by the multiple identities developed in successive lifetimes. It is characterized by three qualities: being, consciousness, and bliss *(sat cit ānanda),* meaning that it is pure, unchanging being and its nature is never altered, despite the changing external circumstances of our lives; it is pure consciousness that takes no notice of the vicissitudes of our lives; and it remains unaffected by our joys, sorrows, hopes, disappointments, pleasures, or pains and thus is in a continuous state of equanimity. Moreover, the Upaniṣadic sages identified the self with the cosmic ultimate, something supremely mysterious, hidden from ordinary perception but all-pervasive, supremely subtle, the essence of all that is. This ultimate was said to be beyond words or conceptual thought and was referred to as "Brahman," because it is the purest and most sublime principle of existence, just as in human society brahmins are the purest and holiest class.

According to this system, the perceptions of ordinary beings are profoundly distorted by ignorance, and the only way to attain correct knowledge is through a process of discipline *(yoga)* in which one's thoughts and body are gradually brought under control and one's attention is turned away from sense objects and directed within.

These premises are shared with the system outlined in the *Yoga Aphorisms (Yoga-sūtra)* of Patañjali, who is credited with gathering the principal practices and premises of the yoga system. Patañjali's system, however, differs in significant ways from that of the Upaniṣads, although both use the term *yoga* to describe their respective training programs. The Upaniṣads outline a monistic system in which the sole reality is said to be Brahman, while everything else is based on mistaken perceptions.

Patañjali, in contrast, contends that both matter *(prakṛti)* and spirit *(puruṣa)* are real entities, and the goal of his system is separation *(kaivalya)* of spirit from matter; the Upaniṣads aim at a final apotheosis in which all dualities are transcended and one realizes the fundamental identity of the self and Brahman. The final goal of the Upaniṣads is expressed in the greatest of the "great statements" *(mahāvākya)* that sum up the central insights of the Upaniṣadic sages: "That is you" *(tat tvam asi).* This expresses the identity of the individual soul and Brahman. Patañjali's goal is separation that liberates one's spiritual essence from matter.

The aim of both systems is liberation *(mokṣa)* from the cycle of existence, but each conceives of this release differently. Both consider yoga to be the primary practice for attaining the final goal, and for both yoga is a program of introspective meditation that begins with physical discipline; control of random, ignorant thoughts; and development of insight into unchanging truth. But the ontological presuppositions and ultimate goals of the two systems differ in significant details.

Social Structure

The Upaniṣads and Patañjali's yoga system represent a shift from the primacy of sacrifices to the gods in the early Vedic period to a general acceptance of the idea that the final aim of the religious path is liberation. As final release from cyclic existence came to be viewed as the supreme goal, sacrifices aimed at maintaining the order of the world and the acquisition of mundane benefits became devalued as inferior to the pursuit of knowledge of truth.

In an apparent reaction to this trend, orthodox elements began to stress the importance of performing one's social duties *(dharma).* Texts like the *Laws of Manu* and the *Bhagavad-gītā* emphasized the importance of selfless, devout adherence to the duties of one's social class *(varṇa):* the brahmins, the warriors and rulers *(kṣatriya),* the merchants and tradespeople *(vaiśya),* and the servants *(śūdra).* Both texts asserted that if people ignore their sacred duty the world will fall into chaos, society will crumble, and essential social functions will not be performed. The *Laws of Manu* delineate a system in which people eventually should renounce the world and pursue final liberation, but only after first performing the duties assigned to their social class. In its system of "duties of social classes and stages of life" *(varṇāśrama-dharma),* specific duties for each class are outlined that should be performed diligently in order to maintain the world.

The system assumes that only in an ordered universe will some people have the leisure and resources to pursue liberation.

The ideal life begins with the student stage, in which a man finds a spiritual preceptor *(guru)* who teaches him the lore appropriate to his class. The three highest classes (brahmins, kṣatriyas, and vaiśyas) are said to be "twice-born" *(dvija)* because they undergo a ceremony (the *upanayana*) that initiates them into adulthood and is considered a "second birth." Only these three classes are permitted to study the Vedas or to participate in Vedic rituals (but officiating in Vedic ceremonies is the special duty of brahmins). After a period of study (which varies in length and content among the four classes), a man should marry, produce male heirs to continue the lineage and perform sacrifices for him and his ancestors after his death, and support the brahmins whose rituals maintain the whole cosmos.

According to Manu, after a man has successfully performed his duty and when he sees his grandson born (assuring that the lineage will continue) and gray hairs on his head, he may withdraw from society (often with his wife) and begin to sever the ties that he cultivated during his life in the world. As a "forest dweller" *(vana-prastha),* he should be celibate and detached from worldly enjoyments, cultivate meditation on ultimate truth, and pursue liberation. When he knows that his attachment to mundane things has ceased, he may take the final step of becoming a "world renouncer" *(saṃnyāsin),* completely devoted to the ultimate goal, wandering from place to place and subsisting on alms, intent on final liberation from cyclic existence.

In this system, everything has its time and place, and while liberation is recognized as the ultimate goal of the religious life, it should not be pursued in a way that might destabilize society. When the demands of dharma have been met, one may seek one's own ends, but Manu declares that renouncing the world too soon would lead to a degeneration of the whole society, and the resulting chaos would make the attainment of liberation difficult, if not impossible, for anyone.

The Path of Devotion

Another important path to liberation lies in the "yoga of devotion" *(bhakti-yoga),* in which one finds salvation through completely identifying oneself with God. The yoga of devotion requires that one focus one's attention so completely on God that all thoughts of ego are transcended in a pure experience of union.

There are a variety of ways of conceiving devotion: Sometimes it takes the form of a love affair in which the devotee experiences an ecstatic union surpassing any human love; for others, devotion takes the form of selfless service to an omnipotent master. Often, Hindu devotionalism exhibits elements of both, along with a feeling of an intensely personal relationship between a human being and God.

The selections presented here are arranged in roughly chronological order and are taken from a wide range of Hindu scriptures. Of necessity many important scriptures have been omitted from this survey. Those that have been included were chosen because they exemplify central themes of contemporary and traditional Hindu religious thought.

HOLIDAYS

Festival of Lights (Divālī or Dīpāvalī) Celebrated in the second half of the lunar month of Aśvina, which generally occurs in October/November. It celebrates the homecoming of Rāma and Sītā to Ayodhya after their years in exile as recounted in the *Adventures of Rāma (Rāmāyaṇa)*. Lights adorn houses, temples, and streets; gifts are exchanged; and food and jewels are offered to Lakṣmī, the goddess of fortune. The holiday is also associated with the slaying of a demon by Kṛṣṇa.

Festival of Colors (Holī) Celebrates the immolation of Holikā, a demonness who possessed a magical shawl that made her immune to fire. Her father, the demon Hiraṇyakaśipu, ordered that his son Prahlāda be burned alive because of his devotion to the god Viṣṇu, but Holikā's shawl flew to him and protected him, while she was burned by the fire. On the first day, huge bonfires are lit all over India, and on the second day people throw colored powders on each other. The festival generally falls in late February or early March.

Birth of Krishna (Kṛṣṇa-janmāṣṭamī) Celebrates the birth of Kṛṣṇa, the eighth incarnation *(avatāra)* of Viṣṇu. It falls on the eighth day of the dark half of the month of Bhadrapada in the Hindu calendar (generally August or September). Devotees often begin with a fast the day prior to the festival and a night-long vigil commemorating Kṛṣṇa's birth. At midnight an image of Kṛṣṇa is bathed, and in the morning women draw tiny footprints outside the house, symbolizing his entry into his home.

Kumbh Festival (Kumbh Mela) Often referred to as the largest religious gathering in the world, occurring when the sun stands at Aquarius *(kumbh)*. It is celebrated every three years and rotates among Hardwar, Prayaga, Ujjaini, and Nasik. Millions of Hindus come from all over the country to bathe in the sacred waters, and large numbers of world renouncers from various religious orders congregate, many performing feats of asceticism.

Great Night of Śiva (Mahā-Śivarātri) Celebrated in the month of Māgha in the Hindu calendar, during a night divided into four quarters. Devotees keep a vigil through the night, chanting the divine names of Śiva and making offerings.

TIMELINE

4000 B.C.E.	Composition of earliest Vedic hymns
2700–1500 B.C.E.	Flourishing of Indus civilization
1900 B.C.E.	Age of the *Rāmāyaṇa*
1500–1200 B.C.E.	Composition of the *Ṛg Veda*
1400 B.C.E.	Great Bhārata War; early version of *Mahābhārata*
500 B.C.E.–500 C.E.	Composition of Epics and early Purāṇas
322–298 B.C.E.	Reign of Candragupta Maurya
100–500 C.E.	Expansion of Hinduism into Southeast Asia
400–500	Vyāsa's *Commentary* on the *Yoga Aphorisms*; origins of Tantrism
999–1026	Raids by Mahmud of Ghazni; destruction of temples
1336–1565	Kingdom of Vijayanagara, last Hindu empire in India
1526	Battle of Panipat; Mughals become rulers of Delhi and Agra
1526–1757	Mughals rule in north India; destruction of most Hindu temples
1542	Jesuit missionary Francis Xavier arrives in Goa
1651	British East India Company opens first factory in Bengal
1828	Ram Mohan Roy founds Brahmo Samāj
1857	Indian Mutiny; British expelled from India for almost two years
1920	Mahātma Gandhi begins his first All-India Civil Disobedience Movement
1947	India's independence; Partition into India and Pakistan
1948	Mahātma Gandhi assassinated; Pandit Nehru elected first Prime Minister of independent India
1992	Hindu extremists demolish Babri mosque in Ayodhyā
1998–2004	Hindu nationalist party Bharatiya Janata Party forms minority government

GLOSSARY

Agni God of fire in the Vedas, who transmutes sacrificial offerings into food for the gods.

Āryan The people who composed the Vedas and whose religion became predominant on the subcontinent.

Ātman "Soul," the divine essence of every individual.

Avidyā "Ignorance," the primary factor that enmeshes living beings in the cycle of birth, death, and rebirth.

Bhagavad-gītā *"Song of God,"* a section of the epic *Mahābhārata* that describes the ethical dilemma of Arjuna, who is torn between the demands of karma and dharma.

Bhakti Selfless devotion to God.

Brahman The ultimate reality described in the Upaniṣads.

Brahmin The priestly caste of traditional Hinduism.

Deva The gods of Hinduism.

Devī The Goddess, who manifests in various female forms.

Dharma "Duty" or "Law," the occupational, social, and religious roles required of individuals as a result of their places in society.

Dravidian Term coined by Western scholars for the inhabitants of India who developed the Indus Valley civilization, portrayed as the enemies of the Āryans in the Vedas.

Hindu An adherent of Hinduism.

Indra King of the gods in the Vedic stories, and the paradigmatic warrior.

Karma "Actions," which bring about concordant results.

Kṣatriya The caste whose members traditionally were warriors and rulers.

Loka-saṃgraha "Upholding the World," the goal of the sacrifices enjoined by the Vedas.

Māyā "Magic" or "illusion," the creative power of Brahman that manifests as the phenomena of the world.

Mokṣa "Release" from the cycle of birth, death, and rebirth.

Rāmāyaṇa Epic story of the heroic deeds of Rāma, believed by tradition to be an incarnation of the god Viṣṇu.

Ṛṣi "Seers" who revealed the Vedas.

Ṛta Cosmic order, which is maintained by the gods.

Saṃnyāsin One who renounces the world in order to seek liberation from cyclic existence.

Saṃsāra "Cyclic Existence," the beginningless cycle of birth, death, and rebirth in which ignorant beings are trapped.

Sanātana-dharma "Universal Truth," a term for Hinduism, implying that it is able to embrace the limited "truths" of other religions and philosophies.

Śaṅkara Most influential of traditional commentators on the Upaniṣads.

Śiva God who exemplifies yogic practice, who will destroy the world at the end of the present cosmic cycle.

Śūdra The caste whose traditional duty was to serve the castes above them.

Upaniṣads Mystical texts that speculate on the nature of human existence and the ultimate reality.

Vaiśya The caste whose members traditionally were merchants and skilled artisans.

Varṇa The four main social groupings of traditional Indian society (brahmins, kṣatriyas, vaiśyas, and śūdras).

Veda The four early sacred texts of Hinduism, which describe the gods and rituals connected with them.

Vedānta Tradition of commentary on the Upaniṣads.

Viṣṇu God whose traditional role is to protect dharma.

Yoga System of meditative cultivation involving physical and mental discipline.

FURTHER READINGS

BASHAM, A. L. *The Wonder That Was India.* London: Sidgwick & Jackson, 1967.

DANIÉLOU, ALAIN. *The Myths and Gods of India.* Rochester, VT: Inner Traditions International, 1985.

DASGUPTA, SURENDRANATH. *A History of Indian Philosophy.* 5 vols. Delhi: Motilal Banarsidass, 1975.

ELIADE, MIRCEA. *Yoga: Immortality and Freedom.* Princeton, NJ: Princeton University Press, 1969.

HIRIYANA, M. *Essentials of Indian Philosophy.* London: Unwin, 1949.

HOPKINS, THOMAS J. *The Hindu Religious Tradition.* Belmont, CA: Wadsworth, 1971.

KINSLEY, DAVID R. *Hindu Goddesses: Visions of the Divine Feminine in the Hindu Religious Tradition.* Delhi: Motilal Banarsidass, 1987.

———. *Hinduism: A Cultural Perspective.* Englewood Cliffs, NJ: Prentice-Hall, 1982.

MINOR, ROBERT. *Modern Indian Interpreters of the Bhagavad Gītā.* Albany: State University of New York Press, 1986.

POTTER, KARL H. *Encyclopedia of Indian Philosophies, Vol I: Bibliography.* Princeton, NJ: Princeton University Press, 1983.

———. *Encyclopedia of Indian Philosophies, Vol. III: Advaita Vedānta up to Śaṇkara and His Pupils.* Delhi: Motilal Banarsidass, 1981.

———. *Presuppositions of India's Philosophies.* Delhi: Motilal Banarsidass, n.d.

SHIVARAMAN, KRISHNA. *Saivism in Philosophical Perspective: A Study of the Formative Concepts, Problems and Methods of Śaiva Siddhānta.* Delhi: Motilal Banarsidass, 1973.

ZIMMER, HEINRICH. *Philosophies of India.* Princeton, NJ: Princeton University Press, 1951.

VEDAS

CREATION OF THE UNIVERSE

The following selections are taken from the Ṛg Veda *and are hymns and ritual texts devoted to the worship of the Vedic gods. These verses describe the attributes of the gods, recounting the mythos of each deity and his or her particular sacrificial functions and associations. The first hymn depicts the creation of the universe as beginning with the sacrifice of Puruṣa ("Man"), a giant god whose body formed the raw material for the formation of the stars, the planets, and living things. According to the story, the four social classes* (varṇa) *of Hinduism were also created through this sacrifice, thus providing a scriptural justification for the stratification of Indian society.*

1. The Man had a thousand heads, a thousand eyes, a thousand feet. He pervaded the earth on all sides and extended beyond it as far as ten fingers.
2. It is the Man who is all this, whatever has been and whatever is to be. He is the ruler of immortality, when he grows beyond everything through food.
3. Such is his greatness, and the Man is yet more than this. All creatures are a quarter of him; three quarters are what is immortal in heaven.
4. With three quarters the Man rose upwards, and one quarter of him still remains here. From this he spread out in all directions, into that which eats and that which does not eat. . . .
6. When the gods spread the sacrifice with the Man as the offering, spring was the clarified butter, summer the fuel, autumn the oblation.
7. They anointed the Man, the sacrifice born at the beginning, upon the sacred grass. With him the gods, Sādhyas, and sages sacrificed.
8. From that sacrifice in which everything was offered, the melted fat was collected, and he made it into those beasts who live in the air, in the forest, and in villages.
9. From that sacrifice in which everything was offered, the verses and chants were born, the metres were born from it, and from it the formulas were born.
10. Horses were born from it, and those other animals that have two rows of teeth; cows were born from it, and from it goats and sheep were born.
11. When they divided the Man, into how many parts did they apportion him? What do they call his mouth, his two arms and thighs and feet?
12. His mouth became the Brahmin; his arms were made into the Warrior *(kṣatriya),* his thighs the People *(vaiśya),* and from his feet the Servants *(śūdra)* were born. . . .
13. The moon was born from his mind; from his eye the sun was born. Indra and Agni came from his mouth, and from his vital breath the Wind was born.
14. From his navel the middle realm of space arose; from his head the sky evolved. From his two feet came the earth, and the quarters of the sky from his ear. Thus they set the worlds in order. . . .
16. With the sacrifice the gods sacrificed to the sacrifice. These were the first ritual laws *(dharma).* These very powers reached the dome of the sky where dwell the Sādhyas, the ancient gods.

Source: *Ṛg Veda* 10.90: *Puruṣa-Sukta,* from *The Rig Veda,* tr. Wendy Doniger O'Flaherty (New York: Penguin, 1981), pp. 30–31.

ORIGIN OF THE GODS

This passage offers another view of creation. It indicates that originally existence arose from nonexistence and that the gods later were produced by a goddess "who crouched with legs spread," an image with obvious anthropomorphic overtones. It suggests that the creation of the gods was similar to a human birth, but the position described may also suggest that creation is linked with the practice of yoga, which is believed to produce energy that may be used in the generation of life.

1. Let us now speak with wonder of the births of the gods—so that some one may see them when the hymns are chanted in this later age.
2. The lord of sacred speech, like a smith, fanned them together. In the earliest age of the gods, existence was born from nonexistence.
3. In the first age of the gods, existence was born from nonexistence. After this the quarters of the sky were born from her who crouched with legs spread.
4. The earth was born from her who crouched with legs spread, and from the earth the quarters of the sky were born. From Aditi, Dakṣa was born, and from Dakṣa Aditi was born.
5. For Aditi was born as your daughter, O Dakṣa, and after her were born the blessed gods, the kinsmen of immortality.
6. When you gods took your places there in the water with your hands joined together, a thick cloud of mist arose from you like dust from dancers.
7. When you gods like magicians caused the worlds to swell, you drew forth the sun that was hidden in the ocean.
8. Eight sons are there of Aditi, who were born of her body. With seven she went forth among the gods, but she threw Mārtaṇḍa, the sun, aside.
9. With seven sons Aditi went forth into the earliest age. But she bore Mārtaṇḍa so that he would in turn beget offspring and then soon die.

Source: *Ṛg Veda* 10.72, from *The Rig Veda*, pp. 38–39.

INDRA, THE PARADIGMATIC WARRIOR

In Vedic mythology, Indra is the king of the gods, and he embodies the warrior virtues valued by the Indo-Āryans. He is fearless in battle, always victorious over his enemies, and although he is sometimes portrayed as proud and boastful, these qualities do not detract from his prowess as a warrior. This hymn recounts the greatest of his mighty deeds, the slaying of the demon Vṛtra, a powerful serpentlike creature that was wreaking havoc throughout the universe, holding back the rainwaters that are essential to the prosperity of living things and obstructing the establishment of cosmic order, which is required for a stable and harmonious world. Wielding his mighty thunderbolt, Indra slays the demon, splits open his body, cuts off his limbs, and thus eliminates the threat he poses.

1. Let me now sing the heroic deeds of Indra, the first that the thunderbolt-wielder performed. He killed the dragon and pierced an opening for the waters; he split open the bellies of mountains.
2. He killed the dragon who lay upon the mountain; Tvaṣṭṛ fashioned the roaring thunderbolt for him. Like lowing cows, the flowing waters rushed straight down to the sea.

3. Wildly excited like a bull, he took the Soma for himself and drank the extract from the three bowls in the three-day Soma ceremony. Indra the Generous seized his thunderbolt to hurl it as a weapon; he killed the first-born of dragons.
4. Indra, when you killed the first-born of dragons and overcame by your own magic the magic of the magicians, at that very moment you brought forth the sun, the sky, and dawn. Since then you have found no enemy to conquer you.
5. With his great weapon, the thunderbolt, Indra killed the shoulderless Vṛtra, his greatest enemy. Like the trunk of a tree whose branches have been lopped off by an axe, the dragon lies flat upon the ground.
6. For, muddled by drunkenness like one who is no soldier, Vṛtra challenged the great hero who had overcome the mighty and who drank Soma to the dregs. Unable to withstand the onslaught of his weapons, he found Indra an enemy to conquer him and was shattered, his nose crushed.
7. Without feet or hands he fought against Indra, who struck him on the nape of the neck with his thunderbolt. The steer who wished to become the equal of the bull bursting with seed, Vṛtra lay broken in many places.
8. Over him as he lay there like a broken reed the swelling waters flowed for man. Those waters that Vṛtra had enclosed with his power—the dragon now lay at their feet.
9. The vital energy of Vṛtra's mother ebbed away, for Indra had hurled his deadly weapon at her. Above was the mother, below was the son; Danu lay down like a cow with her calf.
10. In the midst of the channels of the waters which never stood still or rested, the body was hidden. The waters flow over Vṛtra's secret place; he who found Indra an enemy to conquer him sank into long darkness.
11. The waters who had the Dāsa for their husband, the dragon for their protector, were imprisoned like the cows imprisoned by the Paṇis. When he killed Vṛtra he split open the outlet of the waters that had been closed.
12. Indra, you became a hair of a horse's tail when Vṛtra struck you on the corner of the mouth. You, the one god, the brave one, you won the cows; you won the Soma; you released the seven streams so that they could flow.
13. No use was the lightning and thunder, fog and hail that he had scattered about, when the dragon and Indra fought. Indra the Generous remained victorious for all time to come.
14. What avenger of the dragon did you see, Indra, that fear entered your heart when you had killed him? Then you crossed the ninety-nine streams like the frightened eagle crossing the realms of earth and air.
15. Indra, who wields the thunderbolt in his hand, is the king of that which moves and that which rests, of the tame and of the horned. He rules the people as their king, encircling all this as a rim encircles spokes.

Source: *Ṛg Veda* 1.3, from *The Rig Veda*, pp. 149–151.

PRAYER TO AGNI, THE GOD OF FIRE

Agni is one of the most important gods of the Vedas. As the god of fire, he transmutes sacrificial offerings into smoke, which is consumed by the gods. Thus, he serves as the intermediary between the divine and human realms and is a paradigm for the brahmin priests.

1. I pray to Agni, the household priest who is the god of the sacrifice, the one who chants and invokes and brings most treasure.
2. Agni earned the prayers of the ancient sages, and of those of the present, too; he will bring the gods here.
3. Through Agni one may win wealth, and growth from day to day, glorious and most abounding in heroic sons.
4. Agni, the sacrificial ritual that you encompass on all sides—only that one goes to the gods.
5. Agni, the priest with the sharp sight of a poet, the true and most brilliant, the god will come with the gods.
6. Whatever good you wish to do for the one who worships you, Agni, through you, O Aṅgiras, that comes true.
7. To you, Agni, who shine upon darkness, we come day after day, bringing our thoughts and homage.
8. To you, the king over sacrifices, the shining guardian of the Order, growing in your own house.
9. Be easy for us to reach, like a father to his son. Abide with us, Agni, for our happiness.

Source: *Ṛg Veda* 1.1, from *The Rig Veda*, p. 99.

BURNING DEAD BODIES

This hymn invokes Agni in his role as transporter of the dead. He is asked to burn the corpse of a dead man and to ensure that he is brought to the land of the dead. The concept of afterlife is rather vague in the early Vedas. There are references to a world of the dead, ruled by Yama, who was the first human to die. He found the way to the land of the dead, and now he brings others there. At the end of the ritual the pyre is soaked so thoroughly with water that a small pool is formed, and plants, frogs, and other living things will grow there, symbolizing the renewal of life from the ashes of death.

[To Agni:] Do not burn him entirely, Agni, or engulf him in your flames. Do not consume his skin or his flesh. When you have cooked him perfectly, O knower of creatures, only then send him forth to the fathers. When you cook him perfectly, O knower of creatures, then give him over to the fathers. When he goes on the path that leads away the vital breath, then he will be led by the will of the gods.

[To the dead man:] May your eye go to the sun, your vital breath to the wind. Go to the sky or to earth, as is your nature; or go to the waters, if that is your fate. Take root in the plants with your limbs.

[To the funeral fire:] The goat is your share; burn him with your heat. Let your brilliant light and flame burn him. With your gentle forms, O knower of creatures, carry this man to the world of those who have done good deeds. Set him free again to go to the fathers, Agni, when he has been offered as an oblation in you and wanders with the sacrificial drink. Let him reach his own descendants, dressing himself in a life-span. O knower of creatures, let him join with a body.

[To the dead man:] Whatever the black bird has pecked out of you, or the ant, the snake, or even a beast of prey, may Agni who eats all things make it whole, and Soma who has entered the Brahmins. Gird yourself with the limbs of the cow as an armor against Agni, and cover yourself with fat and suet, so that he will not embrace you with his impetuous heat in his passionate desire to burn you up.

[To the funeral fire:] O Agni, do not overturn this cup, that is dear to the gods and to those who love Soma, fit for the gods to drink from, a cup in which the immortal gods carouse. I send the flesh-eating fire far away. Let him go to those whose king is Yama, carrying away all impurities. But let that other (form of fire), the knower of creatures, come here and carry the oblation to the gods, since he knows the way in advance.

[To the dead man:] The flesh-eating fire has entered your house, though he sees there the other, the knower of creatures; I take that god away to the sacrifice of the fathers. Let him carry the heated drink to the farthest dwelling place. . . .

[To the new fire:] Joyously would we put you in place, joyously would we kindle you. Joyously carry the joyous fathers here to eat the oblation. Now, Agni, quench and revive the very one you have burnt up. Let water plants grow in this place. O cool one, bringer of coolness; O fresh one, bringer of freshness; unite with the female frog. Delight and inspire this Agni.

Source: *Ṛg Veda* 10.16, from Wendy Doniger O'Flaherty, *Textual Sources for the Study of Hinduism* (Chicago: University of Chicago Press, 1988), p. 7.

THE BENEFICIAL EFFECTS OF DRINKING SOMA

Soma is an intoxicating drink that plays a major role in Vedic literature. It was made from a creeping plant that was crushed and strained to make a whitish beverage that apparently produced visions and ecstatic states of mind. The plant used is a matter of current debate, and a number of theories have been proposed, none of which is considered definitive by contemporary scholars. As this passage indicates, those who drank it experienced a feeling of exaltation and expansion of consciousness. The writer of this hymn claims that drinking it has also made him immortal.

1. I have tasted the sweet drink of life, knowing that it inspires good thoughts and joyous expansiveness to the extreme, that all the gods and mortals seek it together, calling it honey.

2. When you penetrate inside, you will know no limits, and you will avert the wrath of the gods. Enjoying Indra's friendship, O drop of Soma, bring riches as a docile cow brings the yoke.
3. We have drunk the Soma; we have become immortal; we have gone to the light; we have found the gods. What can hatred and the malice of a mortal do to us now, O immortal one?
4. When we have drunk you, O drop of Soma, be good to our heart, kind as a father to his son, thoughtful as a friend to a friend. Far-famed Soma, stretch out our lifespan so that we may live.
5. The glorious drops that I have drunk set me free in wide space. You have bound me together in my limbs as thongs bind a chariot. Let the drops protect me from the foot that stumbles and keep lameness away from me.
6. Inflame me like a fire kindled by friction; make us see far; make us richer, better. For when I am intoxicated with you, Soma, I think myself rich. Draw near and make us thrive.
7. We would enjoy you, pressed with a fervent heart, like riches from a father. King Soma, stretch out our lifespans as the sun stretches the spring days.
8. King Soma, have mercy on us for our well-being. Know that we are devoted to your laws. Passion and fury are stirred up. O drop of Soma, do not hand us over to the pleasure of the enemy.
9. For you, Soma, are the guardian of our body; watching over men, you have settled down in every limb. If we break your laws, O god, have mercy on us like a good friend, to make us better.
10. Let me join closely with my compassionate friend [Soma] so that he will not injure me when I have drunk him. O lord of bay horses, for the Soma that is lodged in us I approach Indra to stretch out our lifespan.
11. Weaknesses and diseases have gone; the forces of darkness have fled in terror. Soma has climbed up in us, expanding. We have come to the place where they stretch out lifespans.
12. The drop that we have drunk has entered our hearts, an immortal inside mortals. O fathers, let us serve that Soma with the oblations and abide in his mercy and kindness.
13. Uniting in agreement with the fathers, O drop of Soma, you have extended yourself through sky and earth. Let us serve him with an oblation; let us be masters of riches.
14. You protecting Gods, speak out for us. Do not let sleep or harmful speech seize us. Let us, always dear to Soma, speak as men of power in the sacrificial gathering.
15. Soma, you give us the force of life on every side. Enter into us, finding the sunlight, watching over men. O drop of Soma, summon your helpers and protect us before and after.

Source: *Ṛg Veda* 8.48, from *The Rig Veda*, pp. 134–136.

SEX AND THE YOGIN

This hymn depicts a struggle between a husband and wife named Agastya and Lopāmudrā. Lopāmudrā has just successfully seduced Agastya, who was trying to avoid sexual intercourse in order to store up the vital energy he acquired as a product of yogic exertions. It captures a common theme in classical Indian literature: woman as temptress, whose unrestrained sexual desire and physical charms distract male yogis from their ascetic practice and cause them to dissipate the power they have painstakingly gained through meditation and self-restraint.

1. [Lopāmudrā:] "For many autumns past I have toiled, night and day, and each dawn has brought old age closer, age that distorts the glory of bodies. Virile men should go to their wives.
2. "For even the men of the past, who acted according to the Law and talked about the Law with the gods, broke off when they did not find the end. Women should unite with virile men."
3. [Agastya:] "Not in vain is all this toil, which the gods encourage. We two must always strive against each other, and by this we will win the race that is won by a hundred means, when we merge together as a couple."
4. [Lopāmudrā:] "Desire has come upon me for the bull who roars and is held back, desire engulfing me from this side, that side, all sides."
5. [The poet:] Lopāmudrā draws out the virile bull: the foolish woman sucks dry the panting wise man.
6. [Agastya:] "By this Soma which I have drunk, in my innermost heart I say: Let him forgive us if we have sinned, for a mortal is full of many desires."
7. Agastya, digging with spades, wishing for children, progeny, and strength, nourished both ways, for he was a powerful sage. He found fulfillment of his real hopes among the gods.

Source: *Ṛg Veda* 1.179, from *The Rig Veda*, pp. 250–251.

A CLEVER WOMAN

This hymn is spoken by a woman who has managed to eliminate her rivals and emerge victorious over her husband, who now submits to her will.

1. There the sun has risen, and here my good fortune has risen. Being a clever woman, and able to triumph, I have triumphed over my husband.
2. I am the banner; I am the head. I am the formidable one who has the deciding word. My husband will obey my will alone, as I emerge triumphant.
3. My sons kill their enemies and my daughter is an empress, and I am completely victorious. My voice is supreme in my husband's ears.

4. The oblation that Indra made and so became glorious and supreme, this is what I have made for you, O gods. I have become truly without rival wives.
5. Without rival wives, killer of rival wives, victorious and pre-eminent, I have grabbed for myself the attraction of the other women as if it were the wealth of flighty women.
6. I have conquered and become pre-eminent over these rival wives, so that I may rule as empress over this hero and over the people.

Source: *Ṛg Veda* 10.159, from *The Rig Veda,* p. 291.

THE HORSE SACRIFICE

The horse sacrifice served to establish the dominion of a king by demonstrating how large an area he controlled. For a year prior to the sacrifice, a horse would be set free to wander wherever it wished, indicating the hegemony of the king. To the extent that other rulers were unable to turn the horse away, it served notice of the areas a particular ruler effectively controlled. At the end of the year the horse was offered as a sacrifice to the gods, but although it was killed it is stated in the ritual that it would enjoy a future in heaven.

[To the priests:] The invoker, the officiant, the overseer, the fire kindler, the holder of the pressing-stones, the cantor, the sacrificial priest—fill your bellies with this well-prepared, well-sacrificed sacrifice. The hewers of the sacrificial stake and those who carry it, and those who carve the knob for the horse's sacrificial stake, and those who gather together the things to cook the charger—let their approval encourage us. The horse with his smooth back went forth into the fields of the gods, just when I made my prayer. The inspired sages exult in him. We have made him a welcome companion at the banquet of the gods.

[To the horse:] The charger's rope and halter, the reins and bridle on the head, and even the grass that has been held up to the mouth—let all that stay with you even among the gods. Whatever of the horse's flesh the fly has eaten, or whatever stays stuck to the stake or the axe, or to the hands or nails of the slaughterer—let all of that stay with you even among the gods. Whatever food remains in the stomach, sending forth gas, or whatever smell there is from the raw flesh—let the slaughterers make that well done; let them cook the sacrificial animal until he is perfectly cooked. Whatever runs off your body when it has been placed on the spit and roasted by the fire, let it not lie there in the earth or on the grass, but let it be given to the gods who long for it.

[To the priests:] Those (priests) who see that the racehorse is cooked, who say, "It smells good! Take it away!," and who wait for the doling out of the flesh of the charger—let their approval encourage us. The testing fork for the cauldron that cooks the flesh, the pots for pouring the broth, the cover of the bowls to keep it warm, the hooks, the dishes—all these attend the horse.

[To the horse:] The place where the horse walks, where he rests, where he rolls, and the fetters on the horse's feet, and what he has drunk and the fodder he has eaten—let all of that stay with you even among the gods. Let not the fire that reeks of smoke darken you, nor the red-hot cauldron split into pieces. The gods receive the horse who has been sacrificed, worshipped, consecrated, and sanctified with the cry of "Vaṣaṭ!" The cloth that they spread beneath the horse, the upper covering, the golden trappings on him, the halter and the fetters on his feet—let these things that are his own bind the horse among the gods.

[To the horse:] If someone riding you has struck you too hard with heel or whip when you shied, I make all these things well again for you with prayer, as they do with the ladle for the oblation in sacrifices.

[To the priests:] The axe cuts through the thirty-four ribs of the racehorse who is the companion of the gods. Keep the limbs undamaged and place them in the proper pattern. Cut them apart, calling out piece by piece. One (priest) is the slaughterer of the horse of Tvaṣṭṛ; two (priests) restrain him. This is the rule.

[To the horse:] As many of your limbs as I set out, according to the rules, so many balls I offer into the fire. Let not your dear soul burn you as you go away. Let not the axe do lasting harm to your body. Let no greedy, clumsy slaughterer hack in the wrong place and damage your limbs with his knife. You do not really die through this, nor are you harmed. You go to the gods on paths pleasant to go on. The two bay stallions, the two roan mares are now your chariot mates. The racehorse has been set in the donkey's yoke.

[To the gods:] Let this racehorse bring us good cattle and good horses, male children and all nourishing wealth. Let Aditi make us free from sin. Let the horse with our offerings achieve sovereign power for us.

Source: *Ṛg Veda* 1.162, from *Textual Sources for the Study of Hinduism*, pp. 9–10.

TO THE FIRE ALTAR

This hymn is used to help the officiating priest mentally prepare prior to performance of the sacrifice. He visualizes the fire altar as the entire universe and views the sacrifice as a way to attain spiritual knowledge. It is notable in that it shows the increasingly cosmic significance given to the rituals: They were no longer merely localized sacrifices performed for particular ends, but instead were microcosmic expressions of macrocosmic forces and processes. The sacrificer meditates on the greater ramifications of the ritual about to be performed, its cosmic repercussions, and its transformative effects on the person who performs it. The hymn also shows an expanding view of the cosmos and a corresponding expansion in the religious vision of brahmin priests, who are no longer content simply to perform sacrifices for limited goals but increasingly are interested in the effects they will have beyond this world and in the mind of the sacrificer.

1. The fire altar built here is this world. The stones surrounding it are the waters. Its Yajuṣmati bricks are humans. Its Sūdadohas [a drink of immortality] are cows. Plants and trees are its cement, offerings, and fuel. Agni is its connecting bricks. Thus this constitutes all of Agni. Agni pervades space. Whoever knows this becomes all of Agni, the pervader of space.
2. Moreover, the fire altar is also the air. The horizon is its surrounding circle of bricks. . . . The birds are its Yajuṣmati bricks. . . .
3. Moreover, the fire altar is also the sky. . . .
4. Moreover, the fire altar is also the sun. . . .
5. Moreover, the fire altar is also the stars. . . .
7. Moreover, the fire altar is also the meters [of verses]. . . .
10. Moreover, the fire altar is also the year. . . .
12. Moreover, the fire altar is also the body. . . .
14. Moreover, the fire altar is also all beings and all gods. All the gods and all beings are the waters, and the constructed fire altar is the same as the waters. . . .
16. Referring to this, the verse states: By way of wisdom they ascend to the place where desires disappear. Neither sacrificial gifts nor the devoted performers of sacrifices who lack wisdom go there. One who is ignorant of this does not go to that world either by sacrificial offerings or devout actions. It belongs to those with wisdom.

Source: *Śatapatha Brāhmaṇa* 10.5.4.1–16. Tr. JP.

WHAT IS THE ORIGIN OF THE WORLD?

This poem represents an early speculative tendency from the Vedic period. The writer of the poem is considering what, if anything, existed before the world as we know it, before creation, and even before the birth of the gods.

There was neither nonexistence nor existence then; there was neither the realm of space nor the sky which is beyond. What stirred? Where? In whose protection? Was there water, bottomlessly deep? There was neither death nor immortality then. There was no distinguishing sign of night nor of day. That one breathed, windless, by its own impulse. Other than that there was nothing beyond. Darkness was hidden by darkness in the beginning; with no distinguishing sign, all this was water. The life force that was covered with emptiness, that one arose through the power of heat.

Desire came upon that one in the beginning; that was the first seed of mind. Poets seeking in their heart with wisdom found the bond of existence in nonexistence. Their cord was extended across. Was there below? Was there above? There were seed-placers; there were powers. There was impulse beneath; there was giving-forth above. Who really knows? Who will here proclaim it? Whence was it produced? Whence is this creation? The gods came afterwards, with the creation of this universe. Who then knows whence it has arisen? Whence this creation has arisen—perhaps it formed itself, or perhaps it did not—the one who looks down on it, in the highest heaven, only he knows—or perhaps he does not know.

Source: *Ṛg Veda* 10.129, from *Textual Sources for the Study of Hinduism*, p. 33.

VEDĀNTA: THE UPANIṢADS AND THEIR COMMENTARIES

YAMA'S INSTRUCTIONS TO NACIKETAS

The Kaṭha Upaniṣad *presents the story of a brahmin boy named Naciketas. His father, Āruṇi, is performing a sacrifice in which he is required to give away all his possessions, but Naciketas notices that he is not complying with the spirit of the sacrifice. Naciketas asks his father, "To whom will you give me?", to which his father angrily replies, "I give you to Yama [the god of death]." Unfortunately for both Naciketas and his father, words spoken in the context of a sacrifice have great power, so Naciketas is immediately sent to the palace of Yama.*

Yama, however, is not in the palace when Naciketas arrives and does not return for three days. When Yama arrives and sees that Naciketas has been waiting for a long while and has not been given the courtesy due to a brahmin, he apologizes and offers to make restitution by granting Naciketas three wishes. Being a dutiful son, Naciketas first asks that he be able to return to his father and that his father receive him with happiness and love instead of anger. His next wish is significant: He asks Yama to teach him about the Naciketas fire for which he is named. This is significant because it shows that in this text the traditional values and practices of brahmins are not being questioned. Naciketas does not doubt the efficacy of the sacrifices; instead, he wishes to learn more about them, and only after this does he make his third request, asking Yama to tell him what happens to a human being after death.

Yama responds by testing Naciketas in order to determine his sincerity in asking about this. He offers Naciketas worldly goods instead—things like wealth, land, power, long-lived sons and grandsons, fame, and so on—but none of these things interest Naciketas. He understands that they are transitory and fleeting, and he wishes instead for knowledge of the ātman *(the self), which is truly valuable. Having tested his resolve, Yama praises him for choosing the good* (śreyas) *over the pleasant* (preyas). *Yama then teaches Naciketas about the* ātman, *the essence of each individual, the eternal, unchanging reality that exists forever, unaffected by the circumstances and events of a person's countless rebirths. The* ātman, *he declares, cannot be known through the senses or the intellect: it must be known through direct, intuitive realization. The culmination of the teaching is Yama's revelation that the* ātman *is not only a personal essence; it is also said to be identical with the cosmic Ultimate, called* Brahman.

2.1.1. Yama said: "The good is one thing, and the pleasant another. Both of these different goals blind a person. From among the two, it is better for one who chooses the good. A person who chooses the pleasant does not fulfill his goals.

2. "A person receives both the good and the pleasant. Thoroughly examining the two, a wise person distinguishes them. The wise person chooses the good rather than the pleasant. The stupid person, due to grasping, chooses the pleasant. . . ."
14. Naciketas asked Yama: "Tell me what you see beyond righteousness and unrighteousness, beyond what is done and not done, and what is beyond what was and what will be."
15. Yama said: "I will briefly explain to you all that is taught in the Vedas, all that asceticism declares, and that which sages seek through religious practice: It is *Oṃ*.
16. "This syllable truly is Brahman, it is the supreme syllable. Whoever knows it obtains all wishes.
17. "This is the best support, this is the supreme support. Knowing this support, a person attains happiness in the world of Brahmā.
18. "The wise one is not born, does not die; it does not come from anywhere, does not become anything. It is unborn, enduring, permanent; this one is not destroyed when the body is destroyed.
19. "If someone thinks to destroy and if the destroyed thinks of being destroyed, then neither understands. This [ātman] neither destroys nor is it destroyed.
20. "The ātman hidden in the heart of all living beings is smaller than the smallest and greater than the greatest. A person who does not act with desire and is free from sadness sees it and its greatness through the purity of mind and senses. . . .
23. "The self is not gained through study, nor by the intellect, nor by much learning; it is gained only by whomever it chooses: to such a person the self reveals itself.
24. "Not to one who has not renounced wrongdoing, nor by one who is not tranquil, nor to one who is not calm, nor to one whose mind is not at peace: They cannot gain it through intelligence *(prajñā)*."

2.3.1. "You should know that the ātman is like the rider of a chariot, and the body is like the chariot. You should know that the intellect *(buddhi)* is like the chariot driver, and the mind is like the reins. . . .

4. "The senses are said to be the horses, and sense-objects are the area in which they travel. The self, together with senses and mind, are termed 'enjoyer' by the wise.
5. "If one lacks understanding and does not constantly control the mind, then one's senses become uncontrolled like the bad horses of a charioteer.
6. "If one is wise and constantly controls the mind, then one's senses remain controlled like the good horses of a charioteer.
7. "If one lacks understanding, lacks mental control, and is impure, then one can never reach the goal, but continues in cyclic existence *(saṃsāra)*.
8. "If one is wise, however, with a fully disciplined mind, then one reaches the goal and will not be reborn again. . . .
13. "The wise should restrain speech and mind, mind should be restrained in the understanding self, understanding should be

restrained in the great self, and that should be restrained in the tranquil ātman.

14. "Arise, awaken, go and attain your wishes; understand them! The poets say that the path is like the sharp edge of a razor, difficult to travel, difficult to obtain.
15. "It is soundless, intangible, formless, inexhaustible. In the same way, it is tasteless, eternal, and odorless, beginningless, endless, beyond the great, unchanging. By understanding it, one escapes the jaws of death."

4.1. Yama said: "The Self-Existent opened the senses outward; thus humans look outward, not toward the inner ātman. But a wise person, seeking immortality, turns in the reverse direction and sees the inner ātman.

2. "Childish people go after outward pleasures. They walk into the net of death that is spread everywhere. But the wise, knowing immortality, do not seek the permanent among the impermanent.
3. "One knows color, taste, smell, sounds, touches, and sexual pleasures only through this (ātman). What else remains? This indeed is That.
4. "By recognizing the great, all-pervading ātman, by which one perceives both sleeping and dream states, the wise overcome sorrow. This indeed is That.
5. "One who knows this experiencer, the living ātman that is nearest to one, which is lord of the past and the future, is never afraid of it. This indeed is That. . . .
9. "The sun arises from it and sets into it. All gods are based in it, and none ever move beyond it. This indeed is That. . . .
11. "Through it the mind attains [realization]. There is absolutely no difference here. If one perceives difference here, one goes from death to death."

6.1. Yama said: "Its root is above, its branches below, this eternal tree. That [root] is the Pure. That is Brahman. That is called the Immortal. All worlds rest on it, and none go beyond it. This, indeed, is That.

2. "The whole world, whatever exists, was created from and moves in life. The great fear, the raised thunderbolt: those who know That become immortal.
3. "From fear of It fire burns, from fear of It the sun gives off heat. From fear of It Indra and Vāyu, and Yama the fifth, speed along. . . .
9. "One cannot see its form, and no one ever sees it with the eye. It is framed by the heart, by thought, by the mind: those who know That become immortal.
10. "When one stops the five knowledges [derived from the senses], together with the mind, and the intellect is still, that is said to be the highest path.
11. "This is said to be yoga, the firm restraint of the senses. Then one becomes undistracted. Yoga, truly, is the beginning and the end.

12. "It is not perceived through speech, through mind, nor by sight. How can it be understood other than by saying, 'It is'?"

Source: *Kaṭha Upaniṣad* selections. Tr. JP.

TRUTH AND TRANSCENDENCE

Dharma *is one of the most important concepts in Hinduism, but it is difficult to define because of the multitude of ways in which it is construed and its many associations. It is a universal principle that determines how things ought to be and is linked with the natural order of the universe. It also refers to duty: the actions, attitudes, and ritual performances expected of people according to their respective social grouping (varṇa), gender, stage of life, and role in society. Although* dharma *is unalterable and universal, the way in which one actualizes it in one's life may vary over time, as when a person decides to renounce the world and pursue liberation from cyclic existence. In the following passage, we are informed that* Brahman, *the creator of the universe and the sum total of all that is, originated* dharma *and that its universality places it above even its creator.* Brahman *cannot alter* dharma *or change it. Kings who follow* dharma *must obey its rules. This makes it possible for society to function; the weak have recourse to the truth and can appeal to it. If one's case is just, one can triumph even over those who stand above one in the social hierarchy. This section links* dharma *with the ultimate goal of liberation. After* dharma *was created,* Brahman *projected the four social groupings, each of which had a specific* dharma *to perform which, being unalterable and universal provides a fixed standard of behavior. Similarly, one aspect of the makeup of the universe is the apparent multitude of selves* (ātman), *which are all ultimately one with* Brahman. *Those who understand* dharma *perform their prescribed duties. Spiritually advanced beings recognize the underlying universal reality of* Brahman, *and through this they are able to pass beyond rebirth after they die.*

> [Brahman] was still not fully actualized, and so it created *dharma*, which was a form that was superior to it and surpassed it. *Dharma* is the kingly power that restrains the kingly power [of Brahman]. Thus there is nothing that transcends *dharma*. A weaker man can make demands on a stronger one through an appeal to *dharma*, in the way one makes an appeal to a king. *Dharma* is nothing other than truth, and so when a man speaks the truth, people say that he speaks *dharma*; when he expresses *dharma*, he speaks the truth. They are truly the same thing. . . . If a person leaves this world without realizing his own world [i.e., the Self, *ātman*], because he does not know it, it cannot protect him, just as if the Vedas are not recited or a deed is not performed they do not [produce a positive result.] If one who does not know it [*ātman*] performs many virtuous acts, they will surely perish with him. So one should meditate on the world called the Self. One who meditates on this world called the Self will not see his works perish with him because by this very Self he projects whatever he wishes.

Source: *Bṛhadāraṇyaka Upaniṣd*, 1.4.14–15. Tr. JP.

SACRIFICES CANNOT LEAD TO THE ULTIMATE GOAL

This passage expresses a somewhat different opinion of the value of sacrifices: It calls them "unsteady boats" that should not be relied on by a person wishing to leave cyclic existence. It does not, however, urge brahmins to stop performing sacrifices but instead warns them not to rely on them exclusively and advises them also to remove themselves from the world and practice asceticism and devotion in the forest in order to work at achieving a tranquil mind that knows truth.

1.2.1. This is the truth: The sacrificial rites that the sages saw in the hymns are variously elaborated in the three [Vedas]. Perform them constantly, O lovers of truth. This is the path to the world of good deeds.

2. When the flame flickers after the offering fire has been kindled, then between the offerings of the two portions of clarified butter one should give one's main oblations—an offering made with faith. . . .

7. These sacrificial rituals, eighteen in number, are, however, unsteady boats, in which only the lesser work is expressed. The fools who delight in this as supreme go again and again to old age and death.

8. Abiding in the midst of ignorance, wise only according to their own estimate, thinking themselves to be learned, but really dense, these deluded men are like blind men led by one who is himself blind.

9. Abiding variously in ignorance, childishly they think, "We have accomplished our aim." Since the performers of actions do not understand because of desire, therefore, they, the wretched ones, sink down [from heaven] when their worlds are exhausted.

10. Regarding sacrifice and merit as most important, the deluded ones do not know of anything better. Having enjoyed themselves only for a time on top of the heaven won by good deeds, they re-enter this world or a lower one.

11. Those who practice austerities *(tapas)* and devotion in the forest, the tranquil ones, the knowers of truth, living the life of wandering beggars: they depart, freed from desire, through the door of the sun, to where the immortal Person *(puruṣa)* lives, the imperishable ātman.

12. Having examined the worlds won by actions, a brahmin should arrive at nothing but indifference. The world that was not made is not won by what is done [i.e., by sacrifice]. For the sake of that knowledge, one should go with sacrificial fuel in hand to a spiritual teacher *(guru)* who is well-versed in the scriptures and also firm in the realization of Brahman.

13. Approaching the wise [teacher] properly, one with tranquil thoughts, who has attained peace, is taught this very truth, the knowledge of Brahman by means of which one knows the imperishable Person, the only Reality.

Source: *Muṇḍaka Upaniṣad,* ch. 1. Tr. JP.

INSTRUCTIONS ON RENOUNCING THE WORLD

This passage instructs the aspiring world renouncer (saṃnyāsin) *on the proper motivation for leaving society. It indicates that one should give up performance of the Vedic rituals and leave family, friends, and occupation behind, focusing one's attention on the final goal of realization of the* ātman. *In a special ritual, one takes into oneself the sacred fire that one had maintained as a householder, which now becomes identified with the fire of the digestive processes. One discards the sacred thread that one has worn since the initiation* (upanayana) *ceremony, which designates one as a member of one of the three "twice-born" classes. After this one has no caste identity and can wander anywhere—and take food from anyone—without fear of ritual pollution.*

Āruṇi went to the realm of Prajāpati and, approaching him, said: "Lord, by what means does one completely renounce religious activities?"

Prajāpati said: "One should forsake sons, brothers, relatives, and so forth; one should give up the topknot, the sacred string, sacrifices, ritual codes, and Vedic recitation. . . . One should have a staff and a garment; and renounce everything else.

"A householder or a student *(brahma-cāri)* or a forest hermit should discard his sacred string on the ground or in water. He should place the external fires in the fire of his stomach and the *gāyatri* [a sacred mantra] in the fire of his speech. . . .

"From that point on, he should live without mantras. He should bathe at the start of the three periods of the day and, deeply immersed in meditation, he should realize his union with the Self."

Source: *Āruṇi Upaniṣad* 1–2. Tr. JP.

SELF-EFFORT AND LIBERATION

The following passage comes from the Crest-Jewel of Discrimination, *attributed by Hindu tradition to Śaṅkara, one of the greatest expositors of the thought of the Upaniṣads and the primary exponent of the nondualist* (advaita) *school of commentary. The author contends that the path to liberation is a solitary one. He states that every person must win salvation alone and that no one else can help. Even the scriptures are only guideposts, and one who becomes attached to them will remain enmeshed in cyclic existence. They point the way, but the goal is reached only by those who transcend all mundane supports and actualize direct, nonconceptual understanding of the* ātman.

Children may free their father from his debts, but no other person can free a man from his bondage: he must do it himself. Others may relieve the suffering caused by a burden that weighs upon the head; but the suffering which comes from hunger and the like can only be relieved by one's self. The sick man who takes medicine and follows the rules of diet is seen to be restored to health—but not through the efforts of another. A clear vision of the Reality may be obtained only through our own eyes, when they have been opened by spiritual insight—never through the eyes of some other seer. Through our own eyes we learn what the moon looks like: how could we learn this through the eyes of others? Those cords that bind us, because of our ignorance, our lustful desires and the fruits of our karma—how could anybody but ourselves untie them, even in the course of innumerable ages? Neither by the practice of Yoga or of Sāṃkhya philosophy, nor by good works, nor by learning, does liberation come; but only through a realization that Ātman and Brahman are one—in no other way. . . .

Erudition, well-articulated speech, a wealth of words, and skill in expounding the scriptures—these things give pleasure to the learned, but they do not bring liberation. Study of the scriptures is fruitless as long as Brahman has not been experienced. And when Brahman has been experienced, it is useless to read the scriptures. A network of words is like a dense forest which causes the mind to wander hither and thither. Therefore, those who know this truth should struggle hard to experience Brahman. When a man has been bitten by the snake of ignorance he can only be cured by the realization of Brahman. What use are Vedas or scriptures, charms or herbs? A sickness is not cured by saying the word "medicine." You must take the medicine. Liberation does not come by merely saying the word "Brahman." Brahman must be actually experienced.

Until you allow this apparent universe to dissolve from your consciousness—until you have experienced Brahman—how can you find liberation just by saying the word "Brahman"? The result is merely a noise.

Source: *Viveka-cūḍāmaṇi,* from *Śaṅkara's Crest-Jewel of Discrimination,* tr. Swami Prabhavananda and Christopher Isherwood (Hollywood: Vendanta Press, 1975), pp. 40–41.

MĀYĀ

Māyā plays a central role in Śaṅkara's interpretation of the Upaniṣads. The term literally means "magic" or "illusion," and he claims that it is the power by which Brahman *hides the truth from ordinary beings. It is a creative power that causes the apparent phenomena of cyclic existence to be superimposed on the unitary* Brahman.

Māyā, in her potential aspect, is the divine power of the Lord. She has no beginning. She is composed of the three qualities *(guṇa),* subtle, beyond perception. It is from the effects she produces that her existence is inferred by the wise. It is she who gives birth to the whole universe. She is neither being nor nonbeing, nor a mixture of both. She is neither divided nor undivided, nor a mixture of both. She is neither an indivisible whole, nor composed of parts, nor a mixture of both. She is most strange. Her nature is inexplicable. Just as knowing a rope to be a rope destroys the illusion that it is a snake, so Māyā is destroyed by direct experience of Brahman—the pure, the free, the one without a second.

Source: *Viveka-cūḍāmaṇi,* from *Śaṅkara's Crest-Jewel of Discrimination,* p. 49.

THAT IS YOU

The Upaniṣadic statement "That is you" (tat tvam asi) *is viewed by exponents of nondualist Vedānta as a statement of the nondifference of* ātman *and* Brahman. *The following excerpt discusses this statement from the nondualist perspective.*

The scriptures establish the absolute identity of Ātman and Brahman by declaring repeatedly: "That is you." The terms "Brahman" and "Ātman," in their true meaning, refer to "That" and "you" respectively. In their literal, superficial meaning, "Brahman" and "Ātman" have opposite attributes, like the sun and the glow-worm, the king and his servant, the ocean and the well, or Mount Meru [a huge mountain that stands at the center of the world according to Indian mythology] and the atom. Their identity is established only when they are understood in their true significance, and not in a superficial sense.

"Brahman" may refer to God, the ruler of Māyā and creator of the universe. The "Ātman" may refer to the individual soul, associated with the five coverings which are effects of Māyā. Thus regarded, they possess opposite attributes. But this apparent opposition is caused by Māyā and her effects. It is not real, therefore, but superimposed. These attributes caused by Māyā and her effects are superimposed upon God and upon the individual soul. When they have been completely eliminated, neither soul nor God remains. If you take the kingdom from a king and the weapons from a soldier, there is neither soldier nor king. The scriptures repudiate any idea of a duality in Brahman. Let a man seek illumination in the knowledge of Brahman, as the scriptures direct. Then those attributes, which our ignorance has superimposed upon Brahman, will disappear. . . .

Then let him meditate upon the identity of Brahman and Ātman, and so realize the truth. Through spiritual discrimination, let him understand the true inner meaning of the terms "Brahman" and "Ātman," thus realizing their absolute identity. See the reality in both, and you will find that there is but one. . . .

Just as a clay jar or vessel is understood to be nothing but clay, so this whole universe, born of Brahman, essentially Brahman, is Brahman only—for there is nothing else but Brahman, nothing beyond That. That is the reality. That is our Ātman. Therefore, "That is you"—pure, blissful, supreme Brahman, the one without a second.

Source: *Viveka-cūḍāmaṇi,* from *Śaṅkara's Crest-Jewel of Discrimination,* pp. 72–74.

QUALIFIED NONDUALISM: RĀMĀNUJA'S INTERPRETATION

Rāmānuja disagrees with the nondualist system of Upaniṣadic interpretation. In this passage, he contends that it is absurd to completely equate the absolute Brahman *with the individual* ātman. *As an exponent of devotionalism, Rāmānuja rejects the nondualist system, since it would make devotion absurd. If* ātman *and* Brahman *were one, there would be no real basis for worship. Rāmānuja contends that the Upaniṣadic statement "That is you" does not mean what nondualists think it does; rather, it indicates that there are two separate entities,* ātman *and* Brahman, *and that the former is wholly dependent upon the latter, like a wave in relation to the ocean. The wave appears to stand apart from the ocean, but its substance and being derive from the ocean, although it has at least a qualifiedly separate identity. Similarly, the* ātman *derives from* Brahman, *but because the history of each* ātman *is distinctly its own, it contradicts reason and actual experience to claim that* ātman *is completely identical with* Brahman.

1.1.1. The word "Brahman" refers to the highest Person, in whom all faults are naturally eliminated, who possesses all the most auspicious qualities, is unlimited, unsurpassed, and incalculable. Everywhere the word Brahman is associated with the quality of magnitude. . . . [Brahman] is the "Lord of All.". . .

Our [nondualist Vedāntin] opponents say: "Brahman is only consciousness, is completely opposed to all particularity, and is the highest reality; all difference—such as different types of knowers, objects of knowledge, different knowledge produced by them, and anything beyond that—is false when posited of [Brahman]."

[We reply:] Brahman, which is to be understood by means of its distinctive characteristics, has a nature distinguished from all objects other than itself, and those contradictions are eliminated by these three words: The word "truth" excludes anything that is "non-truth," that which is amenable to modification. The word "knowledge" indicates what is excluded from non-sentient things whose illumination depends upon others. And the word "limitless" indicates what is excluded from anything that is circumscribed by space, time or matter. This exclusion is not a positive or negative quality, but [indicates] Brahman itself as distinguished from everything that is other than itself. . . . The ramification of this is that Brahman is self-luminous, with all contradictions excluded. . . .

Those who propound the doctrine of a substance devoid of all difference cannot legitimately assert that there is a proof for such a substance, because all means of valid cognition have for their objects things that are affected by difference. . . . All consciousness implies difference. All states of consciousness have for their objects things that are marked by some difference, as we see in the case of judgments like, "I saw this.". . . It therefore must be admitted that reality is affected with difference, which is well established by valid proofs. . . .

Instead, what all these scriptures deny is only plurality in the sense of contradicting the unity of the world which is utterly dependent on Brahman as an effect and which has Brahman as the inner controlling principle that is its true Self. They do not deny plurality on the part of Brahman in the sense of deciding to become manifold. . . .

Moreover, in texts like the one that states, "That is you" the connection between the constituent parts does not indicate an absolute unity of undifferentiated substance. Instead, the words "that" and "you" indicate that Brahman is distinguished by difference. The word "that" refers to Brahman, which is omniscient and so forth. . . . Moreover, it is impossible that ignorance could belong to Brahman, whose essential nature is knowledge, which is free from all imperfections, omniscient, and contains within itself all auspicious qualities; nor [is it possible that Brahman] could be the basis of the faults and afflictions that arise from ignorance.

Source: Rāmānuja, *Śrībhāṣya*, ch. 1. Tr. JP.

YOGA

THE MEANING OF YOGA

The following excerpts are taken from the Yoga Aphorisms, *attributed to Patañjali, and an explanatory text titled the* Yoga Commentary, *attributed to Vyāsa. The verses of the* Aphorisms *are given in boldface, and the* Commentary *is given in plain text.*

As the text indicates, the term yoga *may be used to refer to a range of practices for disciplining mind and body. In Patañjali's system the focus is on developing progressively greater control over the agitations and fluctuations of mind and body in order to arrive at a state of perfect equanimity. One accomplishes this by turning the attention inward, away from sense objects, which leads to detachment and wisdom. A person who becomes detached from external things has no basis for continued existence and thus becomes liberated from the cycle of birth and death. Unlike the system of the Upaniṣads, however, Patañjali does not understand liberation as a union of the individual* ātman *with the cosmic ultimate* Brahman *but rather as separation of one's spiritual essence* (puruṣa) *from insentient matter* (prakṛti). *In the yoga system, both are considered to be real, and the association of the two is said to be beginningless. Because matter's tendency is to procreate and acquire, and because it is transitory and prone to decay, beings whose spirits are associated with matter necessarily experience suffering. This suffering can, however, be transcended by following the path of the "eight limbs" of physical and mental discipline, which culminate in a state of perfect mental equipoise.*

1. **Here is an instruction on yoga.**
   Yoga is meditative concentration *(samādhi)*, and it is a characteristic of the mind pervading all its states. . . . The five states of the mind are: (1) wandering; (2) deluded; (3) distracted; (4) one-pointed; and (5) cut off.
2. **Yoga is the cessation of states of mind.**
   Since the mind has the three functions of perception, movement, and rest, it is constituted by the three qualities of purity *(sattva)*, lightness *(rajas)*, and heaviness *(tamas)*. . . .
3. **Then the seer abides in his own nature.**
5. **The states are of five types, and are afflicted and non-afflicted.**
   The afflicted are those that are based on afflictions like ignorance and so forth and serve as the basis of latencies. The non-afflicted are

those that have conceptuality for their object and that oppose the operation of the qualities. . . .

12. **The [states of mind] are restrained by practice and detachment.**

 The stream of mind flows both ways: it flows toward good and it flows toward evil. That which flows on to separation down the plane of discriminative knowledge moves toward happiness. That which leads to rebirth flows down the plane of nondiscrimination and moves toward wrong-doing.

17. **Meditative concentration is attained with the help of conceptual understanding, analytical thought, bliss, and self-awareness.**

 Conceptual understanding is the mind's coarse direct experience when it is directed toward an object. Analytical thought is subtle [cognition]. Joy is happiness. Self-awareness is consciousness pertaining to the self. . . . All these states have an object of observation *(ālambana).*

30. **Sickness, laxity, doubt, carelessness, laziness, worldliness, wrong views, failure to attain any level [of concentration], instability: these distractions of mind are the obstacles.**
31. **Pain, despair, unsteadiness of the body, inspiration, and expiration are the companions of these distractions.**
32. **In order to prevent them, one should become familiar with one entity.**
33. **By cultivating friendliness, compassion regarding suffering, joy regarding merit, and indifference toward demerit, one [attains] a calm, undisturbed mind.**

Source: *Yoga-sūtras* and *Yoga-bhāṣya,* ch. 1. Tr. JP.

YOGIC TECHNIQUES

In section 2, Patañjali describes the process by which one develops one's powers of concentration through disciplining thoughts, bringing mind and body under control, and weaning oneself from attachment to external objects.

2.1. **Asceticism *(tapas)*, study, and devotion to God constitute the yoga of action.**

3. **The afflictions are ignorance, self-cherishing, desire, aversion, and love of life.**

 Ignorance is simply misconception. Self-cherishing and the others are also based on ignorance and, since they cannot exist without it, they are ignorant. Thus when ignorance is destroyed, their destruction also follows.

5. **Ignorance is taking the impermanent, the impure, the painful, and the not-self to be permanent, pure, pleasurable, and the self.**
6. **When one views the appearances of a unitary self through the power of perception, this is self-cherishing.**
7. **Attachment is abiding in pleasure.**
8. **Aversion is abiding in revulsion toward pain.**

9. **Love of life, moving along by its own potency, exists even in the wise.**
11. **Their mental states are destroyed by meditation.**

As the gross dirt of clothes is at first shaken off, and then the fine dirt is washed off by effort and work, so the coarse essential mental states need only slight counteracting efforts, whereas the subtle mental states need very powerful counteragents.

17. **The conjunction of the knower and the knowable is the cause of what is to be escaped.**
18. **The knowable has the nature of purity, lightness, and heaviness; it consists of the elements and the powers of sensation; its purposes are experience and liberation.**

Liberation is the ascertainment of the nature of the enjoyer, the self. Beyond the knowledge of these two there is no wisdom.

20. **The perceiver is only perception; even though pure, it perceives by way of conditions.**

"Only perception": This means that it is nothing other than the power of becoming conscious; that is to say, it is not touched by the qualities. This self cognizes the intellect by reflection. He is neither quite similar nor quite dissimilar to the intellect.

"It is not quite similar." Why? The intellect, having for its sphere of action objects known and not yet known, is of course changeable. . . . "It is not quite dissimilar." Why? . . . Since the self cognizes ideas as the intellect, grasped by consciousness, it is transformed into them; it appears by the act of cognition to be the very self of the intellect, although in reality it is not so. . . .

28. **With the diminution of impurity by the sustained practice of the limbs *(aṅga)* of yoga, the light of wisdom reaches up to discriminating knowledge.**
29. **Restraint, observance, posture, breath control, withdrawal [of the senses], mental stability, meditation, and meditative concentration are the eight limbs of yoga.**
30. **Of these, the restraints *(yama)* are: non-injury *(ahiṃsā)*, truthfulness, not stealing, celibacy, and having few possessions.**
32. **The observances *(niyama)* are: cleanliness, contentment, asceticism, study, and devotion to God.**

Of these, cleanliness is brought about by earth and water, etc., and by eating clean things, etc. This is external. It is internal when it involves washing away impurities of the mind. Contentment is absence of desire to get more of the necessities of life than one already possesses. Asceticism involves bearing extreme conditions, hunger, thirst, cold, and heat, standing or sitting . . . or severe penances. Study is reading texts that are concerned with liberation, or the repetition of the sacred syllable *Oṃ*. Devotion to God involves offering one's actions to the supreme Teacher.

33. **When thoughts of wrongdoing bother you, familiarize yourself with their antidotes.**

40. **By cleanliness is meant disgust with one's body and cessation of contact with others.**
46. **Posture is steadily relaxed.**
47. **By relaxation of effort and by limitless absorption.**

    Posture is perfected when effort ceases, so that there may be no more agitation of the body. Or, when the mind achieves balance with regard to the infinite, it brings about the perfection of posture.
49. **Breath control *(prāṇāyāma)* involves restraining the inhalation and exhalation movements [of breath,] which follows when that [control of posture] has been achieved.**
54. **Withdrawal [of the senses] *(pratyāhāra)* is that by which the senses do not come into contact with their objects and follow the nature of the mind.**

Source: *Yoga-sūtras* and *Yoga-bhāṣya*, ch. 2. Tr. JP.

YOGIC ATTAINMENTS

In this section Patañjali discusses the results of yogic practice, which include unshakable mental stability, equanimity, dispassion, and eventually liberation from the cycle of birth and death.

3.1. **Mental stability *(dhāraṇā)* is mental steadiness.**

    Mental stability involves the mind becoming focused on such places as the sphere of the navel, the lotus of the heart, the light in the brain, the tip of the nose, the tip of the tongue, and similar parts of the body; or on any other external object. . . .

49. **Only one who fully understands the distinction between purity and the self attains supremacy over all states of being and becomes omniscient.**

    Omniscience refers to simultaneously discriminating knowledge of the "qualities"—which are of the nature of all phenomena—and showing forth as they do separately the quiescent, the disturbed, and the unpredictable characteristics. This attainment is known as the "sorrowless" *(viśoka)*. Reaching this, the yogi moves omniscient and powerful, with all his afflictions ended.

50. **When the seed of bondage has been destroyed by desirelessness even for those [attainments], absolute separation *(kaivalya)* results.**

    Then all the seeds of afflictions pass, together with the mind, into latency. When they have become latent, the self does not then suffer. . . . This state—in which the qualities manifest in the mind as afflictions, actions, and fruitions without having fulfilled their object and come back to action—is the final separation of consciousness from the qualities. This is the state of absolute separation, when the self remains consciousness alone, as in its own nature.

Source: *Yoga-sūtras* and *Yoga-bhāṣya*, ch. 3. Tr. JP.

PURĀṆAS AND EPICS

THE FOUR AGES

In contemporary India, the Purāṇas and Epics are among the most widely known of Hindu scriptures. The Purāṇas recount the mythologies of popular gods such as Śiva, Viṣṇu, and Devī (the Goddess). Rich in symbolism and containing a wide variety of divergent traditions, they describe the attributes of the gods and indicate how they should be worshipped.

The two great epics of Hinduism, the Rāmāyaṇa *and the* Mahābhārata, *are monumental stories that weave history, myth, and religion into complex, multifaceted tales that recount important historical and mythical events and indicate the lessons that should be drawn from them. The* Rāmāyaṇa *tells the story of Rāma—considered by tradition to be an incarnation* (avatāra) *of Viṣṇu—who takes birth among humans in order to fight against evil forces and establish dharma in the world. Forced to leave his kingdom with his dutiful wife Sītā, he wanders in the wilderness, spreading righteousness wherever he goes. In a climactic battle he faces the demon Rāvaṇa, who has captured Sītā. Rāma slays Rāvaṇa, thus enabling dharma to be established in the demon's realm.*

The Mahābhārata*—which contains the* Bhagavad-gītā, *one of the most important religious texts in contemporary Hinduism—tells the story of a conflict between related clans for supremacy in northern India. Unlike the heroes of the* Rāmāyaṇa, *the protagonists of the* Mahābhārata *(the Pāṇḍavas) often make mistakes, question what is the right course of action, and regret wrong decisions.*

In this passage from the Liṅga Purāṇa, *Indra teaches a human sage about the cyclical nature of time. According to this system, when the universe is first created a golden age begins. During this time beings have long lifespans, beautiful bodies, and great happiness. As time goes on, however, things begin imperceptibly to worsen, and eventually it becomes necessary to divide people according to their predispositions.*

First, you should know, comes the Golden Age, and then the Age of the Trey; and the Age of the Deuce and the Fourth Age come next: these are the four Ages, in brief. The Golden Age is the age of goodness *(sattva);* the Age of the Trey is the age of energy *(rajas);* the Age of the Deuce is a mixture of energy and darkness *(tamas);* and the Dark Age is the age of darkness; each age has its characteristic ways of behaving. Meditation is the main thing in the Golden Age; sacrifice in the Age of the Trey; worship in the Age of Deuce; purity and charity in the Dark Age. The Golden Age lasts for four thousand years, and is followed by a twilight of four hundred years. And the lifespan of living creatures lasts for four thousand human years in the Golden Age.

After the twilight of the Golden Age has passed, one of the four feet of the dharma of the Ages is gone in all of its aspects. The excellent Age of the Trey is one fourth less than the Golden Age; the Age of the Deuce lasts for half the time of the Golden Age, and the Dark Age lasts for one half the time of the Age of the Deuce. The last three twilights last for three hundred, two hundred, and one hundred years; this happens in aeon after aeon, Age after Age. In the first Age, the Golden Age, the eternal dharma walks on four feet; in the Age of Trey, on three feet; in the Age of Deuce, on two feet. In the Fourth Age it lacks three feet and is devoid of the element of goodness.

In (every) Golden Age, people are born in pairs; their livelihood consists in reveling in the taste of what exists right before one's eyes. All creatures are satisfied, always, and take delight in all enjoyments. There is no distinction between the lowest and the highest among them; they are all good, all equal in their lifespan, happiness, and form, in the Golden Age. They have no preferences, nor do they experience the opposing pairs of emotions; they do not hate or get tired. They have no homes or dwelling-places, but live in the mountains and oceans; they have no sorrow, but consist mostly of goodness and generally live alone. They go wherever they wish, constantly rejoicing in their minds; in the Golden Age, people do not engage in any actions, good or bad.

At that time there was no system of separate classes and stages of life, and no mixture (of classes or castes). But in the course of time, in the Age of the Trey, they no longer reveled in the taste (of existence). When that fulfillment was lost, another sort of fulfillment was born. When water reaches its subtle state, it is transformed into clouds; from thundering clouds, rain is emitted. As soon as the surface of the earth was touched by that rain, trees appeared on it, and they became houses for the people, who used those trees for their livelihood and all their enjoyments. People lived off those trees at the beginning of the Age of the Trey.

But then, after a long time, people began to change; the emotions of passion and greed arose, for no apparent cause, as a result of a change in the people that arose out of time. Then all the trees that they regarded as their houses vanished, and when they had vanished, the people who were born in pairs became confused. They began to think about their fulfillment, considering the matter truthfully, and then the trees that they regarded as their houses appeared again. These trees brought forth clothing and fruits and jewelry; and on the very same trees there would grow, in bud after bud, honey made by no bees, powerful honey of superb aroma, color, and taste. People lived on that honey, lived happily all their life long, finding their delight and their nourishment in that perfection, always free from fever.

But then, as another time came, they became greedy. They lopped off the limbs of the trees and took by force the honey that no bees had made. As a result of that crime that they committed in their greed, the magic trees, together with their honey, vanished, first here, then there, and as time exerted its power, very little of that fulfillment was left. As the Age of the Trey came on, the opposing pairs of emotions arose, and people became quite miserable as a result of the sharp cold and rain and heat. Tortured by these opposing pairs, they began to cover themselves; and then they made houses on the mountain to ward off the opposing pairs. Formerly, they had gone wherever they wished, living without fixed dwellings; now they began to live in fixed dwellings according to their need and their pleasure. . . .

Then, by the force of that Age, all the people were so crazy with rage that they seized one another and took their sons, wives, wealth, and so forth, by force. When he realized all this, the lotus-born (Brahmā) created the Kṣatriyas to protect people from getting wounded, in order to establish a firm support for the moral boundaries. Then by means of his own brilliance, the god who is the soul of all established the system of the classes and stages of life, and he himself established the livelihood for each profession to live on. Gradually, the institution of sacrifice evolved in the Age of the Trey, but even then some good people did not perform animal sacrifices. For eventually Viṣṇu, who sees everything, performed a sacrifice by force, and then as a result of that the Brahmins prescribed the non-violent sacrifice.

But then, in the Age of the Deuce, men began to have differences of opinion, to differ in mind, action, and speech, and to have difficulty making a living. Then, gradually, as a result of the exhaustion of their bodies, all creatures became subject to greed, working for wages, working as merchants, fighting, indecision about basic principles, lack of interest in the schools of the Vedas, confounding of dharmas, destruction of the system of the classes and stages of life, and, finally, lust and hatred.

For in the Age of the Deuce, passion, greed, and drunkenness arise. And in (every) Age of the Deuce, a sage named Vyāsa divides the Veda into four. For it is known that there was a single Veda, in four parts, in the Ages of the Trey; but as a result of the shrinking of the lifespan, it was divided up in the Ages of the Deuce. And these divisions were further divided by the sons of the (Ṛg Vedic) seers, according to their deviant opinions; they transposed the order of the (Ṛg Vedic) mantras and the Brāhmaṇas, and they changed the accents and the syllables. Wise men compiled the collections of the *Ṛg Veda, Yajur Veda,* and *Sāma Veda;* though they were composed in common, they have been (subsequently) separated by people of various opinions, divided into *Brāhmaṇas, Kalpasūtras,* and explications of the mantras. . . .

Drought, death, disease, and other plagues cause sufferings born of speech, mind, and action, and as a result one becomes numb. From this numbness people begin to think about release from suffering. From this thinking there arises detachment, and from detachment they begin to see their faults. As a result of seeing their faults, knowledge arises in the Age of the Deuce. Now, it will be recalled that the behavior characteristic of the Age of the Deuce was a mixture of energy and darkness. But there was dharma in the first age, the Golden Age, and that dharma still functions in the Age of the Trey; in the Age of the Deuce, however, it becomes disturbed, and in the Dark Age it vanishes. In the Fourth Age, men's senses are disturbed by darkness and they fall prey to illusion and jealousy; they even kill ascetics. In the Dark Age, there is always carelessness, passion, hunger, and fear; the terrible fear of drought pits one country against another. Scripture has no authority, and men take to the violation of dharma; they act without dharma, without morality; they are very angry and not very smart. . . . When scripture is destroyed, and the dharma that is known from the Śāstras, then people will kill one another, for they will have no moral boundaries, no check to their violence, no affection, and no shame. When dharma is destroyed, and people attack one another, they will become stunted and live only twenty-five years; their senses will become confused with arguing, and they will abandon their sons and wives. When they are struck by drought, they will abandon agriculture; they will leave their own countries and go to lands beyond their borders, seeking water in rivers, oceans, wells, and mountains.

Suffering greatly, they will live on honey, raw meat, roots, and fruits; they will wear garments of bark, leaves, and antelope skins; they will perform no rituals and have no possessions. They will fall away from the system of classes and stages of life and fall prey to the terrible mingling of classes. Then there will be very few people left, caught up in this calamity. Afflicted by old age, disease, and hunger, their minds will be numbed by suffering. But from this numbness there will arise thought, and thought makes the mind balanced. Understanding comes from a balanced mind, and from understanding comes a dedication to dharma. The people who are left at the end of the Dark Age will have a kind of formless mental peace. Then, in a day and a night, the age will be transformed for them, deluding their wits as if they were dreaming or insane. And then, by the power of the goal of the future, the Golden Age will begin. And when the Golden Age has begun again, the people left over from the Dark Age become the people born in the Golden Age. . . .

Source: *Liṅga Purāṇa* 1.39.5–34, 48–70; 1.40.1–3, 66cd–76, from *Textual Sources for the Study of Hinduism*, pp. 69–71.

THE LIṄGAM OF ŚIVA

In this passage, Viṣṇu tells a human sage about the origin of the liṅgam, *the phallus of Śiva. The* liṅgam *symbolizes both his procreative force and the energy he stores through asceticism. The story begins with a conversation between Brahmā, said to be the creator of the universe in Hindu mythology, and Viṣṇu, who is the creator of Brahmā. Brahmā believes himself to be supreme, self-created, and omnipotent, but Viṣṇu informs him that he is in fact his creature. Both gods are then amazed to see a huge flaming* liṅgam *that stretches out of sight. They agree to try to find its top and bottom, but after one thousand years flying respectively up and down they are unable to fathom its dimensions. At this point they realize that there is a greater power than themselves, which turns out to be Śiva.*

Once upon a time, when the whole triple world was unmanifest, in darkness, swallowed up by me, I lay there alone, with all the creatures in my belly. I had a thousand heads and a thousand eyes, and a thousand feet; I held in my hands the conch shell, discus, and mace, as I lay in the immaculate water. Then, all of a sudden, I saw from afar the four-headed (Brahmā), the great yogi, the Person with golden luminosity, infinitely luminous, as bright as a hundred suns, blazing with his own brilliance. The god was wearing a black antelope skin and carrying a water-pot; and in the space of the blinking of an eye, that supreme Person arrived. Then Brahmā, to whom all people bow, said to me, "Who are you? And where do you come from? And why are you staying here? Tell me, sir. I am the maker of the worlds, self-created, facing in all directions."

When Brahmā had spoken like that to me, I said to him: "I am the maker of the worlds, and also the one who destroys them, again and again." As the two of us were talking together in this way, each wishing to surpass the other, we saw a flame arising in the northern quarter. As we looked at that flame we were amazed, and its brilliance and power made us cup our hands in reverence and bow to that light from Śiva. The flame grew, a surpassing marvel, and Brahmā and I hastened to run up to it. It broke through heaven and earth with its halo of flame, and in the middle of the flame we saw a liṅgam of great lustre, measuring just a handsbreadth, unmanifest and full of supreme light. In the middle, it was neither gold nor stone or silver; it was indescribable, unimaginable, visible and invisible again and again. It had a thousand garlands of flames, amazing, miraculous; it had great brilliance, and kept getting much bigger. It was covered with a halo of flame, terrifying all creatures with its monstrous form, excessive, bursting through heaven and earth.

Then Brahmā said to me, "Quickly, go down and find out the (bottom) end of this noble liṅgam. I will go up until I see its (top) end." We agreed to do this, and went up and down. I kept going down for a thousand years, but I did not reach the end of the liṅgam; and then I became afraid. In the very same way, Brahmā did not find its end above, and came back to join me right there in the expanse of water. Then we were amazed and frightened of the noble one; deluded by his power of illusion, we lost our wits and became confused. But then we meditated on the lord who faces in all directions, the origin and resting place of the worlds, the unchanging lord. Cupping our hands in reverence, we paid homage to Śiva, the trident-bearer, who makes the great, terrifying sound, who has a frightening form, and fangs, who is manifest, and great:

"We bow to you, O lord of the gods and people; we bow to you god, noble lord of all creatures. We bow to you, the eternally successful yogi, the support of all the universe, the highest ruler, the highest ultimate reality, the undying, the highest place. You are the eldest, the lovely god, the ruddy one, the jumper, the lord Śiva . . . you are the sacrifice, the vows, and the observances; the Vedas, the worlds, the gods, the true god everywhere. You are the quality of sound in space; you are the origin and dissolution of creatures. You are the perfume in the earth, the fluidity of the waters, the brightness of fire, great lord. You are the touch of the wind, lord of gods, and the form of the moon. You are the knowledge in intelligence, lord of gods, and the seed in nature. You destroy all the worlds; you are Time, the Ender, made of death. You alone maintain the three worlds, and you alone create them, O lord. . . .

"We bow to you who have the power of a million million suns, who are as white as a thousand moons; we bow to you who hold the thunderbolt and the bow called Pināka; we bow to you who hold the bow and arrows in your hand. We bow to you whose body is adorned with ashes; we bow to you who destroyed the body of Kāma (the god of erotic love); we bow to you, god of the golden embryo, the golden robe, the golden womb, the golden navel, the golden semen, variegated with a thousand eyes; we bow to you, god of the golden color and the golden hair, you the golden hero and the giver of gold; we bow to you, god, master of gold with the sound of gold. We bow to you with the Pināka bow in your hand, Śaṅkara, the blue-necked."

When he had been praised like that, he became manifest, the one of great intellect, the god of gods, womb of the universe, shining as bright as a million suns; and filled with pity, the great god, the great light, spoke to us, as if he would swallow up the sky with his thousands of millions of mouths. His neck was shaped like a conch shell; his belly was lovely; he was adorned with various kinds of jewels; his body was variegated with all sorts of gems, and he wore various kinds of garlands and unguents. The lord had the Pināka bow in his hand and he held the trident; he was fit to be worshipped by the gods. He wore a great serpent for his sacred thread, but he did not frighten the gods.

He sent forth a great laugh, with the noise of the sound of the *dundubhi* drum, like the roar of thunder, a laugh that filled the entire universe. The two of us were terrified by that great sound, but then the great god said, "I am satisfied with you two, best of the gods. See my great yoga, and lose all your fear. Both of you, eternal, were born from my limbs in the past; Brahmā here, the grandfather of all people, is my right arm, and Viṣṇu is my left arm, always unconquered in battles. I am satisfied with the two of you, and so I will give you a boon, whatever you ask." Then the two of us were ecstatic, and we bowed to the feet of the lord, and we said to the great god, who was standing there inclined to favor us, "If you are really satisfied, and if you are going to give us a boon, then let the two of us always have devotion for you, O god, lord of the gods." The god of gods said, "So be it, fortunate ones. Create masses of progeny." And when he had said this, the lord god vanished.

Source: *Brahmāṇḍa Purāṇa* 1.2.26.10–61, from *Textual Sources for the Study of Hinduism*, pp. 85–87.

THE BUDDHA: A FALSE TEACHER

As we saw in the previous selection, a common polemical trope in Puranic literature involves portraying other gods as subordinate to one's own. In the Viṣṇu Purāṇa, *the Buddha, founder of Buddhism, is depicted as a false incarnation of Viṣṇu who is sent to earth to delude the Daityas, a race of superhuman beings who are the enemies of the gods. Viṣṇu grants their request and then creates an apparently wise and benevolent ascetic, dressed in the robes associated with Buddhist monasticism, who teaches them a plausible doctrine but one that deviates from the true path to liberation. Because they foolishly follow his teachings, they abandon their previous practice of Vedic rituals and austerities, which weakens them and leads to their defeat by the gods.*

When mighty Viṣṇu heard their plea, he emitted an illusory form from his body and gave it to the gods, saying, "This deceptive vision will completely fool the Daityas, and because they are led astray from the Vedas they will all be put to death, because all gods, demons, or others who oppose the authority of the Vedas will perish through my power, which is exercised in order to preserve the world. . . ."

[Buddha approached the Daityas and said,] "The dharma I will teach you is the secret path to liberation. There is nothing beyond this or superior to it; by following it you will attain either heaven or liberation from future existence. Mighty Daityas, you deserve such a doctrine." Using such insinuations, and with many specious arguments, this delusive being misled the Daityas from the tenets of the Vedas . . . and so the Daityas were seduced from their proper duties by the repeated lessons of this illusory preacher, who maintained that contradictory tenets are equally true. . . .

When the Daityas had thus deviated from the path of the sacred scriptures, the gods gained courage and assembled for battle. Then fighting ensued, and the demons were defeated and killed by the gods, who had adhered to the path of dharma. The armor of religious practice which had formerly protected the Daityas had been discarded by them, and their utter destruction followed this abandonment.

Source: *Viṣṇu Purāṇa*, Book III, chs. 17–18. Tr. JP.

THE POWER OF THE GODDESS

The following reading is from the Ancient Text of the Goddess (Devī Purāṇa), *which generally is classed as a "secondary ancient text"* (upapurāṇa) *but is regarded as an authoritative scripture by several sects of Śāktas (devotees of the Goddess). The text emphasizes the Goddess in her fierce and terrible aspects—as Kālī, who is worshiped by blood sacrifices, or as Durgā, a mighty warrior who rides a tiger and slays demons, or in a variety of other forms. The text describes a number of her manifestations and her essential nature, along with her activities in the world on behalf of devotees. It also describes her relation with Śiva, who, like the Goddess, is associated with the magical powers gained through asceticism and yoga. The section below lists a number of magical powers that accrue to adepts who recite mantras contained in a collection of spells and magical techniques. The acquisition of magical powers is an essential aspect of the path of the tantric adept* (siddha), *who employs various techniques—including recitation of mantras, visualizations, and rituals—to acquire supernatural abilities, which then can be used in pursuit of liberation.*

1. By taking the vow of a hero while speaking the first mantra 100,000 times, an adept becomes respected and popular.

2. By proclaiming the second mantra, an adept is able to separate the subtle body [a form within the physical body composed of subtle matter] from the physical body in order to visit a cremation ground [a power place for tantric practitioners]. . . .
4. The fourth mantra gives an adept the power to repel all weapons hurled by others.
5. By acquiring the power of the fifth mantra, one can stop rain at will.
6. By becoming skillful in reciting the sixth mantra, an adept acquires the power to vanish and reappear at will. . . .
9. The ninth mantra allows one to cut through all obstacles.
10. By performing rituals in accordance with the tenth mantra, a devotee is able to spread epidemic diseases among enemies.
11. By constant chanting of the eleventh mantra during conflict, the enemy's weapons become paralyzed. . . .
13. By chanting the thirteenth mantra, one is able to attract women.
14. By repeatedly chanting the fourteenth mantra, one can kill someone from a distance. . . .
18. If one successfully chants the eighteenth mantra, a female tantric consort will become available.
19. Through successful repetition of the nineteenth mantra, the Goddess becomes pleased and grants whatever the devotee desires. . . .

Source: *Devī Purāṇa, "Padamalā Mantra Vidyā."* Tr. JP.

RĀMA, A GOD AMONG HUMANS

The opening section of the Rāmāyaṇa *contains a synopsis of the main events of the story. The following verses tell of how prince Rāma was banished from his kingdom through the machinations of his stepmother Kaikeyī, who had been told by his father Daśaratha that she could ask him for anything she wished. Kaikeyī requested that Rāma, the rightful ruler, not assume the throne and that her son Bharata instead become king. As a righteous king, Daśaratha could not refuse, so he reluctantly acceded to the request. Kaikeyī knew that the people of the kingdom wanted Rāma to rule, so to ensure that Bharata would remain king she asked that Rāma be banished in order that popular opinion would not undermine her son's authority. The king agreed but as a result died of a broken heart soon after.*

Accompanied by his brother Lakṣmaṇa and by Sītā, the model of a devout Hindu wife, Rāma went off to the forest. During his travels he was beset by a horde of demons (rākṣasa), *but he defeated them all. This angered the demon lord Rāvaṇa, who captured Sītā and imprisoned her in his city of Laṅkā. Rāvaṇa then fell in love with Sītā and tried to convince her to renounce Rāma and become his queen, but Sītā spurned his advances. With the help of Hanumān, lord of monkeys, Rāma eventually located Sītā, slew Rāvaṇa, and rescued her. He then returned in triumph to his kingdom, and Bharata abdicated in Rāma's favor, since he had never wished to usurp Rāma.*

Following Rāma's return, however, his subjects began to gossip about Sītā, insinuating that while she was in Rāvaṇa's castle she may have succumbed to his advances.

Rāma knew that Sītā was innocent but reluctantly realized that the gossip could undermine his moral authority, which was closely connected to his wife's conduct. Following the dictates of dharma, Rāma was forced to banish Sītā from the kingdom. Rāma was heartbroken, knowing that her love for him kept her chaste in the castle of Rāvaṇa, but his royal duty required him to maintain his reputation for righteousness. The following verses describe how he left the kingdom, joined forces with Hanumān, and then defeated Rāvaṇa.

8. There is a famous king named Rāma . . . who is self-controlled, very powerful, radiant, resolute, and illustrious.
9. Wise and established in good conduct, he is eloquent and regal. He vanquishes his enemies. He has wide shoulders and powerful arms. . . .
12. He understands dharma and always keeps his promises. He always thinks of his subjects' welfare. He is famous, pure, disciplined, and contemplative.
13. Protector of all living beings, guardian of dharma, he knows the essence of the Vedas and their subsidiary lore and is equally skilled in the science of combat. . . .

18–19. His generosity is equal to that of Kubera, the provider of wealth, and his devotion to truth is like that of Dharma [the god of righteousness]. Daśaratha, the lord of the earth, loved him and wanted to name Rāma, his eldest son, as his successor. . . .

20. As Queen Kaikeyī, the king's wife, watched the coronation preparations, she [decided] to ask for a wish that had been promised long ago. She demanded that Bharata [her son] be crowned instead and that Rāma be exiled.
21. Daśaratha was a man who kept his promises, and so, caught in the trap of his own righteousness, he had to exile his beloved son Rāma.
22. To please Kaikeyī, the hero Rāma honored the promise made by his father and went into the forest. . . .

37–38. Then in battle Rāma killed all the *rākṣasas:* . . . About fourteen thousand *rākṣasas* were killed while he resided in Daṇḍaka.

39–42. Then Rāvaṇa, king of *rākṣasas*, heard of the massacre of his relatives, and flew into a rage and . . . he lured the king's sons far away. Then he kidnapped Rāma's wife. . . .

47. Then [Rāma] met the monkey Hanumān on the shores of Lake Pampā. . . .
56. This bull among monkeys wished to find Janaka's daughter [Sītā] and sent all the monkeys searching in all directions. . . .
58. When he reached the city of Laṅkā, which was ruled by Rāvaṇa, he saw Sītā pensive and sad in a grove of *aśoka* trees. . . .
62. The great monkey burned the city of Laṅkā, but spared Sītā, and then returned to tell Rāma the good news. . . .
65. Then the god of the ocean appeared before Rāma, and Rāma followed his advice by having Nala build a bridge [to Laṅkā].
66. Using this [bridge], he went to the city of Laṅkā, and after killing Rāvaṇa in battle he crowned Vibhīṣaṇa as lord of the *rākṣasas* in Laṅkā.

67. One who reads the story of Rāma, which brings merit and purity, will be freed from all sin. One who reads it with devotion and faith will ultimately be worshipped, together with his sons, grandsons, and servants after death.

Source: *Rāmāyaṇa*, ch. 1. Tr. JP.

most famous reading

THE *BHAGAVAD-GĪTĀ*: ARJUNA'S REFUSAL TO FIGHT

The following passages are taken from the Bhagavad-gītā, *one of the most influential of Hindu religious texts. A part of the monumental epic* Mahābhārata, *it tells the story of a climactic battle between the Pāṇḍavas and the Kauravas, two rival clans contending for supremacy in northern India. As the story opens, the Pāṇḍava Arjuna, perhaps the greatest warrior of his generation, decides to scout the opposition. He asks his charioteer Kṛṣṇa [Krishna] (who, unbeknownst to him, is really an incarnation of the god Viṣṇu) to drive the chariot in front of the enemy lines. As he rides past the Kauravas, however, he experiences a crisis of conscience: He recognizes that many of his opponents are relatives, friends, and teachers and that killing them would result in a great deal of negative karma.*

It is important to note that Arjuna is not concerned with killing per se; as a warrior he has killed in the past, but these particular people are linked to him by close karmic bonds, and so he perceives a contradiction between the demands of his warrior's duty (dharma) and the dictates of the law of karma. He decides that the only solution is to opt out of the conflict altogether and become a world renouncer. In response, Kṛṣṇa lectures him on the necessity of correctly performing dharma and indicates that Arjuna will receive more negative karma by dereliction of duty than by killing. Furthermore, Kṛṣṇa asserts, his opponents have already assured their own destruction by their evil deeds, and Arjuna is merely the instrument through which God will exact punishment.

Then Kṛṣṇa gives Arjuna a solution to the problem he faces, which involves a mental reorientation. Arjuna's problem, as explained by Kṛṣṇa, is that he sees himself as an agent and is attached to the results of his actions. If, however, he learns the technique of "disciplined action" (karma-yoga), *he can develop the ability to act without involving the false sense of ego. Arjuna is told to act selflessly, perceiving himself as an impersonal agent of dharma who is simply following God's will. If he offers all of his actions to God as an act of devotion and cultivates complete detachment, then Arjuna may act without acquiring any negative karma. Moreover, Kṛṣṇa tells him, such a mental perspective is the mind-set of the true world renouncer, and this alone leads to liberation from cyclic existence.*

20. Arjuna, his war flag a rampant monkey, saw Dhṛtarāṣṭra's sons assembled as weapons were ready to clash, and he lifted his bow.
21. He told his charioteer: "Kṛṣṇa, halt my chariot between the armies! . . ."
26. Arjuna saw them standing there: fathers, grandfathers, teachers, uncles, brothers, sons, grandsons, and friends.

27. He surveyed his elders and companions in both armies, all his kinsmen assembled together.

28. Dejected, filled with strange pity, he said this: "Kṛṣṇa, I see my kinsmen gathered here, wanting war.

nervous → 29. "My limbs sink, my mouth is parched, my body trembles, the hair bristles on my flesh.

30. "The magic bow slips from my hand, my skin burns, I cannot stand still, my mind reels.

31. "I see omens of chaos, Kṛṣṇa; I see no good in killing my kinsmen in battle.

32. "Kṛṣṇa, I seek no victory, or kingship or pleasures. What use to us are kingship, delights, or life itself? . . .

36. "What joy is there for us, Kṛṣṇa, in killing Dhṛtarāṣṭra's sons? Evil will haunt us if we kill them, though their bows are drawn to kill.

37. "Honor forbids us to kill our cousins, Dhṛtarāṣṭra's sons; how can we know happiness if we kill our own kinsmen? . . .

40. "When the family is ruined, the timeless laws of family duty perish; and when duty is lost, chaos overwhelms the family.

41. "In overwhelming chaos, Kṛṣṇa, women of the family are corrupted; and when women are corrupted, disorder is born in society. . . .

44. "Kṛṣṇa, we have heard that a place in hell is reserved for men who undermine family duties. . . .

46. "If Dhṛtarāṣṭra's armed sons kill me in battle when I am unarmed and offer no resistance, it will be my reward."

47. Saying this in the time of war, Arjuna slumped into the chariot and laid down his bow and arrows, his mind tormented by grief.

2.2. [Kṛṣṇa:] "Why this cowardice in time of crisis, Arjuna? The coward is ignoble, shameful, foreign to the ways of heaven.

3. "Don't yield to impotence! It is unnatural to you! Banish this petty weakness from your heart. Rise to the fight, Arjuna! . . .

11. "You grieve for those beyond grief, and you speak words of insight; but learned men do not grieve for the dead or the living.

12. "Never have I not existed, nor you, nor these kings; and never in the future shall we cease to exist. . . .

16. "Nothing of nonbeing comes to be, nor does being cease to exist; the boundary between these two is seen by men who see reality. ← *Killing is an illusion (not imp.)*

17. "Indestructible is the presence that pervades all this; no one can destroy this unchanging reality. ✶✶

18. "Our bodies are known to end, but the embodied self is enduring, indestructible, and immeasurable; therefore, Arjuna, fight the battle!

19. "He who thinks this self a killer and he who thinks it killed, both fail to understand; it [the self] does not kill, nor is it killed.

20. "It is not born, it does not die; having been, it will never not be; unborn, enduring, constant, and primordial, it is not killed when the body is killed. . . .

22. "Just as a man discards worn-out clothes to put on new and different ones, so the embodied self discards its worn-out bodies to take on other new ones. . . .

Family

taking away from what was used.

your spirit is #1!!

existence in eternal

30. "The self embodied in the body of every being is indestructible; you have no cause to grieve for all these creatures, Arjuna!
31. "Look to your own duty; do not tremble before it; nothing is better for a warrior than a battle of sacred duty [dharma].
32. "The doors of heaven open for warriors who rejoice to have a battle like this thrust on them by chance.
33. "If you fail to wage this war of sacred duty, you will abandon your own duty and fame only to gain evil.
34. "People will tell of your undying shame, and for a man of honor shame is worse than death.
35. "The great chariot warriors will think you deserted in fear of battle; you will be despised by those who held you in esteem.
36. "Your enemies will slander you, scorning your skill in so many unspeakable ways—could any suffering be worse?
37. "If you are killed, you win heaven; if you triumph, you enjoy the earth; therefore, Arjuna, stand up and resolve to fight the battle!
38. "Impartial to joy and suffering, gain and loss, victory and defeat, arm yourself for the battle, lest you fall into evil. . . .
47. "Be intent on action, not on the fruits of action; avoid attraction to the fruits and attachment to inaction!
48. "Perform actions, firm in discipline *(yoga)*, relinquishing attachment; be impartial to failure and success—this equanimity is called discipline. . . .
50. "Wise men disciplined by understanding relinquish the fruit born of action; freed from these bonds of rebirth, they reach a place beyond decay. . . .
55. "When he gives up desires in his mind, is content with the self within himself, then he is said to be a man whose insight is sure, Arjuna.
56. "When suffering does not disturb his mind, when his craving for pleasures has vanished, when attraction, fear, and anger are gone, he is called a sage whose thought is sure. . . .
61. "Controlling all [the senses], with discipline he should focus on me; when his senses are under control, his insight is sure. . . .
71. "When he renounces all desires and acts without craving, possessiveness, or individuality, he finds peace.
72. "This is the place of the infinite spirit [Brahman]; achieving it, one is freed from delusion; abiding in it even at the time of death, one finds the pure calm of infinity. . . .

4.6. "Though myself unborn, undying, the lord of creatures, I fashion nature, which is mine, and I come into being through my own magic.

7. "Whenever sacred duty decays and chaos prevails, then I create myself, Arjuna. . . .

13. "I created mankind in four classes, different in their qualities and actions; though unchanging, I am the agent of this, the actor who never acts!

14. "I desire no fruit of actions, and actions do not defile me; one who knows this about me is not bound by actions. . . .
6.2. "Know that discipline, Arjuna, is what men call renunciation; no man is disciplined without renouncing willful intent. . . .
4. "He is said to be mature in discipline when he has renounced all intention and is detached from sense objects and actions. . . .
20. "When his thought ceases, checked by the exercise of discipline, he is content within the self, seeing the self through himself.
21. "Absolute joy beyond the senses can only be grasped by understanding; when one knows it, he abides there and never wanders from this reality. . . .
9.27. "Whatever you do—what you take, what you offer, what you give, what penances you perform—do as an offering to me, Arjuna!
28. "You will be freed from the bonds of action, armed with the discipline of renunciation, your self liberated, you will join me."

Source: *Bhagavad-gītā* selections, from *The Bhagavad-gītā: Kṛṣṇa's Counsel in Time of War,* tr. Barbara Stoler Miller (New York: Columbia University Press, 1986), pp. 23–27, 29, 31–34, 36, 37, 39, 50, 52, 86.

THE LIFE OF A SAGE

Although the Bhagavad-gītā *counsels against running away from one's* dharma *when conflicts arise, the larger work within which it appears, the* Mahābhārata, *contains a number of passages that recognize the validity of the renunciant path and extol the actions of the sages who pursue it. They leave behind society and subsist on alms, and through their austerities and meditation engage in practices that can lead to liberation. The following passage is spoken by the god Śiva to his wife Umā following an incident in which she playfully covers his eyes, which plunges the world into darkness. In answer to a series of questions about his role in the universe, he describes how sages should live. They inhabit the fringes of society, sleep on the ground and subsist on leftovers, practice meditation and subdue their senses, and thus develop patience and insight.*

[Śiva:] In all the *dharmas* of seers, selves should be conquered; sense faculties should be conquered. . . . Renouncing food prepared with cows' milk and delighting in lying on the bare ground, practicing yoga, enjoying vegetables and leaves, eating fruits and roots, ingesting wind, water, and duck-weed: these are some of the observances of the seers through which they master the way of those who are disciplined. When the smoke has gone, when the pestle has been set down, when there are no more coals, when the people have eaten their meals, when the [cooking and eating] vessels are no longer passed around, after the time for begging alms has passed, then, while they are still eager to have guests, [the renunciant] eats the food that is left over. Delighting in the *dharma* of truth, patient, he is yoked to the *dharma* of sages. He is not arrogant or conceited, is not confused or surprised, is friendly to friends and enemies, and is the foremost knower of dharma.

Source: *Mahābhārata*, ch. 13, "Umā-Maheśvara-saṃvāda." Tr. JP.

DEVOTIONAL LITERATURE

PRAISE OF THE GODDESS

This passage declares that the Goddess is the real source of all creation. All the male deities of Hinduism—as well as all that exists—have their origin in her. It also indicates how she should be worshiped: with all one's heart, as the Divine Mother who protects her devotees as a mother protects her children.

> This blessed goddess Mahāmāyā, having forcibly seized the minds even of men of knowledge, leads them to delusion.
> Through her is created the entire three-tiered universe, that which both does and does not move.
> Just she is the gracious giver of boons to men, for the sake of (their) release.
> From bondage to mundane life; she is indeed the queen (governing) all who have power. . . .
> Brahmā said: By you is everything supported, by you the world created;
> By you is it protected, O Goddess, and you always consume (it) at the end (of time). . . .
> Terrible with your sword and spear, likewise with cudgel and discus,
> With conch and bow, having arrows, sling, and iron mace as your weapons,
> Gentle, more gentle than other gentle ones, exceedingly beautiful,
> You are superior to the high and low, the supreme queen.
> Whatever and whenever anything exists, whether it be real or unreal, O you have everything as your very soul,
> Of all that, you are the power; how then can you be adequately praised?

Source: *Devī-Māhātmya* I.42–I.63, from *Encountering the Goddess*, tr. Thomas B. Coburn (Albany: State University of New York Press, 1991), pp. 35–37.

PRAYER FOR IDENTITY WITH THE GODDESS

The Goddess is described as both fearful and benevolent, indicating that she is connected with both the pleasant and the unpleasant aspects of existence. This poem, traditionally attributed to Śaṅkara, asks for her help in attaining perfect identification with her in a state of perfect devotion in which notions of separateness and personality are transcended.

> If Śiva is united with Śakti, he is able to exert his powers as lord; if not, the god is not able to stir.
> Hence to you, who must be propitiated by Hari [Viṣṇu], Hara [Śiva], Virañca [Brahmā], and the other [gods],
> How can one who has not acquired merit be fit to offer reverence and praise? . . .
>
> For the ignorant you are the island city of the sun, for the mentally stagnant you are a waterfall of streams of nectar [flowing] from a bouquet of intelligence,
> For the poor you are a rosary of wishing-jewels; for those who in the ocean of birth are submerged, you are the tusk of that boar who was the enemy of Mura, O Lady.
>
> Banded with a tinkling girdle, heavy with breasts like the frontal lobes of young elephants,

Slender of waist, with face like the full moon of autumn, bearing on the palms of her hands bow, arrows, noose, and goad,
Let there be seated before us the pride of him who shook the cities [Śiva]. . . .

May you, O Blessed Lady, extend to me, your slave, a compassionate glance!
When one desiring to praise you utters the words "you, O Lady" [which also mean, "May I be you"],
At that moment you grant him a state of identity with you.
With your feet illuminated by the crests of Mukunda, Brahmā, and Indra.

Source: *Saundaryalaharī*, attributed to Śaṅkara, tr. W. N. Brown (Cambridge, MA: Harvard University Press, 1958), pp. 48, 50, 56.

MĪRĀBĀĪ'S MYSTICAL MARRIAGE TO KṚṢṆA

Mīrābāī remains one of the most popular devotional poets of medieval India. She was probably born around 1550 and is said to have been the wife of a Rājput prince who was the son of the ruler (Rana) of Mewar. According to legend, before her marriage she had fallen in love with Kṛṣṇa and refused to consummate her marriage to the prince because her relationship with the Lord took precedence. One story that is told of her relates that one time she was exchanging words of love to a visitor on the other side of a locked door. Her father-in-law, the ruler, overheard her and, outraged by the shame she had brought on his family, threatened to kill her. She told him that the person to whom she was speaking was the Lord Kṛṣṇa, not a human lover, and her life was spared. In this poem she alludes to an incident in which the Rana tried to poison her, but she believes that she was saved by Kṛṣṇa. She indicates that her devotion to the Lord has caused her to leave behind her family and friends and the privileged life she led in the palace and to seek the company of fellow devotees.

My love is reserved for Gopāl, the Mountain Lifter
And for no one else.
O saints and ascetics,
I have seen the world and its ways.
I left my brothers and relatives
And all my possessions.
Abandoning worldly shame,
I came to sit with ascetics.
Together with devotees [of Kṛṣṇa,] I was happy.
[But] when I looked at the world, I wept.
I planted the vine of love
And watered it with my tears.
I churned curds
And extracted the ghee;
I threw out the buttermilk.
The King sent me a cup of poison,
And I gladly drank it all.
Mira's love is deeply rooted;
She accepts whatever comes to her.

Source: Poem from *Mīrābāī ki Padāvalī*. Tr. JP.

CHEATING ON HER HUSBAND

Mahādēvyakka was an important poet of the iconoclastic Vīraśaiva tradition. In her poetry, her devotion to Śiva was often expressed in sexual terms. This led to conflicts with traditional mores and values, particularly those regarding the proper conduct of women. In the following verses, she indicates that her intense devotion to Śiva prevented her from the devotion to her husband required of a traditional Hindu wife. She compares her apparently loveless marriage with her husband to her devotion to Śiva and indicates how little she values the former relationship in comparison to her devotional love affair with the Lord.

> I have Māyā for mother-in-law; the world for father-in-law; three brothers-in-law, like tigers;
> And the husband's thoughts are full of laughing women: no god, this man.
> And I cannot cross the sister-in-law.
> But I will give this wench the slip and go cuckold my husband with Hara, my Lord.
> My mind is my maid: by her kindness, I join my Lord, my utterly beautiful Lord from the mountain-peaks, my lord white as jasmine, and I will make Him my good husband.

Source: Poem by Mahādēvyakka, from *Speaking of Śiva*, tr. A. K. Rāmānujan (Baltimore: Penguin Books, 1973), p. 141.

TREATISES ON DHARMA

ACTIONS AND THEIR RESULTS

The Laws of Manu *codify the hierarchy of medieval Indian society and outline the duties of the four primary social groups: (1) brahmins, the priests; (2) kṣatriyas, the warriors and rulers; (3) vaiśyas, tradespeople and merchants, and (4) śūdras, or servants. Each of them is said to have a role to play in creating a stable, ordered society. Manu also outlines the duties for four stages of life: the student, the householder, the forest-dweller, and the world renouncer. According to this scheme, liberation is recognized as the supreme goal of the religious life, but its pursuit should be postponed until the proper time, which is said to be when one has seen a grandson born (indicating that one's lineage will continue) and gray hairs have appeared on one's head (indicating that one has lived long enough to fulfill the requirements of dharma).*

4.97. It is better (to discharge) one's own (appointed) duty *(dharma)* incompletely than to perform completely that of another; for he who lives according to the law of another (caste) is instantly excluded from his own. . . .

12.3. Action, which springs from the mind, from speech, and from the body, produces either good or evil results; by actions are caused (the various) conditions of men, the highest, middling, and the lowest.

4. Know that the mind is the instigator here below, even for [actions] that are connected with the body. . . .
40. Those endowed with purity *(sattva)* reach the state of gods, those endowed with activity *(rajas)* the state of men, and those endowed with darkness *(tamas)* always sink to the condition of beasts; that is the threefold course of transmigrations. . . .
95. All those traditions *(smṛti)* and all those despicable systems of philosophy, which are not based on the Veda, produce no reward after death; for they are declared to be founded on darkness. . . .
104. Austerity and sacred learning are the best means by which a brahmin gains supreme happiness; by austerity he destroys guilt, by sacred learning he obtains the cessation of (births and) deaths. . . .
173. If (the punishment falls) not on (the offender) himself, (it falls) on his sons, if not on the sons, (at least) on his grandsons; but an iniquity (once) committed never fails to produce consequences for him who wrought it.
174. He prospers for a while through unrighteousness, then he gains great good fortune, next he conquers his enemies, but (at last) he perishes (branch and) root. . . .
240. Single is each being born; single it dies; single it enjoys (the reward of its) virtue; single (it suffers the punishment of its) sin. . . .
1.31. For the sake of the prosperity of the worlds, he (the Lord) caused the brahmin, the kṣatriya, the vaiśya, and the śūdra to proceed from his mouth, his arms, his thighs, and his feet. . . .
87. But in order to protect this universe He, the most glorious one, assigned separate (duties and) occupations to those who came from his mouth, arms, thighs, and feet. . . .
10.1. The three twice-born castes, carrying out their (prescribed) duties, study (the Veda); but among them the brahmin (alone) shall teach it, and not the other two; this is an established rule. . . .
3. On account of his pre-eminence, on account of the superiority of his origin, on account of his observance of restrictive rules, and on account of his particular sanctification, the brahmin is the lord of (all) castes.
4. The brahmin, the kṣatriya, and the vaiśya castes are the twice-born ones, but the fourth, the śūdra, has one birth only; there is no fifth (caste).
5. In all castes those (children) only which are begotten in the direct order on wedded wives, equal (in caste and married as) virgins, are to be considered to belong to the same caste (as the fathers). . . .
45. All those tribes in this world, which are excluded from the (community of) those born from the mouth, the arms, the thighs, and the feet (of Brahman), are called Dasyus ["slaves"], whether they speak the language of the barbarians *(mleccha)* or that of the Āryans. . . .

Source: *The Laws of Manu*, chs. 4, 12, 10. Tr. JP.

The Four Stages of Life

6.87. The student, the householder, the forest dweller, and the world renouncer: these constitute the four separate orders. . . .

89. And in accordance with the precepts of the Veda and of the traditional texts, the householder is declared to be superior to all of them, because he supports the other three. . . .

7.352. Men who commit adultery with the wives of others, the king shall cause to be marked by punishments which cause terror, and afterwards banish.

353. For by (adultery) is caused a mixture of the castes among men; from that (follows) sin, which cuts up even the roots and causes the destruction of everything. . . .

2.36. In the eighth year after conception, one should perform the initiation *(upanayana)* of a brahmin, in the eleventh (year) after conception (that) of a kṣatriya, but in the twelfth that of a vaiśya. . . .

69. Having performed the (rite of) initiation, the teacher must first instruct the (pupil) in (the rules of) personal purification, conduct, of the fire sacrifice, and of the twilight (morning and evening) devotions. . . .

176. Every day, having bathed and being purified, he must offer libations of water to the gods, sages . . . worship the gods, and place fuel (on the sacred fire).

177. He should abstain from honey, meat, perfumes, garlands, substances (used for) flavoring (food), women, all substances turned acid, and from doing injury to living creatures, . . .

179. From gambling, idle disputes, backbiting, and lying, looking at and touching women, and from hurting others. . . .

199. Let him not pronounce the mere name of his teacher (without adding an honorific title), behind his back even, and let him not mimic his gait, speech, and deportment. . . .

201. By censuring (his teacher), though justly, he will become a donkey (in his next birth); by falsely defaming him, a dog; he who lives on his teacher's substance will become a worm, and he who is envious (of his merit), a (larger) insect. . . .

3.1. The vow (of studying) the three Vedas under a teacher must be kept for thirty-six years, or for half that time, or for a quarter, until the (student) has perfectly learned them.

3.2. (A student) who has studied in due order the three Vedas, or two, or even one only, without breaking the (rules of) studentship, shall enter the order of the householders. . . .

4. Having bathed, with the permission of his teacher, and performed according to the rule the rite on homecoming, a twice-born man shall marry a wife of equal caste who is endowed with auspicious (bodily) marks. . . .

75. Let (every man) in this (second order, at least) daily apply himself to the private recitation of the Veda, and also to the performance of the

offering to the gods; for he who is diligent in the performance of sacrifices supports both the movable and the immovable creation. . . .

78. Because men of the three (other) orders are daily supported by the householder with (gifts of) sacred knowledge and food, therefore (the stage of) householder is the most excellent stage. . . .

4.2. A brahmin must seek a means of subsistence which causes either no, or at least little, pain (to others), and live (by that) except in times of distress.

3. For the purpose of gaining bare subsistence, let him accumulate property by (following those) irreproachable occupations (which are prescribed for) his (caste), without (unduly) fatiguing his body. . . .

11. Let him never, for the sake of subsistence, follow the ways of the world; let him live the pure, straightforward, honest life of a brahmin. . . .

Source: *The Laws of Manu,* chs. 6, 7, 3, 4. Tr. JP.

Leaving Home Life

6.1. A twice-born *snātaka* [a brahmin who has finished his studentship and taken a ceremonial bath], who has thus lived according to the law in the order of householders, may, taking a firm resolution and keeping his organs in subjection, live in the forest, duly [observing the rules given below].

2. When a householder sees his (skin) wrinkled, and (his hair) white, and the sons of his sons, then he may resort to the forest.

3. Abandoning all food raised by cultivation, and all his belongings, he may depart into the forest, either committing his wife to his sons, or accompanied by her. . . .

8. Let him be always industrious in privately reciting the Veda; let him be patient in hardships, friendly, of collected mind, ever liberal, and never a receiver of gifts, and compassionate towards all living creatures. . . .

26. Making no effort (to procure) things that give pleasure, chaste, sleeping on the bare ground, not caring for any shelter, dwelling at the roots of trees. . . .

33. Having thus passed the third part of his life in the forest, he may live as an ascetic during the fourth part of his existence, after abandoning all attachment to worldly objects.

34. He who after passing from order to order, after offering sacrifices and subduing the senses, becomes, tired with (giving) alms and offerings of food, an ascetic, gains bliss after death. . . .

36. Having studied the Vedas in accordance with the rule, having begat sons in accordance with the sacred law, and having offered sacrifices according to his ability, he may direct his mind to (the attainment of) final liberation.

37. A twice-born man who seeks final liberation, without having studied the Vedas, without having begotten sons, and without having offered sacrifices, sinks downwards.

38. Having performed the *Iṣṭi,* sacred to the Lord of Creatures, where (he gives) all his property as a sacrificial fee, having deposited the sacred fires in himself, a brahmin may depart from his house (as an ascetic). . . .
41. Departing from his house fully provided with the means of purification, let him wander about absolutely silent, and caring nothing for enjoyments that may be offered (to him). . . .
45. Let him not desire to die, let him not desire to live; let him wait for (his appointed) time, as a servant (waits) for the payment of his wages. . . .
49. Delighting in what refers to the Self, sitting (in yogic meditation), independent (of external help), entirely abstaining from sensual enjoyments, with himself for his only companion, he shall live in this world, desiring the bliss (of final liberation). . . .
65. By deep meditation let him recognize the subtle nature of the Supreme Self, and its presence in all organisms. . . .
85. A twice-born man who becomes an ascetic, after the successive performance of the above-mentioned acts, shakes off sin here below and reaches the highest Brahman.

Source: *The Laws of Manu,* ch. 6. Tr. JP.

Duties of the Four Social Classes

i. The Brahmin

4.74. Brahmins who are intent on the means (of gaining union with) Brahman and firm in [discharging] their duties shall live by correctly performing the following six acts in their (proper) order.

75. Teaching, studying, sacrificing for oneself, sacrificing for others, making gifts and receiving them are the six acts of a brahmin. . . .
79. To carry arms for striking and for throwing (is prescribed) for kṣatriyas as a means of subsistence; to trade, (to raise) cattle, and agriculture for vaiśyas; but their duties are liberality, study of the Vedas, and performance of sacrifices.
80. Among the several occupations, the most commendable are: teaching the Veda for a brahmin, protecting (the people) for kṣatriya, and trade for a vaiśya.
81. But a brahmin, unable to subsist by his peculiar occupations just mentioned, may live according to the law applicable to kṣatriyas, for the latter is next to him in rank.
82. If it is asked, "What should he do if he cannot maintain himself by either (of these occupations," the answer is), he may adopt the vaiśya's mode of life, employing himself in agriculture and raising cattle.
83. But a brahmin, or a kṣatriya, living by a vaiśya's mode of subsistence, shall carefully avoid agriculture, (which causes) injury to many beings and depends on others. . . .
92. By (selling) flesh, salt, and lac a brahmin at once becomes an outcaste; by selling milk he becomes (equal to) a śūdra in three days.

93. But by willingly selling in this world other (forbidden) commodities, a brahmin assumes after seven nights the character of vaiśya. . . .
95. A kṣatriya who has fallen into distress may subsist by all these (means); but he must never arrogantly adopt the mode of life of his betters. . . .
102. A brahmin who has fallen into distress may accept (gifts) from anybody; because according to the law it is not possible that anything pure can be sullied.

ii. The Kṣatriya

7.18. Punishment alone governs all created beings, punishment alone protects them, punishment watches over them while they sleep; the wise declare punishment to be the law (dharma).
19. If (punishment) is properly inflicted after consideration it makes all people happy; but inflicted without consideration, it destroys everything.
20. If the king did not, without tiring, inflict punishment on those worthy to be punished, the stronger would roast the weaker, like fish on a spit. . . .
22. The whole world is kept in order by punishment, for a guiltless man is hard to find; through fear of punishment the whole world yields enjoyments. . . .
88. Not to turn back in battle, to protect the people, to honor the brahmins is the best means for a king to secure happiness.
89. Those kings who, seeking to slay each other in battle, fight with the utmost exertion and do not turn back, go to heaven. . . .
144. The highest duty of a kṣatriya is to protect his subjects, for the king who enjoys the rewards just mentioned is required to do that duty. . . .
198. He should, (however), try to conquer his foes by conciliation, by (well-applied) gifts and by creating dissension, used either separately or conjointly, never by fighting (if it can be avoided).
199. For when two (princes) fight, victory and defeat in the battle are, as experience teaches, uncertain; he should therefore avoid an engagement.

iii. The Vaiśya

9.326. After a vaiśya has received the sacraments and has taken a wife, he shall be always attentive to the business whereby he may subsist and to (that of) cattle.
327. For when the Lord of Creatures created cattle, he gave them to vaiśyas; to the brahmins and to the king he entrusted all created beings.
328. A vaiśya must never wish, "I will not keep cattle"; and if a vaiśya is willing (to keep them), they must never be kept by other (castes).
329. (A vaiśya) must know the respective value of gems, of pearls, of coral, of metals, of (cloth) made of thread, of perfumes, and of spices.
330. He must know how to plant seeds and the good and bad qualities of fields, and he must perfectly know all measures and weights. . . .
333. Let him exert himself to the utmost in order to increase his property in a righteous manner, and he should zealously give food to all created beings.

iv. The Śūdra

8.334. Serving brahmins who are learned in the Vedas, who are householders, and who are famous (for virtue) is the highest duty of a śūdra, which leads to beatitude.

335. [A śūdra who is] pure, the servant of his betters, gentle in his speech, free from pride, and who always seeks a refuge with brahmins, attains (in his next life) a higher caste. . . .

413. But a śūdra, whether bought or unbought, he may compel to do servile work; for he was created by the Self-existent to be the slave of brahmins.

414. A śūdra, even though emancipated by his master, is not released from servitude; since that is innate in him, who can set him free from it? . . .

10.128. The more a (śūdra), keeping himself free from envy, imitates the behavior of the virtuous, the more he gains . . . in this world and the next.

Source: *The Laws of Manu*, chs. 4, 7, 9, 8, 10. Tr. JP.

How Women Should Live

3.55. Women must be honored and adorned by their fathers, brothers, husbands, and brothers-in-law, who desire (their own) welfare.

56. Where women are honored, there the gods are pleased; but where they are not honored, no sacred rite yields rewards.

57. Where the female relations live in grief, the family soon wholly perishes; but that family where they are not unhappy ever prospers.

58. The houses on which female relations, not being duly honored, pronounce a curse, perish completely, as if destroyed by magic. . . .

60. In that family where the husband is pleased with his wife and the wife with her husband, happiness will assuredly be lasting. . . .

67. The nuptial ceremony is stated to be the Vedic sacrament for women (and to be equal to the initiation), serving the husband is (equivalent to) the residence in (the house of the) teacher, and household duties are (the same) as the (daily) worship of the sacred fire. . . .

5.147. By a girl, by a young woman, or even by an aged one, nothing must be done independently, even in her own house.

148. In childhood a female must be subject to her father, in youth to her husband, when her lord is dead to her sons; a woman must never be independent. . . .

150. She must always be cheerful, clever in household affairs, careful in cleaning her utensils, and economical in expenditure.

151. Him to whom her father may give her, or her brother with her father's permission, she shall obey as long as he lives, and when he is dead, she must not insult (his memory). . . .

154. Though destitute of virtue, or seeking pleasure (elsewhere), or devoid of good qualities, a husband must be constantly worshipped as a god by a faithful wife.

155. No sacrifice, no vow, no fast must be performed by women apart (from their husbands); if a wife obeys her husband, she will be exalted for that (reason alone) in heaven.
156. A faithful wife, who desires to dwell (after death) with her husband, must never do anything that might displease him who took her hand, whether he be alive or dead.
157. At her pleasure let her emaciate her body by (living on) pure flowers, roots, and fruit; but she must never even mention the name of another man after her husband has died. . . .
160. A virtuous wife who after the death of her husband constantly remains chaste, even if she has no sons, reaches heaven, just like those chaste men. . . .
164. By violating her duty towards her husband, a wife is disgraced in this world; (after death) she enters the womb of a jackal, and is tormented by diseases for her sin.
165. She who, controlling her thoughts, words, and deeds, never fights her lord, lives (after death) with her husband (in heaven) and is called virtuous. . . .
167. A twice-born man, versed in the sacred law, shall burn a wife of equal caste who conducts herself thus and dies before him with (the sacred fires used for) the Agnihotra and with the sacrificial implements.
168. Having thus, at the funeral, given the sacred fires to his wife who dies before him, he may marry again, and again kindle (the fires).

Source: *The Laws of Manu*, chs. 3, 5. Tr. JP.

MANU'S INSTRUCTIONS ON FINDING THE RIGHT MATE

Marriage is a matter of great concern in classical Hindu texts, because stable marriages are thought to be essential to the proper ordering of society. According to Manu, marriage should occur only within one's caste, and he provides a number of other criteria for men to consider when looking for a wife.

When, with the permission of his teacher, he has bathed and performed the ritual for homecoming (at the end of his studies) according to the ritual rules, a twice-born man should take a wife who is of the same class and has the right marks. A woman who does not come from the same blood line on her mother's side, nor belong to the same ritual line on her father's side, is considered proper as a wife and a sexual partner for a twice-born man. When it comes to relations with a woman, a man should avoid the ten following families, even if they are great or prosperous with cattle, rich in sheep, or possessing other wealth: a family that has abandoned the rituals, one that does not have boys, or a family that does not chant the Veda; and those families in which they have hairy bodies, piles, consumption, weak digestion, bad memories, and families with white leprosy, or black leprosy. A man should not marry a maiden who is a redhead or has an extra limb or is sickly or who is bald or too hairy or talks too much or is sallow or who is named after a constellation, a tree, or a river, who has a low caste name, who is named after a mountain, a bird, a snake, or has a slave name, or who has a fearsome name. He should have nothing to do with a woman who is too fat or too thin, too tall or too dwarfish, who is past her prime or lacks a limb, or who is fond of quarreling.

He should take a woman whose limbs are complete and who has a pleasant name, who walks like a swan or an elephant, whose body hair and hair on the head are fine and whose teeth are not big, with delicate limbs. A wise man, out of concern for the dharma of daughters, will not marry a woman who has no brother or whose father is unknown.

Taking a woman of the same class is recommended to twice-born men for the first marriage; but for men in whom sexual desire has arisen, these should be the choices, listed in order: according to the tradition, only a śūdra woman can be the wife of a śūdra; she and one of his own class can be the wife of a vaiśya; these two and one of his own class for a kṣatriya; and these three and one of his own class for the high-born (brahmin). A śūdra woman is not mentioned as the wife of a brahmin or a kṣatriya even when they are under duress, even in a story. Twice-born men who are so infatuated as to take as wives women of low caste quickly reduce their families, including the children, to the status of śūdras. . . .

A brahmin who beds a śūdra woman goes to hell; if he begets a child on her, he forsakes the status of brahmin. The ancestors and the gods do not eat the offerings to the gods, to the ancestors, and to guests made by such a man, and so he does not go to heaven. No expiation is ordained for a (twice-born) man who drinks the froth from the lips of a śūdra woman or who is tainted by her breath or who begets a son on her. Now listen to the summary of these eight marriage rituals for the four classes, that are both for good and for ill, in this life and after death. Now, the eight are the marriages named after Brahmā, the gods, the sages, Prajāpati, the demons, the gandharvas, the ogres, and the ghouls. I will tell you all about which one is within the dharma of each class, and the faults and qualities of each, and their merits and demerits when it comes to offspring. It should be understood that the first six as they are listed above are within the dharma of a brahmin, the last four are for a kṣatriya, and these same four, with the exception of the ogre marriage, are for a vaiśya or a śūdra. . . .

A marriage is known as following the dharma of a Brahmā marriage when a man dresses his daughter and adorns her and summons a man who knows the Vedas and is moral, and himself gives her to him as a gift.

They say a marriage is in the dharma of the gods when a man adorns his daughter and gives her as a gift to a sacrificial priest, in the course of a properly performed sacrifice. . . .

It is called a demonic dharma when the maiden is given to a man because he desires her himself, when he has given as much wealth as he can to her relatives and to the maiden herself. The ritual is known as a gandharva marriage when the bride and her groom unite with one another because they want to, as a result of the desire for sexual intercourse.

The wedding is called the rule of the ogres when a man forcibly carries off a maiden out of her house, screaming and weeping, after he has killed, wounded, or beaten (her and/or her relatives). The lowest and most evil of marriages, known as that of the ghouls, takes place when a man secretly seduces a girl who is asleep, drunk, or out of her mind. . . .

A man should approach his wife sexually during her fertile period, and always find his sexual pleasure in his own wife; and when he desires sexual pleasure he may go to her to whom he is vowed, except on the days at the junctures. The natural fertile season of a woman lasts for sixteen nights, according to the tradition. . . . On the even nights, sons are conceived, and on the uneven nights, daughters; therefore, a man who wants sons should unite with his wife during her fertile season on the even nights. A male child is born when the seed of the man is greater (than that of the woman), and a female child when the seed of the woman is greater (than that of the man); if both are equal, a hermaphrodite is born, or a boy and a girl; and if the seed is weak or scanty, there will be a miscarriage.

Source: *The Laws of Manu,* ch. 3, from *Textual Sources for the Study of Hinduism,* pp. 101–103.

0

Buddhism

Buddhism

INTRODUCTION

Nearly 2,500 years ago, according to Buddhist tradition, a young man sat under a tree in northern India, determined to find a way to transcend the sufferings that he recognized as being endemic to the world. Born a prince named Siddhārtha Gautama in a small kingdom in what is today southern Nepal, he had renounced his royal heritage in order to escape the cycle of birth, death, and rebirth that inevitably leads to suffering, loss, and pain. As he sat under the tree, he recognized that all the world's problems begin with a fundamental ignorance *(avidyā)* that causes beings to misunderstand the true nature of reality. This causes them to engage in actions that lead to their own suffering and to fail to recognize what leads to happiness.

Siddhārtha remained in meditation throughout the night, and during this time the veils of ignorance lifted from his perception. He came to understand how the lives of all beings in the world are constantly influenced by the effects of their own actions *(karma)* and that seeking happiness within the changing phenomena of the mundane world is a fundamental mistake. He saw everything in the world as impermanent *(anitya)* and understood that because of the fact of constant change even things that seem to provide happiness—such as wealth, fame, power, sex, relationships—are in fact sources of suffering *(duḥkha)*.

In addition, he perceived that everything comes into being in dependence on causes and conditions—a doctrine referred to in Buddhism as "dependent arising" *(pratītya-samutpāda)*—and he understood that because phenomena are in a constant state of flux there is no enduring essence underlying them. Nor is there a supreme being who oversees the process of change and decides the fates of beings. Rather, every being is responsible for its own destiny, and the entire system of universal interdependent causation is driven by its own internal forces. Individual beings are what they are because of the actions they performed in the past.

Moreover, beings lack an enduring self or soul. This doctrine is referred to in Buddhist literature as "no-self" *(anātman)* and is a denial of the sort of permanent, partless, and immortal entity called *ātman* (literally, "I" or "self") in Hinduism and *soul* in Christianity. This doctrine is connected with the idea that all phenomena lack substantial entities and are characterized by an "emptiness" *(śūnyatā)* of inherent existence *(svabhāva;* literally, "own-being"*)*.

At dawn of the following morning, full awareness arose in him, and all traces of ignorance disappeared. He had become a *buddha*, a term derived from the Sanskrit root word *budh*, meaning "to wake up" or "to regain consciousness." Thus, he was now fully awakened from the sleep of ignorance in which most beings spend life after life. At first he thought to remain under the tree and pass away without revealing what he had understood, since he knew that the teachings of an awakened being are subtle and difficult for ordinary beings to comprehend. As he sat there in blissful contemplation, however, the Indian god Brahmā came to him, bowed down before him, and begged him to teach others. Brahmā pointed out that there would be some intelligent people who would derive benefit from his teachings and that such people would find true happiness by following the path he had discovered.

Feeling a sense of profound compassion for suffering beings, Buddha agreed to share his wisdom with them and so embarked on a teaching career that would last for about 40 years. He traveled around India, instructing all who wished to listen. Many people recognized the truth of his words and became his disciples. According to Buddhist tradition, he was an accomplished teacher who was able to perceive the proclivities and mind-sets of his listeners and who could skillfully adapt his teachings for each person and group while still retaining the essential message. He had many lay disciples, but he emphasized the centrality of a monastic lifestyle for those who were intent on liberation. According to his biography, he died in a grove of trees near the town of Vaiśālī at the age of 80.

Shortly after his death, his followers convened a council to codify the teachings of the Buddha. According to tradition, the council met in Rājagṛha, a place where the Buddha had delivered many discourses. The participants were 500 of his closest disciples who had become *arhats* (meaning that they had eradicated mental afflictions and transcended all attachment to mundane things). Such people, it was believed, would not be afflicted by faulty memories or biased by sectarian considerations. The members of the assembly recounted what they had heard the Buddha say on specific occasions, and they prefaced their remarks with the phrase "Thus have I heard: At one time the Exalted One was residing in . . . ." This formula indicated that the speaker had been a member of the audience and provided the context and background of the discourse. Other members would certify the veracity of the account or correct minor details. At the end of the council, all present were satisfied that the Buddha's words had been definitively recorded. The canon of Buddhism was declared closed, and the council issued a pronouncement that henceforth no new teachings would be admitted as the "word of the Buddha" *(buddha-vacana)*.

Despite the intentions of the council, however, new teachings and doctrines continued to appear in the following centuries, and the Buddhist community underwent numerous divisions. The most significant of these was the split into two schools termed "Hīnayāna," or "Lesser Vehicle," and "Mahāyāna," or "Greater Vehicle." These names obviously were coined by the latter group, which considered itself superior to its rivals because it propounded a goal of universal salvation, while the Hīnayāna emphasized the importance of working primarily for one's own emancipation. The Hīnayāna ideal is the *arhat*, a being who overcomes all ties to the phenomenal world and so attains *nirvana*, which is said to be a state beyond birth and death and also is described as perfect bliss.

Their Mahāyāna rivals condemned this as a selfish and limited goal. The Mahāyāna ideal is the *bodhisattva* (a being—*sattva*—whose goal is awakening—*bodhi*), who seeks to attain the state of buddhahood in order to help others find the path to final happiness. This form of Buddhism later predominated in Central and East Asia—in countries such as Tibet, Mongolia, Korea, Japan, Vietnam, and China—while Hīnayāna schools took hold in Southeast Asia—in countries such as Sri Lanka, Thailand, Burma, Cambodia, and Laos.

Buddhists in these latter countries do not accept the designation of their tradition as a "Lesser Vehicle." Rather, they contend that the dominant Theravāda tradition (the only one of the numerous schools collectively designated "Hīnayāna" that survives today) is in fact the true teaching of Buddha. They further believe that the Mahāyāna *sūtras* (discourses believed by Mahāyānists to have been spoken by the historical Buddha) are in fact forgeries that proclaim practices and doctrines that the Buddha never taught but that actually were falsely propounded by others long after his death.

The oldest distinctively Mahāyāna literature is a group of texts that discuss the "perfection of wisdom" *(prajñā-pāramitā)*. The earliest of these is probably *Perfection of Wisdom in 8,000 Lines*, the oldest version of which may have been composed as early as the first century B.C.E. The Perfection of Wisdom texts do not make their appearance until several centuries after the death of the Buddha, but they claim to have been spoken by him during his lifetime. Mahāyāna tradition explains the chronological discrepancy by contending that they were indeed taught by the Buddha to advanced disciples but that he ordered that they be hidden in the underwater realm of *nāgas* (beings with snakelike bodies and human heads) until the time was right for their propagation. The legend further reports that the second-century philosopher Nāgārjuna (fl. ca. 150 C.E.) was the person preordained by Buddha to recover and explicate the Perfection of Wisdom texts. After one of his lectures, some *nāgas* approached him and told him of the texts hidden in their kingdom, and Nāgārjuna traveled there and returned with the sūtras to India. He is credited with founding the Madhyamaka (Middle Way) school of Buddhist philosophy, which emphasizes the centrality of the doctrine of emptiness.

Nāgārjuna and his commentators (the most influential of whom was Candrakīrti, ca. 550–600) developed the philosophical ramifications of this doctrine, which is closely connected to the notion of dependent arising. Because all phenomena come into being as a result of causes and conditions, abide due to causes and conditions, and pass away due to causes and conditions, everything in the universe is empty of a substantial entity. Ordinary beings, however, perceive them as existing in the way they appear—that is, as real, substantial things that inherently possess certain qualities.

Nāgārjuna declared that a failure to understand emptiness correctly leads to mistaken perceptions of things and that erroneous philosophical views are the reifications of such notions.

The Madhyamaka philosophers applied this insight not only to mistaken perceptions but also to the doctrines of rival schools, which they contended were founded on self-contradictory assumptions. Through a process of dialectical reasoning, Madhyamaka thinkers exposed both Buddhist and non-Buddhist systems of thought to a rigorous critique, the goal of which was to lead people to recognize the ultimate futility of attempting to encapsulate truth in philosophical propositions.

Approximately two centuries after Nāgārjuna, a new Mahāyāna school arose in India, commonly known as the Yogic Practice School *(Yogācāra)*. The main scriptural source for this school is the *Sūtra Explaining the Thought (Saṃdhinirmocana-sūtra)*, which consists of a series of questions put to the Buddha by a group of bodhisattvas. The name "Yogic Practice School" may have been derived from an important treatise by Asaṅga (ca. 310–390) titled *Levels of Yogic Practice (Yogācāra-bhūmi)*. Along with his brother Vasubandhu (ca. 320–400), Asaṅga is credited with founding this school and developing its central doctrines.

Yogācāra emphasizes the importance of meditative practice, and several passages in Yogācāra texts indicate that the founders of the school perceived other Mahāyāna Buddhists as being overly concerned with dialectical debate while neglecting meditation. The Yogācāra school is commonly referred to in Tibet as "Mind Only" (*sems tsam*; Sanskrit: *citta-mātra*) because of an idea found in some Yogācāra texts that all the phenomena of the world are "cognition-only" *(vijñapti-mātra)*, implying that everything we perceive is conditioned by consciousness. In the following centuries, a number of syncretic schools developed. They tended to mingle Madhyamaka and Yogācāra doctrines. The greatest examples of this syncretic period are the philosophers Śāntarakṣita (ca. 680–740) and Kamalaśīla (ca. 740–790), who are among the last significant Buddhist philosophers in India.

In addition to these developments in philosophy, sometime around the sixth or seventh century a new trend in practice developed in India, which was written down in texts called *tantras*. These texts purported to have been spoken by the historical Buddha (or sometimes by other buddhas), and while they incorporated the traditional Mahāyāna ideal of the bodhisattva who seeks buddhahood for the benefit of all beings, they also proposed some radically new practices and paradigms. The central practices of *tantra* include visualizations intended to foster cognitive reorientation, prayers *(mantra)* to buddhas that are intended to facilitate the transformation of the meditator into a fully awakened buddha, and often elaborate rituals.

In the tantric practice of deity yoga *(devatā-yoga)*, meditators first visualize buddhas in front of themselves (this is referred to as the "generation stage," *utpatti-krama*) and then invite the buddhas to merge with them, a process that symbolically transforms them into buddhas (this is referred to as the "completion stage," *niṣpanna-krama*). The practice of deity yoga is intended to help meditators become familiar with having the body, speech, and mind of buddhas and with performing the compassionate activities of buddhas. Because meditators train in the desired effect of buddhahood, adherents of tantra claim that their path is much shorter than that of traditional Mahāyāna, which was said to require a minimum of three "countless eons" *(asaṃkhyeya-kalpa)* to complete. With the special practices of tantra, one may become a buddha in as little as one human lifetime.

Following this last flowering of Buddhist thought in India, Buddhism began to decline. It increasingly became a tradition of elite scholar-monks who studied in great monastic universities like Nālandā and Vikramaśīla in northern India. Buddhism failed to adapt to changing social and political circumstances and apparently lacked a wide base of support. Thus, when a series of invasions by Turkish Muslims descended on India in the ninth through twelfth centuries, with the invaders sacking the great north Indian monastic universities and killing many prominent monks, Buddhism was dealt a death blow from which it never recovered.

The Spread of Buddhism Outside of India

During the third century B.C.E. the spread of Buddhism was furthered by Aśoka (r. 272–236), the third of the Mauryan kings who created the first pan-Indian empire. Aśoka was converted to Buddhism by a Theravāda monk, and after a bloody war of conquest against the neighboring state of Kaliṅga, he recognized that such aggression violated the principles of Buddhism. From this point on, he renounced war as an instrument of foreign policy and began to implement Buddhist principles in the administration of the kingdom. In order to inform the populace of his political and ruling philosophy, he had edicts inscribed on stone pillars and placed throughout his realm. A number of them still survive today. His reign is considered by Buddhists to have been a model of good government, one informed by Buddhist principles of righteousness and respect for life.

Aśoka's advocacy of Buddhism was one of the primary reasons for the spread of the tradition into Southeast Asia. He sent teams of missionaries all over the Indian subcontinent and to Sri Lanka, Burma, and other neighboring areas. Due to Aśoka's influence and personal power, the missionaries generally were well received in the countries they visited and often were successful in convincing people to convert to Buddhism. One of the most successful missions he sponsored was led by his son Mahinda, who traveled to Sri Lanka along with four other monks and a novice. According to Buddhist tradition, the mission was so successful that the king of Sri Lanka became a Buddhist, and Mahinda then supervised the translation of the Theravāda canon (written in the Pāli language) into Sinhala. He also helped found a monastery, named the Mahāvihāra, that became the main bastion of Theravāda orthodoxy in Sri Lanka for over a thousand years.

It is unclear exactly when Buddhism first arrived in East Asia. China was the first country in the region to record contact with Buddhism. A royal edict issued in 65 C.E. states that a prince in what is now northern Kiangsu Province performed Buddhist sacrifices and entertained Buddhist monks and laypeople. The earliest Buddhists in China were probably from Central Asia, and for centuries Buddhism was widely perceived as a religion of foreigners. In 148 C.E., a monk named An Shigao, from the Central Asian kingdom of Kusha, began translating Indian Buddhist texts into Chinese in Luoyang, which was to become the capital of the later Han dynasty. An Shigao and a number of other monks (mostly from Central Asia) translated about thirty Buddhist texts over the next three decades.

The early translators used a translation system termed "matching concepts" *(keyi)*, which was to have important ramifications for the development of Chinese Buddhism. Realizing that China had a highly developed culture and that the Chinese tended to view people from other countries as uncouth barbarians, the early translators used indigenous terminology—particularly Daoist terminology—to translate Sanskrit technical terms. One result of this practice was that it made many foreign ideas more palatable to Chinese readers, but it also inevitably colored the translations to such an extent that for the first few centuries after Buddhism's arrival in China, many Chinese believed it to be merely another version of Daoism.

In later centuries, Chinese Buddhism developed its own identity, and from China Buddhism was passed on to Korea and Japan. In 552, according to *Chronicles of Japan (Nihonshōki)*, the Korean state of Paekche sent Buddhist texts and images to Japan, hoping to persuade the Japanese emperor to become an ally in its war against the neighboring state of Silla. Some members of the Soga clan wanted to worship the Buddha as a powerful foreign god *(kami)*, hoping to gain influence by associating themselves with what they believed to be a deity of the powerful Chinese empire. The early Japanese interest in Buddhism was connected mostly with purported magical powers of buddhas and Buddhist monks, but after the emperor Yōmei (r. 585–587) converted to Buddhism, Japanese began to travel to China in order to study with Buddhist teachers there, and indigenous Buddhist schools developed in Japan.

Yōmei's son Prince Shōtoku (574–622) enthusiastically propagated Buddhism. He is credited with building numerous Buddhist temples and with sponsoring Japanese monks to travel to China for study. He is also the author of commentaries on three Buddhist texts. In later times he was viewed in Japan as an incarnation of the bodhisattva Avalokiteśvara.

During the reign of the Tibetan king Trisong Detsen (740–798), the Indian scholar Śāntarakṣita traveled to Tibet, but opposition from some of the king's ministers forced him to leave. Before departing, he urged the king to invite the tantric adept Padmasambhava to Tibet. Upon his arrival, Padmasambhava claimed that Śāntarakṣita's efforts had been frustrated by the country's demons. Padmasambhava then challenged the demons to personal combat, and none were able to defeat him. This so impressed the king and his court that Śāntarakṣita was invited back at Padmasambhava's urging, and the first Buddhist monastery in Tibet was built at Samye. This marked the beginning of the "first dissemination" of Buddhism to Tibet, which ended when the devout Buddhist king Relbachen (815–836) was assassinated.

Relbachen's death in 836 marked the beginning of an interregnum period for Tibetan Buddhism, which ended in 1042 when Atiśa (982–1054), one of the directors of the monastic university of Nālandā, traveled to Tibet. This is considered by Tibetan historians to mark the beginning of the "second dissemination" of Buddhism to Tibet. Atiśa was so successful in bringing the dharma to Tibet that Buddhism quickly became the dominant religious tradition in the country.

Today Buddhism continues to flourish in Asia, despite setbacks such as the suppression of religion in China since the inauguration of the People's Republic of China. The current government follows Karl Marx's notion that religion is "the opiate of the masses" and an impediment to social development. In recent years government persecution of Buddhism has eased somewhat, and currently Buddhism is enjoying increased support from the Chinese populace. The government is also allowing young people to become ordained as Buddhist monks and nuns.

Buddhism is becoming increasingly popular in Western countries, and a number of prominent Buddhist teachers have established successful centers in Europe and North America. The Dalai Lama, Thich Nhat Hanh, Sogyal Rinpoche, a number of Zen masters *(rōshi),* and Theravāda meditation teachers have attracted substantial followings outside Asia, and books and articles about Buddhism are appearing with increasing frequency in Western countries.

Buddhist Scriptures

The early Buddhist canon is traditionally referred to as the "Three Baskets" *(tripiṭaka;* Pāli: *tipiṭaka),* consisting of (1) *vinaya:* rules of conduct mainly concerned with the regulation of the monastic order; (2) *sūtras:* discourses purportedly spoken by the Buddha, and sometimes by his immediate disciples; and (3) *abhidharma,* including scholastic treatises that codify and interpret the teachings attributed to the Buddha. According to Buddhist tradition, this division was instituted at the first council. This canon was written in a language called Pāli, which is believed to have been derived from a dialect used in the region of Magadha. A second council introduced some modifications to the rules of monastic discipline, and later councils added other texts to the canon. At first the canon was transmitted orally, but after a time of political and social turmoil King Vaṭṭagāmaṇi of Sri Lanka ordered that it be committed to writing. This was accomplished between 35 and 32 B.C.E. The *sūtras* and *vinaya* were written in Pāli, but some of the commentaries were in Sinhala. The Sinhala texts were translated into Pāli in the fifth century C.E.

The *Vinaya* section of the Pāli canon consists of rules of conduct, most of which are aimed at monks and nuns. Many of these are derived from specific cases in which the Buddha was asked for a ruling on the conduct of particular members of the order, and the general rules he promulgated still serve as the basis for monastic conduct.

The *Sūtra* (Pāli: *Sutta*) section of the Pāli canon traditionally is divided into five "groupings" *(nikāya):* (1) the "long" *(dīgha)* discourses; (2) the "medium length" *(majjhima)* discourses; (3) the "grouped" *(saṃyutta)* discourses; (4) the "enumerated" *(aṅguttara)* discourses, which are arranged according to the enumerations of their topics; and (5) the "minor" *(khuddaka)* discourses, which constitute the largest section of the canon and the one that contains the widest variety of materials. It includes stories of the Buddha's former births *(Jātaka),* which report how he gradually perfected the exalted qualities of a buddha; accounts of the lives of the great disciples *(apadāna);* didactic verses *(gāthā);* an influential work titled *Path of Truth (Dhammapada);* and a number of other important texts.

The *Abhidharma* (Pāli: *abhidhamma*) section includes seven treatises that organize the doctrines of particular classes of the Buddha's discourses. The *Abhidharma* writers attempted to systematize the profusion of teachings attributed to the Buddha into a coherent philosophy. Their texts classify experience in terms of impermanent groupings of factors referred to as *dharmas* (Pāli: *dhammas*), which in aggregations are the focus of the doctrine *(dharma)* taught by Buddha. They are simple real things, indivisible into something more basic. Collections of dharmas are the phenomena of experience. Everything in the world—people, animals, plants, inanimate objects—consists of impermanent groupings of dharmas. Thus, nothing possesses an underlying soul or essence. The collections of dharmas change in every moment, and so all of reality is viewed as a vast interconnected network of causation.

Other early schools developed their own distinctive canons, many of which have very different collections of texts—although the doctrines and practices they contain are similar. Some schools, such as the Sarvāstivādins ("Everything Exists School"), used Sanskrit for their canons, but today only fragments of these collections exist, mostly in Chinese translations. Although Mahāyāna schools developed an impressive literature, there does not seem to have been an attempt to create a Mahāyāna canon in India. The surviving Mahāyāna canons were all compiled in other countries.

Canons compiled in Mahāyāna countries contain much of the material of the Pāli canon but also include Mahāyāna sūtras and other texts not found in the Pāli canon. The Tibetan canon, for example, contains a wealth of Mahāyāna sūtras translated from Sanskrit, treatises *(śāstra)* by important Indian Buddhist thinkers, tantras and tantric commentaries, and miscellaneous writings deemed important enough to include in the canon. The Chinese canon also contains Mahāyāna sūtras, Indian philosophical treatises, and a variety of other texts, but its compilation was much less systematic than that of the Tibetan canon. The Tibetan translators had access to a much wider range of literature, due to the fact that the canon was collected in Tibet centuries after the Chinese one. In addition, Buddhist literature came to China in a rather haphazard way. The transmission of Buddhist texts to China occurred over the course of several centuries, and during this time the tradition in India was developing, creating new schools and doctrines.

The Chinese canon was transmitted to Korea and Japan. Tibet and Mongolia both follow the Tibetan canon, which according to tradition was redacted and codified by Pudön (1290–1364). The Theravāda countries of

Southeast Asia follow the Pāli canon and generally consider the texts of Mahāyāna to be heterodox. In addition to this canonical literature, each school of Buddhism has created literature that it considers to be authoritative. In the selections below we provide examples of such texts from a wide range of schools and periods of Buddhist literature, but the vast scope of canonical and extracanonical literature prevents us from including many important works. The selections are intended to present a representative sampling of early texts that contain central doctrines or that recount important events in the history of Buddhism, along with statements by Buddhist thinkers of later times that illustrate influential developments in Buddhist thought and practice.

HOLIDAYS

Āsāḷha Offering (Āsāḷha Pūjā; Sri Lanka: Esala Perahera) A festival held in Theravāda countries to commemorate the Buddha's first sermon in the Deer Park. It is held in Āsāḷha, the eighth lunar month, generally around July.

Buddhist New Year In Theravāda countries, the new year is celebrated for three days beginning with the first new moon in April. In Mahāyāna countries, the celebration generally begins on the first new moon in January.

Robe Offering (Kaṭhina) An annual event in Theravāda countries in which laypeople mark the end of the rains' retreat by giving new robes to monks.

Great Prayer Festival (Mönlam Chenmo) Annual new year celebration instituted by Tsong Khapa in 1409. It combines religious activities with sporting contests and parties.

Festival of the Hungry Ghosts (Ullambana; China: Yulan; Japan: Obon) A festival celebrated in East Asian Mahāyāna countries commemorating Maudgalyāyana's efforts to help his mother, who had been reborn as a hungry ghost *(preta)*. Traditionally celebrated on the 15th day of the seventh lunar month, it involves making offerings of food, money, clothing, and prayers for hungry ghosts and hell beings.

Vesak (Thai: Visākhā Pūjā) A major celebration in Theravāda countries, commemorating the day on which, according to tradition, the Buddha was born, attained awakening, and entered final nirvana. It is celebrated on the full moon day of the month of Visākhā (April–May). In Tibet it is known as Saga Dawa and celebrated in June–July.

TIMELINE

485–405 B.C.E.	Life of Śākyamuni Buddha
405 B.C.E.	First Buddhist Council at Rājagṛha
305 B.C.E.	Second Buddhist Council at Vaiśālī
272–236 B.C.E.	Reign of Aśoka
200 B.C.E.	Beginnings of Mahāyāna Buddhism in India
101–77 B.C.E.	Reign of Duṭṭagāmaṇi in Sri Lanka; establishment of Buddhism as state religion
1st century C.E.	Buddhism enters Central Asia and China
148	An Shigao arrives in China and establishes first translation bureau
3rd century	Buddhism transmitted to Burma, Cambodia, Laos, Indonesia
350–650	Gupta Dynasty in India; flourishing of Buddhist philosophy and art
552	Buddhism enters Japan from Korea
618–650	Life of Songtsen Gampo, first of Tibet's "religious kings"
618–906	Chinese Tang Dynasty; apogee of Buddhism in China
720–1200	Tantric Buddhism arises and develops in India
845	Persecution of Buddhism in China
1042	Atiśa arrives in Tibet; beginning of "second dissemination" of Buddhism
1173–1262	Life of Shinran; founding of Jōdo-shinshū in Japan
1200	Destruction of Nālandā Monastic University by Mahmud Ghorī
1603–1867	Buddhism becomes state religion in Japan during Tokugawa period
18th century	Colonial occupation of Sri Lanka, Burma, Laos, Cambodia, and Vietnam by European powers
1851	First Buddhist temple founded in San Francisco for Chinese immigrants
1891–1956	Life of B. R. Ambedkar; mass conversion of former Untouchables in India

GLOSSARY

anātman "No-self," the doctrine that there is no permanent, partless, substantial essence or soul.

Arhat The ideal of "Hīnayāna" Buddhism, who strives to attain a personal nirvana.

Avidyā "Ignorance," the primary factor that enmeshes living beings in the cycle of birth, death, and rebirth.

Bodhisattva A compassionate being who resolves to bring others to liberation.

Buddha "Awakened One," epithet of those who successfully break the hold of ignorance, liberate themselves from cyclic existence, and teach others the path to liberation.

Chan/Zen A school that developed in East Asia, emphasizing meditation aimed at a nonconceptual, direct understanding of reality.

Completion Stage *(niṣpanna-krama)* Tantric practice in which one visualizes oneself as being transformed into a buddha.

Deity Yoga *(devatā-yoga)* The tantric practice of visualizing oneself as a buddha.

Dependent Arising *(pratītya-samutpāda)* Doctrine that phenomena arise and pass away in dependence on causes and conditions.

Dharma Buddhist doctrine and practice.

Duḥkha "Suffering," the first "noble truth" of Buddhism, which holds that cyclic existence is characterized by suffering.

Eightfold Noble Path Fourth of the "four noble truths," which involves cultivation of correct views, actions, and meditative practices in order to bring an end to suffering.

Five Aggregates The components of the psycho-physical personality and the factors on the basis of which unawakened beings impute the false notion of a "self": (1) form, (2) feelings, (3) discriminations, (4) consciousness, (5) compositional factors.

Four Noble Truths Basic propositions attributed to the Buddha: (1) suffering, (2) the cause of suffering, (3) the cessation of suffering, (4) the eightfold noble path.

Generation Stage *(utpatti-krama)* Tantric practice of visualizing a vivid image of a buddha in front of oneself.

Hīnayāna "Lesser Vehicle," a term coined by Mahāyānists to describe their opponents, whose path they characterized as selfish and inferior to their own.

Karma "Actions," which bring about concordant results.

Keyi "Matching Concepts," a translation style adopted for early Chinese versions of Buddhist texts, which involved using indigenous Chinese terms for Sanskrit words.

Madhyamaka "Middle Way School," one of the most influential systems of Indian Buddhism.

Mahāyāna "Greater Vehicle," the school of Buddhism that emphasizes the ideal of the bodhisattva.

Nirvana Liberation from cyclic existence.

Pure Land A school of Buddhism popular in East Asia whose adherents strive for rebirth in the realm of the Buddha Amitābha.

Śākyamuni "Sage of the Śākyas," an epithet of the historical Buddha, whose name at birth was Siddhārtha Gautama.

Saṃsāra "Cyclic Existence," the beginningless cycle of birth, death, and rebirth in which ignorant beings are trapped.

Skill in Means *(upāya-kauśalya)* The ability to adapt Buddhist teachings and practices to the level of understanding of one's audience.

Śūnyatā "Emptiness," the lack of inherent existence that characterizes all persons and phenomena.

Sūtra Discourses attributed to the historical Buddha.

Tantra Discourses attributed to the historical Buddha that appeared sometime around the seventh century and that advocate practices involving visualizing oneself as a buddha.

Yogācāra "Yogic Practice School," a system of Indian Buddhism whose main early exponents were the brothers Asaṅga and Vasubandhu.

Zen See **Chan.**

FURTHER READINGS

BECHERT, HEINZ, AND GOMBRICH, RICHARD. *The World of Buddhism.* New York: Thames and Hudson, 1984.

CH'EN, KENNETH. *Buddhism in China: A Historical Survey.* Princeton, NJ: Princeton University Press, 1984.

COLLINS, STEVEN. *Selfless Persons: Imagery and Thought in Theravāda Buddhism.* Cambridge: Cambridge University Press, 1982.

DUMOULIN, HEINRICH. *Zen Buddhism: A History.* 2 vols. New York: Macmillan, 1988.

GOMBRICH, RICHARD. *Theravāda Buddhism: A Social History from Ancient Benares to Modern Colombo.* London: Routledge & Kegan Paul, 1988.

KIYOTA, MINORU (ed.). *Mahāyāna Buddhist Meditation.* Honolulu: University of Hawaii Press, 1978.

LAMOTTE, ÉTIENNE. *History of Indian Buddhism.* Sara Webb-Boin, tr. Louvain: Peeters Press, 1988.

MATSUNAGA, DAIGAN AND ALICIA. *Foundation of Japanese Buddhism,* 2 vols. Los Angeles: Buddhist Books International, 1974.

PAUL, DIANA. *Women in Buddhism: Images of the Feminine in Mahāyāna Tradition.* Berkeley, CA: Asian Humanities Press, 1979.

POWERS, JOHN. *Introduction to Tibetan Buddhism.* Ithaca: Snow Lion, 1995.

RUEGG, DAVID S. *The Literature of the Madhyamaka School of Philosophy in India.* Wiesbaden: Otto Harrassowitz, 1981.

WILLIAMS, PAUL. *Mahāyāna Buddhism: The Doctrinal Foundations.* London and New York: Routledge, 1989.

THE LIFE OF THE BUDDHA

According to traditional accounts, the Buddha was born a prince named Siddhārtha Gautama in a small kingdom in what is today southern Nepal. His final incarnation was a culmination of a training program that spanned countless lifetimes, during which he gradually perfected the exalted qualities that would mark him as a buddha. Shortly after his birth, his father consulted a number of astrologers, all of whom declared that the newborn prince would become a great king who would rule with truth and righteousness. One astrologer, however, declared that if the prince were to see a sick person, an old person, a corpse, and a world-renouncing ascetic, he would become dissatisfied with his life and pursue the path of a wandering mendicant in order to seek final peace.

These four things became known in Buddhism as the "four sights." The first three epitomize the problems inherent in the world, while the fourth points to the way out of the endless cycle of birth, death, and rebirth, which is characterized by suffering and loss.

According to the Extensive Sport Sūtra (Lalitavistara-sūtra), *Siddhārtha's father, king Śuddhodana, decided to prevent his son from encountering any of the four sights and surrounded him with pleasant diversions during his early years. The prince, however, eventually convinced his father to let him visit a part of the city that lay outside the palace gates.*

Before allowing the prince to ride out in his chariot, Śuddhodana first ordered that the streets be cleared of all sick and old people and that the prince not be allowed to see any corpses or world renouncers. Despite the king's efforts, however, at one point the path of the royal chariot was blocked by a sick man. Siddhārtha had never before encountered serious illness, and he turned to Channa, his charioteer, and asked,

O charioteer, who is this man, weak and powerless?
His flesh, blood, and skin withered, his veins protruding,
With whitened hair, few teeth, his body emaciated,
Walking painfully and leaning on a staff?

Channa informed the prince that the man had grown old and that such afflictions were the inevitable result of age. He added,

O prince, this man is oppressed by age
His organs are weak; he is in pain, and his strength and vigor are gone.
Abandoned by his friends, he is helpless and unable to work,
Like wood abandoned in a forest. . . .
Lord, this is not unique to his race or his country.
Age exhausts youth and the entire world.
Even you will be separated from the company
Of your mother and father, friends and relatives.
There is no other fate for living beings.

Siddhārtha was amazed to find that most people see such sights every day but persist in shortsighted pursuits and mundane affairs, apparently unconcerned that they will inevitably become sick, grow old, and die. In three subsequent journeys outside the palace, Siddhārtha saw an old man and a corpse, and when he learned that eventually his young, healthy body would become weak and decrepit he fell into a profound depression.

On a fourth trip, Siddhārtha saw a world renouncer, a man who stood apart from the crowd, who owned nothing and was unaffected by the petty concerns of the masses, and who radiated calm, serenity, and a profound inner peace. This sight lifted Siddhārtha's spirits, because it revealed to him that there is a way to transcend the vicissitudes of mundane existence and find true happiness. Intrigued by the ascetic, Siddhārtha asked Channa what sort of man he was, and the charioteer replied,

Lord, this man is one of the order of *bhikṣus* [mendicants].
Having abandoned sensual desires,
He has disciplined conduct.
He has become a wandering mendicant.
Who views himself and the external world with the same regard.
Devoid of attachment or enmity, he lives by begging.

Realizing the folly of remaining in the palace, Siddhārtha resolved to renounce the world and find inner peace.

Channa, for countless ages I have enjoyed sensual objects
Of sight, sound, color, flavor, and touch, in all their varieties;
But they have not made me happy. . . .
Realizing this, I will embark on the raft of dharma, which is steadfast,
Endowed with the range of austerities, good conduct,
Equanimity, effort, strength, and generosity,
Which is sturdy, made of the firmness of effort, and strongly held together.

Siddhārtha then declared his desire to become awakened in order to show other suffering beings a way to end suffering:

I desire and wish that,
After attaining the level of awakening,
Which is beyond decay and death,
I will save the world.
The time for that has arrived.

Siddhārtha left the palace and subsequently practiced meditation with several teachers, but none could show him a path leading to the cessation of suffering. At one point he fell in with five spiritual seekers who told him that the way to salvation lies in severe asceticism. He followed their practices and eventually was eating only a single grain of rice per day. After swooning due to weakness, however, Siddhārtha realized that extreme asceticism is just as much a trap as the hedonistic indulgence of his early years. Thus, he left his ascetic companions behind and resolved to find a path leading to the cessation of suffering. He recognized that he would have to discover the truth for himself. Before embarking on his final quest for truth, Siddhārtha made a solemn vow:

As I sit here, my body may wither away,
My skin, bones, and flesh may decay,
But until I have attained awakening—
Which is difficult to gain even during many ages—
I will not move from this place.

Siddhārtha stood in a spot that is now known as "the Circle of Awakening," located in modern-day Bodhgayā. Sitting under a tree, during the night Siddhārtha entered into progressively deeper meditative states in which the patterns of the world fell into place for him, and thus he came to understand the causes and effects of actions, why beings suffer, and how to transcend all the pains and sorrows of the world. By the dawn of the next morning, he had completely transcended the misconceptions of ordinary people. At this point Buddhist texts refer to him as "buddha," indicating that he was now fully awake and aware of the true nature of all things. Scanning the world with his heightened perception, the Buddha recognized that his realization was too profound to be understood by the vast majority of beings in the world, so initially he decided to remain under the tree in profound equanimity and to pass away without teaching what he had learned.

Profound, peaceful, perfectly pure,
Luminous, uncompounded, ambrosial
Is the dharma I have attained.

Even if I were to teach it,
Others could not understand
Thus, I should remain silent in the forest.

After the Buddha had made this statement, however, the Indian god Brahmā appeared before him and begged him to teach what he had learned for the benefit of those few beings who could understand and profit from his wisdom. Moved by compassion for the sufferings of creatures caught up in the round of cyclic existence, the Buddha agreed, and for the next forty years he traveled around India, teaching all who cared to listen.

Source: *Lalita-vistara* selections. Tr. JP.

PĀLI CANON

THE FIRST SERMON

Shortly after making the decision to teach, Buddha surveyed the world in order to choose a place to begin his teaching career. He decided to travel to Sārnāth, where his five former companions were still practicing pointless austerities, hoping in this way to find happiness. The following excerpt purports to be Buddha's first public teaching. It is referred to as the "Sūtra Turning the Wheel of Doctrine" because it set in motion the Buddha's teaching career. In this passage, he lays out some of the themes that would be central to his later teachings, such as the importance of following a "middle way" that avoids the extremes of sensual indulgence and extreme asceticism, as well as the "four noble truths": (1) that all mundane existence involves suffering, (2) that suffering is caused by desire, (3) that there can be a cessation of suffering, and (4) the eightfold noble path that leads to this cessation.

Thus have I heard: At one time, the Exalted One was living near Vārāṇasī, at Isipatana near the Deer Park. Then the Exalted One spoke to the group of five monks: These two extremes, O monks, should not be practiced by one who has gone forth [from the household life]. What are the two? That which is linked with sensual desires, which is low, vulgar, common, unworthy, and useless, and that which is linked with self-torture, which is painful, unworthy, and useless. By avoiding these two extremes the Tathāgata [Buddha] has gained the knowledge of the middle path which gives vision and knowledge, and leads to calm, to clairvoyances, to awakening, to nirvana.

O monks, what is the middle path, which gives vision . . . ? It is the noble eightfold path: right views, right intention, right speech, right action, right livelihood, right effort, right mindfulness, right concentration. This, O monks, is the middle path, which gives vision. . . .

1. Now this, O monks, is the noble truth of suffering: birth is suffering, old age is suffering, death is suffering, sorrow, grieving, dejection, and despair are suffering. Contact with unpleasant things is suffering, not getting what you want is also suffering. In short, the five aggregates of grasping are suffering.

2. Now this, O monks, is the noble truth of the arising of suffering: that craving which leads to rebirth, combined with longing and lust for this and that—craving for sensual pleasure, craving for rebirth, craving for cessation of birth. . . .
3. Now this, O monks, is the noble truth of the cessation of suffering: It is the complete cessation without remainder of that craving, the abandonment, release from, and non-attachment to it.
4. Now this, O monks, is the noble truth of the path that leads to the cessation of suffering: This is the noble eightfold path. . . .

Now monks, as long as my threefold knowledge and insight regarding these noble truths . . . were not well purified, so long, O monks, I was not sure that in this world . . . I had attained the highest complete awakening.

But when my threefold knowledge and insight in these noble truths with their twelve divisions were well purified, then, O monks, I was sure that in this world . . . I had attained the highest complete awakening.

Now knowledge and insight have arisen in me, so that I know: My mind's liberation is assured; this is my last existence; for me there is no rebirth.

Source: *Saṃyutta-nikāya* 5.420–423. Tr. JP.

THE BUDDHA'S GOOD QUALITIES

From a Buddhist perspective, the Buddha is not only important as a person who taught a corpus of texts. The events of his life also serve as an inspiration to devout Buddhists, who see him as the supreme example of how meditative realization should be put into practice in daily life. The following passage describes how he lived and related to the people and things around him.

Renouncing the killing of living beings, the ascetic Gotama abstains from killing. He has put down the club and the sword, and he lives modestly, full of mercy, desiring in his compassion the welfare of all living beings.

Having renounced the taking of what is not given, the ascetic Gotama abstains from grasping after what does not belong to him. He accepts what is given to him and waits for it to be given; and he lives in honesty and purity of heart. . . .

Having renounced unchastity, the ascetic Gotama is celibate and aloof and has lost all desire for sexual intercourse, which is vulgar.

Having renounced false speech, the ascetic Gotama abstains from lying, he speaks the truth, holds to the truth, is trustworthy, and does not break his word in the world. . . .

Having renounced slander, the ascetic Gotama abstains from libel. When he hears something in one place he will not repeat it in another in order to cause strife . . . but he unites those who are divided by strife and encourages those who are friends. His pleasure is in peace, he loves peace and delights in it, and when he speaks he speaks words that make for peace. . . .

Having renounced harsh speech, the ascetic Gotama avoids abusive speech. He speaks only words that are blameless, pleasing to the ear, touching the heart, cultured, pleasing to people, loved by people. . . .

Having renounced frivolous talk, the ascetic Gotama avoids gossip. He speaks at the right time, in accordance with the facts, with meaningful words, speaking of the truth *(dhamma)*, of the discipline *(vinaya)*. His speech is memorable, timely, well illustrated, measured, and to the point.

The ascetic Gotama has renounced doing harm to seeds or plants. He takes only one meal per day, not eating at night, nor at the wrong time.

He abstains from watching shows or attending fairs with song, dance, and music. He has renounced the wearing of ornaments and does not adorn himself with garlands, scents, or cosmetics. He abstains from using a large or high bed. He abstains from accepting silver or gold, raw grain or raw meat. He abstains from accepting women or girls, male or female slaves, sheep or goats, birds or pigs, elephants or cows, horses or mares, fields or property. He abstains from acting as a go-between or messenger, from buying and selling, from falsifying with scales, weights, or measures. He abstains from crookedness and bribery, from cheating and fraud. He abstains from injury, murder, binding with bonds, stealing, and acts of violence.

Source: *Dīgha-nikāya* 1.4–10. Tr. JP.

THE PERFECT MAN'S PERFECT BODY

Indian Buddhist authors assume a direct connection between a person's spiritual attainments and physical appearance. Those who are beautiful, wealthy, and healthy enjoy these qualities as a result of past performance of virtue. The Buddha is characterized as the "ultimate man" (puruṣ ottama), *and he has the best of all possible bodies. This is essential to his mission as a religious teacher, because while fools may be able to parrot words of wisdom, only a buddha can prove his attainments by displaying a perfect body. His physique is distinguished by the thirty-two "physical characteristics of a great man"* (mahāpuruṣa-lakṣaṇa), *which include a fist-sized lump on top of his head, webbed fingers and toes, arms that reach to his knees, a silver tuft of hair between his eyebrows, and a male organ hidden by a sheath. While this physiognomy sounds odd by contemporary standards, it was portrayed as the epitome of human perfection in Indian sources, and it plays a key role in several accounts of conversions in which skeptical observers become followers of the Buddha merely by viewing his form. The following passage from the* Extensive Sport *describes a scene in which he walks into a town and all activity ceases because everyone is overcome by his perfect beauty. Many of those who see him become his followers before even hearing him speak.*

Crowds of men and women gaze at the man who is like pure gold. His self-mastery is complete; he is marked with the thirty-two physical characteristics. And no one tires of looking at him. . . . [They ask,] "Who is this being? Never before have we seen one like him; he makes the city radiant with his splendor." Thousands of women, wishing to see the most outstanding of men, leave their houses empty; they stand on the rooftops, in doorways, at windows, and in the streets to gaze at him. The merchants stop doing business; in the houses and in the streets all drinking and revelry cease, so intent are the people on watching the most remarkable of men.

Source: *Lalitavistara*, pp. 175–176. Tr. JP.

CRITERIA FOR ASSESSING VALID TEACHINGS AND TEACHERS

Although there are many passages in Buddhist literature in which faith is extolled as an important virtue, this faith ideally should be based on evidence and valid reasoning. In addition, there are several places in Buddhist literature in which the Buddha exhorts his listeners to examine teachers and teachings closely before putting trust in them. In the following passage, the Buddha addresses a group of people collectively referred to as Kālāmas, who are confused by the conflicting claims of the religious systems of their day. The Buddha advises them to verify all claims themselves by examining which doctrines lead to positive results and which lead to negative ones. The former should be adopted, and the latter rejected.

Do not be [convinced] by reports, tradition, or hearsay; nor by skill in the scriptural collections, argumentation, or reasoning; nor after examining conditions or considering theories; nor because [a theory] fits appearances, nor because of respect for an ascetic [who holds a particular view]. Rather, Kālāmas, when you know for yourselves: These doctrines are non-virtuous; these doctrines are erroneous; these doctrines are rejected by the wise; these doctrines, when performed and undertaken, lead to loss and suffering—then you should reject them, Kālāmas.

Source: *Aṅguttara-nikāya* 1.189. Tr. JP.

NIRVANA

Nirvana is said to be the final cessation of suffering, a state beyond the cycle of birth and death. As such, it could be said to be the ultimate goal of the path taught by the Buddha, whose quest was motivated by a concern with the unsatisfactoriness of cyclic existence and a wish to find a way out of the round of suffering that characterizes the mundane world. Despite its importance, however, there are few descriptions of nirvana in Buddhist literature. The selection below is one of the most detailed analyses of what nirvana is and how one attains it.

Monks, there exists something in which there is neither earth nor water, fire nor air. It is not the sphere of infinite space, nor the sphere of infinite consciousness, nor the sphere of nothingness, nor the sphere of neither perception nor non-perception [these are advanced meditative states]. It is neither this world nor another world, nor both, neither sun nor moon.

cohen → forces us to think beyond the obvious meaning

Monks, I do not state that it comes nor that it goes. It neither abides nor passes away. It is not caused, established, arisen, supported. It is the end of suffering. . . .

What I call the selfless is difficult to perceive, for it is not easy to perceive the truth. But one who knows it cuts through craving, and for one who knows it, there is nothing to hold onto. . . .

Monks, there exists something that is unborn, unmade, uncreated, unconditioned. Monks, if there were not an unborn, unmade, uncreated, unconditioned, then there would be no way to indicate how to escape from the born, made, created, and conditioned. However, monks, since there exists something that is unborn, unmade, uncreated, and unconditioned, it is known that there is an escape from that which is born, made, created, and conditioned. . . .

There is wandering for those who are attached, but there is no wandering for those who are unattached. There is serenity when there is no wandering, and when there is serenity, there is no desire. When there is no desire, there is neither coming nor going, and when there is no coming nor going there is neither death nor rebirth. When there is neither death nor rebirth, there is neither this life nor the next life, nor anything in between. It is the end of suffering.

Source: *Udāna*, ch. 8.80. Tr. JP.

DEPENDENT ARISING

After attaining awakening, the Buddha indicated that he had come to realize that all the phenomena of the universe are interconnected by relationships of mutual causality. Things come into being in dependence on causes and conditions, abide due to causes and conditions, and eventually pass away due to causes and conditions. Thus, the world is viewed by Buddhists as a dynamic and ever-changing system. The following passage describes the process of causation in relation to human existence, which is said to proceed in a cyclical fashion. Because of a basic misunderstanding of the workings of reality (referred to as "ignorance"), people falsely imagine that some worldly things can bring them happiness, and thus they generate desire and try to acquire these things. Such attitudes provide the basis for the arising of negative mental states, and these states in turn provide a basis for beings to return to the world in a future birth. This next life will begin with the conditioning of the last, and thus the entire cycle will repeat itself unless a person recognizes the folly of conventional wisdom and chooses to follow the Buddhist path, which is designed to provide a way out of the trap of cyclic existence.

[Ānanda, quoting Buddha, said:] "Kaccāna, on two things the world generally bases its view: existence and non-existence. Kaccāna, one who perceives with correct insight the arising of the world as it really is does not think of the non-existence of the world. Kaccāna, one who perceives with correct insight the cessation of the world as it really is does not think of the existence of the world. Kaccāna, the world in general seizes on systems and is imprisoned by dogmas. One who does not seek after, seize on, or fixate on this seizing on systems, this dogma, this mental bias does not say, 'This is my self.' One who thinks, 'Whatever arises is only suffering; whatever ceases is suffering' has no doubts or qualms. In this sense, knowledge not borrowed from others comes to one. This, Kaccāna, is right view.

"Kaccāna, 'Everything exists' is one extreme; Kaccāna, 'Nothing exists' is the other extreme. Not approaching either extreme, Kaccāna, the Tathāgata teaches you a doctrine in terms of a middle path: ignorance depends on action; action depends on consciousness; consciousness depends on name and form; name and form depend on the six sense spheres; the six sense spheres depend on contact; contact depends on feeling; feeling depends on attachment; attachment depends on grasping; grasping depends on existence; existence depends on birth; birth depends on aging and death. Suffering, despair, misery, grief, and sorrow depend on aging and death. In this way, the whole mass of suffering arises. But due to the complete eradication and cessation of ignorance comes a cessation of karmas and so forth. This is the cessation of this whole mass of suffering."

Source: *Saṃyutta-nikāya* 3.90. Tr. JP.

QUESTIONS THAT SHOULD BE AVOIDED

The following passage contains a series of questions about metaphysical topics posed to the Buddha by a wandering ascetic named Vacchagotta. The Buddha's response is interesting: He does not even try to provide answers, nor does he indicate that he does not answer because of ignorance on his part. Rather, he tells Vacchagotta that there is no point in answering the questions, because they are irrelevant to the goal of salvation. He indicates that people who spend their time pondering such questions and arguing about philosophical conundrums are unlikely to find release from suffering, so the wisest course of action is to avoid such questions as a waste of time.

Thus have I heard: At one time the Exalted One was staying near Sāvatthi in the Jeta Grove in Anāthapiṇḍika's hermitage. . . . Then the wanderer Vacchagotta approached the Exalted One . . . and said, "Gotama, does the reverend Gotama have this view: 'The world is eternal; this is the truth, and all else is falsehood'?"

"Vaccha, I do not have this view. . . ."

"Then, Gotama, does the reverend Gotama have this view: 'The world is not eternal; this is the truth, and all else is falsehood'?"

"Vaccha, I do not have this view. . . ."

"Now, Gotama, does the reverend Gotama have this view: 'The world is finite; this is the truth, and all else is falsehood'?"

"Vaccha, I do not have this view. . . ."

"Then, Gotama, does the reverend Gotama have this view: 'The world is not finite; this is the truth, and all else is falsehood'?"

"Vaccha, I do not have this view. . . ."

"Now, Gotama, does the reverend Gotama have this view: 'The soul *(jīva)* and the body are the same; this is the truth, and all else is falsehood'?"

"Vaccha, I do not have this view. . . ."

"Then, Gotama, does the reverend Gotama have this view: 'The soul is one thing and the body is another; this is the truth, and all else is falsehood'?"

"Vaccha, I do not have this view. . . ."

"Now, Gotama, does the reverend Gotama have this view: 'After death, the Tathāgata exists; this is the truth, and all else is falsehood'?"

"Vaccha, I do not have this view. . . ."

"Then, Gotama, does the reverend Gotama have this view: 'After death, the Tathāgata does not exist; this is the truth, and all else is falsehood'?"

"Vaccha, I do not have this view. . . ."

"Now, Gotama, does the reverend Gotama have this view: 'After death, the Tathāgata both exists and does not exist; this is the truth, and all else is falsehood'?"

"Vaccha, I do not have this view. . . ."

"Then, Gotama, does the reverend Gotama have this view: 'After death, the Tathāgata neither exists nor does not exist; this is the truth, and all else is falsehood'?"

"Vaccha, I do not have this view. . . ."

"Gotama, what is the danger that the reverend Gotama sees that he does not hold any of these views?"

"Vaccha, thinking that 'the world is eternal' is going to a [wrong] view, holding a view, the wilderness of views, the writhing of views, the scuffling of views, the bonds of views; it is accompanied by anguish, distress, misery, fever; it does not lead to turning away from [the world], to dispassion, cessation, calm, clairvoyances, awakening, nor to nirvana. . . . Vaccha, contending that this is dangerous, I do not approach any of these views."

"But does Gotama have any views?"

"Vaccha, holding to any view has been eliminated by the Tathāgata . . . so I say that through destruction, dispassion, cessation, abandoning, getting rid of all imaginings, all supposings, all latent pride that 'I am the doer, mine is the deed,' a Tathāgata is released without desire."

"But Gotama, where is a monk whose mind is thus released reborn?"

"Vaccha, the term 'reborn' does not apply."

"Then, Gotama, is he not reborn?"

"Vaccha, the term 'not reborn' does not apply."

"Then, Gotama, is he both reborn and not reborn?"

"Vaccha, 'both reborn and not reborn' does not apply."

"Then, Gotama, is he neither reborn nor not reborn?"

"Vaccha, 'neither reborn nor not reborn' does not apply." . . .

"I am confused at this point, Gotama; I am bewildered, and I have lost all the satisfaction from the earlier conversation I had with Gotama."

"You should be confused, Vaccha, you should be bewildered. Vaccha, this doctrine *(dhamma)* is profound, difficult to see, difficult to understand, peaceful, wonderful, beyond argumentation, subtle, understood by the wise; but it is difficult for you, who hold another view, another allegiance, another goal, having different practices and a different teacher. Well, then, Vaccha, I will now question you in return. . . . If a fire were burning in front of you, would you know, 'This fire is burning in front of me'?"

"Gotama . . . I would know." . . .

"Vaccha, if the fire in front of you were put out, would you know, 'This fire that was in front of me has been put out'?"

"Gotama . . . I would know."

"But, Vaccha, if someone were to ask you—'Regarding that fire that was in front of you and that has been put out, in which direction has the fire gone from here: to the east, west, north, or south'—what would you reply to this question, Vaccha?"

"Gotama, it does not apply. Gotama, the fire burned because of a supply of grass and sticks, but due to having totally consumed this and due to a lack of other fuel, it is said to be put out since it is without fuel."

"Vaccha, in the same way, the form by which one recognizing the Tathāgata would recognize him has been eliminated by the Tathāgata, uprooted, made like a stump of a palm tree that has become non-existent and will not arise again in the future. Vaccha, the Tathāgata is released from designation by form, he is profound, immeasurable, unfathomable like the great ocean. 'Reborn' does not apply; 'not reborn' does not apply. The feelings . . . discriminations . . . compositional factors . . . consciousness by which one recognizing the Tathāgata might recognize him have been eliminated by the Tathāgata, uprooted . . . and will not arise again in the future. Vaccha, the Tathāgata is released from all designation by consciousness; he is profound, immeasurable, unfathomable as the great ocean. 'Reborn' does not apply; 'not reborn' does not apply; 'both reborn and not reborn' does not apply; 'neither reborn nor not reborn' does not apply."

Source: *Majjhima-nikāya* 3.72. Tr. JP.

SELFLESSNESS

Buddhism denies that there is anything corresponding to the common idea of a soul or self. Instead, the Buddha taught that the soul is a false notion imputed to a collection of constantly changing parts. These are the five "aggregates" (skandha): *form, feelings, discriminations, consciousness, and compositional factors. Form refers to one's physical form, and feelings are our emotional responses to the things we experience. Discriminations are classifications of these experiences into pleasant, unpleasant, and neutral. Consciousness refers to the functioning of the mind, and compositional factors are other aspects connected with the false sense of self, such as one's karmas.*

[Buddha:] "Monks, form is selflessness. Monks, if form were the self, then form would not be involved with sickness, and one could say of the body: 'Let my form be thus; let my form not be thus.' Monks, because form is selfless, it is involved with sickness, and one cannot say of form: 'Let my form be thus; let my form not be thus.'

"Feeling is selfless . . . discrimination is selfless . . . the aggregates are selfless . . . compositional factors are selfless . . . consciousness is selfless. Monks, if consciousness were the self, then consciousness would not be involved with sickness, and one could say of consciousness: 'Let my consciousness be thus; let my consciousness not be thus. . . .'

"What do you think, monks: Is form permanent or impermanent?"

"Impermanent, sir."

"And is the impermanent suffering or happiness?"

"Suffering, sir."

"And with respect to what is impermanent, suffering, naturally unstable, is it proper to perceive it in this way: 'This is mine; I am this; this is my self?'"

"Definitely not, sir."

"It is the same way with feelings, discriminations, compositional factors, and consciousness. Therefore, monks, every single form—past, future, or present; internal or external; gross or subtle; low or high; near or far—should be viewed in this way, as it really is, with correct insight: 'This is not mine; this is not I; this is not my self.'

"Every single feeling, every single discrimination, every single compositional factor . . . every single consciousness [should be viewed in this way].

"Perceiving [these] in this way, monks, the well-taught, wise disciple feels disgust for form, feels disgust for feeling, feels disgust for discrimination, feels disgust for compositional factors, and feels disgust for consciousness. Feeling disgust in this way, one becomes averse; becoming averse, one is liberated. Awareness that the liberated person is liberated arises, so that one knows: 'Birth is destroyed; the virtuous life has been lived; my work is done; for such a life there is nothing beyond [this world].'"

Source: *Saṃyutta-nikāya* 3.59. Tr. JP.

INSTRUCTIONS ON MEDITATION

Following the example of the Buddha, Buddhism emphasizes the importance of meditation as a means of attaining clarity of perception, eliminating mental afflictions, and escaping from cyclic existence. The following passage, attributed to Aśvaghoṣa (ca. second century C.E.*), is believed to contain instructions given by Buddha to his half-brother Nanda.*

Now after having closed the windows of the senses with the shutters of mindfulness, you should know the proper measure of food in order to meditate properly and maintain good health. For too much food impedes the intake of breath, makes one lethargic and sleepy, and saps one's strength. Furthermore, just as too much food leads to distraction, eating too little makes one weak. . . . Thus as a practitioner of yoga you should feed your body simply in order to overcome hunger, and not out of desire for food or love of it.

After spending the day in self-controlled mental concentration, you should shake off sleepiness and spend the night engaged in the discipline of yoga. And do not think that your awareness is properly aware when drowsiness manifests itself in your heart. When you are overcome by sleepiness, you should apply your attention to exertion and steadfastness, strength and courage. You should clearly recite the texts you have been taught, and you should teach them to others and ponder them yourself. In order to remain awake, splash water on your face, look around in all directions, and look at the stars. . . .

During the first three watches of the night, you should practice [meditation], but after that you should lie down and rest on your right side, remaining awake in your heart, your mind at peace, keeping your attention on the idea of light. In the third watch, you should get up and, either walking or sitting, continue to practice yoga, with a pure mind and controlled senses. . . .

Sit cross-legged in a solitary place, keep your back straight, and direct your mindfulness in front of you, [focusing] on the tip of the nose, the forehead, or the space between the eyebrows. Keep the wandering mind focused completely on one thing. If a mental affliction—a desirous thought—arises, you should not hold to it, but should brush it off like dust on your clothes. Even if you have eliminated desires from your mind, there is still an innate tendency toward them, like a fire smoldering in ashes. My friend, this should be extinguished by meditation, in the way that fire is extinguished by water. Unless you do this, desire will arise again from the innate tendency, as plants arise from a seed. Only by destroying [the tendencies] will they finally be eradicated, like plants whose roots have been destroyed. . . .

When one washes dirt from gold, one first gets rid of the largest pieces of dirt, and then the smaller ones, and having cleaned it one is left with pieces of pure gold. In the same way, in order to attain liberation, one should discipline the mind, first washing away the coarser faults, and then the smaller ones, until one is left with pure pieces of dharma.

Source: *Saundarananda* chs. 14, 15. Tr. JP.

ORDINATION OF WOMEN

When Buddha began his teaching career, his first disciples were monks, but eventually some women became followers and began to desire ordination as nuns. The woman who put the request to Buddha was Mahāpajapatī Gotamī, who had raised him after his mother died. Buddha first refused her request, but after she obtained the support of Ānanda, Buddha's personal assistant, he eventually agreed, but he added that the decision to admit nuns into the order would shorten the period of "true dharma" by 500 years. It seems clear from the passage, however, that this is not due to any inherent inferiority on the part of women, since Buddha asserts that women are capable of following the spiritual path and attaining the fruits of meditative training.

Some commentators speculate that the reason for his refusal may have been that his early followers were homeless wanderers, so there were no adequate facilities for separating men and women. Because of the pervasiveness and strength of sexual desire, groups of men and women in close proximity inevitably develop attractions and tensions, which lead to conflict. Whatever the reasons for his initial reluctance, Buddha did eventually ordain women, but he added the condition that nuns must observe eight additional rules.

Then Mahāpajapatī Gotamī approached the Lord and, having paid obeisance to him, stood to one side. And Mahāpajapatī Gotamī said this to the Lord: "Lord, it would be good if women could be initiated into the order, in the doctrine and discipline taught by the Tathāgata."

[Buddha replied:] "Gotamī, do not request the initiation of women into the order. . . ."

She made her request two more times, but after being refused she despondently concluded that Buddha would not allow the ordination of women.

Then Mahāpajapatī Gotamī, having cut off her hair, putting on saffron robes, went to Vesālī . . . and when she arrived, her feet were swollen, her body covered with dust, tears covered her face, as she stood outside the grove [where the Buddha was staying].

When the venerable Ānanda saw Mahāpajapatī Gotamī standing there . . . he asked, "Gotamī, why are you standing there, your feet swollen, your body covered with dust, and crying?"

"Venerable Ānanda, it is because the Lord does not allow women to be initiated into the order, in the doctrine and discipline taught by the Tathāgata."

On hearing this, Ānanda offered to intercede on her behalf and approached the Buddha, asking why he had refused her.

Then the venerable Ānanda approached the Lord and, having paid obeisance to him, stood to one side. . . . And he said this to the Lord: "Lord, Mahāpajapatī Gotamī is standing outside the grove, her feet swollen, her body covered with dust, tears on her face, and crying, and she says that the Lord will not allow women to be initiated into the order, in the doctrine and discipline taught by the Tathāgata. Lord, it would be good if women were to be initiated into the order. . . ."

"Ānanda, do not request the initiation of women into the order, in the doctrine and discipline taught by the Tathāgata."

Then the venerable Ānanda thought, "The Lord does not allow the initiation of women into the order . . . but perhaps I can ask in another way. . . ." Then the venerable Ānanda said to the Lord: "Lord, are women who have been initiated into the order, in the doctrine and discipline taught by the Tathāgata, able to attain the fruit of a stream-enterer, or the fruit of a once-returner, or the fruit of a non-returner, or arhathood?"

"Ānanda, women who have been initiated into the order . . . are able to attain the fruit of a stream-enterer, or the fruit of a once-returner, or the fruit of a non-returner, or arhathood."

"So, Lord, women who have been initiated into the order are able to attain [these fruits], and Mahāpajapatī Gotamī was very helpful to the Lord: she was the Lord's aunt, foster mother, and nurse, she suckled him when his mother died [and he should repay her kindness]."

[Hearing this, Buddha said:] "Ānanda, if Mahāpajapatī Gotamī accepts eight cardinal rules she may receive initiation into the order. . . ."

Then Ānanda . . . went to Mahāpajapatī Gotamī and said, "Gotamī, if you will accept eight cardinal rules, you may receive initiation into the order. . . ."

[She replied:] "Honored Ānanda, I accept these eight cardinal rules and will never transgress them during my entire life."

Ānanda then informed Buddha that Mahāpajapatī had accepted these rules, to which he replied:

"Ānanda, if women had not been given the opportunity to receive initiation into the order, in the doctrine and discipline taught by the Tathāgata, then, Ānanda, the monastic system would have lasted longer, and the true doctrine would have endured for one thousand years. But, Ānanda, since women may now receive ordination . . . the monastic system will only endure for five hundred years."

Source: *Vinaya-piṭaka, Cullavagga*, ch. 10, from *Rules of Discipline for Nuns (Bhikṣuṇī Vinaya)*. Tr. JP.

THE CESSATION OF SUFFERING

After the Buddha agreed to create an order of nuns, a number of women took monastic vows, and some eventually were recognized as advanced meditators. The verses below were written by the nun Paṭācārā after she became an arhatī (a female arhat). Her early biography, recounted in Songs of the Nuns (Therīgāthā), *graphically illustrates the problems of cyclic existence. Her entire family is killed one by one under tragic circumstances, and she is driven to the brink of madness. In a state of utter despair, she meets the Buddha, who counsels her and allows her to become a nun. After years of meditative practice, she severs all attachments to worldly things, recognizing them as a source of suffering.*

Ploughing their fields, sowing seeds in the ground,
Men care for their wives and children and prosper.
Why is it that I, endowed with morality and adhering to the teachings,
Do not attain nirvana? I am neither lazy nor conceited.
After washing my feet, I observed the water; watching the water flow downwards,
I focused my mind as one [trains] a noble thoroughbred horse.
Then I took a lamp and entered my cell. After observing the bed, I sat on the couch.
Holding a pin, I pulled out the wick.
The lamp goes out: nirvana. My mind is free!

Source: *Therīgāthā*, psalm 47. Tr. JP.

MY TEACHER

The Songs of the Nuns *collection contains a wealth of information on the religious lives of the early Buddhist nuns. Their biographies describe their struggles and tribulations, and many indicate that they saw monastic ordination as a way to escape the drudgery of household work and loveless marriages. The following passage was written by an anonymous nun who celebrates her liberation from sorrow. It praises her teacher, a fellow nun who showed her the path.*

Four or five times I went from my cell
Without having attained peace of mind or control over my mind.
I approached a nun whom I could trust, and she taught me about the doctrine,
The aggregates, the sense spheres, and the elements.
Having listened to her doctrinal instructions, I sat cross legged for
seven days,
Possessed of joy and bliss.
On the eighth day I stretched out my feet,
Having eliminated the mass of darkness (of ignorance).

Source: *Therīgāthā*, psalm 38. Tr. JP.

THE JOY OF RELEASE

The following poem was written by the mother of Sumaṅgala (a monk who became an arhat). She was the wife of a poor umbrella maker who left her home and became a nun. Later she attained the level of arhathood, which she celebrates in these verses.

Free, I am free!
I am completely free from my kitchen pestle!
[I am free from] my worthless husband and even his sun umbrella!
And my pot that smells like a water snake!
I have eliminated all desire and hatred,
Going to the base of a tree, [I think,] "What happiness!"
And contemplate this happiness.

Source: *Therīgāthā*, psalm 22. Tr. JP.

THE BUDDHA'S LAST DAYS AND FINAL INSTRUCTIONS

After a long and successful teaching career, the Buddha's body had become old and wracked with constant pain. Realizing that his mission had been accomplished, the Buddha decided to enter final nirvana (parinirvana). *He first asked his disciples if they had any final questions and then told them that they should rely on the teachings they had already received. Buddha further informed them that he had told them everything of the path and the true doctrine that could be put into words, holding nothing back, and so it was now up to them to put these teachings into practice.*

[Buddha:] "Ānanda, I have taught the doctrine without distinguishing 'inner' and 'outer.' As to this, the Tathāgata is not a 'closed-fisted teacher' with reference to the doctrine [i.e., he does not hold anything back]. If anyone thinks, 'I should watch over the order,' or 'The order should refer to me,' then let him promulgate something about the order. The Tathāgata does not think in such terms. Thus the Tathāgata does not promulgate something about the order. . . .

"Ānanda, I am now aged, old, an elder, my time has gone, I have arrived at the age of eighty years. Just as an old cart is made to go by tying it together with straps, so the Tathāgata's body is made to go by strapping it together. Ānanda, during periods when the Tathāgata, by withdrawing his attention from all signs, by the cessation of some emotions, enters into the signless concentration of thought and stays in it, on such occasions the Tathāgata's body is made comfortable.

"Therefore, Ānanda . . . you should live with yourselves as islands, with yourselves as refuges, with no one else as refuge; with the doctrine as an island, with the doctrine as a refuge, with no one else as refuge. . . .

"It might be that you will think, Ānanda, 'The Teacher's word has ceased, now we have no teacher!' You should not perceive things in this way. The doctrine and discipline that I have taught and described will be the teacher after I pass away."

He then told Ānanda that after his death it would be permissible for monks to abolish the minor rules of monastic discipline, but Ānanda neglected to ask him which these were. Buddha again exhorted his followers to rely on the teachings he had already taught them, and Ānanda informed him that none of the monks present had any doubts about the doctrine, the path, or monastic discipline. Buddha then delivered his final teaching to his disciples:

"Monks, all compounded things are subject to decay and disintegration. Work out your own salvations with diligence." These were the Tathāgata's last words.

Source: *Dīgha-nikāya, Mahāparinibbāna-sutta.* Tr. JP.

THE QUESTIONS OF KING MILINDA

According to Buddhist tradition, the Bactrian king Menander (Pāli: Milinda) engaged the Buddhist sage Nāgasena in a series of philosophical discussions in which Nāgasena convinced him of the truth of the Buddha's teachings. The following dialog concerns the Buddhist doctrine of selflessness, which holds that there is no enduring self, no soul, no truly existent personal identity. The king at first expresses disbelief, pointing out that he is clearly speaking to Nāgasena, who seems to be a concretely existing person.

Nāgasena convinces the king by using the analogy of a chariot, which is composed of parts that separately are incapable of performing the functions of a chariot but which when assembled are given the conventional designation "chariot."

Similarly, human beings (and all other phenomena) are merely collections of parts that are given conventional designations, but they lack any enduring entity.

Then King Milinda said to the venerable Nāgasena: "What is your reverence called? What is your name, reverend sir?"

"Sire, I am known as Nāgasena; my fellow religious practitioners, sir, address me as Nāgasena. But although [my] parents gave [me] the name of Nāgasena . . . still it is only a designation, a name, a denotation, a conventional expression, since Nāgasena is only a name because there is no person here to be found. . . ."

"If, reverend Nāgasena, there is no person to be found, who is it that gives you necessities like robe material, food, lodging, and medicines for the sick, who is it that uses them, who is it that keeps the precepts, practices meditation, actualizes the paths, the fruits, nirvana; who kills living beings, takes what is not given, commits immoral acts, tells lies, drinks intoxicants, and commits the five types of immediate karmas? In that case, there is no virtue; there is no non-virtue; there is no one who does or who makes another do things that are virtuous or non-virtuous; there is no fruit or ripening of good or bad karma. Reverend Nāgasena, if someone kills you, there will be no demerit. Also, reverend Nāgasena, you have no teacher, no preceptor, no ordination. . . .

"Is form Nāgasena?"

"No, sire."

"Is feeling Nāgasena?"

"No, sire."

"Is discrimination Nāgasena?"

"No, sire."

"Are compositional factors Nāgasena?"

"No, sire."

"Is consciousness Nāgasena?"

"No, sire."

"Then, reverend sir, are form, feelings, discriminations, compositional factors, and consciousness together Nāgasena?"

"No, sire."

"Then, reverend sir, is there something other than form, feelings, discriminations, compositional factors, and consciousness that is Nāgasena?"

"No, sire."

"Reverend sir, although I question you closely, I fail to find any Nāgasena. Nāgasena is only a sound, sir. Who is Nāgasena? Reverend sir, you are speaking a lie, a falsehood: there is no Nāgasena."

Then the venerable Nāgasena said to king Milinda: ". . . Your majesty, did you come here on foot, or riding?"

"Reverend sir, I did not come on foot; I came in a chariot."

"Sire, if you came in a chariot, show me the chariot. Is the pole the chariot, sire?"

"No, reverend sir."

"Is the axle the chariot?"

"No, reverend sir."

"Are the wheels . . . the frame . . . the banner-staff . . . the yoke . . . the reins . . . the goad the chariot?"

"No, reverend sir."

"Then, sire, are pole, axle, wheels, frame, banner-staff, yoke, reins, goad together the chariot?"

"No, reverend sir."

"Then, sire, is something other than the pole, axle, wheels, frame, banner-staff, yoke, reins, goad together the chariot?"

"No, reverend sir."

"Sire, although I question you closely, I fail to find any chariot. Chariot is only a sound, sire. What is the chariot? . . ."

"Reverend Nāgasena . . . it is because of the pole, axle, wheels, frame, banner-staff, yoke, reins, and goad that 'chariot' exists as a designation, appellation, denotation, as a conventional usage, as a name."

"Good: sire, you understand the chariot. It is just like this for me, sire: because of the hair of the head and because of the hair of the body . . . and because of the brain of the head, form, feelings, discriminations, compositional factors, and consciousness that 'Nāgasena' exists as designation, appellation, denotation, as a conventional usage, as a name. But ultimately there is no person to be found here. . . ."

"Wonderful, reverend Nāgasena! Marvelous, reverend Nāgasena! The replies to the questions that were asked are truly brilliant. If the Buddha were still here, he would applaud. Well done, well done, Nāgasena!"

Source: *Milinda-pañha*, 2.25–28. Tr. JP.

HOW TO AVOID EXTREME VIEWS

Buddhaghosa, the greatest commentator of the Theravāda tradition, expands on the analogy of the chariot and indicates how this analysis relates to meditative practice and the pursuit of liberation.

Thus, just as when the parts—the axle, wheels, frame, pole—are put together in a certain way, the mere word "chariot" is used, but ultimately there is no such thing as "chariot" when any of the parts are examined; so when the parts of a house, such as the exterior, are put together in a certain way enclosing a space, the mere word "house" is used, but ultimately there is no such thing as a house; or when fingers and so forth are placed together in a certain way, the mere word "fist" is used; or the mere words "lute," "army," "town," "tree" are used when their respective parts—such as the body of the lute and the strings, elephants and horses, walls and houses and gates, trunk and branches and leaves—are arranged in certain positions, but there is ultimately no such thing as a tree when one examines each part. So when the five aggregates of grasping exist, the mere word "being," "person" is used, but when one examines each of the states, ultimately there is no such thing as a being: it is the object of a misconception that makes one say, "I am" or "I"; ultimately there is just name and form. The perception of one who perceives in this way is called perception of reality.

And one who abandons perception of reality and holds to the view that a being exists must admit that it will perish or that it will not perish. If one asserts that it will not perish, then one falls to the [extreme view of] permanence; if one asserts that it will perish, then one falls to the [extreme view of] nihilism. There is no other state which is a product of that being, as curd is a product of milk. One who holds that a being is eternal falls [into the pleasures of the senses]; one who holds that it is annihilated is carried away by an extreme [view]. Therefore, the Exalted One has said:

> Monks, there are two [wrong] views through which some gods and humans fall into the pleasures of existence and are carried away by existence; only those who have the eye [of truth] see the truth. Monks, how do some fall into the pleasures of existence? Monks, there are gods and humans who delight in existence, who are thrilled with existence, who are enraptured by existence. When they are taught the dharma that leads to cessation of existence, their minds do not respond, do not have faith, are not steady and focused. Monks, in this way some fall into existence.
>
> And how, monks, are some extremists? Some are oppressed by, ashamed of, disgusted by existence, some delight in non-existence, saying, "Since it is said that when the body dissolves this self is cut off, dies, and does not exist after death, that is peace, that is wisdom, that is the truth." Monks, in this way some are extremists.
>
> Monks, how do those who have the eye [of truth] see these things? Monks, in this a monk sees the five aggregates as they are. Seeing the five aggregates as they are, he practices in order that he will become disgusted with them, have no desire for them, so that they might cease. Monks, this is how one who has the eye [of truth] sees.

Source: *Visuddhi-magga* by Buddhaghosa. Tr. JP.

MAHĀYĀNA SCRIPTURES

THE *HEART OF PERFECT WISDOM SŪTRA*

The following passage is the entire text of the Heart of Perfect Wisdom Sūtra, *one of the shortest texts of the Perfection of Wisdom corpus. It is said by Mahāyānists to contain the essence of the teachings of this voluminous literature.*

Thus have I heard: At one time the Exalted One was dwelling on the Vulture Peak in Rājagṛha together with a great assembly of monks and a great assembly of bodhisattvas. At that time, the Exalted One was immersed in a meditative absorption *(samādhi)* on the enumerations of phenomena called "perception of the profound." Also at that time, the bodhisattva, the great being, the superior Avalokiteśvara was considering the meaning of the profound perfection of wisdom, and he saw that the five aggregates *(skandha)* are empty of inherent existence. Then, due to the inspiration of the Buddha, the venerable Śāriputra spoke thus to the bodhisattva, the great being, the superior Avalokiteśvara: "How should a son of good lineage train if he wants to practice the profound perfection of wisdom?"

The bodhisattva, the great being, the superior Avalokiteśvara spoke thus to the venerable Śāriputra: "Śāriputra, sons of good lineage or daughters of good lineage who want to practice the profound perfection of wisdom should perceive [reality] in this way: They should correctly perceive the five aggregates also as empty of inherent existence. Form is emptiness; emptiness is form. Emptiness is not other than form; form is not other than emptiness. In the same way, feelings, discriminations, compositional factors, and consciousness are empty. Śāriputra, in that way, all phenomena are empty, without characteristics, unproduced, unceasing, undefiled, not undefiled, not decreasing, not increasing.

"Therefore, Śāriputra, in emptiness there is no form, no feelings, no discriminations, no compositional factors, no consciousness, no eye, no ear, no nose, no tongue, no body, no mind, no form, no sound, no odor, no taste, no object of touch, no phenomenon. There is no eye constituent, no mental constituent, up to and including no mental consciousness constituent. There is no ignorance, no extinction of ignorance, up to and including no aging and death and no extinction of aging and death. In the same way, there is no suffering, no source [of suffering], no cessation [of suffering], no path, no exalted wisdom, no attainment, and also no non-attainment.

"Therefore, Śāriputra, because bodhisattvas have no attainment, they depend on and abide in the perfection of wisdom. Because their minds are unobstructed, they are without fear. Having completely passed beyond all error, they go to the fulfillment of nirvana. All the buddhas who live in the three times [past, present, and future] have been completely awakened into unsurpassable, complete, perfect awakening through relying on the perfection of wisdom.

"Therefore, the *mantra* of the perfection of wisdom is the *mantra* of great knowledge, the unsurpassable *mantra*, the *mantra* that is equal to the unequaled, the *mantra* that thoroughly pacifies all suffering. Because it is not false, it should be known to be true. The *mantra* of the perfection wisdom is as follows:

> *Oṃ gate gate paragate parasaṃgate bodhir svāha* [*Oṃ* gone, gone, gone beyond, gone completely beyond; praise to awakening.]

"Śāriputra, bodhisattvas, great beings, should train in the profound perfection of wisdom in that way."

Then the Exalted One arose from that meditative absorption and said to the bodhisattva, the great being, the superior Avalokiteśvara: "Well done! Well done, well done, son of good lineage, it is just so. Son of good lineage, it is like that; the profound perfection of wisdom should be practiced just as you have indicated. Even the Tathāgatas admire this."

When the Exalted One had spoken thus, the venerable Śāriputra, the bodhisattva, the great being, the superior Avalokiteśvara, and all those around them, and those of the world, the gods, humans, demigods, and *gandharvas* were filled with admiration and praised the words of the Exalted One.

Source: *Prajñāpāramitā-hṛdaya-sūtra*. Tr. JP.

EXCERPTS FROM THE *DIAMOND SŪTRA*

Perfection of Wisdom texts contain many warnings against holding too rigidly to doctrines, even Buddhist doctrines. In the following passage, Buddha warns his disciple Subhūti against conceiving sentient beings as truly existing, and then applies the reasoning of emptiness to other Buddhist categories.

[Buddha:] "Subhūti, due to being established in the bodhisattva vehicle, one should give rise to the thought, 'As many sentient beings there are that are included among the realms of sentient beings . . . whatever realms of sentient beings can be conceived, all these should be brought by me to nirvana, to a final nirvana that is a realm of nirvana without remainder; but, although countless sentient beings have reached final nirvana, no sentient being whatsoever has reached final nirvana.' Why is this? Subhūti, if a discrimination of a sentient being arises in a bodhisattva [literally, 'awakening-being'], he should not be called an awakening-being. Why is this? Subhūti, one who gives rise to the discrimination of such a self, the discrimination of a sentient being, the discrimination of a soul, or the discrimination of a person should not be called a bodhisattva. . . .

"Subhūti, all of them produce and acquire an immeasurable and incalculable store of merit. Why is this? Subhūti, it is because these bodhisattvas, great beings, do not give rise to the discrimination of a self, the discrimination of a sentient being, the discrimination of a soul, or the discrimination of a person. Also, Subhūti, these bodhisattvas, great beings, do not give rise to discriminations of phenomena, nor do they give rise to discriminations of non-phenomena, nor do they give rise to discrimination or to non-discrimination.

"Why is this? Subhūti, if these bodhisattvas, great beings, gave rise to discriminations of phenomena, this would be grasping a self, grasping a sentient being, grasping a soul, grasping a person. If they gave rise to discriminations of non-phenomena, this also would be grasping a self, grasping a sentient being, grasping a soul, grasping a person. Why is this? Subhūti, in no way should a bodhisattva, a great being, grasp either phenomena nor non-phenomena. Therefore, this has been said by the Tathāgata with hidden intent: 'For those who understand the teaching of *dharma* that is like a raft, *dharma* should be abandoned, and still more non-*dharma*.'"

Source: *Vajracchedika-prajñāpāramitā-sūtra* selections. Tr. JP.

WHY BODHISATTVAS ARE SUPERIOR TO HEARERS

Some early Mahāyāna texts have a distinctly sectarian tone, particularly when they compare the ideals of the arhat and the bodhisattva. In the following passage from the 8,000 Line Perfection of Wisdom Sūtra, *Buddha describes to Subhūti the differences between the attitudes of Hīnayānists and those of Mahāyānists.*

> [Buddha:] "Subhūti, bodhisattvas, great beings, should not train in the way that persons of the hearer vehicle and solitary realizer vehicle train. Subhūti, in what way do persons of the hearer vehicle and the solitary realizer vehicle train? Subhūti, they think thus, '[I] should discipline only myself; [I] should pacify only myself; [I] should attain nirvana by myself.' In order to discipline only themselves and pacify themselves and attain nirvana, they begin to apply themselves to establishing all the virtuous roots. Also, Subhūti, bodhisattvas, great beings, should not train in this way. On the contrary, Subhūti, bodhisattvas, great beings, should train thus, 'In order to benefit all the world, I will dwell in suchness; and, establishing all sentient beings in suchness, I will lead the immeasurable realms of sentient beings to nirvana.' Bodhisattvas, great beings, should begin applying themselves in that way to establishing all virtuous roots, but should not be conceited because of this. . . .
>
> "Those who say, 'In this very life, having thoroughly freed the mind from contamination, without attachment, [I] will pass beyond sorrow' are 'at the level of hearers and solitary realizers.' With respect to this, bodhisattvas, great beings, should not give rise to such thoughts. Why is this? Subhūti, bodhisattvas, great beings, abide in the great vehicle and put on the great armor; they should not give rise to thoughts of even a little elaboration. Why is this? These supreme beings thoroughly lead the world and are a great benefit to the world. Therefore, they should always and uninterruptedly train well in the six perfections."

Source: *Aṣṭasāhasrikā-prajñāpāramitā-sūtra ('Phags pa shes rab kyi pha rol tu phyin pa brgyad stong pa'i mdo),* ch. 11. Tr. JP.

WHY THE BODHISATTVA WORKS ALONE

In Mahāyāna texts, the bodhisattva is portrayed as a heroic figure, valiantly following the path to buddhahood for the benefit of others. The following passage indicates that this is a long and difficult path that each individual must traverse alone.

> The bodhisattva is alone, with no . . . companion, and puts on the armor of supreme wisdom. He acts alone and leaves nothing to others, working with a will that is firm with courage and strength. He is strong in his own strength . . . and he thinks thus: "I will help all sentient beings to obtain whatever they should obtain. . . .
>
> "The virtue of generosity is not my helper—I am the helper of generosity. Nor do the virtues of ethics, patience, effort, concentration, and

wisdom help me—it is I who help them. The perfections of the bodhisattva do not support me—it is I who support them. . . . I alone, standing in this round and hard world, must subdue Māra, with all his hosts and chariots, and develop supreme awakening with the wisdom of instantaneous insight."

Just as the rising sun, the child of the gods, is not stopped . . . by all the dust rising from the four continents of the earth . . . or by wreaths of smoke . . . or by rugged mountains, so bodhisattvas, great beings . . . are not deterred from bringing virtuous roots to fruition, whether by the malice of others . . . or by their wrong-doing or error, or by their mental agitation. . . . They will not lay down their limbs of awakening because of the corrupt generations of humanity, nor do they waver in their resolution to save the world because of their wretched quarrels. . . . They do not lose heart on account of their faults. . . .

They think, "All creatures are in pain; all suffer from bad and hindering karma . . . so that they cannot see the buddhas or hear the true doctrine or know the monastic community. . . . All that mass of pain and evil karma I take in my own body . . . I take upon myself the burden of sorrow; I resolve to do so; I endure it all. I do not turn back or run away, I do not tremble . . . I am not afraid . . . nor do I despair. I must definitely bear the burdens of all sentient beings . . . for I have resolved to save them all, I must set them all free, I must save the whole world from the forest of birth, aging, sickness, and rebirth, from misfortune and wrong-doing, from the round of birth and death, from the dangers of error. . . . For all sentient beings are caught in the net of desire, enmeshed in ignorance, held by the desire for existence; they are doomed to destruction, shut in a cage of pain . . . they are ignorant, untrustworthy, full of doubts, always fighting one with another, always prone to see evil; they cannot find a refuge in the ocean of existence; they are all on the edge of the gulf of destruction.

"I work to establish the kingdom of perfect wisdom for all sentient beings. I care not at all for my own liberation. I must save all sentient beings from the river of rebirth with the raft of my omniscient mind. I must pull them back from the great precipice. I must free them from all misfortune, ferry them over the stream of rebirth.

"For I have taken upon myself, by my own will, the whole of the pain of all living things. Thus I dare try every place of pain, in . . . every part of the universe, for I must not keep virtuous roots from the world. I resolve to live in each bad state for countless eons . . . for the salvation of all sentient beings . . . for it is better that I alone suffer than that all sentient beings sink to the bad transmigrations [animals, hungry ghosts, hell beings]. There I shall give myself into bondage, to redeem all the world from the forest of suffering, from births as animals, from the realm of death. I shall bear all grief and pain in my own body for the good of all living things. I vow to work for all sentient beings, speaking the truth, trustworthy, not breaking my word. I will not abandon them. . . . I must be their charioteer, I must be their leader, I must be their torchbearer, I must be their guide to safety. . . . I must not wait for the help of another, nor must I lose my resolution and leave my tasks to another. I must not turn back in my efforts to save all sentient beings nor cease to use my merit for the destruction of all pain. And I must not be satisfied with small successes."

Source: *Śikṣāsamuccaya*, pp. 278–283. Tr. JP.

ON THE DIFFERENCES BETWEEN MEN AND WOMEN

The following dialog applies the doctrine of emptiness to the commonly accepted differences between men and women. When these are closely examined, they are found to be merely the results of misguided conceptuality, because there is no inherently existent difference between the sexes.

The dialog occurs in the house of Vimalakīrti, a lay bodhisattva who is pretending to be sick in order to initiate a discourse on the dharma. The Buddha's disciples follow Mañjuśrī—an advanced bodhisattva who is said to embody wisdom—to Vimalakīrti's house in order to hear the two discuss the perfection of wisdom. The interchange is so profound that a young goddess who lives in Vimalakīrti's house rains down flowers on the assembly. The Hīnayāna monks who are present try frantically to brush them off, because monks are forbidden in the Vinaya to wear flowers or adornments. The bodhisattvas in the audience, however, are unaffected by such rigid adherence to rules, and so the flowers fall from their robes.

This causes Śāriputra—described in Pāli texts as the most advanced of the Buddha's Hīnayāna disciples in the development of wisdom—to marvel at the attainments of the goddess and the bodhisattvas. She chides him for viewing the fruits of meditative training as things to be acquired, and in response Śāriputra asks her why she does not change from a woman into a man. The question appears to be based on traditional Indian perceptions of authority, according to which wisdom is associated with elder males. The goddess violates these principles, because she is young and female. But it is clear from the dialog that she is very advanced in understanding the perfection of wisdom.

The goddess responds to Śāriputra's challenge by turning him into a woman and herself into a man. This leads to one of the most poignant scenes in the sūtra, in which Śāriputra experiences discomfort in his new body, apparently because of the Vinaya injunctions preventing monks from physical contact with women. Śāriputra, now in a woman's body, is unable to avoid such contact and tells the goddess that he is a woman without being a woman. The goddess replies that all women are women without being women, because "woman" is merely a conventional designation with no ultimate referent.

A goddess who lived in the house of Vimalakīrti, having heard the doctrinal teaching of the bodhisattvas, the great beings, was very pleased, delighted, and moved. She took on a material form and scattered heavenly flowers over the great bodhisattvas and great hearers. When she had thrown them, the flowers that landed on the bodies of the bodhisattvas fell to the ground, while those that fell on the bodies of the great hearers remained stuck to them and did not fall to the ground. Then the great hearers tried to use their supernatural powers to shake off the flowers, but the flowers did not fall off.

Then the goddess asked the venerable Śāriputra: "Venerable Śāriputra, why do you try to shake off the flowers?"

"Goddess, flowers are not fitting for monks; that is why we reject them."

"Venerable Śāriputra, do not speak thus. Why? These flowers are perfectly fitting. Why? The flowers are flowers and are free from conceptuality; it is only yourselves, the elders, who conceptualize them and create conceptuality toward them. Venerable Śāriputra, among those who have renounced the world to take up monastic discipline, such conceptualizations and conceptuality are not fitting; it is those who do not conceive either conceptualizations nor conceptuality who are fit.

"Venerable Śāriputra, take a good look at these bodhisattvas, great beings: the flowers do not stick to them because they have abandoned conceptuality. . . . Flowers stick to those who have not yet abandoned the defilements; they do not stick to those who have abandoned them. . . ."

"Well done! Well done, Goddess! What have you attained, what have you gained that enables you to have such eloquence?"

"It is because I have not attained anything nor gained anything that I have such eloquence. Those who think that they have attained or gained something are deluded with respect to the well-taught disciplinary doctrine. . . ."

"Goddess, why do you not change your womanhood?"

"During the twelve years [that I have lived in this house], I have looked for womanhood, but have never found it. Venerable Śāriputra, if a skillful magician created an illusory woman through transformation, could you ask her why she does not change her womanhood?"

"Every illusory creation is unreal."

"In the same way, venerable Śāriputra, all phenomena are unreal and have an illusory nature; why would you think of asking them to change their womanhood?"

Then the goddess performed a supernatural feat that caused the elder Śāriputra to appear in every way like the goddess and she herself to appear in every way like the elder Śāriputra. Then the goddess who had changed into Śāriputra asked Śāriputra who had been changed into a goddess: "Why do you not change your womanhood, venerable sir?"

[Śāriputra:] "I do not know either how I lost my male form nor how I acquired a female body."

[Goddess:] "Elder, if you were able to change your female form, then all women could change their womanhood. Elder, just as you appear to be a woman, so also all women appear in the form of women, but they appear in the form of women without being women. It was with this hidden thought that the Exalted One said: 'Phenomena are neither male nor female.'"

Then the goddess cut off her supernatural power and the venerable Śāriputra regained his previous form. Then the goddess said to Śāriputra: "Venerable Śāriputra, where is your female form now?"

[Śāriputra:] "My female form is neither made nor changed."

[Goddess:] "Well done! Well done, venerable sir! In the same way, all phenomena, just as they are, are neither made nor changed. Saying that they are neither made nor changed is the word of the Buddha. . . ."

[Śāriputra:] "Goddess, how long will it be before you reach awakening?"

[Goddess:] "Elder, when you yourself return to being a worldly person, with all the qualities of a worldly person, then I myself will reach unsurpassed, perfect awakening."

[Śāriputra:] "Goddess, it is impossible that I could return to being a worldly person, with all the qualities of a worldly person; it cannot occur."

[Goddess:] "Venerable Śāriputra, in the same way, it is impossible that I will ever attain unsurpassed, perfect awakening; it cannot occur. Why? Because unsurpassed, perfect awakening is founded on a non-foundation. Thus, since there is no foundation, who could reach unsurpassed, perfect awakening?"

[Śāriputra:] "But the Tathāgata has said: 'Tathāgatas as innumerable as the sands of the Ganges river attain, have attained, and will attain unsurpassed, perfect awakening.'"

[Goddess:] "Venerable Śāriputra, the words, 'buddhas past, future, and present' are conventional expressions made up of syllables and numbers. Buddhas are neither past, nor future, nor present, and their awakening transcends the three divisions of time. Tell me, elder, have you already attained the level of arhat?"

[Śāriputra:] "I have attained it because there is nothing to attain."

[Goddess:] "It is the same with awakening: it is attained because there is nothing to attain."

Source: *Vimalakīrti-nirdeśa-sūtra ('Phags pa dri ma med par grags pas bstan pa'i mdo),* ch. 6. Tr. JP.

THE *LOTUS SŪTRA:* PARABLE OF THE BURNING HOUSE

The parable of the burning house is a famous allegory for the practice of "skillful means" (upāya-kauśalya), *one of the important abilities of bodhisattvas and buddhas. It involves adapting the dharma to the interests and proclivities of individual listeners, telling them things that will attract them to the practice of Buddhism. The question posed in this dialog concerns whether such tactics should be considered underhanded or dishonest.*

The answer, not surprisingly, is no: The means used are for the good of the beings and benefit them greatly in the long run. Moreover, with beings who are thoroughly enmeshed in the concerns of the world it is necessary to draw their attention away from mundane pleasures toward the dharma, which can lead to lasting happiness.

[Buddha:] "Śāriputra, let us suppose that in a village somewhere . . . there was a householder who was . . . very wealthy. Suppose that he owned a great mansion, lofty, spacious, built long ago, inhabited by hundreds of living beings. The house had one door and was covered with thatch, its terraces were collapsing, the bases of its pillars were rotting, and the plaster and coverings of the walls were falling apart. Now suppose that all of a sudden the whole house burst into flames and that the householder managed to get himself out, but that his little boys [were still inside]. . . .

"[He thought:] 'I was able to get out of the burning house through the door safely, without being touched by the flames, but my children remain in the house, playing with their toys, enjoying themselves. They do not realize . . . that the house is on fire, and so are not afraid. Even though they are caught up in the fire and are being scorched by flames, though they are actually suffering, they are unaware of it, and so they do not think to come out. . . .'

"So he called to the boys: 'Come, my children, the house is burning with a mass of flames! Come out, so that you will not be burned in the inferno and come to disaster!'

"But the ignorant boys paid no attention to the man's words, even though he only wished for their well-being. . . . They did not care, and did not run from the house, did not understand, and did not comprehend even the meaning of the word 'inferno.' Instead, they continued to run and play here and there, occasionally looking at their father. Why? Because they were ignorant children.

"So then, Śāriputra, the man thought: . . . 'I should use a skillful method to cause the children to come out of the house.' The man knew the mental dispositions of his children and clearly understood their interests. He knew of the kinds of toys they liked. . . . So he said to them: 'Children, all the toys that you like . . . such as little ox carts, goat carts, and deer carts, which are pleasing and captivating to you, have all been put outside by me, so that you can play with them. Come, run out of the house! I will give each of you what you want! Come quickly! Come and get these toys!'

"Then the boys, hearing him mentioning the names of the toys they liked . . . quickly ran from the burning house, not waiting for each other, and calling, 'Who will be first? Who will be foremost?'

"Then the man, seeing that his children had come out of the house safely, knowing that they were out of danger . . . gave his children . . . ox carts only. They were made of seven precious metals, and had railings, were hung with strings of bells, were high and lofty, adorned with wonderful and precious jewels, illuminated by garlands of gems, decorated with wreaths of flowers. . . .

"Now what do you think, Śāriputra, did that man lie to his children by first promising them three vehicles and then later giving them only great vehicles, the best vehicles?"

Śāriputra said: "No indeed, Lord! Not at all! There is no reason to think that in this case the man was a liar, because he was using skillful means in order to cause his children to come out of the burning house, and because of this he gave them the gift of life. Moreover, Lord, in addition to keeping their lives, they also received those toys. But, Lord, even if the man had not given them a single cart, he would still not have been a liar. Why is this? Because, Lord, that man first thought, 'By using skillful means, I will liberate those children from a great mass of suffering. . . .' "

"Well said, Śāriputra, well said! You have spoken well! In the same way, the Tathāgata also . . . is the father of the world, who has attained the supreme perfection of understanding of great skillful means, who is greatly compassionate, who has a mind that is unwearied, who is concerned for the well-being of others. He appears in this triple world, which is like a burning house blazing with the whole mass of suffering and despair . . . in order to liberate from desire, aversion, and obscuration those beings who remain trapped in the mists of ignorance, in order to liberate them from the blindness of ignorance, birth, old age, death, sorrow, grief, suffering, sadness, and dissatisfaction, in order to awaken them to supreme, perfect awakening. . . . In this triple world, which is like a burning house, they enjoy themselves and run here and there. Even though they are afflicted by a great deal of suffering, they do not even think that they are suffering. . . .

"Therefore, Śāriputra, the Tathāgata, who is just like that strong-armed man who . . . employed skillful means to coax his children from the burning house . . . speaks of three vehicles: the hearers' vehicle, the solitary realizers' vehicle, and the bodhisattvas' vehicle. . . . So the Tathāgata is not a liar when he uses skillful means, first holding out the prospect of three vehicles and then leading beings to final nirvana by means of a single great vehicle."

Source: *Saddharma-puṇḍarīka-sūtra*, ch. 3. Tr. JP.

EVERYTHING IS CONTROLLED BY THE MIND

The following passage comes from the Cloud of Jewels Sūtra. *It indicates that all phenomena are productions of mind and that everything is created by mind. Ordinary beings allow the mind to wander at will, thereby enmeshing them in confused and harmful thoughts, but bodhisattvas are advised to train the mind in order to bring it under control.*

All phenomena originate in the mind, and when the mind is fully known all phenomena are fully known. For by the mind the world is led . . . and through the mind karma is piled up, whether good or bad. The mind swings like a firebrand, the mind rears up like a wave, the mind burns like a forest fire, like a great flood the mind carries all things away. Bodhisattvas, thoroughly examining the nature of things, remain in ever-present mindfulness of the activity of the mind, and so do not fall into the mind's power, but the mind comes under their control. And with the mind under their control, all phenomena are under their control.

Source: *Ratnamegha-sūtra*, from the *Śīkṣā-samuccaya*, ch. 6. Tr. JP.

THE BASIS CONSCIOUSNESS

This passage from the Sūtra Explaining the Thought *is one of the earliest descriptions of the "basis consciousness"* (ālaya-vijñāna), *a doctrine that was central to the Indian Yogācāra school and also was influential in other Mahāyāna countries, particularly Tibet and China. The basis consciousness is the most fundamental level of mind and is said to be comprised of the "seeds" of past actions and mental states. The seeds become part of the continuum of the basis consciousness, which is moved along by their force. If one cultivates positive actions and thoughts, for example, one's mind will become habituated to positive actions and thoughts. The converse is true for those who engage in negative actions and thoughts.*

Under appropriate conditions, the seeds give rise to corresponding thoughts and emotions, which are the phenomena of ordinary experience. Mind and its objects are said to arise together, so there is no substantial difference between subject and object. Because of this, phenomena are said to be "cognition-only" (vijñapti-mātra), *meaning that all we ever perceive are mental impressions, and not things in themselves.*

> [Buddha:] "Initially in dependence upon two types of appropriation—the appropriation of the physical sense powers associated with a support and the appropriation of predispositions which proliferate conventional designations with respect to signs, names, and concepts—the mind which has all seeds ripens; it develops, increases, and expands in its operations. . . .
>
> "Consciousness is also called the 'appropriating consciousness' because it holds and appropriates the body in that way. It is called the 'basis consciousness' because there is the same establishment and abiding within those bodies. . . . It is called 'mind' because it collects and accumulates forms, sounds, smells, tastes, and tangible objects."

Source: *Saṃdhinirmocana-sūtra*, ch. 5. Tr. JP.

NĀGĀRJUNA ON EMPTINESS

Nāgārjuna, founder of the Madhyamaka school of Indian Mahāyāna, emphasized the centrality of the doctrine of emptiness in his philosophy. In the following verses he indicates that concepts are empty because language is simply an interconnected system of terms that do not capture actual things but instead simply relate to other words. One who fully recognizes this fact becomes freed from the snares of language and attains correct realization, an important part of the path to liberation.

1. Through the force of worldly conventions, buddhas
   Have spoken of duration, arising, disintegration, existence, non-existence,
   Inferior, middling, and superior,
   But they have not spoken [of these] in an ultimate sense.
2. Self, non-self, and self-non-self do not exist,
   And so conventional expressions do not [really] signify.
   Like nirvana, all expressible things are empty of inherent existence.

3. Since all things completely lack inherent existence—either in causes or conditions, [in their] totality, or separately—they are empty.
4. Because it exists, being does not arise;
   Because it does not exist, non-being does not arise.
5. Because they are discordant phenomena, being and non-being [together] do not arise.
   Thus they neither endure nor cease. . . .
7. Without one, many does not exist; without many, one is not possible.
   Thus, dependently arisen things are indeterminable. . . .
56. In dependence upon the internal and external sense spheres *(āyatana)* consciousness arises.
   Thus, just like mirages and illusions, consciousness is empty.
57. In dependence upon an apprehendable object, consciousness arises.
   Thus, the observable does not exist [in itself].
   [The subject of consciousness] does not exist without the apprehendable and consciousness.
   Thus, the subject of consciousness does not exist [by itself]. . . .
65. Due to correctly perceiving that things are empty, one becomes non-deluded.
   Ignorance ceases, and thus the twelve limbs [of dependent arising] cease. . . .
67. Nothing exists inherently, nor is there non-being there.
   Arising from causes and conditions, being and non-being are empty.
68. All things are empty of inherent existence,
   And so the incomparable Tathāgata teaches dependent arising with respect to things. . . .
72. One with faith who seeks the truth, who considers this principle with reason,
   Relying on the dharma that is free of supports, is liberated from existence and non-existence [and abides in] peace.
73. When one understands that "this is a result of that," the net of wrong views is eradicated.
   Due to abandoning attachment, obscuration, and hatred, undefiled, one attains nirvana.

Source: Nāgārjuna, *Śūnyatā-saptati.* Tr. JP.

THE BODHISATTVA'S VOWS OF UNIVERSAL LOVE

The following verses, written by Śāntideva, are among the most eloquent expressions in Mahāyāna literature of the ideal mind-set of bodhisattvas, who should dedicate all of their energies to helping other beings in every possible way.

16. May those who malign me, or harm me, or accuse me falsely, and others all be recipients of awakening.
17. May I be a protector of the helpless, a guide for those on the path, a boat, a bridge, a way for those who wish to crossover.

18. May I be a lamp for those who need a lamp, a bed for those who seek a bed, and a slave for those who desire a slave.
19. May I become a wish-fulfilling jewel, an inexhaustible jar, a powerful mantra, a cure for all sickness, a wish-fulfilling tree, and a cow of plenty for all creatures.
20. As earth and the other elements are enjoyed in various ways by innumerable beings living throughout space,
    So may I be the sustenance for various kinds of beings in all the realms of space for as long as all are not satisfied.

Source: Śāntideva, *Bodhicaryāvatāra, "Bodhicitta-parigraha."* Tr. JP.

TANTRIC SKILL IN MEANS

Tantric texts claim that the system of tantra skillfully uses aspects of reality that cause bondage for people who are enmeshed in mundane conceptuality—things like desire and other negative emotions. The following excerpt from the Hevajra Tantra *indicates that these may serve as aids to the path of liberation if the proper means are used.*

> Those things by which evil men are bound, others turn into means and gain thereby release from the bonds of existence. By passion the world is bound, by passion too it is released, but by heretical Buddhists this practice of reversals is not known.

Source: *Hevajra-tantra* I.ix.2–3, tr. David Snellgrove, *Indo-Tibetan Buddhism* (Boston: Shambhala, 1987), vol. I, pp. 125–126.

THE STAGE OF COMPLETION

The tantric practice of deity yoga involves first creating a vivid image of a buddha in front of one and then visualizing the buddha as merging with oneself. One views oneself as a buddha—with the body, speech, and mind of a buddha—and as performing the activities of an awakened being. The first procedure is called the "generation stage," and the second, which is described in the following passage from the Guhyasamāja Tantra, *is termed the "completion stage." In order to avoid becoming attached to the visualization, one should be aware that both the buddha and oneself are empty of inherent existence. Thus, at the end of the session, one dissolves both oneself and the buddha into emptiness.*

> Everything from the crown of the head to the feet dissolves into the heart; you engage in the perfect yoga (meditation on emptiness). . . . All sentient beings and all other phenomena dissolve into clear light and then dissolve into you; then you yourself, as the deity, dissolve into your heart. . . . Just as mist on a mirror fades toward the center and disappears, so does everything—the net of illusory manifestation—dissolve into the clear light of emptiness. Just as fish are easily seen in clear water, so does everything—the net of illusory manifestation—emerge from the clear light of emptiness.

Source: *Guhyasamāja-tantra;* quoted in Khenpo Könchog Gyaltsen, *The Garland of Mahamudra Practices* (Ithaca: Snow Lion, 1986), pp. 56–57.

UNBOUNDED ACTION

The ideal practitioner of tantra is referred to as an "adept" (siddha), *who becomes a mighty sorcerer through cultivation of the rituals, visualizations, and manipulations of subtle energies that are the focus of tantric practice. Adepthood is a state of utter transcendence, in which all mundane concerns and limitations are overcome. Adepts wander freely, spontaneously engaging in whatever activities they wish, unconcerned with social norms or the expectations of others. The following passage from the* Arising of Supreme Pleasure Tantra *describes this freedom.*

> He should give away his wealth, his wife, and even his own life as offerings; abandoning those ties, he should always be a trainee of the practice. He has great strength attained by reciting magical spells, and he is intent on speaking the truth . . . he should not make a distinction between purity, impurity, or purification, nor between what may or may not be drunk. Being without anger and free from conceit, he should not care about praise or condemnation. Adhering to the idea that everything is equal, he is always without attachment and without desire. He neither practices the fire offering (*homa*) nor worships. He neither recites [mantras] nor uses prayer beads. . . . Having a tiger skin as a garment and adorned with five seals, the yogi should imagine himself to be [the buddha] Heruka, who combines wisdom and method.

Source: *Saṃvarodaya-tantra.* Tr. JP.

WOMEN SHOULD BE HONORED

One notable feature of the tantric movement is an emphasis on the spiritual capacities of women. Classical Indian literature indicates that extreme misogyny was prevalent in the society, which makes this aspect of tantra even more significant. An example of the emphasis on the equality of women is the fact that one of the basic vows required of all tantric practitioners is a pledge not to denigrate women, "who are the bearers of wisdom." The following passage from the Caṇḍamahāroṣaṇa Tantra *expresses a similar sentiment in its praises of women.*

> When women are honored,
> They provide instant accomplishments *(siddhi)*
> To those who wish for the welfare of all beings.
> Thus one should honor women.
> Women are heaven, women are dharma,
> Women are also the supreme asceticism *(tapas).*
> Women are Buddha, women are the monastic community *(saṃgha);*
> Women are the perfection of wisdom.

Source: *Caṇḍamahāroṣaṇa-tantra*, 8.27–30. Tr. JP.

SAṂSĀRA AND NIRVANA ARE ONE

The following excerpts from the Hevajra Tantra *discuss the tantric idea that there is no fundamental difference between cyclic existence and nirvana. Buddhas perceive them as undifferentiable, but ordinary beings, because of their delusions, think in terms of dichotomies and so imagine that the path and the goal are separate.*

> Then the essence is declared, pure and consisting in knowledge, where there is not the slightest difference between cyclic existence and nirvana.
> Nothing is mentally produced in the highest bliss, and no one produces it,
> There is no bodily form, neither object nor subject,
> Neither flesh nor blood, neither dung nor urine,
> No sickness, no delusion, no purification,
> No passion, no wrath, no delusion, no envy,
> No malignity, no conceit of self, no visible object,
> Nothing mentally produced and no producer,
> No friend is there, no enemy,
> Calm is the Innate and undifferentiated. . . .
> The Awakened One is neither existence nor non-existence; he has a form with arms and faces and yet in highest bliss is formless.
> So the whole world is the Innate, for the Innate is its essence.
> Its essence too is nirvana when the mind is in a purified state.

Source: *Hevajra-tantra*, ch. I.x.32–34, II.ii.43–44, tr. David Snellgrove, *The Hevajra Tantra: A Critical Study* (London: Oxford University Press, 1959), vol. I, p. 92.

USING DESIRE TO ERADICATE DESIRE

Tantric adepts claim that the fact that tantra uses emotions like desire as means in the path is an example of the skillful practices of the system. The following passage from Vīryavajra's Commentary on the Sampuṭa Tantra *contends that there are four levels of the use of desire: visualizing a man and woman looking at each other, laughing with each other, holding hands, and sexual union. Each of these represents a progressively higher level of desire. One should engage in these practices, however, in order to utilize the energy of desire as a force that can eradicate mental afflictions. The skillful use of desire is said in some texts to be like rubbing two sticks together to make a fire, which then consumes the sticks themselves. In this case, the process is compared to the way insects are born in wood and then later consume the wood.*

> Within the sound of laughter non-conceptual bliss is generated; or it is generated from looking at the body, the touch of holding hands and the embrace of the two; or from the touch [of union] . . . just as an insect is generated from the wood and then eats the wood itself, so meditative stabilization is generated from bliss [in dependence on desire] and is cultivated as emptiness [whereupon desire is consumed].

Source: Vīryavajra's *Commentary on the Sampuṭa Tantra;* quoted in *Sngags rim chen mo*, II.7. Tr. JP.

THE STATE OF PURE AWARENESS

The following passage from the Hevajra Tantra *describes the state of mind of one who has transcended all discursive and dichotomizing thought through direct, intuitive awareness of the boundless clarity of mind.*

> From self-experiencing comes this knowledge, which is free from ideas of self and other; like the sky it is pure and void, the essence supreme of non-existence and existence, a mingling of wisdom and method, a mingling of passion and absence of passion. It is the life of living things, it is the Unchanging One Supreme; it is all-pervading, abiding in all embodied things. It is the stuff the world is made of, and in it existence and non-existence have their origin. It is all other things that there are. . . . It is the essential nature of all existing things and illusory in its forms.

Source: *Hevajra-tantra* I.x.8–12, tr. David L. Snellgrove, *The Hevajra Tantra*, p. 81.

THE IMPORTANCE OF THE GURU

The special techniques of tantra are said to be very powerful, but they can also be dangerous. Thus, tantric texts warn meditators to find qualified spiritual guides (gurus) who can help them avoid possible pitfalls. One of the central practices of tantra is "guru yoga," in which one visualizes one's guru as a fully awakened buddha. One who does this successfully is said to move quickly toward actualization of buddhahood. In the following passage the tantric master Tilopa teaches that finding a qualified guru is a prerequisite for successful tantric practice.

> The ignorant may know that sesame oil—the essence—exists in the sesame seed, but because they do not know how, they cannot extract the oil. So also does the innate fundamental wisdom abide in the heart of all migrators; but unless it is pointed out by the guru, it cannot be realized. By pounding the seeds and clearing away the husks, one can extract the essence—the sesame oil. Similarly, when it is shown by the guru, the meaning of suchness is so illuminated that one can enter into it.

Source: Tilopa; quoted in *The Garland of Mahamudra Practices*, p. 58.

TIBETAN BUDDHIST SCRIPTURES

ULTIMATE REALITY

The "great completion" (dzogchen) *tradition of Tibetan Buddhism is practiced by all four main schools—Nyingma, Kagyu, Sakya, and Geluk—but is most closely associated with the Nyingma. In this system all phenomena are said to be creations of mind that, like mind, are a union of luminosity and emptiness. In the following passage, meditators are instructed on the nature of ultimate reality, in which phenomena spontaneously appear to the mind although they have no real substance.*

> Since [things exist] only in the manner of mirages, dreams, and delusions, you should abandon [false appearances] and adopt [virtuous practices], work for the sake [of others], avoid [non-virtue] and practice [virtue]. Wash away the afflictions of desire, anger, and obscuration with the waters of their antidotes: [meditation on] repulsiveness, love, and dependent arising. Because ultimate reality is non-arisen and pure, it is free from elaborations *(spros pa, prapañca)* such as the duality of saṃsāra and nirvana. . . . All phenomena merely appear naturally to your own mind on the maṇḍala that is the sphere of the foundation, the buddha nature. They are falsities, not really things, empty, and only appear as forms, as the aggregates, realms, spheres, and so forth. . . . The unsurpassed, supreme, secret great completion directly actualizes the sphere of the spontaneously existent. This foundational sphere is unchanging, like space. [All good] qualities [reside] in it spontaneously, as the sun, moon, planets, and stars [reside] in the sky. There is no need to seek it, since it has existed since beginningless time. No work or effort [is necessary,] as this path is naturally manifest.

Source: Longchen Rapjampa, *Chos bzhi rin po che'i phreng ba (Four Themed Precious Garland)*. Tr. JP.

BARDO, THE STATE BETWEEN LIVES

The following excerpts are drawn from a Tibetan classic on death and dying titled Liberation through Hearing in the Intermediate State, *attributed to Padmasambhava. According to the tradition, it was hidden by Padmasambhava and rediscovered by the "treasure finder" Karma Lingpa in the fourteenth century. The book describes the "intermediate state"* (bardo; *translated here as "the between") that all beings are said to enter after death.*

During the process of dying, the physiological changes that occur are accompanied by mental changes in which the coarser levels of mind drop away, revealing progressively subtler aspects of consciousness. At the moment of death, the subtlest level of mind dawns. This is called the "mind of clear light," and compared to it all other minds are adventitious.

At this point one enters the intermediate state and experiences strange and terrifying sights. These are all said to be aspects of one's own mind, and they include visions of mild and terrifying beings, deafening sounds, and other intense sense experiences. The intermediate state is a time of great opportunity, however, and if one is able to maintain awareness and focus on the clear light nature of mind and perceive all experiences as merely aspects of mind, one may become a buddha, or at least attain rebirth in the pure land of a buddha. In such places the conditions are optimal for beings who seek buddhahood. If one is unable to maintain mindfulness, one will be reborn in accordance with one's accumulated karma.

> Hey! Now when the life between dawns upon me,
> I will abandon laziness, as life has no more time,

Unwavering, enter the path of learning, thinking, and meditating,
And taking perceptions and mind as a path,
I will realize the Three Bodies of enlightenment! . . .
Conscious of dreaming, I will enjoy the changes as clear light.
Not sleeping mindlessly like an animal,
I will cherish the practice merging sleep and realization! . . .
Now when the death-point between dawns upon me,
I will give up the preoccupations of the all-desiring mind,
Enter unwavering the experience of the clarity of the precepts,
And transmigrate into the birthless space of inner awareness;
About to lose this created body of flesh and blood,
I will realize it to be impermanent illusion! . . .
I will . . . enter into the recognition of all objects as my mind's own visions,
And understand this as the pattern of perception in the between;
Come to this moment, arrived at this most critical cessation,
I will not fear my own visions of deities mild and fierce! . . .
Now courage and positive perception are essential.

Source: *Bardo thos grol*, from *Bar do thos grol: The Tibetan Book of the Dead: Liberation through Understanding in the Between*, tr. Robert A. F. Thurman (New York: Bantam, 1994), pp. 115–116.

MILAREPA ON MEDITATION

Milarepa, one of the most influential figures in Tibetan Buddhism, was born into a fairly well-to-do family, but his greedy aunt and uncle took everything away from him, his mother, and sister. Overcome by rage, his mother coerced Milarepa into learning black magic and sending a curse on the aunt and uncle, with the result that a number of people died, but not the primary objects of his revenge. Milarepa, terrified of the consequences of his evil deeds, searched for a spiritual guide (lama) *who could help him escape the consequences of his actions. He eventually found Marpa, who gave Milarepa a series of difficult and dispiriting tasks that cleansed his negative karma. After this Milarepa spent many years living in a cave and practicing solitary meditation, which culminated in his attainment of awakening. He is considered in Tibet to be the supreme example of the attainment of buddhahood in one lifetime through tantric practice.*

Look up into the sky, and practice meditation free from the fringe and center.
Look up at the sun and moon, and practice meditation free from bright and dim.
Look over the mountains, and practice meditation free from departing and changing.
Look down at the lake, and practice meditation free from waves.
Look here at your mind, and practice meditation free from discursive thought.

Source: *Rje btsun mi la ras pa'i rnam thar (Religious Biography of the Master Milarepa)*, pp. 49bff. Tr. JP.

NIGUMA ON MAHĀMUDRĀ

Niguma is said by Tibetan tradition to have been the founder of the Shangpa lineage of the Kagyu tradition. In the following passage, she describes the view of mahāmudrā *(literally, "great seal"), which is said by the Kagyu school to be the supreme form of Buddhist practice. In* mahāmudrā, *one dispenses with the visualizations and rituals of tantra and focuses on the natural state of mind, which is said to be a union of clear light and emptiness. All phenomena are viewed as the spontaneous play of mind, and by cultivating this awareness it is said that the meditator moves quickly toward the attainment of buddhahood.*

Do nothing at all with the mind;
Abide in a non-artificial and natural state.
Your own unwavering mind is the truth body *(dharma-kāya).*
The important thing for meditation is an unwavering mind.
You should realize the great [reality] that is free from extremes.
The afflictions, desires, aversions, and conceptualizations
That arise like bubbles on the ocean of cyclic existence
Should be cut off with the sharp sword of non-production
That is not different from the nature of things.
When you cut off the trunk and roots,
The branches will not grow.
Just as in the clear ocean
Waves pop up and sink into the water,
So conceptualizations are not really different from reality.
So don't look for faults, remain at ease.
Whatever arises, whatever materializes,
Don't hold on to it, but immediately let it go.
Appearances, sounds, and phenomena are one's own mind;
There are no other phenomena apart from mind.
Mind is free from the elaborations of arising and cessation.
The nature of mind, awareness,
Enjoys the five qualities of the Desire Realm, but
Does not wander from reality. . . .
In the great realm of reality *(dharma-dhātu)*
There is nothing to abandon or adopt,
No meditative equipoise or post-meditation period.

Source: Niguma, *Rang grol phyag rgya chen po (Individual Liberation of the Great Seal).* Tr. JP.

INSTRUCTIONS FROM MAÑJUŚRĪ

The following verses, according to the Sakya tradition of Tibetan Buddhism, were spoken to Günga Nyingpo (1092–1158). They are a summary of the entire Buddhist path, including the renunciation of the world, the development of compassion, and the importance of avoiding extreme views.

If you cling to this life, then you are not a dharma practitioner.
If you cling to existence, then you do not have renunciation.

> If you are attached to your own interests, then you do not have the mind of awakening.
> If you hold to [a position], then you do not have the correct view.

Source: Drakpa Gyeltsen, *Zhen pa bzhi bral (Parting from the Four Attachments).* Tr. JP.

THE TRIPLE APPEARANCE

The Sakya school teaches that there are three main levels of awareness, which are summarized in the following stanzas from Virūpa's Vajra Verses. *The first verse refers to the perceptions of ordinary beings, which are colored by ignorance and mental affliction. The second verse describes the perceptions of people on the path, who have some experience with meditation and thus have overcome some of their mental afflictions. The final verse indicates that buddhas perceive the world unafflicted by ignorance, hatred, desire, and so on, and so are at the level of the "pure appearance." The Sakya tradition stresses that although they appear to be incompatible, the three appearances are fundamentally non-different.*

> For sentient beings with the afflictions is the impure appearance.
> For the meditator with transic absorption is the appearance of experience.
> For the ornamental wheel of the Sugata's [Buddha's] inexhaustible awakened body, voice and mind is the pure appearance.

Source: *Rdo rje tshigs rkang (Vajra Verses)*, ch. 1. Tr. JP.

DEVELOPING THE MIND OF AWAKENING

Ordinary beings are consumed by self-centered desires and think primarily of their own narrow interests. Bodhisattvas spend countless eons working toward buddhahood for the benefit of all beings, cheerfully accepting all the tribulations that occur along the path. Given the vast gulf between the attitudes of bodhisattvas and those of ordinary beings, it is difficult for people enmeshed in mundane concerns to imagine making the transition to true altruism.

The following passage by Tsong Khapa (the founder of the Gelukpa school of Tibetan Buddhism) outlines a seven-step program for developing the "mind of awakening," which marks the beginning of the bodhisattva path. It begins by recognizing that because one has been reborn into an infinite variety of situations since beginningless time, one has been in every possible relationship with every other sentient being. Thus, every sentient being has been one's mother and has been a nurturing and caring friend. One should reflect on the kindness of one's own mother and then think that every other being has been equally kind. One then resolves to repay this kindness and generates a feeling of love toward others, wishing that they have happiness and the causes of happiness. One then develops compassion for sentient beings, because they are experiencing suffering as a result of contaminated actions and afflictions.

In the next stage one attains the "unusual attitude," which involves vowing to work to free all beings from suffering and establish them in buddhahood. The final step is attainment of the mind of awakening, which is a resolve to do whatever is necessary to attain buddhahood in order to help all sentient beings.

From one's own viewpoint, since one has cycled beginninglessly, there are no sentient beings who have not been one's friends hundreds of times. Therefore, one should think, "Whom should I value?" "Whom should I hate?" . . .

Imagine your mother very clearly in front of you. Consider several times how she has been your mother numberless times, not only now, but from beginningless cyclic existence. When she was your mother, she protected you from all danger and brought about your benefit and happiness. In particular, in this life she held you for a long time in her womb. Once you were born, while you still had new hair, she held you to the warmth of her flesh and rocked you on the tips of her ten fingers. She nursed you at her breast . . . and wiped away your filth with her hand. In various ways she nourished you tirelessly. When you were hungry and thirsty, she gave you drink, and when you were cold, clothes, and when poor, money. She gave you those things that were precious to her. Moreover, she did not find these easily. . . . When you suffered with a fever she would rather have died herself than have her child die; and if her child became sick, from the depths of her heart she would rather have suffered herself than have her child suffer. . . .

Source: *Lam rim chen mo (Great Exposition of the Stages of the Path),* pp. 572.5, 575.1. Tr. JP.

CHINESE AND JAPANESE BUDDHIST SCRIPTURES

WHY BUDDHISM IS SUPERIOR TO DAOISM AND CONFUCIANISM

The following passage, by Jizang (549–623), is an example of the sectarian debates between Buddhists and Daoists in China. Drawn from Profound Meaning of the Three Treatises, *it compares the teachings of Buddhism to those of Laozi and Zhuangzi.*

Shi Sengzhao (374–414) says, "Every time I read Laozi and Zhuangzi, it causes me to lament and say: 'It is beautiful, but as for the technique of abiding with the spirit, of quieting the mental ties [that bind us to life and death], they have not yet mastered [them]. . . .'

"Kumārajīva long ago heard that the three mysteries, together with the nine teachings of Buddhism, were both definitive. Laozi, together with Śākyamuni [Buddha], were [held to be] comparable in actions. So [Kumārajīva] lamented thus, and lamenting said, 'Lao[zi] and Zhuang[zi] have entered the profound. Therefore, they certainly do lead astray the ears and eyes.' This is the wisdom of the ordinary person. These are reckless words [claiming that Buddhism and Daoism are comparable]. In saying this, it appears to be the ultimate, and still has not yet begun to approach it. . . .

"Non-Buddhists are not yet able to consider the ultimate, and still wander among the myriad things. Buddhist teachings, without moving away from absolute truth, teach, still establishing the various phenomena. Non-Buddhists reside in the teachings of gain and loss. Buddhists vanquish the two extremes in the principle of negation. Non-Buddhists have not yet extinguished both the knower and known. Buddhists have extinguished both subject and object.

"If we take these [two, Buddhists and non-Buddhists], and further examine them in detail, it is like comparing a small bird's wings to the wings of a *peng* bird, or comparing a well to the ocean. [These metaphors] are not yet sufficient to explain their difference. Kumārajīva doubted the final teachings [of the Daoists]. What more can I say?"

Source: Jizang, *Sanlun Xuanyi (Profound Meaning of the Three Treatises)*, ch. 1. Tr. JP.

THE *PLATFORM SŪTRA* OF THE SIXTH PATRIARCH

The Chan (Japanese: Zen) school developed in China. Asserting that the teachings of the school were a "special transmission outside of the scriptures," Zen masters claimed that their tradition represents the authentic teaching of the Buddha, who is said to have passed on the essence of his awakened mind to his disciple Mahākāśyapa. He in turn taught it to his main disciple, and so it continued in India through an unbroken chain of transmission until Bodhidharma, the last Indian "patriarch," traveled to China.

Bodhidharma, a semi-legendary figure, is said to have arrived at the Shaolin monastery in China, where he sat in silent meditation in front of a wall for several years. At the end of this period, he began teaching the tradition to Chinese disciples, one of whom became the first Chinese patriarch.

The following passage was spoken by Hui Neng, the sixth patriarch, to a group of disciples. It contains many of the important doctrines of the developed Chan tradition, including the doctrine of "sudden awakening," which holds that buddhas become awakened in a flash of insight, and not gradually as traditional Indian Buddhism taught. According to Indian Buddhist meditation texts, meditators should enter into concentrated meditative states called samādhi, *and these states lead to the awakening of wisdom* (prajñā).

Hui Neng, however, declared that such ideas impose a false dualism on the path to buddhahood. He contended that both concentration and wisdom are present in every moment of thought and that they cannot legitimately be separated. He also opposed the goal-oriented practices of traditional Mahāyāna and said that one becomes awakened by eliminating discursive thought. When all conceptual thoughts drop away and one attains the state of "no-thought" (wu nian), *the mind flows freely and unimpededly, in harmony with the rhythms of the world. This is the state of mind characteristic of buddhahood, and any notions of "path" and "goal," or "cultivation" and "attainment," are products of dualistic thinking that will impede one's progress toward awakening.*

The Master Hui Neng called, saying: "Good friends, awakening *(bodhi)* and intuitive wisdom *(prajñā)* are from the outset possessed by men of this world themselves. It is just because the mind is deluded that men cannot attain awakening to themselves. They must seek a good teacher to show them how to see into their own natures. Good friends, if you meet awakening, [Buddha]-wisdom will be achieved.

13. "Good friends, my teaching of the dharma takes meditation *(ding)* and wisdom *(hui)* as its basis. Never under any circumstances say mistakenly that meditation and wisdom are different; they are a unity, not two things. Meditation itself is the substance of wisdom; wisdom itself is the function of meditation. At the very moment when there is wisdom, then meditation exists in wisdom; at the very moment when there is meditation, then wisdom exists in meditation. Good friends, this means that meditation and wisdom are alike. Students, be careful not to say that meditation gives rise to wisdom, or that wisdom gives rise to meditation, or that meditation and wisdom are different from each other. . . .
16. "Good friends, in the Dharma there is no sudden or gradual, but among people some are keen and others dull. The deluded recommend the gradual method, the awakened practice the sudden teaching. To understand the original mind of yourself is to see into your own original nature. Once awakened, there is from the outset no distinction between these two methods; those who are not awakened will for long *kalpas* [eons] be caught in the cycle of transmigration.
17. "Good friends, in this teaching of mine, from ancient times up to the present, all have set up no-thought as the main doctrine, non-form as the substance, and non-abiding as the basis. Non-form is to be separated from form even when associated with form. No-thought is not to think even when involved in thought. Non-abiding is the original nature of humanity.

    "Successive thoughts do not stop; prior thoughts, present thoughts, and future thoughts follow one after the other without cessation. If one instant of thought is cut off, the Dharma body separates from the physical body, and in the midst of successive thoughts there will be no place for attachment to anything. If one instant of thought clings, then successive thoughts cling; this is known as being fettered. If in all things successive thoughts do not cling, then you are unfettered. Therefore, non-abiding is made the basis."

Source: Hui Neng, *Platform Sūtra* 12–16, tr. Philip Yampolsky, *The Platform Sūtra of the Sixth Patriarch* (New York: Columbia University Press, 1967), pp. 135–138.

KŪKAI: EXOTERIC AND ESOTERIC BUDDHISM

Kūkai (774–835), posthumously known as Kōbō daishi, was one of the most influential thinkers of the Heian period (794–1185). He traveled to China in 804 to study Buddhism and learned the doctrines and practices of Esoteric Buddhism (Chinese: Zhenyan*; Japanese:* Shingon*) under the Chinese master Hui Guo. This school is a branch of Vajrayāna ("Vajra Vehicle"), which is based on the tantras of Indian Buddhism. Like its counterparts in South Asia, East Asian Esoteric Buddhism emphasizes the importance of visualizations, mantras, and rituals for bringing about a cognitive transformation of one's mind into the mind of a buddha.*

In the following passage, Kūkai compares the path of Esoteric Buddhism to that of Exoteric Buddhism. He contends that Esoteric Buddhism is far superior to the Exoteric teachings and practices and is more effective in bringing about mundane benefits as well as final awakening. Kūkai believed that human beings have the capacity to become "awakened in this very body" (sokushin jōbutsu) *and that the rituals and symbols of Esoteric Buddhism appeal directly to humans' basic nature of buddha-potential and enable them to quickly attain the state of buddhahood. These practices bring the body, speech, and mind of the meditator into concordance with those of the truth body and thus allow the primordial buddha Mahāvairocana to communicate directly with advanced practitioners.*

I have heard that there are two kinds of preaching of the Buddha. One is shallow and incomplete while the other is esoteric. The shallow teaching is comprised of the scriptures with long passages and verses, whereas the esoteric teaching is the *dhāraṇī* [esoteric prayers thought to have magical properties] found in the scriptures.

The shallow teaching is, as one text says, like the diagnosis of an illness and the prescription of a medicine. The esoteric method of reciting *dhāraṇī* is like prescribing appropriate medicine, ingesting it, and curing the ailment. If a person is ill, opening a medical text and reciting its contents will be of no avail in treating the illness. It is necessary to adapt the medicine to the disease and to ingest it in accordance with proper methods. Only then will the illness be eliminated and life preserved.

However, the present custom of chanting the *Sūtra of Golden Light* at the Imperial Palace is simply the reading of sentences and the empty recital of doctrine. There is no drawing of buddha images in accordance with proper technique nor the practice of setting up an altar for offerings and for the ceremonies of empowerment. Although the reading of the *Sūtra* may appear to be an opportunity to listen to the preaching of the nectar-like teachings of the Buddha, in actuality it lacks the precious taste of the finest essence of Buddhist truth.

I humbly request that from this year on, fourteen monks skilled in esoteric ritual and fourteen novices be selected who, while properly reading the *Sūtra*, will for seven days arrange the sacred images, perform the requisite offerings, and recite *mantra* in a specially adorned room. If this is done, both the exoteric and esoteric teachings, which express the Buddha's true intent, will cause great happiness in the world and thereby fulfill the compassionate vows of the holy ones.

Source: Kūkai, *Petition to Supplement the Annual Reading of Sūtra in the Imperial Palace;* tr. David Gardiner.

DŌGEN'S MEDITATION INSTRUCTIONS

Dōgen (1200–1253), founder of the Sōtō (*Chinese:* Zaodong) *school of Zen, traveled to China in 1223 and studied with Rujing, a Chinese Chan master. One day during meditation practice, another monk fell asleep, and Rujing woke him up, admonishing him to practice meditation diligently in order to "drop off body and mind" (Japanese:* shinjin datsuraku). *This idea became a cornerstone of Dōgen's system of meditative practice. The following passage contains instructions on meditation practice* (zazen), *which in Dōgen's system is based on the experience of "not thinking"* (hishiryō).

In the state of not thinking, a meditator moves beyond discursive and dichotomizing thought (shiryō), *transcends the tendency to stop ordinary thought by suppressing it* (fushiryō), *and thus enters into a spontaneous awareness of reality in which thoughts flow along of their own accord. In this state of spontaneous mindfulness, the meditator experiences his or her own "buddha nature," an inherent propensity toward awakening that is shared by all beings.*

> Once you have settled your posture, you should regulate your breathing. Whenever a thought occurs, be aware of it; as soon as you are aware of it, it will vanish. If you remain for a long period forgetful of objects, you will naturally become unified. This is the essential art of *zazen* [sitting meditation]. *Zazen* is the dharma gate of great ease and joy. . . .
>
> Having thus regulated body and mind, take a breath and exhale fully. Sitting fixedly, think of not thinking. How do you think of not thinking? Nonthinking. This is the art of *zazen. Zazen* is not the practice of *dhyāna* [meditation]. It is the dharma gate of great ease and joy. It is undefiled practice and verification.

Source: Dōgen, *Shōbōgenzō* selections, from *Dōgen's Manual of Zen Meditation,* tr. Carl Bielefeldt (Berkeley: University of California Press, 1988), p. 181.

THE MU KŌAN

The Rinzai (*Chinese:* Linji) *school of Zen is renowned for its use of* kōan, *riddles that cannot be answered by rational or discursive modes of thought. The following passage contains the kōan that is generally given to beginning students, referred to as the "Mu kōan." It reports that a monk asked the Zen master Jōshū if a dog has the buddha nature, to which Jōshū answered, "Mu!"* Mu *may be translated as "not," but in the kōan Jōshū's answer is not a denial, but rather an indication that the question makes no sense from the point of view of awakening.*

The dilemma behind the question is based on traditional Japanese Buddhist ideas about the path. It is widely accepted in Japanese Buddhism that all beings—including dogs—have the buddha nature, that is, an inherent potential for buddhahood. Thus, from the point of view of tradition, Jōshū's answer should be "Yes." But because Zen claims to transcend blind adherence to tradition, this would be an unacceptable answer. On the other hand, if Jōshū were to state that dogs do not have the buddha nature, he could be accused of contravening Buddhist doctrine and setting himself above the buddhas.

Thus, Jōshū's answer is an invitation to move beyond tradition and conceptualization to a direct perception of truth. The Zen tradition refers to this kōan as the "closed opening" or the "gateless barrier," because once a meditator perceives the meaning behind Jōshū's statement, it marks the first dawning of realization that will eventually culminate in full awakening, referred to in Zen as satori. *It is intended to cause a cognitive crisis as the meditator attempts to solve the riddle by means of conceptual thought but finds all such attempts utterly frustrated. This leads to the development of the "great doubt"* (daigi), *which is said to burn inside of one like a red-hot ball of iron. When the kōan is solved, however, the pain and frustration disappear and are replaced by a serene, nonconceptual awareness.*

> A monk once asked Master Jōshū, "Has a dog the Buddha Nature or not?" Jōshū said, "Mu!"
>
> Mumon's commentary: In studying Zen, one must pass the barriers set up by ancient Zen Masters. For the attainment of incomparable satori, one has to cast away his discriminating mind. Those who have not passed the barrier and have not cast away the discriminating mind are all phantoms haunting trees and plants.
>
> Now Tell me, what is the barrier of the Zen Masters? Just this "Mu"—it is the barrier of Zen. It is thus called "the gateless barrier of Zen." Those who have passed the barrier will not only see Jōshū clearly, but will go hand in hand with all the Masters of the past, see them face to face. . . .
>
> Wouldn't it be wonderful? Don't you want to pass the barrier? Then concentrate yourself into this "Mu," with your 360 bones and 84,000 pores, making your whole body one great inquiry. Day and night work intently at it. Do not attempt nihilistic or dualistic interpretations. It is like having swallowed a red hot iron ball. You try to vomit it but cannot. . . .
>
> You kill the Buddha if you meet him; you kill the ancient Masters if you meet them. On the brink of life and death you are utterly free, and in the six realms and the four modes of life you live, with great joy, a genuine life in complete freedom.

Source: From *Zen Comments on the Mumonkan*, tr. Zenkei Shibayama (New York: Mentor, 1974), pp. 19–20.

PURE LAND: SHINRAN ON AMIDA'S VOW

The Pure Land (Chinese: Qingdu; *Japanese:* Jōdo*) tradition focuses on a buddha named Amitābha ("Limitless Light") or Amitāyus ("Limitless Life"), who as a merchant named Dharmākara is said to have made a series of vows concerning the sort of "buddha-land" he would create after his attainment of buddhahood. In the* Sūtra on the Array of the Joyous Land (Sukhāvatīvyūha-sūtra), *Dharmākara indicates that his land will be especially wonderful, a place in which the conditions for buddhahood are optimal. Beings fortunate enough to be born into this land will receive teachings from buddhas and bodhisattvas, and they will progress quickly toward awakening.*

Amitābha also teaches that beings may be reborn in his land if they have sincere faith in him. The Japanese Pure Land teacher Shinran (1173–1262) states that anyone may be reborn in Amitābha's paradise, regardless of past actions. Previous teachers had contended that birth in Sukhāvatī required good moral character and constant repetition of the formula "Praise to Amida Buddha" (Namu Amida Butsu), *but Shinran declares that all that is necessary is one moment of sincere belief* (shinjin, *literally, "believing mind").*

Shinran makes a distinction between "self-power," which characterizes the practices of early Buddhism, and "other-power," in which one relies completely on the saving power of Amitābha. Shinran contends that the former practice was appropriate in the Buddha's day, but that the present age is one of degeneration and human beings have become so depraved that their only hope is to rely on Amitābha. The Tannishō *was written by a direct disciple of Shinran, probably Yuien (d. 1290), in the decades after Shinran's death, and it remains a respected record of Shinran's teachings.*

> "When from faith that you will be saved by the wondrous vow of Amida, and attain rebirth in the Pure Land, in the heart there spontaneously arises the urge to speak the *nembutsu* phrase, at that moment Amida will bestow upon you blessing that once grasped is never relinquished. Amida's vow makes no distinction between old and young, good and bad—you must know that sole importance lies in the believing heart. This is because that vow is to save all sentient beings caught in the throes of deep karmic evil and raging passion. Thus, it is enough simply to have faith in the vow; no other virtue is necessary. For there is no higher virtue than that of the *nembutsu*. Nor should you fear evil, for there is no evil great enough to obstruct the vow of Amida." These were the teacher's words.
>
> Even a virtuous person can gain rebirth in the Pure Land, to say nothing of an evil person. Yet consider the common saying, that "even an evil person can gain rebirth in the Pure Land, to say nothing of a virtuous person." This statement may seem reasonable at first glance, but in fact it goes against the meaning of the Primal Vow's "power from without." The reason for this is that as long as you perform good deeds through "power from within," you are lacking the spirit of depending on the "power from without," and hence you are not in accord with Amida's vow. However, if you overturn this reliance on power from within, and instead place your faith in the power from without, you will achieve rebirth in the true land. Amida's vow arose from an impulse of pity towards those of us who are in the grip of passions, and who cannot transcend the cycle of life and death no matter what practice we embrace; the essence of that vow is that it is precisely the evil person who has faith in power from without who possesses the true basis for rebirth in the Pure Land. This is why the teacher said, "Even a virtuous person can gain rebirth in the Pure Land, to say nothing of an evil person."

Source: Shinran, *Tannishō* selection; tr. Meredith McKinney.

TRUTH DECAY: NICHIREN ON THE TITLE OF THE *LOTUS SŪTRA*

Nichiren (1222–1282) was one of the most charismatic figures of Japanese Buddhism. Initially trained in the Tendai school, he became disenchanted with its doctrines and practices, considering them inappropriate to the current age, which he believed to be the "age of degenerate dharma" (Japanese: mappō*) that the Buddha had predicted would begin 1,500 years after his death. Many Japanese Buddhists of the Kamakura period (1185–1333) believed that the turmoils of the time indicated the arrival of the final age of dharma, and a number of teachers believed that in such a time new models and practices were required.*

Because in the final age people become progressively more degenerate, Nichiren contended that the practices of the past—including intensive meditation practice and adherence to monastic vows—were no longer possible for most people, and thus simpler and more effective practices, appropriate to mappō*, were required. Nichiren focused on the* Lotus Sūtra (Saddharma-puṇḍarīka-sūtra) *as the only viable teaching for* mappō*, and he counseled his followers to place all of their faith in it. Its teachings, however, were deemed too profound for most people to understand, so Nichiren developed the practice of chanting the title of the sūtra* (Namu Myōhōrengekyō *in Japanese) and trusting to the saving power of the sūtra to bring worldly benefits and final salvation.*

> Question: If a person does not understand the real meaning of the *Lotus Sūtra*, or grasp its import, but simply recites the words "Namu Myōhō Rengekyō," perhaps once a day, or once a month, or once a year or once every ten years, or even once in a lifetime, without yielding to the temptation of any evil action, great or small, will such a person not only be able to avoid the four evil realms, but manage thereby to attain that place from which there is no backsliding?
>
> Answer: He will. . . . All the beings of the nine worlds and the buddha world are contained within the syllables "Myōhō Rengekyō." And since these words contain the ten worlds, they naturally include all the states of rebirth possible in those worlds. Given that all doctrines are contained within the five syllables of the name of this sūtra, one single word from it is lord of all sūtras. The whole body of sūtras is contained therein.

Source: Nichiren, *Hokke Damokushū* selections; tr. Meredith McKinney.

Indigenous Traditions

Indigenous Religions of the West

INTRODUCTION

Like other indigenous religions around the world, those from Africa and America are as varied as the hundreds of native tribes within those regions. Also typical of indigenous religions in general, our knowledge of those from Africa and America rests largely on the work of social scientists rather than on documents composed by religious practitioners themselves. Because of both the uniqueness of various tribal practices and the rarity of firsthand documents, religions from these regions lack the kind of official sacred texts that we find in major world religions such as Hinduism or Judaism. Nevertheless, tribal religions have perpetuated an oral tradition, often passed from generation to generation, and some of this tradition has been recorded by researchers. This includes myths about spirits and gods, hymns to spiritual beings, legends containing moral wisdom, and sacred utterances for special events and life passage rituals.

African Religion

Africa is a large and culturally diverse continent, which makes it difficult to generalize about its religious practices. About one-third of the African people follow traditional African religions, and the remaining two-thirds are Muslim or Christian. Traditional African religions are restricted to specific tribal regions; there are as many as 700 languages in Africa, and each represents a different cultural group and religion. The various traditional religions are unique insofar as they developed from within their respective cultures and no attempt was made to send out missionaries or to convert people of other tribal religions. Nevertheless, these tribal religions have some shared features. First, many African religions hold a common belief in a high god—a supreme being in the sky and creator of all. However, since they believe that the high god is remote, religious rituals often focus on specialized tutelary gods, ancestral spirits, and animal spirits. Second, African religions have dramatic rituals involving ecstatic dances, chants, the wearing of masks, and the use of other fetish objects. So prominent are these visual worship practices in African religion that, for some time, the term *fetishism* designated African religion in general. Third, although African religions have some belief in an afterlife, their primary concern is with living well in this life. Fourth, African religions frequently hold that individual people are composed of numerous souls of their ancestors, which were handed on to them by their parents. The ancestral spirits inhabit all parts of a person's body, such as blood or bones, and make their wishes known. The ancestral spirits are particularly offended when living family members quarrel with each other or are immoral. This might prompt a particular ancestral spirit to rise up from within a living family member, take possession of her, and make her vocalize the ancestral spirit's discontent. Spirit possession and trances of this type, it is believed, are important for helping heal and integrate an individual.

For more distinct features of African religions, we must look to regional tribal practices. For simplicity, we can divide the African continent into four geographical regions that designate distinct cultural and religious traditions. One region is the northern portion, dominated by the Sahara desert. This area has seen much Christian and Muslim missionary activity, especially along the well-traveled trade routes; thus, when scholars speak of traditional African religion, they typically refer to the remaining three sub-Saharan areas. A second geographical area is eastern Africa, which contains 200 distinct tribal societies. The religious practices of the Nuer—herdspeople from the grasslands and swamps of southern Sudan—have attracted special attention. A third area is central and southern Africa, which is marked off by its regionally shared language group called *Bantu*. A fourth and final area is West Africa, which accounts for half of Africa's total population.

Native American Religion

The term "Native American" designates the indigenous peoples of the Western Hemisphere, including the peoples of both North and South America. Unlike African religion, which does contain some common themes, few generalizations can be made about indigenous American religion beyond what is central to most religions—namely, belief in the supernatural, the use of religious symbols, and ritual practices. There is no single concept of a high god or nature gods. In some tribes religious symbols are sometimes modeled after natural objects, and in others they tend to be abstract. Religious practices are sometimes formalized and other times integrated into daily activity. When Europeans first arrived in the Americas, there were around 240 tribal groups in North America alone. Anthropologists have classified these into the following nine groups based on geographical location and language:

Arctic: Aleut, Inuit

Subarctic (Alaska to Labrador): Chipewyan, Mountain, Tanana, Yellowknife

Northwest Coast (Alaska to northern California): Chinook, Haida, Nootka, Tlingit

California: Chumash, Esselen, Mojave, Pomo, Wappo

Western Plateau and Great Basin (east of California): Flathead, Nez Perce, Paiute, Shoshoni, Umatilla, Ute

Southwest (Arizona, New Mexico, Texas, northern Mexico): Apache, Hopi, Navajo, Pueblo, Zuni

Plains (north of Texas): Arapaho, Cheyenne, Comanche, Dakota, Kiowa, Lakota, Pawnee

Eastern Woodlands (northeast of Mississippi): Delaware, Iroquois, Ojibwa, Shawnee, Susquehanna, Winnebago

Southeast (Louisiana to Florida): Cherokee, Chickasaw, Choctaw, Creek, Seminole

Though Mexico and South America were no less varied in their regional tribes, these areas are most distinguished by major empires. Among the oldest of these is the *Maya*, which flourished between 250 and 900 C.E. in Mesoamerica (southern Mexico, Guatemala, and Belize). They developed a complex calendar and a hieroglyphic form of writing that has recently been translated. Their religion focused on a collection of nature gods, such as the sun, moon, rain, corn, and double-headed snake. For reasons not entirely clear, the civilization went into decline, its major cities being overtaken with jungle growth. Following on the heels of the Maya, just to the north in central Mexico, arose the *Toltec* empire, which peaked from the tenth to the twelfth centuries. Toltecs practiced human sacrifice in religious ceremonies, and, drawing on earlier mythology, they developed a cult of *Quetzalcoatl*, the "Feathered Serpent." They declined with the invasion of northern Mexican tribes into this region, giving rise to the *Aztec* empire. The Aztecs perpetuated both the practice of human sacrifice and the cult of Quetzalcoatl. Like the Maya, they too developed a system of writing, which gives us a direct avenue to understanding their religion. By the fifteenth century the Aztecs ruled central and southern Mexico; their expansion was finally halted in 1521 by Spanish explorers. During the rise of the Aztecs in Mexico, Peru saw the emergence of the *Inca* empire, which, like the Aztec, was crushed by Spanish conquest in 1532. With the Spanish invasion came Roman Catholic Christianity, which was quickly imposed on the conquered people. In rural areas, though, vestiges of the ancient religions remain, often intermingled with Catholic elements.

The selections here sample the religious mythology of African and Native American tribes. They explore the cause of death, the structure of the spiritual realm, the creation of the world, and the source of human suffering. In each case the myths express anguish about the human predicament and offer some statement about our place in the spiritual nature of things.

TIMELINE: AFRICA

200,000 B.C.E.	Earliest true humans in Africa
4,000–1,000 B.C.E.	Ancient African civilizations of the Nile Valley
1,000 B.C.E.	Spread of Bantu migration through sub-Saharan Africa

(Continued)

TIMELINE *(Continued)*

300–700 C.E.	Expansion of Christianity across northern Africa
600–1000	Spread of Bantu migration to southern Africa
700–800	Expansion of Islam across northern Africa
700	Beginning of Arab slave trade in Africa
1000	Spread of Islam into sub-Saharan Africa
1441	Beginning of European slave trade in Africa
1900	Peak of European colonization of Africa

TIMELINE: AMERICA

20,000 B.C.E.	Arrival of first settlers in the Americas
250–900 C.E.	Classical Mayan civilization
1200–1519	Aztec civilization
1350–1533	Inca empire in Peru
1492	Discovery of America by Columbus
1830	Indian Removal Act passed by U.S. Congress
1979	U.S. American Indian Religious Freedom Act

GLOSSARY

Bantu Region and language group of central and southern Africa.

Cherokee Indigenous North American people of the Iroquois group of the southeastern United States.

Fetishism Use in worship practices of special objects that contain spiritual power, such as masks.

High God A supreme being in the sky and creator of all.

Hopi Indigenous North American people of the Pueblo group in the southwestern United States.

Maya Indigenous pre-Columbian people and civilization of southern Mexico and Guatemala.

Popol Vuh Mayan religious text composed around 1550.

Quetzalcoatl Mythical priest-king of the Toltec people.

San Indigenous people of southern Africa, also called Bushmen; prior to and distinct from Bantu inhabitants.

Tezcatlipoca Mythical evil wizard of the Toltec people.

Toltec Indigenous pre-Columbian people and civilization of central Mexico in the tenth to twelfth centuries C.E.

FURTHER READINGS

Brown, Joseph Epes. *Teaching Spirits: Understanding Native American Religious Traditions.* Oxford: Oxford University Press, 2001.

Gill, Sam. *Native American Religions: An Introduction.* Belmont, CA: Wadsworth/Thomson, 2005.

Hirschfelder, Arlene B. *Encyclopedia of Native American Religions: An Introduction.* New York: Facts on File, 2000.

King, Noel Quinton. *African Cosmos: An Introduction to Religion in Africa.* Belmont, CA: Wadsworth, 1986.

Leon-Portilla, Miguel (ed.). *Native Mesoamerican Spirituality.* New York: Paulist Press, 1980.

Magesa, Laurenti. *African Religion: The Moral Traditions of Abundant Life.* Maryknoll, NY: Orbis Books, 1997.

Martin, Joel W. *The Land Looks After Us: A History of Native American Religion.* New York: Oxford University Press, 1999.

Mbiti, John S. *Introduction to African Religion.* Oxford: Heinemann Educational, 1991.

Ray, Benjamin C. *African Religions: Symbol, Ritual, and Community.* Englewood Cliffs, NJ: Prentice Hall, 1999.

Thomas, Douglas E. *African Traditional Religion in the Modern World.* Jefferson, NC: McFarland, 2005.

Turaki, Yusufu. *Foundations of African Traditional Religion and Worldview.* Nairobi: WordAlive Publishers, 2006.

Young, William A. *Quest for Harmony: Native American Spiritual Traditions.* New York: Seven Bridges Press, 2002.

Zimmerman, Larry J. *Native North America.* Norman: University of Oklahoma Press, 2000.

AFRICA

CAUSE OF DEATH

One of the most distinctive and pervasive themes in African religious myth is that death is unnatural: God originally intended humans to live forever, but there was some misunderstanding that prevented this. The plots, human characters, and gods differ, but there is an unmistakable thread tying these myths together throughout Africa's diverse regions. Three such stories are presented here.

Unkulunkulu [the High God of the Zulu people of the Bantu] sent a chameleon; he said to it, "Go, chameleon, go and say, 'Let not men die!'" The chameleon set out; it went slowly, it loitered in the way; and as it went it ate of the fruit of a bush which is called Ubukwebezane. At length Unkulunkulu sent a lizard after the chameleon, when it had already set out for some time. The lizard went; it ran and made great haste, for Unkulunkulu had said, "Lizard, when you have arrived say, 'Let men die!'" So the lizard went, and said, "I tell you, it is said, 'Let men die!'" The lizard came back again to Unkulunkulu before the chameleon had reached his destination, the chameleon, which was sent first—which was sent and told to go and say, "Let not men die!" At length it arrived and shouted, saying, "It is said, 'Let not men die!'" But men answered, "Oh, we have accepted the word of the lizard; it has told us the word. It is said 'Let men die!' We cannot hear your word. Through the word of the lizard men will die."

Imana [the High God of the Bantu tribes in Rwanda] used to talk with men. One day he said to a man, "Do not go to sleep to-night; I am coming to give you some good news." There was a serpent hidden in the hut, who overheard these words. The man kept awake till cockcrow, after which he was overpowered by sleep, and did not hear when Imana came and called him. The serpent was on the watch and answered the call. Imana thought the man was speaking, and said, "You will die, but you will rise again; you will grow old, but you will get a new skin, you, your children, and your grandchildren." Next morning the man went to see Imana, and complained that he had not received any message. Imana asked, "It was not you, then, to whom I spoke in the night?" "No." "Then it must have been the snake, who is for ever accursed. If a Tusi ever comes across that snake let him kill it—likewise the Hutu and the Twa. Let them kill one wherever they find it. But as for you, you will die, you and your children and your children's children."

Source: Adapted from Alice Werner, *Myths and Legends of the Bantu* (London: G. G. Harrap and Co., Ltd., 1933), chs. 2 and 3.

In the beginning of the world when the Creator had made men and women and the animals, they all lived together in the creation land. The Creator was a big chief, past all men, and being very kindhearted, was very sorry whenever any one died. So one day he sent for the dog, who was his head messenger, and told him to go out into the world and give his word to all people that for the future whenever any one died the body was to be placed in the compound, and wood ashes were to be thrown over it; that the dead body was to be left on the ground, and in twenty-four hours it would become alive again.

When the dog had traveled for half a day he began to get tired; so as he was near an old woman's house he looked in, and seeing a bone with some meat on it he made a meal of it, and then went to sleep, entirely forgetting the message which had been given him to deliver.

After a time, when the dog did not return, the Creator called for a sheep, and sent him out with the same message. But the sheep was a very foolish one, and being hungry, began eating the sweet grasses by the wayside. After a time, however, he remembered that he had a message to deliver, but forgot what it was exactly. So as he went about among the people, he told them that the message the Creator had given him to tell the people, was that whenever any one died they should be buried underneath the ground.

A little time afterwards the dog remembered his message, so he ran into the town and told the people that they were to place wood ashes on the dead bodies and leave them in the compound, and that they would come to life again after twenty-four hours. But the people would not believe him, and said, "We have already received the word from the

Creator by the sheep, that all dead bodies should be buried." In consequence of this the dead bodies are now always buried, and the dog is much disliked and not trusted as a messenger. If he had not found the bone in the old woman's house and forgotten his message, the dead people might still be alive.

Source: Elphinstone Dayrell, *Folk Stories from Southern Nigeria, West Africa* (London; New York: Longmans, Green and Co., 1910).

KING OF DEATH: ANGOLAN MYTH

The above myths about the cause of death express a frustration with the boundaries that separate the living from the dead. This theme plays out in a variety of myths in which a dejected person attempts to cross over this boundary. The following legend from the Bantu Ambundu tribe of Angola describes a heartbroken king's efforts to retrieve his dead wife from the realm of death—which is presided over by Lord Kalunga-ngombe. The king enlists the aid of a medicine man who makes the journey.

Kitamba was a chief who lived at Kasanji. He lost his head-wife, Queen Muhongo, and mourned for her many days. Not only did he mourn himself, but he insisted on his people sharing his grief. "In my village, too, no man will do anything. The young people will not shout; the women will not pound; no one will speak in the village." His headmen argued with him, but Kitamba was inflexible, and declared that he would neither speak nor eat nor allow anyone else to do so till his queen was restored to him. The headmen consulted together, and called in a medicine man. Having received his fee—first a gun, and then a cow—hearing their statement of the case, he said, "All right," and set off to gather herbs. He pounded these in a medicine-mortar, and, having prepared a potion, ordered the king and all the people to wash themselves with it. He next directed some men to dig a grave in his guest-hut at the fireplace, which they did. He entered it with his little boy, giving two last instructions to his wife: to leave off her girdle [*i.e.*, to dress negligently, as if in mourning] and to pour water every day on the fireplace. Then the men filled in the grave.

The medicine man saw a road open before him. He walked along it with his boy till he came to a village, where he found Queen Muhongo sitting, sewing a basket. She saw him approaching, and asked, "Where do you come from?" He answered, in the usual form demanded by native politeness, "I have sought you, yourself. Since you have been dead, King Kitamba will not eat, drink, or speak. In the village they do not pound food; they do not speak. He says, 'fetch my head-wife and I will talk and eat.' That is what brought me here. I have spoken." The queen then pointed out a man seated a little way off, and asked the doctor who he was. As he could not say, she told him, "He is the King of Death, Lord Kalunga-ngombe. He is always consuming us, us all." Directing his attention to another man who was chained, she asked if he knew him, and he answered, "He looks like King Kitamba, whom I left where I came from." It was indeed Kitamba, and the queen further informed the messenger that her husband had not many years to live, and also that "anyone who comes here in the realm of Death never returns again." She gave him the armlet which had been buried with her, to show to Kitamba as a proof that he had really visited the abode of the dead. She urged him, though, not to tell the king that he had seen him there. And he must not eat anything in Kalunga; otherwise he would never be permitted to return to earth.

Meanwhile, the medicine man's wife had kept pouring water on the grave. One day she saw the earth beginning to crack; the cracks opened wider, and, finally, her husband's head appeared. He gradually made his way out, and pulled his small son up after him. The child fainted when he came out into the sunlight, but his father washed him with some herbal medicine, and soon brought him to.

Next day the medicine man went to the headmen and presented his report; he was repaid with two slaves and returned to his home. The headmen told Kitamba what he had said, and produced the token. The only comment he is recorded to have made, on looking at the armlet, is "Truth, it is the same." We do not hear whether he countermanded the official mourning, but it is to be presumed he did so, for he made no further difficulty about eating or drinking. Then, after a few years, he died. They wailed at the funeral, then dispersed.

Source: Adapted from Alice Werner, *Myths and Legends of the Bantu,* ch. 2.

WOMAN'S SEARCH FOR THE HIGH GOD: ZAMBIAN MYTH

Religious traditions around the world struggle with explaining why God allows human suffering. The next story from a Bantu tribe of Zambia is about an old woman who, having suffered miserably through her life, attempts to find the High God and have him explain the meaning of her ordeal. Her efforts, though, fail.

An old woman, whose parents had died when she was a child, lost all her sons and daughters, one after another, and was left with no one belonging to her. When she was very old and weary she thought she must be about to follow them. But instead of that she found herself growing younger, and was seized with a strong desire to find Leza [the High God] and ask him the meaning of it all. Thinking that he had his abode in the sky, she began to cut down trees and make a scaffolding by which she could climb up.

But when she had built it up to a considerable height, the lower poles rotted away, and the whole fell down, she falling with it. She was not hurt, and tried again, but with no better success. At last she gave up in despair, and set out to reach the place where, as she believed, the sky joins the earth. So she wandered through one country after another, and when the people asked her what she wanted she said, "I am seeking Leza." "What do you want of him?" "My brothers, you ask me? Here in the nations is there one who has suffered as I have suffered? I am alone. As you see me, a solitary old woman, that is how I am!"

The people answered, "Yes, we see! That is how you are! Bereaved of friends and kindred? In what do you differ from others? Shikakunamo [High God of the Baila tribe] sits on the back of every one of us, and we cannot shake him off!"

Source: Adapted from Alice Werner, *Myths and Legends of the Bantu,* ch. 3.

TREE TO THE UPPER WORLD: TANZANIAN MYTH

The previous myth expresses the belief that the spiritual realm is located physically above the world in which we live. Just as the old woman attempts to build a scaffolding to breach the gulf, other myths describe similar mechanisms for climbing up to the heavens. The following myth from the Wachagga people of Tanzania's Kilimanjaro region describes a mysterious tree that leads to the world above.

A girl named Kichalundu went out one day to cut grass. Finding it growing very luxuriantly in a certain place, she stepped on the spot and sank into a quagmire. Her companions took hold of her hands and tried to pull her out, but in vain; she vanished from their sight. They heard her singing, "The ghosts have taken me. Go and tell my father and mother," and they ran to call the parents. The whole countryside gathered about the place, and a diviner advised the father to sacrifice a cow and a sheep. This was done, and they heard the girl's voice again, but growing fainter and fainter, till at last it was silent, and they gave her up for lost. But after a time a tree grew up on the spot where she had disappeared. It went on growing, until at last it reached the sky. The herd-boys, during the heat of the day, used to drive their cattle into its shade, and themselves climbed up into the spreading branches. One day two of them ventured higher than the rest, and called out, "Can you see us still?" The others answered, "No, come down again!" but the two daring fellows refused. "We are going on into the sky to *Wuhu,* the World Above!" Those were their last words, for they were never seen again. And the tree was called *Mdi Msumu,* "the Story-tree."

Source: Alice Werner, *Myths and Legends of the Bantu,* ch. 5.

DEAD PEOPLE BECOME CLOUDS: SAN MYTH

The San—or Bushmen—are an indigenous people of southern Africa. Their social composition consists of autonomous groups of families totaling around fifty people, typically with no dominant leader. Although at one point they occupied about one-third of the African continent, their numbers now are greatly diminished and total less than 100,000.

The following San myth describes how, upon death, nature covers over the footprints that we made while alive and then carries us away to become clouds. Unlike the previous myths, which are presented in a somewhat stylized form, the one here conveys the unedited utterances of a specific tribesperson.

The wind does thus when we die, our (own) wind blows; for we, who are human beings, we possess wind; we make clouds when we die. Therefore, the wind does thus when we die, the wind makes dust, because it intends to blow, taking away our footprints, with which we had walked about while we still had nothing the matter with us. And our footprints, which the wind intends to blow away, would (otherwise still) lie plainly visible. For, the thing would seem as if we still lived. Therefore, the wind intends to blow, taking away our footprints. And, our gall, when we die, sits in the sky; it sits green in the sky, when we are dead.

Therefore, mother was wont to do thus when the moon lying down came, (when) the moon stood hollow. Mother spoke, she said: "The moon is carrying people who are dead. For, you are those who see that it lies in this manner; and it lies hollow, because it is killing itself (by) carrying people who are dead. This is why it lies hollow. It is not threatening; for, is it a moon of badness? You may (expect to) hear something, when the moon lies in this manner. A person is the one who has died, he whom the moon carries. Therefore, you may (expect to) hear what has happened, when the moon is like this."

The hair of our head will resemble clouds when we die, when we in this manner make clouds. These things are those which resemble clouds; and we think that (they) are clouds. We, who do not know, we are those who think in this manner, that (they) are clouds. We, who know, when we see that they are like this, we know that (they) are a person's clouds; (that they) are the hair of his head. We, who know, we are those who think thus, while we feel that we seeing recognize the clouds, how the clouds do in this manner form themselves.

Source: Wilhelm Heinrich Immanuel Bleek et al., *Specimens of Bushman Folklore* (London: G. Allen and Company, 1911).

WAR OF THE GODS: YORUBA MYTH

The myth below, from the Yoruba city of Ife, describes an epic war between the gods that engulfed the earth. The Father of the Gods (Aramfe) *had two sons: the Creator of Men* (Orisha) *and the King of Men* (Oduwa). *At creation the Father of the Gods gave the Creator of Men a bag containing the wisdom and craftsmanship for the advancement of human civilization. But when the Creator of Men was sleeping, his brother, the King of Men, stole the bag. Although the King of Men then possessed the bag, he nevertheless did not have the power to teach its secrets. The Creator of Men asked for the bag back, but the King of Men refused. This in turn brought catastrophic war to the city of Ife between armies of the two gods and their human followers. The Father of the Gods tried to stop the conflict by punishing the gods and humans alike with great floods, but that failed.*

The God of Iron (Ogun)—son of the King of Men—grew weary of the war and asked the King of Men to return the bag to the Creator of Men. But the King of Men still refused and, transforming into stone, he sank beneath the soil, forever taking the bag with him.

When the God of Iron and other gods first made known their handicrafts, men learned to patiently acquire thatch, food and wine in forests and rivers. So man thrived. But in those days strife and turmoil came to the gods. For out of jealousy and pride, the King of Men [had stolen and] held the bag [of knowledge and wisdom] that the Father of the Gods gave to the great Creator of Men. Often the Creator of Men made a plea, and often a petitioner came before his brother the King of Men. But it was in vain. But then once the King of Men sat with the God of Iron in that same palace where the ancestors reign. The sound of drums was heard and the great Creator of Men approached with a skilled brass worker, and said: "The time has come to teach the art of the Father of the Gods to men. Give back the bag, for it is mine, so that I may do our father's bidding. Otherwise, beware: is it not told how caution slept in the still woods when the proud leopard fell, lured on by silence, beneath the monster's foot?" Then the King of Men was greatly angered: "Am I not king? Did not the Father of the Gods make me lord of gods and men? Go away! Who dares to speak inappropriate words before the king is preparing to travel."

The gods and their followers of men took up arms, and on that day the first wars began in Ife and the forest. Such was the fall of the gods from divine ways, and such was the despair for men that the King of Men created through his theft. But the gods cared little about their deep guilt until darkness fell and everything was quiet. For then they remembered their heritage, the calm of heaven that was born and destined for the world. Gloom, too, came down with the still night. A sense of unholy wrong and ungodly sin weighed down the weary warriors, and everything was changed. All around, the forest seemed dead, and its branches were still. The quiet air was also dead amidst the forest's strangling and knotted growth. While in that hush, the storm's silent messenger, there came the distant thunderous voice of the old Father of the Gods. He thought: "In vain did I send my sons—the children of my happy valley—into the waste beneath to make a world of amusement. For the homes of Ife are held in desolation, and women with their babies are outcast in the naked woods." But when the whirling clouds were wheeling in the sky and the great trees were smitten by the wind, the thunderous Father of the Gods in his anger reprimanded his erring sons: "At my command you came to darkness, where the evil of the void—lifeless violence—had made its home, to shape in the abyss a world of joy and lead creation in the ways of heaven. Why, then, this fighting? Did the void's black soul outmatch you, or possess your hearts to come again into that void? I grieve for man's misfortune. But you have carried them on the wave of your wrong-doing, and your punishment is theirs to share. For now I hurl my thunderbolts, with floods upon the land to fill the marshes and lagoons, and stop forever your unholy war."

Dawn came, the storm was gone, and in his grief the old Father of the Gods departed on black clouds. But still the wrath and anger of his sons continued, and the rebel gods fought on in the dripping forests and the marshes. In the clouds far away the Father of the Gods reasoned to himself: "I spoke in thunders, and my deluge filled the marshes that a priest had once dried. But still they fight. Punish them as I may, what can I achieve? Maybe something in all-powerful heaven, but what about here? What does this mean? I cannot tell. In the unknown, beyond the sky where I have set the sun, is he-who-speaks-not. He knows all. Can this be truth that the world was withdrawn amidst the unnatural strife of brothers, and by strife it must continue?"

Oh, scribe, your pen has written about how the first wars began, and how the old Father of the Gods tried to stop the flow of blood. But of the weary days of all that war, what mouth can speak? It is said the anger of the gods endured two hundred years. We know a priest made strange amulets for all the mortal soldiers of the gods: one charm could turn a spear aside, a second robbed the wounding sword of all its sting, another made one so terrible that twenty must flee. But not one word is handed down of the great deeds, of hopes and fears, of imminent defeat or victory snatched away. No legend has survived, and no voice has called through the dimness of those mysterious years. But when an end came to the terrible days that were foreknown to him-who-speaks-not, memories of the calm of heaven came upon the sleepless gods. For while the moon lay soft with all her spell on Ife of the many battles; while with sorrowful reproach the wise trees stood and gazed upon the gods who made the soil the voices of the forest sang their dreams of peace: "sleep, sleep" all weary nature craved, and "sleep" the slumberous reed-folk urged, and between the shadow and the silvered leaf, for sleep the drowsing breezes yearned.

And with the break of dawn, the God of Iron, the warrior, with his comrades stood before the King, and thus he spoke: "King of Men, we weary of the battle, and its agony weighs heavy on our people. Have you forgotten the effortless hours of the Father of the Gods' realm? What is the point of this war, this empty war between one mother's sons? You may say that the Creator of Men willed it so. It was said of old "he who has no house will buy no broom." Why then did the great Creator of Men bring plagues on those he made in love? In heaven afar the Father of the Gods gave to you the empire, but to the Creator of Men knowledge of the ways of mysteries and hidden things. You stole the bag, but not the clues to its use—the skill, the wisdom of great the Creator of Men which alone could wake the sleeping wisdom. The nations of the world are yours: give back the bag, and the great Creator of Men will trouble us no more."

But neither the God of Iron nor the soft voices of the night could loosen the King of Men from the bondage of envy. The rule of men and empire were of no influence when the hot thought of the Father of the Gods' wisdom newly roused his black anger. He held the bag, but all the faithless years had not revealed its promised treasures. Bitterly he answered: "these many years my brother, the Creator of Men, has made war upon me; while for the crown, its power and greatness, I have continuously labored for. Today my son [i.e., the King of Iron] (who is the hope of my cause and my cause itself) now tires of war, and joins my enemies. Weak son, the scepter you were born to hold and hand down strengthened to a line of kings could not uphold your will and be your encouragement until the end. Is it not said, "shall one priest bury, and immediately his mate dig up the corpse?" You have undone more than a brief day's work, which all my heart has longed for through a life of labor. So let it be, God of Soft Iron! Upon your royal brow descends this day the crown of a diminished chieftaincy, with the sweet honors of a king only in name. For I go back to the Father of the Gods' hills and the calm realm about which you babble on and on." Then the King of Men transformed to stone and sank beneath the soil, taking away the fateful bag. And thus, beneath, through all the ages of the world a voiceless wisdom and arts which found no teacher have lain in bondage.

Source: John Wyndham, *Myths of Ife* (London, 1921).

AMERICA

CREATION: MAYAN MYTH

The Popol Vuh *is one of the more important documents of pre-Columbian Mayan religion. Composed around 1550 by a Mayan author, it was written in the Quiché language of Mayan Guatemala, using Spanish letters. In the early 1700s, it was translated into Spanish by a Catholic priest, and, although the original Quiché has since been lost, the translation survives. The work chronicles the formation of the world of the Quiché people and lists their kings up to the year 1550. The selection below is the account of creation, which describes the gods' efforts to create humans; dissatisfied with their early productions, though, they resolve to destroy the immoral and arrogant creatures.*

Over a universe wrapped in the gloom of a dense and primeval night passed the god Hurakan, the mighty wind. He called out "earth," and the solid land appeared. The chief gods took counsel; they were Hurakan, Gucumatz, the serpent covered with green feathers, and Xpiyacoc and Xmucane, the mother and father gods. As the result of their deliberations animals were created. But as yet man was not. To supply the deficiency the divine beings resolved to create manikins carved out of wood. But these soon incurred the displeasure of the gods, who, irritated by their lack of reverence, resolved to destroy them. Then by the will of Hurakan, the Heart of Heaven, the waters were swollen, and a great flood came upon the manikins of wood. They were drowned and a thick resin fell from heaven. The bird Xecotcovach tore out their eyes; the bird Camulatz cut off their heads; the bird Cotzbalam devoured their flesh; the bird Tecumbalam broke their bones and sinews and ground them into powder. Because they had not thought on Hurakan, therefore the face of the earth grew dark, and a pouring rain commenced, raining by day and by night. Then all sorts of beings, great and small, gathered together to abuse the men to their faces. The very household utensils and animals jeered at them, their mill-stones, their plates, their cups, their dogs, their hens. Said the dogs and hens, "Very badly have you treated us, and you have bitten us. Now we bite you in turn." Said the mill-stones, "Very much were we tormented by you, and daily, daily, night and day, it was *squeak, screech, screech,* for your sake. Now you will feel our strength, and we will grind your flesh and make meal of your bodies." And the dogs upbraided the manikins because they had not been fed, and tore the unhappy images with their teeth. And the cups and dishes said, "Pain and misery you gave us, smoking our tops and sides, cooking us over the fire burning and hurting us as if we had no feeling. Now it is your turn, and you will burn." Then ran the manikins hither and thither in despair. They climbed to the roofs of the houses, but the houses crumbled under their feet; they tried to mount to the tops of the trees, but the trees hurled them from them; they sought refuge in the caverns, but the caverns closed before them. Thus was accomplished the ruin of this race, destined to be overthrown. And it is said that their posterity are the little monkeys who live in the woods.

After this catastrophe, before the earth was yet quite recovered from the wrath of the gods, there existed a man "full of pride," whose name was Vukub-Cakix. The name signifies "Seven-times-the-color-of-fire," or "Very brilliant," and was justified by the fact that its owner's eyes were of silver, his teeth of emerald, and other parts of his anatomy of precious metals. In his own opinion Vukub-Cakix's existence rendered unnecessary that of the sun and the moon, and this egoism so disgusted the gods that they resolved upon his overthrow. His two sons, Zipacna and Cabrakan (earth-heaper and earthquake), were daily employed, the one in heaping up mountains, and the other in demolishing them, and these also incurred the wrath of the immortals. Shortly after the decision of the deities the twin hero-gods Hun-Ahpu and Xbalanque came to earth with the intention of chastising the arrogance of Vukub-Cakix and his progeny.

Now Vukub-Cakix had a great tree of the variety known in Central America as "nanze" or "tapal," bearing a fruit round, yellow, and aromatic, and upon this fruit he depended for his daily sustenance. One day on going to partake of it for his morning meal he mounted to its summit in order to seek out the choicest fruits, when to his great indignation he discovered that Hun-Ahpu and Xbalanque had been before him, and had almost stripped the tree of its produce. The hero-gods, who lay concealed within the foliage, now added injury to theft by hurling at Vukub-Cakix a dart from a blow-pipe, which had the effect of precipitating him from the summit of the tree to the earth. He arose in great wrath, bleeding profusely from a severe wound in the jaw. Hun-Ahpu then threw himself upon Vukub-Cakix, who in terrible anger seized the god by the arm and wrenched it from the body. He then proceeded to his dwelling, where he was met and anxiously interrogated by his spouse Chimalmat. Tortured by the pain in his teeth and jaw he, in an access of spite, hung Hun-Ahpu's arm over a blazing fire, and then threw himself down to bemoan his injuries, consoling himself, however, with the idea that he had adequately avenged himself upon the interlopers who had dared to disturb his peace.

But Hun-Ahpu and Xbalanque were in no mind that he should escape so easily, and the recovery of Hun-Ahpu's arm must be made at all hazards. With this end in view they consulted two venerable beings in whom we readily recognize the father-mother divinities, Xpiyacoc and Xmucane, disguised for the nonce as sorcerers. These personages accompanied Hun-Ahpu and Xbalanque to the abode of Vukub-Cakix, whom they found in a state of intense agony. The ancients persuaded him to be operated upon in order to relieve his sufferings, and for his glittering teeth they substituted grains of maize. Next they removed his eyes of emerald, upon which his death speedily followed, as did that of his wife Chimalmat. Hun-Ahpu's arm was recovered, re-affixed to his shoulder, and all ended satisfactorily for the hero-gods.

But their mission was not yet complete. The sons of Vukub-Cakix, Zipacna and Cabrakan, remained to be accounted for. Zipacna consented, at the entreaty of four hundred youths, incited by the hero-gods, to assist them in transporting a huge tree which was destined for the roof-tree of a house they were building. While assisting them, he was beguiled by them into entering a great ditch which they had dug for the purpose of destroying him, and when once he descended was overwhelmed by tree-trunks by his treacherous acquaintances, who imagined him to be slain. But he took refuge in a side-tunnel of the excavation, cut off his hair and nails for the ants to carry up to his enemies as a sign of his death, waited until the youths had become intoxicated with pulque because of joy at his supposed demise, and then, emerging from the pit, shook the house that the youths had built over his body about their heads, so that all were destroyed in its ruins.

But Hun-Ahpu and Xbalanque were grieved that the four hundred had perished, and laid a more efficacious trap for Zipacna. The mountain-bearer, carrying the mountains by night, sought his sustenance by day by the shore of the river, where he lived upon fish and crabs. The hero-gods constructed an artifical crab which they placed in a cavern at the bottom of a deep ravine. The hungry titan descended to the cave, which he entered on all fours. But a neighboring mountain had been undermined by the divine brothers, and its bulk was cast upon him. Thus at the foot of Mount Meavan perished the proud "Mountain Maker," whose corpse was turned into stone by the catastrophe.

Of the family of boasters only Cabrakan remained. Discovered by the hero-gods at his favourite pastime of overturning the hills, they enticed him in an easterly direction, challenging him to overthrow a particularly high mountain. On the way they shot a bird with their blow-pipes, and poisoned it with earth. This they gave to Cabrakan to eat. After partaking of the poisoned fare his strength deserted him, and failing to move the mountain he was bound and buried by the victorious hero-gods.

Source: *The Popol Vuh*, Book I, from Lewis Spence, *The Popol Vuh, the Mythic and Heroic Sagas of the Kichés of Central America* (London: David Nutt, 1908).

QUETZALCOATL AND TEZCATLIPOCA: MEXICAN MYTH

Quetzalcoatl and Tezcatlipoca were major rival deities in pre-Columbian Mesoamerica. Quetzalcoatl, the feathered serpent, was the subject of a religious cult among the Toltec people of central Mexico in the tenth to twelfth centuries C.E. *Several myths depict Quetzalcoatl as a priest-king of Tollan, the urban center of the Toltec region. Sacrificing only animals, he runs into conflict with the evil wizard Tezcatlipoca, who prefers human sacrifice. Tezcatlipoca then expels Quetzalcoatl. In the following myth, Tezcatlipoca tricks Quetzalcoatl and usurps his power. The dejected Quetzalcoatl then leaves for his homeland.*

In the days of Quetzalcoatl there was abundance of everything necessary for subsistence. The maize was plentiful, the calabashes were as thick as one's arm, and cotton grew in all colors without having to be dyed. A variety of birds of rich plumage filled the air with their songs, and gold, silver, and precious stones were abundant. In the reign of Quetzalcoatl there was peace and plenty for all men.

But this blissful state was too fortunate, too happy to endure. Envious of the calm enjoyment of the god and his people the Toltecs, three wicked "necromancers" plotted their downfall—the deities Huitzilopochtli, Tezcatlipoca, and Tlacahuepan. These laid evil enchantments upon the city of Tollan, and Tezcatlipoca in particular took the lead in these envious conspiracies. Disguised as an aged man with white hair, he presented himself at the palace of Quetzalcoatl, where he said to the pages in-waiting: "Pray present me to your master the king. I desire to speak with him."

The pages advised him to retire, as Quetzalcoatl was indisposed and could see no one. He requested them, however, to tell the god that he was waiting outside. They did so, and procured his admittance.

On entering the chamber of Quetzalcoatl the wily Tezcatlipoca simulated much sympathy with the suffering god-king. "How are you, my son?" he asked. "I have brought you a drug which you should drink, and which will put an end to the course of your malady."

"You are welcome, old man," replied Quetzalcoatl. "I have known for many days that you would come. I am exceedingly indisposed. The malady affects my entire system, and I can use neither my hands nor feet."

Tezcatlipoca assured him that if he partook of the medicine which he had brought him he would immediately experience a great improvement in health. Quetzalcoatl drank the potion, and at once felt much revived. The cunning Tezcatlipoca pressed another and still another cup of the potion upon him, and as it was nothing but *pulque,* the wine of the country, he speedily became intoxicated, and was as wax in the hands of his adversary. . . .

The Toltecs were so tormented by the enchantments of Tezcatlipoca that it was soon apparent to them that their fortunes were on the wane and that the end of their empire was at hand. Quetzalcoatl, chagrined at the turn things had taken, resolved to leave Tollan and go to the country of Tlapallan, from which he had come on his civilizing mission to Mexico. He burned all the houses which he had built, and buried his treasure of gold and precious stones in the deep valleys between the mountains. He changed the cacao-trees into mesquites, and he ordered all the birds of rich plumage and song to quit the valley of Anahuac and to follow him to a distance of more than a hundred leagues. On the road from Tollan he discovered a great tree at a point called Quauhtitlan. He rested there, and requested his pages to hand him a mirror. Regarding himself in the polished surface, he exclaimed, "I am old," and from that circumstance the spot was named Old Quauhtitlan. Proceeding on his way accompanied by musicians who played the flute, he walked until fatigue arrested his steps, and he seated himself upon a stone, on which he left the imprint of his hands. This place is called Temacpalco (The Impress of the Hands). At Coaapan he was met by the Nahua gods, who were inimical to him and to the Toltecs.

"Where do you go?" they asked him. "Why do you leave your capital?"

"I go to Tlapallan," replied Quetzalcoatl, "from which I came."

"For what reason?" persisted the enchanters.

"My father the Sun has called me thence," replied Quetzalcoatl.

"Go, then, happily," they said, "but leave us the secret of your art, the secret of founding in silver, of working in precious stones and woods, of painting, and of feather-working, and other matters."

But Quetzalcoatl refused, and cast all his treasures into the fountain of Cozcaapa (Water of Precious Stones). At Cochtan he was met by another enchanter, who asked him where he was bound, and on learning his destination proffered him a draught of wine. On tasting the vintage Quetzalcoatl was overcome with sleep. Continuing his journey in the morning, the god passed between a volcano and the Sierra Nevada (Mountain of Snow), where all the pages who accompanied him died of cold. He regretted this misfortune exceedingly, and wept, lamenting their fate with most bitter tears and mournful songs. On reaching the summit of Mount Poyauhtecatl he slid to the base. Arriving at the sea-shore, he embarked upon a raft of serpents, and was wafted away toward the land of Tlapallan.

Source: Lewis Spence, *The Myths of Mexico and Peru* (New York: T. Y. Crowell Co., 1913).

CREATION: HOPI MYTH

The Hopi people of North America are part of the Pueblo Indian group, located in what is now the southwestern United States. Their villages were often cliff dwellings and contained at least two dominant kivas, or underground social chambers. The best-known of their rituals is the Snake Dance, in which performers danced with live snakes in their mouths. The Hopi creation myth below describes how two principal goddesses—the Hard-Being Women of the east and west—dried the land, created animals, and then created one race of people. Another goddess—Spider Woman—created other races, which introduced discord into society.

A very long time ago there was nothing but water. In the east, the Hard-Being Woman [Huruing Wuhti], the deity of all hard substances, lived in the ocean. Her house was a kiva like the kivas of the Hopi of to-day. To the ladder leading into the kiva were usually tied a skin of a gray fox and one of a yellow fox. Another Hard-Being Woman lived in the ocean in the west in a similar kiva, but to her ladder was attached a turtle-shell rattle.

The Sun also existed at that time. Shortly before rising in the east, the Sun would dress up in the skin of the gray fox, whereupon it would begin to dawn—the so-called white dawn of the Hopi. After a little while the Sun would lay off the gray skin and put on the yellow fox skin, whereupon the bright dawn of the morning—the so-called yellow dawn of the Hopi—would appear. The Sun would then rise, that is, emerge from an opening in the north end of the kiva in which the Hard-Being Woman lived. When arriving in the west again, the sun would first announce his arrival by fastening the rattle on the point of the ladder beam, whereupon he would enter the kiva, pass through an opening in the north end of the kiva, and continue his course eastward under the water, and so on.

By and by these two deities caused some dry land to appear in the midst of the water, the waters receding eastward and westward. The Sun passing over this dry land constantly took notice of the fact that no living being of any kind could be seen anywhere, and mentioned this fact to the two deities. So one time the Hard-Being Woman of the west sent word through the Sun to the Hard-Being Woman in the east to come over to her as she wanted to talk over this matter. The Hard-Being Woman of the east complied with this request and proceeded to the West over a rainbow. After consulting each other on this point the two concluded that they would create a little bird; so the deity of the east made a wren of clay, and covered it up with a piece of native cloth. Hereupon they sang a song over it, and after a little while the little bird showed signs of life. Uncovering it, a live bird came forth, saying: "Why do you want me so quickly?" "Yes," they said, "we want you to fly all over this dry place and see whether you can find anything living." They thought that as the Sun always passed over the middle of the earth, he might have failed to notice any living beings that might exist in the north or the south. So the little Wren flew all over the earth, but upon its return reported that no living being existed anywhere. Tradition says, however, that by this time Spider Woman

[Kohk'ang Wuhti] lived somewhere in the south-west at the edge of the water, also in a kiva, but this the little bird had failed to notice.

Hereupon the deity of the west proceeded to make very many birds of different kinds and form, placing them again under the same cover under which the Wren had been brought to life. They again sang a song over them. Presently the birds began to move under the cover. The goddess removed the cover and found under it all kinds of birds and fowls. "Why do you want us so quickly?" the latter asked. "Yes, we want you to inhabit this world." Hereupon the two deities taught every kind of bird the sound that it should make, and then the birds scattered out in all directions.

Hereupon the Hard-Being Woman of the west made of clay all different kinds of animals, and they were brought to life in the same manner as the birds. They also asked the same question: "Why do you want us so quickly?" "We want you to inhabit this earth," was the reply given them, whereupon they were taught by their creators their different sounds or languages, after which they proceeded forth to inhabit the different parts of the earth. They now concluded that they would create people. The deity of the east made of clay first a woman and then a man, who were brought to life in exactly the same manner as the birds and animals before them. They asked the same question, and were told that they should live upon this earth and should understand everything. Hereupon the Hard-Being Woman of the east made two tablets of some hard substance, whether stone or clay tradition does not say, and drew upon them with the wooden stick certain characters, handing these tablets to the newly created man and woman, who looked at them, but did not know what they meant. So the deity of the east rubbed with the palms of her hands, first the palms of the woman and then the palms of the man, by which they were enlightened so that they understood the writing on the tablets. Hereupon the deities taught these two a language. After they had taught them the language, the goddess of the east took them out of the kiva and led them over a rainbow, to her home in the east. There they stayed four days, after which the Hard-Being Woman told them to go now and select for themselves a place and live there. The two proceeded forth saying that they would travel around a while and wherever they would find a good field they would remain. Finding a nice place at last, they built a small, simple house, similar to the old houses of the Hopi. Soon the Hard-Being Woman of the west began to think of the matter again, and said to herself: "This is not the way yet that it should be. We are not done yet," and communicated her thoughts to the Hard-Being Woman of the east. By this time Spider Woman had heard about all this matter and she concluded to anticipate the others and also create some beings. So she also made a man and woman of clay, covered them up, sang over them, and brought to life her handiwork. But these two proved to be Spaniards. She taught them the Spanish language, also giving them similar tablets and imparting knowledge to them by rubbing their hands in the same manner as the woman of the East had done with the "White Men." Hereupon she created two burros, which she gave to the Spanish man and woman. The latter settled down close by. After this, Spider Woman continued to create people in the same manner as she had created the Spaniards, always a man and a woman, giving a different language to each pair. But all at once she found that she had forgotten to create a woman for a certain man, and that is the reason why now there are always some single men.

She continued the creating of people in the same manner, giving new languages as the pairs were formed. All at once she found that she had failed to create a man for a certain woman, in other words, it was found that there was one more woman than there were men. "Oh my!" she said, "How is this?" and then addressing the single woman she said: "There is a single man somewhere, who went away from here. You try to find him and if he accepts you, you live with him. If not, both of you will have to remain single. You do the best you can about that." The two finally found each other, and the woman said, "Where will we live?" The man answered: "Why here, anywhere. We will remain together." So he went to work and built a house for them in which they lived. But it did not take very long before they commenced to quarrel with each other. "I want to live here alone," the woman said. "I can prepare food for myself." "Yes, but who will get the wood for you? Who will work the fields?" the man said. "We had better remain together." They made up with each other, but peace did not last. They soon quarreled again, separated for while, came together again, separated again, and so on. Had these people not lived in that way, all the other Hopi would now live in peace, but others learned it from them, and that is the reason why there are so many contentions between the men and their wives. These were the kind of people that Spider Woman had created. The Hard-Being Woman of the west heard about this and commenced to meditate upon it. Soon she called the goddess from the east to come over again, which the latter did. "I do not want to live here alone," the deity of the west said, "I also want some good people to live here." So she also created a number of other people, but always a man and a wife. They were created in the same manner as the deity of the east had created hers. They lived in the west. Only wherever the people that Spider Woman had created came in contact with these good people there was trouble. The people at that time led a nomadic life, living mostly on game. Wherever they found rabbits or antelope or deer they would kill the game and eat it. This led to a good many contentions among the people. Finally the Woman of the west said to her people: "You remain here; I am going to live, after this, in the midst of the ocean in the west. When you want anything from me, you pray to me there." Her people regretted this very much, but she left them. The Hard-Being Woman of the east did exactly the same thing, and that is the reason why at the present day the places where these two live are never seen.

Those Hopi who now want something from them deposit their prayer offerings in the village. When they say their wishes and prayers they think of those two who live in the far distance, but of whom the Hopi believe that they still remember them.

The Spanish were angry at the Hard-Being Woman and two of them took their guns and proceeded to the abiding place of the deity. The Spaniards are very skillful and they found a way to get there. When they arrived at the house of the Hard-Being Woman the latter at once surmised what their intentions were. "You have come to kill me," she said; "don't do that; lay down your weapons and I will show you something; I am not going to hurt you." They laid down their arms, whereupon she went to the rear end of the kiva and brought out a white lump like a stone and laid it before the two men, asking them to lift it up. One tried it, but could not lift it up, and what was worse, his hands adhered to the stone. The other man tried to assist him, but his hands also adhered to the stone, and thus they were both prisoners. Hereupon the Hard-Being Woman took the two guns and said: "These do not amount to anything," and then rubbed them between her hands to powder. She then said to them: "You people ought to live in peace with one another. You people of Spider Woman know many things, and the people whom we have made also know many, but different, things. You ought not to quarrel about these things, but learn from one another; if one has or knows a good thing he should exchange it with others for other good things that they know and have. If you will agree to this I will release you." They said they did, and that they would no more try to kill the deity. Then the latter went to the rear end of the kiva where she disappeared through an opening in the floor, from where she exerted a secret influence upon the stone and thus released the two men. They departed, but the Hard-Being Woman did not fully trust them, thinking that they would return, but they never did.

Source: H. R. Voth, *The Traditions of the Hopi*, in *Field Columbian Museum, Publication, Anthropological Series* (Chicago: The Museum, 1895–1905), vol. 8.

CREATION: CHEROKEE MYTH

The Cherokee people of North America are of the Iroquois language group and lived in what is now the southeastern United States. In the 1830s, the United States government forced them to relocate to Oklahoma. This Cherokee creation myth emphasizes the role of animals in the creation process. While the world was covered with water, they existed in a realm above the earth, slowly inhabiting it as it became dry. Vegetation followed, and finally humans appeared.

The earth is a great island floating in a sea of water, and suspended at each of the four cardinal points by a cord hanging down from the sky vault, which is of solid rock. When the world grows old and worn out, the people will die and the cords will break and let the earth sink down into the ocean, and all will be water again. The Indians are afraid of this.

When all was water, the animals were above, in the place Beyond the Arch; but it was very much crowded, and they were wanting more room. They wondered what was below the water, and at last "Beaver's

Grandchild," the little Water-beetle, offered to go and see if it could learn. It darted in every direction over the surface of the water, but could find no firm place to rest. Then it dived to the bottom and came up with some soft mud, which began to grow and spread on every side until it became the island which we call the earth. It was afterward fastened to the sky with four cords, but no one remembers who did this.

At first the earth was flat and very soft and wet. The animals were anxious to get down, and sent out different birds to see if it was yet dry, but they found no place to land and came back again to the place Beyond the Arch. At last it seemed to be time, and they sent out the Buzzard and told him to go and make ready for them. This was the Great Buzzard, the father of all the buzzards we see now. He flew all over the earth, low down near the ground, and it was still soft. When he reached the Cherokee country, he was very tired, and his wings began to flap and strike the ground, and wherever they struck the earth there was a valley, and where they turned up again there was a mountain. When the animals above saw this, they were afraid that the whole world would be mountains, so they called him back, but the Cherokee country remains full of mountains to this day.

When the earth was dry and the animals came down, it was still dark, so they got the sun and set it in a track to go every day across the island from east to west, just overhead. It was too hot this way, and the "Red Crawfish" had his shell scorched a bright red, so that his meat was spoiled; and the Cherokee do not eat it. The conjurers put the sun another hand-breadth higher in the air, but it was still too hot. They raised it another, until it was seven handbreadths high and just under the sky arch. Then it was right, and they left it so. This is why the conjurers call the highest place "The Seventh Height," because it is seven hand-breadths above the earth. Every day the sun goes along under this arch, and returns at night on the upper side to the starting place.

There is another world under this, and it is like ours in everything—animals, plants, and people—save that the seasons are different. The streams that come down from the mountains are the trails by which we reach this underworld, and the springs at their heads are the doorways by which we enter it, but to do this one must fast and go to water, and have one of the underground people for a guide. We know that the seasons in the underworld are different from ours, because the water in the springs is always warmer in winter and cooler in summer than the outer air.

When the animals and plants were first made—we do not know by whom—they were told to watch and keep awake for seven nights, just as young men now fast and keep awake when they pray to their medicine. They tried to do this, and nearly all were awake through the first night, but the next night several dropped off to sleep, and the third night others were asleep, and then others, until, on the seventh night, of all the animals only the owl, the panther, and one or two more were still awake. To these were given the power to see and to go about in the dark, and to make prey of the birds and animals which must sleep at night. Of the trees only the cedar, the pine, the spruce, the holly, and the laurel were awake to the end, and to them it was given to be always green and to be greatest for medicine, but to the others it was said: "Because you have not endured to the end you will lose your hair every winter."

Men came after the animals and plants. At first there were only a brother and sister until he struck her with a fish and told her to multiply, and so it was. In seven days a child was born to her, and thereafter every seven days another, and they increased very fast until there was danger that the world could not keep them. Then it was made that a woman should have only one child in a year, and it has been so ever since.

Source: James Mooney, *Myths of the Cherokee,* from *Nineteenth Annual Report of the Bureau of American Ethnology: To the Secretary of the Smithsonian Institution, 1897–98* (Washington, DC: Government Printing Office, 1900).

ORIGIN OF DISEASE AND MEDICINE: CHEROKEE MYTH

The following myth illustrates the exceptionally close relationship that the Cherokee people had to their natural surroundings. According to the myth, as the human population increased and became insensitive toward the animal world, the animals rose up against them. They afflicted humans with rheumatism, fears, nightmares, and diseases. Only the plants were sympathetic to the humans and thus provided cures for their ailments.

In the old days the beasts, birds, fishes, insects, and plants could all talk, and they and the people lived together in peace and friendship. But as time went on the people increased so rapidly that their settlements spread over the whole earth, and the poor animals found themselves beginning to be cramped for room. This was bad enough, but to make it worse humans invented bows, knives, blowguns, spears, and hooks, and began to slaughter the larger animals, birds, and fishes for their flesh or their skins, while the smaller creatures, such as the frogs and worms, were crushed and trodden upon without thought, out of pure carelessness or contempt. So the animals resolved to consult upon measures for their common safety.

The Bears were the first to meet in council in their townhouse under Kuwahi Mountain, the "Mulberry Place," and the old White Bear chief presided. After each in turn had complained of the way in which humans killed their friends, ate their flesh, and used their skins for their own purposes, it was decided to begin war at once against them. Someone asked what weapons humans used to destroy them. "Bows and arrows, of course," cried all the Bears in chorus. "And what are they made of?" was the next question. "The bow of wood, and the string of our entrails," replied one of the Bears. It was then proposed that they make a bow and some arrows and see if they could not use the same weapons against humans themselves. So one Bear got a nice piece of locust wood and another sacrificed himself for the good of the rest in order to furnish a piece of his entrails for the string. But when everything was ready and the first Bear stepped up to make the trial, it was found that in letting the arrow fly after drawing back the bow, his long claws caught the string and spoiled the shot. This was annoying, but some one suggested that they might trim his claws, which was accordingly done, and on a second trial it was found that the arrow went straight to the mark. But here the chief, the old White Bear, objected, saying it was necessary that they should have long claws in order to be able to climb trees. "One of us has already died to furnish the bowstring, and if we now cut off our claws we must all starve together. It is better to trust to the teeth and claws that nature gave us, for it is plain that human weapons were not intended for us."

No one could think of any better plan, so the old chief dismissed the council and the Bears dispersed to the woods and thickets without having concerted any way to prevent the increase of the human race. Had the result of the council been otherwise, we should now be at war with the Bears, but as it is, the hunter does not even ask the Bear's pardon when he kills one.

The Deer next held a council under their chief, the Little Deer, and after some talk decided to send rheumatism to every hunter who should kill one of them unless he took care to ask their pardon for the offense. They sent notice of their decision to the nearest settlement of Indians and told them at the same time what to do when necessity forced them to kill one of the Deer tribe. Now, whenever the hunter shoots a Deer, the Little Deer, who is swift as the wind and can not be wounded, runs quickly up to the spot and, bending over the blood-stains, asks the spirit of the Deer if it has heard the prayer of the hunter for pardon. If the reply be "Yes," all is well, and the Little Deer goes on his way; but if the reply be "No," he follows on the trail of the hunter, guided by the drops of blood on the ground, until he arrives at his cabin in the settlement, when the Little Deer enters invisibly and strikes the hunter with rheumatism, so that he becomes at once a helpless cripple. No hunter who has regard for his health ever fails to ask pardon of the Deer for killing it, although some hunters who have not learned the prayer may try to turn aside the Little Deer from his pursuit by building a fire behind them in the trail.

Next came the Fishes and Reptiles, who had their own complaints against humans. They held their council together and determined to make their victims dream of snakes coiling about them in slimy folds and blowing foul breath in their faces, or to make them dream of eating raw or decaying fish, so that they would lose appetite, sicken, and die. This is why people dream about snakes and fish.

Finally the Birds, Insects, and smaller animals came together for the same purpose, and the Grubworm was chief of the council. It was decided that each in turn should give an opinion, and then they would vote on the question as to whether or not humans were guilty. Seven votes should be enough to condemn them. One after another denounced human cruelty and injustice toward the other animals and voted in favor of their death. The Frog spoke first, saying: "We must do something to check the increase of the race, or people will become so numerous that we will be crowded from off the earth. See how they have kicked me about because I'm ugly, as they say, until my back is covered with sores"; and here he showed the spots on his skin. Next came the Bird—no one remembers now which one it was—who condemned humans "because he burns my feet off," meaning the way in which the hunter barbecues birds by impaling them on a stick set over the fire, so that their feathers and tender feet are singed off. Others followed in the same strain. The Ground-squirrel alone ventured to say a good word for humans, who seldom hurt him because he was so small, but this made the others so angry that they fell upon the Ground-squirrel and tore him with their claws, and the stripes are on his back to this day.

They began then to devise and name so many new diseases, one after another, that had not their invention at last failed them, no one of the human race would have been able to survive. The Grubworm grew constantly more pleased as the name of each disease was called off, until at last they reached the end of the list, when some one proposed to make menstruation sometimes fatal to women. On this he rose up in his place and cried: "Thanks! I'm glad some more of them will die, for they are getting so thick that they tread on me." The thought fairly made him shake with joy, so that he fell over backward and could not get on his feet again, but had to wriggle off on his back, as the Grubworm has done ever since.

When the Plants, who were friendly to humans, heard what had been done by the animals, they determined to defeat the latter's evil designs. Each Tree, Shrub, and Herb, down even to the Grasses and Mosses, agreed to furnish a cure for some one of the diseases named, and each said: "I will appear to help humans when they call upon me in their needs." Thus came medicine; and the plants, every one of which has its use if we only knew it, furnish the remedy to counteract the evil wrought by the revengeful animals. Even weeds were made for some good purpose, which we must find out for ourselves. When the medicine man does not know what medicine to use for a sick person the spirit of the plant tells him.

Source: James Mooney, *Myths of the Cherokee.*

ORIGIN OF CORN: CREEK MYTH

Many Native American myths concern the origin of corn, a staple in Native American diets. One account from the Creek Indians of the southeastern United States attributes it to the Corn Woman. The myth takes many forms, but the central theme is this: An old woman of mysterious origins enters a village and secretly provides the inhabitants with corn, which they all enjoy. They discover, though, that she produces the corn from scabs on her body, her feces, or some other disgusting source. Repulsed by this, they can no longer eat what she supplies. Versions of the myth have the Corn Woman solve the problem in different ways. In one account she instructs her sons to kill and decapitate her and drag her body around, and corn then grows where her blood has seeped into the soil. The Corn Woman's solution in the version here is much more humane.

> It is said that corn was obtained by one of the women of a local clan. She had a number of neighbors and friends, and when they came to her house she would serve some corn into an earthen bowl and they would eat it. They found it delicious, but did not know where she got the stuff of which to make it. Finally they noticed that she washed her feet in water and rubbed them, whereupon what came from her feet was corn. She said to them, "You may not like to eat from me in this way, so build a corncrib, put me inside and fasten the door. Don't disturb me, but keep me there for four days, and at the end of the fourth day you can let me out." They did so, and while she was there they heard a great rumbling like distant thunder, but they did not know what it meant. On the fourth day they opened the door as directed and she came out. Then they found that the crib was well stocked with corn. There was corn for making bread, hard flint corn for making other kinds. She instructed them how to plant grains of corn from what she had produced. They did so, the corn grew and reproduced and they have had corn ever since.

Source: Adapted from John R. Swanton, *Myths and Tales of the Southeastern Indians*, Smithsonian Institution Bureau of American Ethnology, Bulletin 88 (Washington, DC: U.S. Government Printing Office, 1929).

Religions of the West -- Judaism

Judaism

INTRODUCTION

Judaism, with its 3,000-year existence, is one of the world's oldest living religions. Like all religions, Judaism has evolved over time, but several key beliefs pervade its rich history. First and foremost is the belief that YHWH (usually pronounced Yahweh) is the only God and creator of all. Second, humans should obey God's law as found in both written and oral law. Third, God made a series of covenants with the Jews to designate their lineage as chosen. The most significant of these covenants are with Abraham, who received the promise of a nation; with Moses, who received the Law; and with David, who received the kingdom. Fourth is the belief that a coming King-Messiah will free the Jews from foreign domination. Unlike the other major monotheistic religions in the Western tradition—Christianity and Islam—Judaism is distinguished by being *this-worldly*. Although a doctrine of the afterlife can be found in its teachings, greater emphasis is placed on the nation, the land, and traditions.

Judaism's Beginnings

Judaism is inseparably tied to the history of the Jewish people; their scriptures, feasts, and worship practices recall events of the past. The earliest historical archaeological record derived from the period of Israel's settlement in its land is from the twelfth century B.C.E., during the period of the Judges. At this time the Israelites were occupied with capturing territory from the previous inhabitants of perhaps a thousand years, the Canaanites, and settling into agrarian life. The land, *Israel* to the Jews and *Canaan* to the Canaanites, is an area about the size of New Jersey, located on the southeast shore of the Mediterranean sea. Some of the Israelite stories defined their identity as a nation and entitled them to the land. In these stories, their lineage is traced back to Abraham, a Mesopotamian nomad from a few hundred years earlier. Abraham made a special pact with God whereby God would make him the father of a nation. Abraham and his clan migrated to Canaan, the land later given to him by God. Two generations later, famine drove his descendants to Egypt. For a while all was fine, until the Pharaoh of Egypt resorted to forced labor for his building projects. Abraham's descendants were enslaved for this purpose. Eventually, they were led by Moses out of Egypt and into the desert, where they wandered for forty years. During the journey, Moses received detailed codes of law directly from God. The story further recounts that Moses' successors led the Israelites into Canaan to capture the land promised to Abraham.

Politically, Canaan was a decentralized collection of tiny independent kingdoms. Religiously, the Canaanites performed plant and animal sacrificial rites in temples and open-air places, and fertility rites of prostitution. Key deities of the Canaanites were El the creator, Asherah the consort of El, Baal the son of El and god of storm, and Anat daughter of El and goddess of war. The Israelites and Canaanites already shared a common ethnic and language family, which was Semitic. As the Israelites occupied the land and eventually controlled the region, many intermarried with the locals and adopted the Canaanite ways, including worship of their deities. Politically the Israelites were a loose confederation of twelve tribes. A political balance of power was maintained among the chosen tribal leaders, legal and military judges, prophets, and priests from a thirteenth, landless group or tribe, Levi. Geographically there was a more delicate balance of power between two southern tribes—Judah (the largest of the twelve) and Benjamin—and the remaining ten tribes located primarily in the north, who felt threatened by Judah's size and political dominance.

United and Divided Kingdoms

An unexpected influx of warring invaders from the northeast Mediterranean area forced the Israelites to unify politically. These invading Philistines had a special military advantage in iron weaponry. Bronze weapons were less effective, especially in the hands of an Israelite army of drafted civilians. The need for a monarchy arose to facilitate a more concerted effort to block the Philistine power. The first King, Saul, died in battle with the Philistines. The kingdom and military leadership passed to his son-in-law, David, who instituted a standing professional army. Equipped with iron weapons, David's army effectively put an end to the Philistine threat. Through military and diplomatic maneuvers, the Kingdom of Israel took control of territory as far south as Egypt and as far north as Mesopotamia. At David's death, the throne passed to his young son, Solomon. Legendary for his wisdom and multiple diplomatic marriages, Solomon launched monumental building projects, including several fortified cities, a palace, and Israel's first permanent temple. Although Solomon taxed the entire country to fund his projects, benefits were seen primarily in Judah, which further alienated the northern tribes.

Solomon died about 922 B.C.E., and the throne passed to his son, Rehoboam. When Rehoboam announced that he would continue his father's policy of taxation, the northern tribes split from the south and proclaimed their own kingdom. The southern kingdom was thereafter referred to as *Judah,* while the northern kingdom retained the name *Israel.* During this period, both the northern and southern kingdoms continued to be influenced by Canaanite religious practices, and efforts were made at monotheistic reform in both kingdoms by prophets and kings.

After a 200-year existence, the northern kingdom was conquered by the Assyrian empire. For several decades, the north had tried several strategies of resistance, but in 722 B.C.E. its kingdom was annexed as an Assyrian province.

Some Israelites were deported, while others fled to Judah. Colonists from Mesopotamia settled in the region and intermarried with the remaining inhabitants, forming the group known as Samaritans, a remnant of which remains today. The southern kingdom escaped immediate annexation by becoming a vassal of the Assyrians. Two decades later, though, Judah's King Hezekiah broke with the Assyrians, prompting a military confrontation that ended in a loss of territory for Judah and a return to vassal status. He, and later King Josiah, made valiant efforts at monotheistic reform, but each time the populus reverted to Canaanite practices.

Exile and Restoration

In Mesopotamia, the power structure shifted and the Babylonians overtook the Assyrians. The new Babylonian Empire invaded surrounding countries to bring them within its control, and in three separate invasions (596, 587, and 583 B.C.E.), two of which were provoked by the Judeans, Judah was crushed. Cities and homes were destroyed, thousands of skilled craftsmen and potential troublemakers were deported to Babylon, and thousands more fled to Egypt, some of whom went to the Island of Elephantine. Most significantly, Solomon's temple was destroyed.

Although records of events during the Babylonian captivity are sketchy, the trauma of the exile apparently forced the Israelites to reexamine and solidify their religious beliefs. In the absence of the temple, the *Torah,* or books of Moses, became more important. Their understanding of Yahweh may also have changed so that they now viewed him as sovereign authority over the universe. The term *Jew,* which means someone from Judah, became common at this time.

Yet again the power structure in Mesopotamia shifted. In 539 B.C.E., the Persian emperor Cyrus overthrew the Babylonians, returned 40,000 Jews to Judah (now known by its Greek pronunciation, *Judea*), and authorized the rebuilding of the temple. Judea, however, remained a province of the Persian empire. The Jews who stayed in Babylon continued to prosper and grow in number, and their views may have been influenced by Zoroastrianism, the Persian religion at the time. Angelology and demonology become more prominent themes in post-exilic writings. Greater emphasis was placed on the resurrection of the dead, cataclysms of the end times, and the age of a redeemer or Messiah. In 458 B.C.E. an additional 17,000 people returned to the land under the leadership of the priest Ezra. He returned from Babylon with a complete *Torah* in the form we have today, which is the five books of Moses. He and governor Nehemiah instituted a theocratic state with power vested in the priests. The Jews were required to take an oath to observe the Torah, tithe, sacrifice, and attend feasts. Marriage with foreigners was condemned in order to ensure cultural and religious survival. He also established a council called *The Great Synagogue* to formulate doctrine and perhaps compile the texts of the *Tanakh*. Ezra's and Nehemiah's reforms set a new direction for the Jewish religion.

Maccabean Revolt and the Hasmonean Dynasty

The Persian Empire collapsed in 333 B.C.E. during Alexander the Great's campaign for world domination. The next year Judea also fell under his control. After Alexander's death, the empire was divided among four of his generals, whose dynasties were committed to Hellenization, that is, the propagation of Greek culture. Judea was passed back and forth between two dynasties of the divided empire: the Selucid Dynasty of Persia and the Ptolemaic Dynasty of Egypt. From 301 to 198 B.C.E., life was peaceful under the Ptolemies. Then it changed hands to the Selucids. By 165 B.C.E., the extreme Hellenizing policies of the Selucid king Antiochus Epiphanes reduced central Jewish religious rites to capital crimes. For many young Jews their heritage became an embarrassment, as evidenced by a frequently practiced surgical reversal of circumcision. The ultimate assault against the Jewish religion was the erection in the temple of an altar to Zeus upon which pigs were sacrificed. Further plans were made to confiscate land from Jews who followed their traditions. In revolt, an old priest named Mattathias killed a commissioner who had ordered him to sacrifice to Zeus. Gathering his five sons and followers, he fled to the desert. From there his son Judas Maccabeus launched a guerrilla attack, recapturing Jerusalem and restoring worship. Although the Selucid army responded to the revolt, the Selucids could not engage in a protracted guerrilla war and ultimately recognized Judea as a semi-independent temple-state. The Maccabean leaders declared themselves a dynasty of Priest Kings, also called the Hasmonean Dynasty, and for the next hundred years engaged in relatively independent, though frequently despotic, rule.

The Hasmoneans greatly expanded Judea's borders and fortified key cities. It is probably during this time that synagogues emerged as centers of local religious education and worship. According to Josephus, a noted Jewish historian of the first century C.E., three religious orders also emerged: the Pharisees, the Sadducees, and the Essenes. The Pharisees were priests and lay people who adopted a priestly life; they were proponents of oral tradition, purity rituals, a messianic kingdom, and the resurrection of the dead. They were also dedicated teachers of these doctrines to the masses. The Sadducees were aristocratic and priestly rivals of the Pharisees and denied many of their doctrines, especially those listed above. They also competed with the Pharisees for political influence in the Sanhedrin, the legislative assembly of Judea. The Essenes shared key doctrines with the Pharisees, such as food rituals, a messianic kingdom, and the resurrection of the dead. However, they became disgusted with the tyrannical rule of the Hasmoneans and the quarreling religious leaders and established a monastic community in the desert along the Dead Sea.

Roman Domination

Hasmonean rule of Judea ended in 63 B.C.E. when a civil war broke out between Jewish parties. Roman general Pompey was called in to arbitrate, but instead he occupied Judea and declared it a Roman province. The first Roman governors were particularly brutal, enslaving or crucifying those who disobeyed them.

A cunning Jewish governor from Galilee, Herod the Great, was appointed King of the Jews in 37 B.C.E. Herod had non-Jewish ancestry and was never completely accepted by the Jews. Preoccupied with conspiracies against him, Herod built massive fortifications for protection. He also rebuilt Jerusalem and the temple on a grand scale. But taxation for these projects economically crippled the peasant population. After Herod's death in 4 B.C.E., the Romans appointed a series of governors who were insensitive to the religious practices and economic concerns of the people. Growing anti-Roman sentiment among the peasants led to revolts in which thousands of Jews were massacred. Incited by a prophecy that a Jewish Messiah would rule the world, a territory-wide peasant revolt finally erupted in 66 C.E. Although it was initially successful, the Romans marched on the rebellious Jewish territories, destroying everything in their path. Most important, the elaborate new temple in Jerusalem was destroyed, bringing an end to temple sacrifices in 70 C.E. Many Jews were sold as slaves, and the Jewish territories forfeited statehood status within the Roman Empire. With the temple in ruins for three generations, in 132 C.E. Jewish peasants and leaders were easily seduced by the messianic leader Simeon Bar Kokhba, who promised to restore the temple. His unsuccessful three-year revolt brought more destruction to the country and a massive dispersion, or Diaspora, of the Jews throughout Europe. Jerusalem became officially off limits to all Jews, and the country was ironically renamed *Palestine,* after the ancient Philistines, arch-enemies of the early Israelites.

Diaspora

With the Diaspora, the center of Judaism shifted from Jerusalem to Babylonia, where a large population of Jews had remained after the 586 B.C.E. exile. At its peak, 1 million Jews lived in Babylon in the years following the exile and restoration. The figure of the Rabbi emerged at this time as an authority in scriptural interpretation and Jewish law, culminating in the creation of the Babylonian *Talmud,* the ultimate repository of Jewish oral law and commentary. Babylonian Jews remained the dominant voice of Judaism until the Arab conquest of the region in the seventh century C.E.

In the centuries following, Jews of the Diaspora attempted to settle in communities throughout Europe, only to be forced out as host countries became intolerant of them. In the reshuffling, two distinct groups emerged, each with its own distinct language and religious rituals. The Saphardic Jews were expelled from Spain and Portugal and moved to the Ottoman Empire. The Ashkenasic Jews were expelled from other countries and moved to eastern Europe.

Beginning in the eighteenth century, Judaism evolved in several directions. In reaction to impersonal rabbinic legalism and widespread disillusionment in the absence of the expected Messiah, the Hasidic movement was founded by Baal Shem Tov. Hasidism offered a more mystical and joyous approach to Judaism, particularly for the laity. Although Hasidim were at first persecuted by traditional rabbinic schools, eventually half of the traditional Rabbis joined them.

It was not until the eighteenth-century Enlightenment that European countries finally granted civil rights to their Jewish citizens. As an outgrowth of their freedom, Reform Judaism was founded in Germany by Abraham Geiger in the nineteenth century. Geiger believed that Judaism should pertain more to the sphere of religion than to culture and that Jewish worship practices should be modified to parallel those of Protestant Christians. In reaction, the Orthodox denomination reaffirmed the traditional elements of Judaism. Mediating between the reformed and orthodox views, the Conservative denomination emerged as an attempt to "conserve" historical traditions that the Reform denomination had eliminated. Finally, in the twentieth century the Reconstructionist denomination was founded by Mordecai Kaplan as a development from the Conservative denomination. Reconstructionists offer a more pragmatic approach in the modern world, placing more emphasis on the cultural development of Judaism than on its religious elements.

The Tanakh

The most sacred collection of writings for Judaism is the *Tanakh*. The word *Tanakh* is an acronym coined in the middle ages from the initials of its three divisions: the Torah (Law), the Neviim (Prophets), and the Ketuvim (Writings). The twenty-four books of the *Tanakh* are traditionally categorized as follows:

Torah: Genesis, Exodus, Leviticus, Numbers, Deuteronomy

Neviim:

Former Prophets: Joshua, Judges, Samuel, Kings

Latter Prophets: Isaiah, Jeremiah, Ezekiel, The Twelve (Hosea, Joel, Amos, Obadiah, Jonah, Micah, Nahum, Habakkuk, Zephaniah, Haggai, Zechariah, Malachi)

Ketuvim: Psalms, Job, Proverbs, Ruth, Song of Songs, Ecclesiastes, Lamentations, Esther, Daniel, Ezra-Nehemiah, Chronicles

The books of the *Tanakh* were written and compiled over a period of a thousand years, from approximately 1100 to 100 B.C.E. Each book has a detailed history of authorship, editing, and reediting. The writings appear in a variety of literary genres, including song lyrics, historical chronicles, wisdom literature, laws, prophecies, and apocalypses. The oldest stories and poems, such as the *Song of Deborah,* included here, may have been orally transmitted before taking written form. Much of the *Tanakh* bears the mark of post-exilic Judaism, either in composition or in editing. The books and main divisions of the *Tanakh* were in place when in 90 C.E. a Sanhedrin council in the Palestinian city of Jabneh gave the list its official stamp.

Of all writings within Judaism, the five books of the Torah have always been considered the most sacred. Thus, an understanding of its development is important. The term *Torah* means law, in the sense of instruction or teaching, which traces its authority to Moses. More specifically, *Torah* has come to mean the collection of writings consisting of Genesis, Exodus, Leviticus,

Numbers, and Deuteronomy. Any account of the origin and authorship of the Torah must take place against the backdrop of a theory in biblical scholarship known as the Documentary Hypothesis, most famously articulated by Julius Wellhausen (1844–1918). According to this theory, the Torah is a fabric sewn from four distinct textual sources identified as J, E, P, and D. The J source acquired its name from its continued use of the word *Yahweh* (often mispronounced *Jehovah*) for God in early parts of the narrative (prior to the revelation of the divine name of God to Moses). The E source is so named for its pervasive use of the term *Elohim* for God. The D source refers to the bulk of the text of Deuteronomy, with its unique style. Finally, the P source derives its name from the priestly content of its text.

Since Wellhausen, biblical scholars have identified more precisely the authors and dates of the four sources. One interpretation is that the J source was written by an author of the southern kingdom and reflects the political interests of Judah. Sometimes this involves besmirching the north. The E source, by contrast, was written by an author of the northern kingdom, possibly a Levitic priest, who endorsed the north's political structure but attacked its religious establishment. Both J and E appear to have been written between 922 and 722 B.C.E. Shortly after the fall of the north to the Assyrians in 722 and during Hezekiah's reign in the south, J and E were spliced or *redacted* together into a single document as a conciliation to the northern Israelites who had migrated to Judah. In reaction to the influx of northern priests, the P source was created as an alternative to the J and E story. One hundred years later, during the reign of Josiah, the framework of the D source was written around an old law code as a catalyst for religious reform. The D source is the first part of a larger historical sequence encompassing Joshua, Judges, Samuel, and Kings, compiled and edited by a single historian. The complete sequence of texts, called the Deuteronomistic History, details God's covenant with David for an unbroken royal lineage and rejection of local altars in favor of a single sacrificial site at the temple in Jerusalem. Finally, all four sources (J, E, P, and D) were redacted together into the five books of Moses, the Torah, by a priest (possibly Ezra) during or shortly after the Babylonian exile.

Post-Exilic Writings

From 300 B.C.E. until about 200 C.E., the notion of an official Jewish canon of scriptures was fluid, even after the council of Jabneh in 90 C.E. Hundreds of religious texts appeared that were considered authoritative by many at this time. Although the authority of these texts was rejected by later Jewish scholars, even today they continue to have historical importance. These writings are classified into three collections: Apocrypha, Pseudepigrapha, and Dead Sea Scrolls.

The term "*Apocrypha*" is Greek for "concealed" and refers to thirteen texts that at one time were associated with the Jewish canon but were officially rejected at the council of Jabneh. The original source of the Apocrypha is a Greek translation of the Jewish scriptures called the Septuagint (meaning "Seventy"), so called because seventy-two Jewish scholars were brought to Egypt to create a

Greek translation of Jewish scriptures between 285 and 246 B.C.E. Legend has it that each translated the first five books within seventy-two days, compared the various translations, and found them to be exactly the same. Completed around 100 B.C.E., the Septuagint contains the thirteen Apocryphal books interspersed among the other books of the *Tanakh,* with no clear distinction in importance. The thirteen books include Esdras 1 and 2, Tobit, Judith, the rest of the book of Esther, the Wisdom of Solomon, Ecclesiasticus (Sirach), Baruch, a Letter of Jeremiah, additions to the Book of Daniel (the Song of the Three Children, Susanna, and Bel and the Dragon), the Prayer of Manasseh, and Maccabees 1 and 2.

The term *Pseudepigrapha* means "writings with false subscriptions" and refers to a collection of fifty-two Jewish religious writings from 200 B.C.E. to 200 C.E., attributed to ideal figures in Jewish history such as Abraham and Moses. In literary styles paralleling those of the *Tanakh,* its four theological themes are the origins of sin and evil, God's transcendence, a coming Messiah, and the resurrection of the dead. The Pseudepigrapha is important in showing the diversity of Jewish theology at this time and the development of doctrines such as the coming of a Messiah, which are only hinted at in the *Tanakh.*

The Dead Sea Scrolls are a collection of writings and fragments discovered between 1947 and 1960 C.E. in the Qumran Valley area on the northwest shore of the Dead Sea. The religious community of Qumran was established around 200 B.C.E. as a desert haven against the oppressive political and religious realities of the time and was destroyed in 70 C.E. by the Romans during the Jewish revolt. The messianic community was preparing to be joined by angels for a final war against evil on earth. Although the Qumran community is often identified with the Essenes as described by Josephus, its association with that or any other sect is uncertain. Scriptures of the Qumran community were discovered in 1947 and were made fully public in 1991. The writings include the earliest copies of many texts of the *Tanakh* as well as an array of previously unknown religious texts. When first discovered, the new documents were thought to represent the unique views of the post-exilic monastic community. More recently, however, some historians believe they originated in Jerusalem, the center of Jewish religious activity, and thus, like the Pseudepigrapha, reflect the breadth of Jewish scripture at the time.

Rabbinic Writings

During the first five centuries C.E., Judaism witnessed a dramatic flourishing of literary activity among Rabbis. One such was the composition of verse-by-verse commentaries on the *Tanakh,* known collectively and stylistically as *midrash.* Another and more important type of activity was the development of oral law, culminating in the texts of the *Mishnah* and the *Talmud.* Traditionally, the oral law of Judaism is believed to have been given to Moses by God at Mount Sinai and orally transmitted for 1,500 years. In view of its divine origin, the oral law is on the same scriptural plane as the *Tanakh.* Historically, the foundation of the oral law tradition is thought to have been laid with Ezra's *Great Synagogue,* continuing through the Pharisees and then extensively developed by the *Tannaim,* scholarly Rabbis who lived during the first two centuries C.E. Although the *Tannaim* resisted committing the oral traditions to writing, in 200 C.E. the Palestinian Rabbi Judah Ha-Nasi did just that. The resulting work is the *Mishnah,* a collection of sayings attributed to specific *Tannaim* and rabbinic schools from the first two centuries C.E. The sayings are stylistically rhythmic, which facilitated their early memorization. Much of its content derives from the legal codes in the Torah, although it rarely quotes the *Tanakh* directly. The text contains six key divisions: agricultural rules, laws governing the Sabbath and holidays, laws on marriage and divorce, the system of civil and criminal law, rules of temple sacrifices, and rules of purities and impurities.

Early Rabbis developed a tradition of commenting on the contents of the *Mishnah.* One collection, called the *Tosefta,* was written by the *Tannaim* themselves. After the *Tannaim,* two other groups of Rabbis continued commenting on the *Mishnah:* the *Amoraim* (200–500 C.E.) and the *Saboraim* (500–700 C.E.). Their comments became the basis of the *Talmud,* the grandest expression of this rabbinic tradition. A first version of the *Talmud* appeared in 450 C.E. in Jerusalem, and a second and longer version in 600 C.E. in Babylon. Material was added to each version in the following century. Both the Jerusalem and Babylonian Talmuds have two parts: first, the text of the *Mishnah,* and second, the *Gemara,* a several-thousand-page collection of comments on the *Mishnah* written by the *Amoraim* and *Saboraim.* Both Talmuds are structured according to the main divisions of the *Mishnah,* although the Babylonian *Talmud* covers more divisions than its Jerusalem counterpart and thus is more definitive.

Medieval and Recent Writings

At the close of the Rabbinic period, Jewish writers continued penning commentaries on the *Tanakh* and *Talmud.* Only two of these writers will be mentioned here. First is the great philosopher Moses Maimonides (1135–1204), whose family left Spain for North Africa to avoid persecution. When only 23, Maimonides began writing an extensive commentary on the *Mishnah,* included in which is a statement of thirteen articles of faith that subsequently became a regular part of Jewish prayer services. The second influential author of the period was the thirteenth-century Spaniard Moses de Leon, who, writing in the Jewish mystical tradition of Kabbala, composed the multivolume *Book of Splendor (Sefer ha-Zohar).* The hero of the book, Rabbi Shimon, a second-century C.E. *Tannaim,* presents to his followers a verse-by-verse mystical commentary on several books of the *Tanakh.* To gain a receptive audience and lend authenticity to its content, de Leon claimed that his work was a recently discovered ancient text written by Rabbi Shimon himself. For almost 600 years, Kabbalists took de Leon at his word. The various Jewish movements of the past few centuries—Hasidism, Reform Judaism, Orthodox Judaism, Conservative Judaism, Zionism, Reconstructionist Judaism—have each given birth to revered works in several genres, including commentaries, tales, statements of faith, and polemics.

HOLIDAYS

Sabbath (Shabbat; literally, "seventh," i.e., "Saturday") Weekly day of worship that commemorates God's rest on the seventh day of creation.

New Year's Day (Rosh Hashanah; usually September) Beginning of the Jewish year.

Day of Atonement (Yom Kippur; late September or early October) Commemorates the Jewish people's wanderings in the desert.

Festival of Booths (Sukkot; September or October) Commemorates the Israelites' living in booths after their exodus from Egypt.

Pentecost (Shavu'ot; usually May) Commemorates Moses receiving the Torah at Mount Sinai.

Festival of Lights (Hanukkah; December) Commemorates the re-dedication of the Second Temple in Jerusalem to holy service by the Maccabees.

Festival of Lots (Purim; usually March) Commemorates the rescue of the Jews of ancient Persia.

TIMELINE

922 B.C.E.	Kingdom of Israel divided between north and south
722 B.C.E.	Assyrian invasion of northern kingdom
587 B.C.E.	Babylonian invasion of southern kingdom
200–100 B.C.E.	*Tanakh* canonized
164 B.C.E.	Jews under Judas Maccabeus
63 B.C.E.	Judea becomes a Roman province
66–70 C.E.	Jewish revolt; destruction of temple and fall of Jerusalem
132–135	Simeon Bar Kokhba revolt and mass dispersion (Diaspora) of Jews
200	*Mishnah* compiled
450–600	Jerusalem and Babylonian Talmuds compiled
900–1090	Golden age of Jewish culture in Spain
1135–1204	Maimonides, leading Rabbi of Sephardic Judaism
1250–1300	Moses de Leon, publisher of the *Zohar*

TIMELINE *(Continued)*

1492	Jews expelled from Spain
1700–1760	Ba'al Shem Tov, founder of Hasidic Judaism
1820–1860	Development of Orthodox Judaism and Reform Judaism
1897	Theodor Herzl advocates creating an independent Jewish state in Israel
1938–1945	Nazi Holocaust
1948	Israel declares itself an independent nation

GLOSSARY

Amoraim Rabbinic sages from 200 to 500 C.E. whose comments on the *Mishnah* are in the *Talmud.*

Deuteronomistic History The historical sequence of books in the *Tanakh* from Deuteronomy through Chronicles, connected in terms of authorship and theology.

Diaspora Dispersion of the Jews outside of Israel.

Elohim Hebrew for *God.*

Israelite People of Israel until the return from the Babylonian exile.

Jew Descendants of the Israelites from the return from the Babylonian exile to the present. *Jew* is from the Hebrew *jehudi,* meaning a descendant of Jacob's son Judah.

Judea The name for the land of the Jews from the post-exilic period to the early Roman period.

Kabbala Literally, "Tradition"; the largest school of Jewish mysticism, from the twelfth century C.E. to the present.

Midrash A verse-by-verse style of commentary on the *Tanakh,* especially as used by early Rabbis.

Mishnah The written expression of the oral law, compiled in 200 C.E. by Rabbi Judah Ha-Nasi.

Saboraim Rabbinic sages from 500 to 700 C.E. whose comments on the *Mishnah* were added to those of the Amoraim in the *Talmud.*

Sefirot The ten emanations of God, as described in early Kabbalist theology.

Talmud An extensive collection of commentaries on the *Mishnah* compiled from the sayings of Rabbis from 200 to 500 C.E.

Tanakh The Hebrew Bible. The term comes from the initials of its three divisions: Torah (Law), Neviim (Prophets), Ketuvim (Writings).

Tannaim Rabbinic sages of the first two centuries C.E. whose sayings are compiled in the *Mishnah.*

Torah Hebrew for law, teaching, or instruction. In the broad sense, *Torah* refers to the law of Moses, both written and oral. In the narrow sense, it refers to the first five books of the *Tanakh,* traditionally called the Books of Moses.

Yahweh The personal name of God in Judaism.

FURTHER READINGS

ALEXANDER, PHILLIP S. *Textual Sources for the Study of Judaism.* Totowa, NJ: Barnes and Noble, 1986.
BANK, RICHARD D. *The Everything Judaism Book.* Avon, MA: Adams Media Corp., 2002.
BLECH, BENJAMIN. *Understanding Judaism.* New York: Alpha Books, 1999.
COHN-SHERBOK, DAN. *Judaism: History, Belief and Practice.* London: Routledge, 2003.
DE LANGE, N. R. M. *An Introduction to Judaism.* Cambridge: Cambridge University Press, 2000.
DOSICK, WAYNE D. *Living Judaism.* San Francisco: Harper San Francisco, 1995.
FACKENHEIM, EMIL L. *What Is Judaism?* New York: Summit Books, 1987.
GOLDBERG, DAVID, AND RAYNER, JOHN. *The Jewish People.* New York: Viking, 1987.
HOLTZ, BARRY. *Back to the Sources: Reading the Classic Jewish Texts.* New York: Touchstone, 1984.
NEUSNER, JACOB. *The Life of the Torah: Readings in the Jewish Religious Experience.* Encino, CA: Dickenson Publ. Co., 1974.
ROBINSON, GEORGE. *Essential Judaism: A Complete Guide to Beliefs, Customs, and Rituals.* New York: Pocket Books, 2000.
SANDMEL, SAMUEL. *The Hebrew Scriptures.* Oxford: Oxford University Press, 1978.
SILVER, DANIEL, AND MARTIN, BERNARD. *A History of Judaism.* 2 vols. New York: Basic Books, 1974.
SOLOMON, NORMAN. *Judaism: A Very Short Introduction.* Oxford: Oxford University Press, 1996.
STEINSALTZ, ADIN. *The Essential Talmud.* San Francisco: HarperCollins, 1976.
WIGODER, GEOFFREY, AND SKOLNIK, FRED. *The New Encyclopedia of Judaism.* New York: New York University Press, 2002.

BOOKS OF MOSES

CREATION

The first eleven books of the Tanakh *present a continuous historical narrative from the creation of the world until the Babylonian exile. Genesis opens with two creation stories, one from the P or Priestly source, and one from the J or Yahwist source. Central to both is the idea that humans are the pinnacle of God's creative activity. The P source creation story, presented below, emphasizes the cosmic structure of creation, as opposed to the earlier and perhaps agrarian-oriented account of the J source. Also, the writer sees creation as involving three mandates. First, humans are to fill the earth and master it. Second, humans are to eat plants for food. Finally, the seventh day of the week is declared holy.*

> When God began to create heaven and earth—the earth being unformed and void, with darkness over the surface of the deep and a wind from God sweeping over the water—God said, "Let there be light"; and there was light. God saw that the light was good, and God separated the light from the darkness. God called the light Day, and the darkness He called Night. And there was evening and there was morning, a first day.

God said, "Let there be an expanse in the midst of the water, that it may separate water from water." God made the expanse, and it separated the water which was below the expanse from the water which was above the expanse. And it was so. God called the expanse Sky. And there was evening and there was morning, a second day.

God said, "Let the water below the sky be gathered into one area, that the dry land may appear." And it was so. God called the dry land Earth, and the gathering of waters He called Seas. And God saw that this was good. And God said, "Let the earth sprout vegetation: seed-bearing plants, fruit trees of every kind on earth that bear fruit with the seed in it." And it was so. The earth brought forth vegetation: seed-bearing plants of every kind, and trees of every kind bearing fruit with the seed in it. And God saw that this was good. And there was evening and there was morning, a third day.

God said, "Let there be lights in the expanse of the sky to separate day from night; they shall serve as signs for the set times—the days and the years; and they shall serve as lights in the expanse of the sky to shine upon the earth." And it was so. God made the two great lights, the greater light to dominate the day and the lesser light to dominate the night, and the stars. And God set them in the expanse of the sky to shine upon the earth, to dominate the day and the night, and to separate light from darkness. And God saw that this was good. And there was evening and there was morning, a fourth day. God said, "Let the waters bring forth swarms of living creatures, and birds that fly above the earth across the expanse of the sky." God created the great sea monsters, and all the living creatures of every kind that creep, which the waters brought forth in swarms, and all the winged birds of every kind. And God saw that this was good. God blessed them, saying, "Be fertile and increase, fill the waters in the seas, and let the birds increase on the earth." And there was evening and there was morning, a fifth day.

God said, "Let the earth bring forth every kind of living creature: cattle, creeping things, and wild beasts of every kind." And it was so. God made wild beasts of every kind and cattle of every kind, and all kinds of creeping things of the earth. And God saw that this was good. And God said, "Let us make man in our image, after our likeness. They shall rule the fish of the sea, the birds of the sky, the cattle, the whole earth, and all the creeping things that creep on earth." And God created man in His image, in the image of God He created him; male and female He created them. God blessed them and God said to them, "Be fertile and increase, fill the earth and master it; and rule the fish of the sea, the birds of the sky, and all the living things that creep on earth."

God said, "See, I give you every seed-bearing plant that is upon all the earth, and every tree that has seed-bearing fruit; they shall be yours for food. And to all the animals on land, to all the birds of the sky, and to everything that creeps on earth, in which there is the breath of life, [I give] all the green plants for food." And it was so. And God saw all that He had made, and found it very good. And there was evening and there was morning, the sixth day.

The heaven and the earth were finished, and all their array. On the seventh day God finished the work that he had been doing, and He ceased on the seventh day from all the work that He had done. And God blessed the seventh day and declared it holy, because on it God ceased from all the work of creation that He had done. Such is the story of heaven and earth when they were created.

Source: Genesis 1:1–2:3, from *Tanakh: The Holy Scriptures* (Philadelphia: Jewish Publication Society, 1985). Reprinted by permission.

COVENANT WITH NOAH

The first great covenant in the Tanakh *is between God and Noah. The P text story relates how God finds all the earth's inhabitants wicked, except for Noah, and destroys the earth in a flood. When the water subsides, God promises that he will not again destroy the world by water and permits humans to eat animal flesh. The authors of the P text note later (in Exodus 40) that all slaughter of animals must be done within the context of a sacrificial rite conducted by a priest.*

God blessed Noah and his sons, and said to them, "Be fertile and increase, and fill the earth. The fear and the dread of you shall be upon all the beasts of the earth and upon all the birds of the sky—everything with which the earth is astir—and upon all the fish of the sea; they are given into your hand. Every creature that lives shall be yours to eat; as with the green grasses, I give you all these. You must not, however, eat flesh with its life-blood in it. But for your own life-blood I will require a reckoning: I will require it of every beast; of man, too, will I require a reckoning for human life, of every man for that of his fellow man!

Whoever sheds the blood of man,
By man shall his blood be shed;
For in His image
Did God make man.

Be fertile, then, and increase; abound on the earth and increase on it."

And God said to Noah and to his sons with him, "I now establish My covenant with you and your offspring to come, and with every living thing that is with you—birds, cattle, and every wild beast as well—all that have come out of the ark, every living thing on earth. I will maintain My covenant with you: never again shall all flesh be cut off by the waters of a flood, and never again shall there be a flood to destroy the earth."

God further said, "This is the sign that I set for the covenant between Me and you, and every living creature with you, for all ages to come. I have set My bow in the clouds, and it shall serve as a sign of the covenant between Me and the earth. When I bring clouds over the earth, and the bow appears in the clouds, I will remember My covenant between Me and you and every living creature among all flesh, so that the waters shall never again become a flood to destroy all flesh. When the bow is in the clouds, I will see it and remember the everlasting covenant between God and all living creatures, all flesh that is on earth. That," God said to Noah, "shall be the sign of the covenant that I have established between Me and all flesh that is on earth."

Source: Genesis 9:1–17, from *Tanakh: The Holy Scriptures.*

COVENANT WITH ABRAHAM

The second great covenant of the Tanakh, *as it appears in the P text, is between God and Abraham, when Abraham is selected by God to be father of a multitude. God indicates that he will inherit the land of Canaan and that circumcision is to be the sign of that covenant. Circumcision is a rite to be performed by priests.*

When Abram was ninety-nine years old, the Lord appeared to Abram and said to him, "I am El Shaddai [God heeds]. Walk in My ways and be blameless. I will establish My covenant between Me and you, and I will make you exceedingly numerous."

Abram threw himself on his face; and God spoke to him further, "As for Me, this is My covenant with you: You shall be the father of a multitude of nations. And you shall no longer be called Abram, but your name shall be Abraham, for I make you the father of a multitude of nations. I will make you exceedingly fertile, and make nations of you; and kings shall come forth from you. I will maintain My covenant between Me and you, and your offspring to come, as an everlasting covenant throughout the ages, to be God to you and to your offspring to come. I assign the land you sojourn in to you and your offspring to come, all the land of Canaan, as an everlasting holding. I will be their God."

God further said to Abraham, "As for you, you and your offspring to come throughout the ages shall keep My covenant. Such shall be the covenant between Me and you and your offspring to follow which you shall keep: every male among you shall be circumcised. You shall circumcise the flesh of your foreskin, and that shall be the sign of the covenant between Me and you. And throughout the generations, every male among you shall be circumcised at the age of eight days. As for the homeborn slave and the one bought from an outsider who is not of your offspring, they must be circumcised, homeborn and purchased alike. Thus shall My covenant be marked in your flesh as an everlasting pact. And if any male who is uncircumcised fails to circumcise the flesh of his foreskin, that person shall be cut off from his kin; he has broken My covenant."

And God said to Abraham, "As for your wife Sarai, you shall not call her Sarai, but her name shall be Sarah. I will bless her; indeed, I will give you a son by her. I will bless her so that she shall give rise to nations; rulers of peoples shall issue from her." Abraham threw himself on his face and laughed, as he said to himself, "Can a child be born to a man a hundred years old, or can Sarah bear a child at ninety?" And Abraham said to God,

"O that Ishmael might live by Your favor!" God said, "Nevertheless, Sarah your wife shall bear you a son, and you shall name him Isaac; and I will maintain My covenant with him as an everlasting covenant for his offspring to come. As for Ishmael, I have heeded you. I hereby bless him. I will make him fertile and exceedingly numerous. He shall be the father of twelve chieftains, and I will make of him a great nation. But My covenant I will maintain with Isaac, whom Sarah shall bear to you at this season next year." And when He was done speaking with him, God was gone from Abraham.

Source: Genesis 17:1–22, from *Tanakh: The Holy Scriptures*.

PASSOVER AND EXODUS

Abraham's descendants migrate to Egypt to avoid famine in Canaan, and within a few generations their population dramatically increases. Intimidated by their numbers, the Pharaoh enslaves the Israelites and issues an edict that male infants are to be drowned. To save her child, one woman places her toddler, Moses, in a basket and floats it down the Nile, where it is discovered and he is adopted by the Pharaoh's daughter. When Moses grows up, God appears to him and instructs him to lead his people out of Egypt and into Canaan. To break the Pharaoh's resistance to releasing the Israelites, God kills the first-born humans and cattle in Egypt. In preparation for the event, the Israelites are instructed to perform a series of activities as described below. Passover, one of Judaism's most sacred feasts, is a celebration of this event.

12. In the middle of the night the Lord struck down all the first-born in the land of Egypt, from the first-born of Pharaoh who sat on the throne to the first-born of the captive who was in the dungeon, and all the first-born of the cattle. And Pharaoh arose in the night, with all his courtiers and all the Egyptians—because there was a loud cry in Egypt; for there was no house where there was not someone dead. He summoned Moses and Aaron in the night and said, "Up, depart from among my people, you and the Israelites with you! Go, worship the Lord as you said! Take also your flocks and your herds, as you said, and be gone! And may you bring a blessing upon me also!"

The Egyptians urged the people on, impatient to have them leave the country, for they said, "We shall all be dead." So the people took their dough before it was leavened, their kneading bowls wrapped in their cloaks upon their shoulders. The Israelites had done Moses' bidding and borrowed from the Egyptians objects of silver and gold, and clothing. And the Lord had disposed the Egyptians favorably toward the people, and they let them have their request; thus they stripped the Egyptians.

The Israelites journeyed from Rameses to Succoth, about six hundred thousand men on foot, aside from children. Moreover, a mixed multitude went up with them, and very much livestock, both flocks and herds. And they baked unleavened cakes of the dough that they had taken out of Egypt, for it was not leavened, since they had been driven out of Egypt and could not delay; nor had they prepared any provisions for themselves.

The length of time that the Israelites lived in Egypt was four hundred and thirty years; at the end of the four hundred and thirtieth year, to the very day, all the ranks of the Lord departed from the land of Egypt. That was for the Lord a night of vigil to bring them out of the land of Egypt; that same night is the Lord's, one of vigil for all the children of Israel throughout the ages. . . .

14. When the king of Egypt was told that the people had fled, Pharaoh and his courtiers had a change of heart about the people and said, "What is this we have done, releasing Israel from our service?" He ordered his chariot and took his men with him; he took six hundred of his picked chariots, and the rest of the chariots of Egypt, with officers in all of them. The Lord stiffened the heart of Pharaoh king of Egypt, and he gave chase to the Israelites. As the Israelites were departing defiantly, the Egyptians gave chase to them, and all the chariot horses of Pharaoh, his horsemen, and his warriors overtook them encamped by the sea, near Pihahiroth, before Baal-zephon.

As Pharaoh drew near, the Israelites caught sight of the Egyptians advancing upon them. Greatly frightened, the Israelites cried out to the Lord. And they said to Moses, "Was it for want of graves in Egypt that you brought us to die in the wilderness? What have you done to us, taking us out of Egypt? Is this not the very thing we told you in Egypt, saying, 'Let us be, and we will serve the Egyptians, for it is better for us to serve the Egyptians than to die in the wilderness'?" But Moses said to the people, "Have no fear! Stand by, and witness the deliverance which the Lord will work for you today; for the Egyptians whom you see today you will never see again. The Lord will battle for you; you hold your peace!"

Then the Lord said to Moses, "Why do you cry out to Me? Tell the Israelites to go forward. And you lift up your rod and hold out your arm over the sea and split it, so that the Israelites may march into the sea on dry ground. And I will stiffen the hearts of the Egyptians so that they go in after them; and I will gain glory through Pharaoh and all his warriors, his chariots and his horsemen. Let the Egyptians know that I am Lord, when I gain glory through Pharaoh, his chariots, and his horsemen."

The angel of God, who had been going ahead of the Israelite army, now moved and followed behind them; and the pillar of cloud shifted from in front of them and took up a place behind them, and it came between the army of the Egyptians and the army of Israel. Thus there was the cloud with the darkness, and it cast a spell upon the night, so that the one could not come near the other all through the night.

Then Moses held out his arm over the sea and the Lord drove back the sea with a strong east wind all that night, and turned the sea into dry ground. The waters were split, and the Israelites went into the sea on dry ground, the waters forming a wall for them on their right and on their left. The Egyptians came in pursuit after them into the sea, all of Pharaoh's horses, chariots, and horsemen. At the morning watch, the Lord looked down upon the Egyptian army from a pillar of fire and cloud, and threw the Egyptian army into a panic. He locked the wheels of their chariots so that they moved forward with difficulty. And the Egyptians said, "Let us flee from the Israelites, for the Lord is fighting for them against Egypt."

Then the Lord said to Moses, "Hold out your arm over the sea, that the waters may come back upon the Egyptians and upon their chariots and upon their horsemen." Moses held out his arm over the sea, and at daybreak the sea returned to its normal state, and the Egyptians fled at its approach. But the Lord hurled the Egyptians into the sea. The waters turned back and covered the chariots and the horsemen—Pharaoh's entire army that followed them into the sea; not one of them remained. But the Israelites had marched through the sea on dry ground, the waters forming a wall for them on their right and on their left.

Source: Exodus 12:29–41, 14:5–29, from *Tanakh: The Holy Scriptures.*

MOSAIC COVENANT

The third great covenant in the Tanakh *text consists of God giving the Law to Moses at Mount Sinai, a means by which the Israelites could become a holy people. Mosaic Law is articulated throughout the books of Exodus, Leviticus, Numbers, and Deuteronomy, interspersed with narratives about the Israelites' forty years of wandering. Exodus 19, a JE text, describes the people's preparation for receiving the Law from God. Exodus 20, which is possibly a reworked version of an ancient P text, presents the best-known part of the Mosaic Law, the Ten Commandments.*

19. On the third new moon after the Israelites had gone forth from the land of Egypt, on that very day, they entered the wilderness of Sinai. Having journeyed from Rephidim, they entered the wilderness of Sinai and encamped in the wilderness. Israel encamped there in front of the mountain, and Moses went up to God. The Lord called to him from the mountain, saying, "Thus shall you say to the house of Jacob and declare to the children of Israel: 'You have seen what I did to the Egyptians, how I bore you on eagles' wings and brought you to Me. Now then, if you will obey Me faithfully and keep My covenant, you shall be My treasured possession among all the peoples. Indeed, all the earth is Mine, but you shall be to Me a kingdom of priests and a holy nation.' These are the words that you shall speak to the children of Israel."

Moses came and summoned the elders of the people and put before them all that the Lord had commanded him. All the people answered as one, saying, "All that the Lord has spoken we will do!" And Moses brought back the people's words to the Lord. And the Lord said to Moses, "I will come to you in a thick cloud, in order that the people may hear when I speak with you and so trust you ever after." Then Moses reported the people's words to the Lord, and the Lord said to Moses, "Go to the people and warn them to stay pure today and tomorrow. Let them wash their clothes. Let them be ready for the third day; for on the third day the Lord will come down, in the sight of all the people, on Mount Sinai. You shall set bounds for the people round about, saying, 'Beware of going up the mountain or touching the border of it. Whoever touches the mountain shall be put to death: no hand shall touch him, but he shall be either stoned or shot; beast or man, he shall not live.' When the ram's horn sounds a long blast, they may go up on the mountain."

Moses came down from the mountain to the people and warned the people to stay pure, and they washed their clothes. And he said to the people, "Be ready for the third day: do not go near a woman."

On the third day, as morning dawned, there was thunder, and lightning, and a dense cloud upon the mountain, and a very loud blast of the horn; and all the people who were in the camp trembled. Moses led the people out of the camp toward God, and they took their places at the foot of the mountain.

Now Mount Sinai was all in smoke, for the Lord had come down upon it in fire; the smoke rose like the smoke of a kiln, and the whole mountain trembled violently. The blare of the horn grew louder and louder. As Moses spoke, God answered him in thunder. The Lord came down upon Mount Sinai, on the top of the mountain, and the Lord called Moses to the top of the mountain and Moses went up. The Lord said to Moses, "Go down, warn the people not to break through to the Lord to gaze, lest many of them perish. The priests also, who come near the Lord, must stay pure, lest the Lord break out against them." But Moses said to the Lord, "The people cannot come up to Mount Sinai, for You warned us saying, 'Set bounds about the mountain and sanctify it.'" So the Lord said to him, "Go down, and come back together with Aaron; but let not the priests or the people break through to come up to the Lord, lest He break out against them." And Moses went down to the people and spoke to them.

20. God spoke all these words, saying:

"I the Lord am your God who brought you out of the land of Egypt, the house of bondage: You shall have no other gods besides Me.

"You shall not make for yourself a sculpted image, or any likeness of what is in the heavens above, or on the earth below, or in the waters under the earth. You shall not bow down to them or serve them for I the Lord your God am an impassioned God, visiting the guilt of the parents upon the children, upon the third and upon the fourth generations of those who reject Me, but showing kindness to the thousandth generation of those who love Me and keep My commandments.

"You shall not swear falsely by the name of the Lord your God; for the Lord will not clear one who swears falsely by His name.

"Remember the sabbath day and keep it holy. Six days you shall labor and do all your work, but the seventh day is a sabbath of the Lord your God: you shall not do any work—you, your son or daughter, your male or female slave, or your cattle, or the stranger who is within your settlements. For in six days the Lord made heaven and earth and sea, and all that is in them, and He rested on the seventh day; therefore the Lord blessed the sabbath day and hallowed it.

"Honor your father and your mother, that you may long endure on the land that the Lord your God has assigned to you.

"You shall not murder.

"You shall not commit adultery.

"You shall not steal.

"You shall not bear false witness against your neighbor.

"You shall not covet your neighbor's house; you shall not covet your neighbor's wife, or his male or female slave, or his ox or his ass, or anything that is your neighbor's."

All the people witnessed the thunder and lightning, the blare of the horn and the mountain smoking; and when the people saw it, they fell back and stood at a distance. "You speak to us," they said to Moses, "and we will obey; but let not God speak to us, lest we die." Moses answered the people, "Be not afraid; for God has come only in order to test you, and in order that the fear of Him may be ever with you, so that you do not go astray."

Source: Exodus 19, 20:1–17, from *Tanakh: The Holy Scriptures.*

HOLINESS CODE

The Mosaic Law contains a series of codes on social, ethical, and religious topics, such as the Covenant Code (Exodus 21–23), the Purity Code (Leviticus 11–16), the Holiness Code (Leviticus 17–27), and the Law Code (Deuteronomy 12–26). The literary and legal style of these codes is frequently compared to other codes of the ancient Near East, such as the Code of Hammurabi, king of Ur. For example, on the issue of kidnapping, the Hammurabi code states, "If a man has stolen the young son of a freeman, he shall be put to death." By comparison, the Covenant Code in Exodus 21:16 states, "He who kidnaps a man—whether he has sold him or is still holding him—shall be put to death." The following is from the Holiness Code, a P text in the Book of Leviticus.

19. The Lord spoke to Moses, saying, Speak to the whole Israelite community and say to them: You shall be holy, for I, the Lord your God, am holy.

You shall each revere his mother and his father, and keep My Sabbaths: I the Lord am your God.

Do not turn to idols or make molten gods for yourselves: I the Lord am your God.

When you sacrifice an offering of well-being to the Lord, sacrifice it so that it may be accepted on your behalf. It shall be eaten on the day you sacrifice it, or on the day following; but what is left by the third day must be consumed in fire. If it should be eaten on the third day, it is an offensive thing, it will not be acceptable. And he who eats of it shall bear his guilt, for he has profaned what is sacred to the Lord; that person shall be cut off from his kin.

When you reap the harvest of your land, you shall not reap all the way to the edges of your field, or gather the gleanings of your harvest. You shall not pick your vineyard bare, or gather the fallen fruit of your vineyard; you shall leave them for the poor and the stranger: I the Lord am your God.

You shall not steal; you shall not deal deceitfully or falsely with one another. You shall not swear falsely by My name, profaning the name of your God: I am the Lord.

You shall not defraud your fellow. You shall not commit robbery. The wages of a laborer shall not remain with you until morning.

You shall not insult the deaf, or place a stumbling block before the blind. You shall fear your God: I am the Lord.

You shall not render an unfair decision: do not favor the poor or show deference to the rich; judge your kinsman fairly. Do not deal basely with your countrymen. Do not profit by the blood of your fellow: I am the Lord.

You shall not hate your kinsfolk in your heart. Reprove your kinsman but incur no guilt because of him. You shall not take vengeance or bear a grudge against your countrymen. Love your fellow as yourself: I am the Lord.

You shall observe My laws.

You shall not let your cattle mate with a different kind; you shall not sow your field with two kinds of seed; you shall not put on cloth from a mixture of two kinds of material.

If a man has carnal relations with a woman who is a slave and has been designated for another man, but has not been redeemed or given her freedom, there shall be an indemnity; they shall not, however, be put to death, since she has not been freed. But he must bring to the entrance of the Tent of Meeting, as his guilt offering to the Lord, a ram of guilt offering. With the ram of guilt offering the priest shall make expiation for him before the Lord for the sin that he committed; and the sin that he committed will be forgiven.

When you enter the land and plant any tree for food, you shall regard its fruit as forbidden. Three years it shall be forbidden for you, not to be eaten. In the fourth year all its fruit shall be set aside for jubilation before the Lord; and only in the fifth year may you use its fruit—that its yield to you may be increased: I the Lord am your God.

You shall not eat anything with its blood. You shall not practice divination or soothsaying. You shall not round off the side-growth on your head, or destroy the side-growth of your beard. You shall not make gashes in your flesh for the dead, or incise any marks on yourselves: I am the Lord.

Do not degrade your daughter and make her a harlot, lest the land fall into harlotry and the land be filled with depravity. You shall keep my Sabbaths and venerate My sanctuary: I am the Lord.

Do not turn to ghosts and do not inquire of familiar spirits, to be defiled by them: I the Lord am your God.

You shall rise before the aged and show deference to the old; you shall fear your God: I am the Lord.

When a stranger resides with you in your land, you shall not wrong him. The stranger who resides with you shall be to you as one of your citizens; you shall love him as yourself, for you were strangers in the land of Egypt: I the Lord am your God.

You shall not falsify measures of length, weight, or capacity. You shall have an honest balance, honest weights, an honest *ephah,* and an honest *hin.* I the Lord am your God who freed you from the land of Egypt. You shall faithfully observe all my laws and all my rules: I am the Lord.

Source: Leviticus 19:1–37, from *Tanakh: The Holy Scriptures.*

CONQUEST AND UNITED KINGDOM

ENTRY INTO CANAAN

After forty years of wandering, the Israelites enter Canaan under the leadership of Joshua, Moses' successor. This account is part of a larger text sequence called the Deuteronomistic History, edited just before the Babylonian exile and encompassing the books of Deuteronomy through second Kings. The story emphasizes Deuteronomist themes, such as the importance of the Ark of the Covenant as the focus of God's presence and the command to annihilate the present occupants of Canaan as a means of ensuring religious purity.

After the death of Moses the servant of the Lord, the Lord said to Joshua son of Nun, Moses' attendant:

"My servant Moses is dead. Prepare to cross the Jordan, together with all this people, into the land that I am giving to the Israelites. Every spot on which your foot treads I give to you, as I promised Moses. Your territory shall extend from the wilderness and the Lebanon to the Great River, the River Euphrates [on the east]—the whole Hittite country—and up to the Mediterranean Sea on the west. No one shall be able to resist you as long as you live. As I was with Moses, so I will be with you; I will not fail you or forsake you.

"Be strong and resolute, for you shall apportion to this people the land that I swore to their fathers to assign to them. But you must be very strong and resolute to observe faithfully all the Teaching that My servant Moses enjoined upon you. Do not deviate from it to the right or to the left, that you may be successful wherever you go. Let not this Book of the

Teaching cease from your lips, but recite it day and night, so that you may observe faithfully all that is written in it. Only then will you prosper in your undertakings and only then will you be successful.

"I charge you: Be strong and resolute; do not be terrified or dismayed, for the Lord your God is with you wherever you go."

Joshua thereupon gave orders to the officials of the people: "Go through the camp and charge the people thus: Get provisions ready, for in three days' time you are to cross the Jordan, in order to enter and possess the land that the Lord your God is giving you as a possession."

Then Joshua said the to Reubenites, the Gadites, and the half-tribe of Manasseh, "Remember what Moses the servant of the Lord enjoined upon you, when he said: 'The Lord your God is granting you a haven; He has assigned this territory to you.' Let your wives, children, and livestock remain in the land that Moses assigned to you on this side of the Jordan; but every one of your fighting men shall go across armed in the van of your kinsmen. And you shall assist them until the Lord has given your kinsmen a haven, such as you have, and they too have gained possession of the land that the Lord your God has assigned to them. Then you may return to the land on the east side of the Jordan, which Moses the servant of the Lord assigned to you as your possession, and you may possess it."

They answered Joshua, "We will do everything you have commanded us and we will go wherever you send us. We will obey you just as we obeyed Moses; let but the Lord your God be with you as He was with Moses! Any man who flouts your commands and does not obey every order you give him shall be put to death. Only be strong and resolute!"

Early next morning, Joshua and all the Israelites set out from Shittim and marched to the Jordan. They did not cross immediately, but spent the night there. Three days later, the officials went through the camp and charged the people as follows: "When you see the Ark of the Covenant of the Lord your God being borne by the levitical priests, you shall move forward. Follow it—but keep a distance of some two thousand cubits from it, never coming any closer to it—so that you may know by what route to march, since it is a road you have not traveled before."

And Joshua said to the people, "Purify yourselves, for tomorrow the Lord will perform wonders in your midst."

Then Joshua ordered the priests, "Take up the Ark of the Covenant and advance to the head of the people." And they took up the Ark of the Covenant and advanced to the head of the people.

The Lord said to Joshua, "This day, for the first time, I will exalt you in the sight of all Israel, so that they shall know that I will be with you as I was with Moses. For your part, command the priests who carry the Ark of the Covenant as follows: When you reach the edge of the waters of the Jordan, make a halt in the Jordan."

And Joshua said to the Israelites, "Come closer and listen to the words of the Lord our God. By this," Joshua continued, "you shall know that a living God is among you, and that He will dispossess for you the Canaanites,

Hittites, Hivites, Perizzites, Girgashites, Amorites, and Jebusites: the Ark of the Covenant of the Sovereign of all the earth is advancing before you into the Jordan. Now select twelve men from the tribes of Israel, one man from each tribe. When the feet of the priests bearing the Ark of the Lord, the Sovereign of all the earth, come to rest in the waters of the Jordan, the waters of the Jordan—the water coming from upstream—will be cut off and will stand in a single heap."

When the people set out from their encampment to cross the Jordan, the priests bearing the Ark of the Covenant were at the head of the people. Now the Jordan keeps flowing over its entire bed throughout the harvest season. But as soon as the bearers of the Ark reached the Jordan, and the feet of the priests bearing the Ark dipped into the water at its edge, the waters coming down from upstream piled up in a single heap a great way off, at Adam, the town next to Zarethan; and those flowing away downstream to the Sea of the Arabah (the Dead Sea) ran out completely. So the people crossed near Jericho. The priests who bore the Ark of the Lord's Covenant stood on dry land exactly in the middle of the Jordan, while all Israel crossed over on dry land, until the entire nation had finished crossing the Jordan.

Source: Joshua 1, 3, from *Tanakh: The Holy Scriptures.*

SONG OF DEBORAH

After their entry into Canaan, the Israelites fight to dislodge the Canaanites. Israel is then governed by a series of legal and military judges, including Deborah, one of a few female leaders in Jewish history. With the aid of the military leader Barak, Deborah and a small group defeat the army of Jabin, King of Canaan. The Canaanite army, headed by Sisera, has an initial advantage of 900 chariots. Due to a sudden divinely caused cloudburst and flash flood, the Israelites gain the advantage. The Song of Deborah, which commemorates this victory, is one of the oldest passages of the Tanakh. *Composed about 1100 B.C.E., it is similar in structure to Canaanite poems of the period. Historically it denotes the Israelites' successful habitation of the hillsides, overshadowing Canaanite occupation of the valley regions.*

When locks go untrimmed in Israel,
When people dedicate themselves—
Bless the Lord.

Hear, O kings! Give ear, O potentates!
I will sing, will sing to the Lord,
Will hymn the Lord, the God of Israel.

O Lord, when you came forth from Seir,
Advanced from the country of Edom,
The earth trembled;
The heavens dripped,
Yea, the clouds dripped water,
The mountains quaked—
Before the Lord, Him of Sinai,
Before the Lord, God of Israel.

In the days of Shamgar son of Anath,
In the days of Jael, caravans ceased,
And wayfarers went
By roundabout paths.
Deliverance ceased,
Ceased in Israel,
Till you arose, O Deborah,
Arose, O mother, in Israel!
When they chose new gods,
Was there a fighter then in the gates?
No shield or spear was seen
Among forty thousand in Israel!

My heart is with Israel's leaders,
With the dedicated of the people—
Bless the Lord!
You riders on tawny she-asses,
You who sit on saddle rugs,
And you wayfarers, declare it!
Louder than the sounds of archers,
There among the watering places
Let them chant the gracious acts of the Lord,
His gracious deliverance of Israel.
Then did the people of the Lord
March down to the gates!
Awake, awake, O Deborah!
Awake, awake, strike up the chant!
Arise, O Barak;
Take your captives, O son of Abinoam!

Source: Judges 5:2–12, from *Tanakh: The Holy Scriptures.*

DAVIDIC COVENANT

In response to the need for a ruler who could unify the country against Philistine attacks, Saul is appointed the first king. The Deuteronomistic History relates how Saul's disobedience quickly puts him in disfavor with God, after which God selects David as Saul's more obedient successor. This reflects the most consistent theological theme throughout all seven books of the Deuteronomistic History: Obedience to God results in prosperity, while disobedience results in hardship. The fourth and final great covenant in the Tanakh *is with King David, wherein a promise is given that David's house and kingship will be secure and his throne established forever.*

. . . Thus said the Lord of Hosts: I took you from the pasture, from following the flock, to be ruler of My people Israel, and I have been with you wherever you went, and have cut down all your enemies before you. Moreover, I will give you great renown like that of the greatest men on earth. I will establish a home for My people Israel and will plant them firm, so that they shall dwell secure and shall tremble no more. Evil men shall not oppress them any more as in the past, ever since I appointed chieftains over My people Israel. I will give you safety from all your enemies.

The Lord declares to you that He, the Lord, will establish a house for you. When your days are done and you lie with your fathers, I will raise up your offspring after you, one of your own issue, and I will establish his kingship. He shall build a house for my name, and I will establish his royal throne forever. I will be a father to him, and he shall be a son to Me. When he does wrong, I will chastise him with the rod of men and the affliction of mortals; but I will never withdraw My favor from him as I withdrew it from Saul, whom I removed to make room for you. Your house and your kingship shall ever be secure before you; your throne shall be established forever.

Source: 2 Samuel 7:8–16, from *Tanakh: The Holy Scriptures.*

PSALMS ASCRIBED TO DAVID

The Book of Psalms is a collection of 150 songs and prayers written over a 600-year period, many after the Babylonian exile. The book may have taken its final form under the editorship of Ezra and sometimes is referred to as the hymn book of the second temple. Although the authorship of most of the psalms is uncertain, 73 are ascribed in the text to David and are traditionally said to reflect happy or troubled periods of his life. The psalms are classified as they relate to the themes of deliverance, penitence, praise, pilgrimages, historical episodes, and messianic hope. The following is a selection of psalms of David.

8.

O Lord, our Lord,
How majestic is Your name throughout the earth,
You who have covered the heavens with Your splendor!
From the mouths of infants and sucklings
You have founded strength on account of Your foes,
to put an end to enemy and avenger.
When I behold Your heavens, the work of Your fingers,
the moon and stars that You set in place,
what is man that You have been mindful of him,
mortal man that You have taken note of him,
that You have made him little less than divine,
and adorned him with glory and majesty;
You have made him master over Your handiwork,
laying the world at his feet,
sheep and oxen, all of them,
and wild beasts, too;
the birds of the heavens, the fish of the sea,
whatever travels the paths of the seas.
O Lord, our Lord, how majestic is Your name throughout the earth!

23.

The Lord is my shepherd;
I lack nothing.
He makes me lie down in green pastures;
He leads me to water in places of repose;
He renews my life;

He guides me in right paths
as befits His name.
Though I walk through a valley of deepest darkness,
I fear no harm, for You are with me;
Your rod and Your staff—they comfort me.
You spread a table for me in full view of my enemies;
You anoint my head with oil;
my drink is abundant.
Only goodness and steadfast love shall pursue me
all the days of my life,
and I shall dwell in the house of the Lord
For many long years.

27.

The Lord is my light and my help;
whom would I fear?
The Lord is the stronghold of my life,
whom should I dread?
When evil men assail me
to devour my flesh—
it is they, my foes and my enemies,
who stumble and fall.
Should an army besiege me,
my heart would have no fear;
should war beset me,
still would I be confident.
One thing I ask of the Lord,
only that do I seek:
to live in the house of the Lord
all the days of my life,
to gaze upon the beauty of the Lord,
to frequent His temple.
He will shelter me in His pavilion
on an evil day,
grant me the protection of His tent,
raise me high upon a rock.
Now is my head high
over my enemies roundabout;
I sacrifice in His tent with shouts of joy,
singing and chanting a hymn to the Lord.
Hear, O Lord, when I cry aloud;
have mercy on me, answer me.
In Your behalf my heart says:
seek My face!
O Lord, I seek Your face.
Do not hide Your face from me;
do not thrust aside Your servant in anger;
You have ever been my help.
Do not forsake me, do not abandon me,
O God, my deliverer.
Though my father and mother abandon me,

the Lord will take me in.
Show me Your way, O Lord,
and lead me on a level path
because of my watchful foes.
Do not subject me to the will of my foes,
for false witnesses and unjust accusers have appeared against me.
Had I not the assurance that I would enjoy the goodness of the Lord in the land of the living. . . .
Look to the Lord;
be strong and of good courage!
O look to the Lord!

32.

Happy is he whose transgression is forgiven,
whose sin is covered over.
Happy the man whom the Lord does not hold guilty,
and in whose spirit there is no deceit.
As long as I said nothing,
my limbs wasted away
from my anguished roaring all day long.
For night and day
Your hand lay heavy on me;
my vigor waned
as in the summer drought.
Then I acknowledged my sin to you;
I did not cover up my guilt;
I resolved, "I will confess my transgressions to the Lord,"
and You forgave the guilt of my sin.
Therefore let every faithful man pray to You
upon discovering [his sin]
that the rushing mighty waters not overtake him.
You are my shelter;
You preserve me from distress;
You surround me with the joyous shouts of deliverance.
Let me enlighten you
and show you which way to go;
let me offer counsel; my eye is on you.
Be not like a senseless horse or mule
whose movement must be curbed by bit and bridle,
far be it from you!
Many are the torments of the wicked,
but he who trusts in the Lord
shall be surrounded with favor.
Rejoice in the Lord and exult, O you righteous;
shout for joy, all upright men!

51.

Have mercy upon me, O God,
as befits Your faithfulness;
in keeping with Your abundant compassion,

blot out my transgressions.
Wash me thoroughly of my iniquity,
and purify me of my sin;
for I recognize my transgressions,
and am ever conscious of my sin.
Against You alone have I sinned,
and done what is evil in Your sight;
so You are just in Your sentence,
and right in Your judgment.
Indeed I was born with iniquity;
with sin my mother conceived me.
Indeed You desire truth about that which is hidden;
teach me wisdom about secret things.
Purge me with hyssop till I am pure;
wash me till I am whiter than snow.
Let me hear tidings of joy and gladness;
let the bones You have crushed exult.
Hide Your face from my sins;
blot out all my iniquities.
Fashion a pure heart for me, O God;
create in me a steadfast spirit.
Do not cast me out of your presence,
or take Your holy spirit away from me.
Let me again rejoice in Your help;
let a vigorous spirit sustain me.
I will teach transgressors Your ways,
That sinners may return to you.
Save me from bloodguilt,
O God, God, my deliverer,
that I may sing forth Your beneficence.
O Lord, open my lips,
and let my mouth declare Your praise.
You do not want me to bring sacrifices;
you do not desire burnt offerings;
True sacrifice to God is a contrite spirit;
God, You will not despise
a contrite and crushed heart.
May it please You to make Zion prosper;
rebuild the walls of Jerusalem.
Then you will want sacrifices offered in righteousness,
burnt and whole offerings;
the bulls will be offered on Your altar.

Source: Psalms 8, 23, 27, 32, 51, from *Tanakh: The Holy Scriptures.*

SOLOMON'S TEMPLE

Israel's glory peaked during the reign of King Solomon, David's son. Its borders extended farther than they ever would again (though not as far as under David), and Israel was a key player in ancient Near Eastern politics. The jewel in the crown of

Solomon's achievements was his temple, said to have taken thirteen years to complete. According to the Deuteronomistic History, all sacrifices were to be performed only at the temple in Jerusalem; thus, the temple became the focus of all religious activity in Israel. The following describes the extent and wealth of Solomon's kingdom, his wisdom, and his construction of the temple.

Judah and Israel were as numerous as the sands of the sea; they ate and drank and were content. . . .

Solomon's rule extended over all the kingdoms of the Euphrates to the land of the Philistines and the boundary of Egypt. They brought Solomon tribute and were subject to him all his life. Solomon's daily provisions consisted of 30 *kors* of semolina, and 60 *kors* of [ordinary] flour, 10 fattened oxen, 20 pasture-fed oxen, and 100 sheep and goats, besides deer and gazelles, roebucks and fatted geese. For he controlled the whole region west of the Euphrates—all the kings west of the Euphrates, from Tiphsah to Gaza—and he had peace on all his borders roundabout. All the days of Solomon, Judah and Israel from Dan to Beer-sheba dwelt in safety, everyone under his own vine and under his own fig tree. Solomon had 40,000 stalls of horses for his chariotry and 12,000 horsemen.

All those prefects, each during his month, would furnish provisions for King Solomon and for all who were admitted to King Solomon's table; they did not fall short in anything. They would also, each in his turn, deliver barley and straw for the horses and the swift steeds to the places where they were stationed.

The Lord endowed Solomon with wisdom and discernment in great measure, with understanding as vast as the sands on the seashore. Solomon's wisdom was greater than the wisdom of all the Kedemites and than all the wisdom of the Egyptians. He was the wisest of all men: [wiser] than Ethan the Ezrahite, and Heman, Chalkol, and Darda the sons of Mahol. His fame spread among all the surrounding nations. He composed three thousand proverbs, and his songs numbered one thousand and five. He discoursed about trees, from the cedar in Lebanon to the hyssop that grows out of the wall; and he discoursed about beasts, birds, creeping things, and fishes. Men of all peoples came to hear Solomon's wisdom, [sent] by all the kins of the earth who had heard of his wisdom.

King Hiram of Tyre sent his officials to Solomon when he heard that he had been anointed king in place of his father; for Hiram had always been a friend of David. Solomon sent this message to Hiram: "You know that my father David could not build a house for the name of the Lord his God because of the enemies that encompassed him, until the Lord had placed them under the soles of his feet. But now the Lord my God has given me respite all around; there is no adversary and not mischance. And so I propose to build a house for the name of the Lord my God, as the Lord promised my father David, saying, 'Your son, whom I will set on your throne in your place, shall build the house for My name.' Please, then, give orders for cedars to be cut for me in the Lebanon. My servants will work with yours, and I will pay you any wages you may ask for your servants; for as you know, there is none among us who knows how to cut timber like the Sidonians."

When Hiram heard Solomon's message, he was overjoyed. "Praised be the Lord this day," he said, "for granting David a wise son to govern this great people." So Hiram sent word to Solomon: "I have your message; I will supply all the cedar and cypress logs you require."

. . . King Solomon imposed forced labor on all Israel; the levy came to 30,000 men. He sent them to the Lebanon in shifts of 10,000 a month: they would spend one month in the Lebanon and two months at home. Adoniram was in charge of the forced labor. Solomon also had 70,000 porters and 80,000 quarriers in the hills, apart from Solomon's 3,300 officials who were in charge of the work and supervised the gangs doing the work.

The king ordered huge blocks of choice stone to be quarried, so that the foundations of the house might be laid with hewn stones. Solomon's masons, Hiram's masons, and the men of Gebal shaped them. Thus the timber and the stones for building the House were made ready.

. . . When Solomon had completed the construction of the House, he paneled the walls of the house on the inside with planks of cedar. He also overlaid the walls on the inside with wood, from the floor of the House to the ceiling. And he overlaid the floor of the House with planks of cypress. Twenty cubits from the rear of the House, he built [a partition] of cedar planks from the floor to the walls; he furnished its interior to serve as a Shrine, as the Holy of Holies. The front part of the House, that is, the Great Hall, measured 40 cubits. The cedar of the interior of the House had carvings of gourds and calyxes; it was all cedar, no stone was exposed. In the innermost part of the House, he fixed a Shrine in which to place the Ark of the Lord's Covenant. The interior of the Shrine was 20 cubits long, 20 cubits wide, and 20 cubits high. He overlaid it with solid gold; he similarly overlaid [its] cedar altar. Solomon overlaid the interior of the House with solid gold; and he inserted golden chains into the door of the Shrine. He overlaid [the Shrine] with gold, so that the entire House was overlaid with gold; he even overlaid with gold the entire altar of the Shrine. And so the entire House was completed.

Source: 1 Kings 4:20; 5:1–20, 27–33; 6:14–22, from *Tanakh: The Holy Scriptures.*

PROVERBS ATTRIBUTED TO SOLOMON

In the preceding passage, Solomon is said to have been the wisest of all men and author of 3,000 proverbs. The Book of Proverbs contains seven distinct collections of sayings, the first four of which are traditionally attributed to Solomon. Compiled during the time of Ezra, Proverbs contains sayings from throughout periods of the united and divided kingdom, in the form of two-line sentences about an aspect of human experience, usually secular. Three literary styles are exhibited in the proverbs: synonymous parallelism, in which the second line repeats the content of the first; antithetic parallelism, in which good behavior in the first line is contrasted with bad behavior in the second line; and ascending parallelism, in which the second line completes the train of thought in the first line. The following is from the second collection within Proverbs—thought to be the oldest part of the book—titled "The Proverbs of Solomon."

1. A gentle response allays wrath;
A harsh word provokes anger.
2. The tongue of the wise produces much knowledge,
But the mouth of dullards pours out folly.
3. The eyes of the Lord are everywhere,
Observing the bad and the good.
4. A healing tongue is a tree of life,
But a devious one makes for a broken spirit.
5. A fool spurns the discipline of his father,
But one who heeds reproof becomes clever.
6. In the house of the righteous there is much treasure,
But in the harvest of the wicked there is trouble.
7. The lips of the wise disseminate knowledge;
Not so the minds of dullards.
8. The sacrifice of the wicked is an abomination to the Lord,
But the prayer of the upright pleases Him.
9. The way of the wicked is an abomination to the Lord,
But he loves him who pursues righteousness.
10. Discipline seems bad to him who forsakes the way;
He who spurns reproof will die.
11. Sheol and Abaddon lie exposed to the Lord,
How much more the minds of men!
12. The scoffer dislikes being reproved;
He will not resort to the wise.
13. A joyful heart makes a cheerful face;
A sad heart makes a despondent mood.
14. The mind of a prudent man seeks knowledge;
The mouth of the dullard pursues folly.
15. All the days of a poor man are wretched,
But contentment is a feast without end.
16. Better a little with fear of the Lord
Than great wealth with confusion.
17. Better a meal of vegetables where there is love
Than a fattened ox where there is hate.
18. A hot-tempered man provokes a quarrel;
A patient man calms strife.
19. The way of a lazy man is like a hedge of thorns,
But the path of the upright is paved.
20. A wise son makes his father happy;
A fool of a man humiliates his mother.
21. Folly is joy to one devoid of sense;
A prudent man walks a straight path.
22. Plans are foiled for want of counsel,
But they succeed through many advisers.
23. A ready response is a joy to a man,
And how good is a world rightly timed!

24. For an intelligent man the path of life leads upward,
    In order to avoid Sheol below.
25. The Lord will tear down the house of the proud,
    But he will establish the homestead of the widow.
26. Evil thoughts are an abomination to the Lord,
    But pleasant words are pure.
27. He who pursues ill-gotten gain makes trouble for his household;
    He who spurns gifts will live long.
28. The heart of the righteous man rehearses his answer,
    But the mouth of the wicked blurts out evil things.
29. The Lord is far from the wicked,
    But He hears the prayer of the righteous.
30. What brightens the eye gladdens the heart;
    Good news puts fat on the bones.
31. He whose ear heeds the discipline of life
    Lodges among the wise.
32. He who spurns discipline hates himself;
    He who heeds reproof gains understanding.
33. The fear of the Lord is the discipline of wisdom;
    Humility precedes honor.

Source: Proverbs 15, from *Tanakh: The Holy Scriptures.*

DIVIDED KINGDOM AND EXILE

ELIJAH VERSUS THE PRIESTS OF ASHERAH AND BAAL

After Solomon's reign, Israel divided into northern and southern kingdoms. The explanation given for this in the Deuteronomistic History is Solomon's continual worship of regional deities. Writers of the Tanakh *condemn these worship practices and praise the Yahwist prophets and kings who challenge them. Israelite worship of the goddess Asherah is of particular interest. Asherah is the wife of the Canaanite high god, El, and in some popular Israelite religion may have been a consort of Yahweh. Worship rituals of Asherah center on sacred pillars, which in the Deuteronomistic History are strictly forbidden (Deuteronomy 16:21–22). The following story from the Deuteronomistic History dramatically presents a showdown between the prophets of Asherah and Baal on one side, and the prophet Elijah on the other. Elijah is the lone defender of Yahweh in the northern kingdom at this time.*

16. . . . Ahab son of Omri became king over Israel in the thirty-eighth year of King Asa of Judah, and Ahab son of Omri reigned over Israel in Samaria for twenty-two years. Ahab son of Omri did what was displeasing to the Lord, more than all who preceded him. Not content to follow the sins of Jeroboam son of Nebat, he took a wife Jezebel daughter of King Ethball of the Phoenicians, and he went and served Baal and worshipped him. He erected an altar to Baal in the temple of

Baal which he built in Samaria. Ahab also made a sacred post. Ahab did more to vex the Lord, the God of Israel, than all the kings of Israel who preceded him.

17. Elijah the Tisbite, an inhabitant of Gilead, said to Ahab, "As the Lord lives, the God of Israel whom I serve, there will be no dew or rain except at my bidding." . . .
18. Much later, in the third year, a word of the Lord came to Elijah: "Go, appear before Ahab; then I will send rain upon the earth." Thereupon Elijah set out to appear before Ahab. . . .

When Ahab caught sight of Elijah, Ahab said to him, "Is that you, you troubler of Israel?" He retorted, "It is not I who have brought trouble on Israel, but you and your father's House, by forsaking the commandments of the Lord and going after the Baalim. Now summon all Israel to join me at Mount Carmel, together with the four hundred and fifty prophets of Baal and the four hundred prophets of Asherah, who eat at Jezebel's table.

Ahab sent orders to all the Israelites and gathered the prophets at Mount Carmel. Elijah approached all the people and said, "How long will you keep hopping between two opinions? If the Lord is God, follow Him; and if Baal, follow him!" But the people answered him not a word. Then Elijah said to the people, "I am the only prophet of the Lord left, while the prophets of Baal are four hundred and fifty men. Let two young bulls be given to us. Let them choose one bull, cut it up, and lay it on the wood, but let them not apply fire; I will prepare the other bull, and lay it on the wood, and will not apply fire. You will then invoke your god by name, and I will invoke the Lord by name; and let us agree: the god who responds with fire, that one is God." And all the people answered, "Very good!"

Elijah said to the prophets of Baal, "Choose one bull and prepare it first, for you are the majority; invoke your god by name, but apply no fire." They took the bull that was given them; they prepared it, and invoked Baal by name from morning until noon, shouting, "O Baal, answer us!" But there was no sound, and none who responded; so they performed a hopping dance about the altar that had been set up. When noon came, Elijah mocked them, saying, "Shout louder! After all, he is a god. But he may be in conversation, he may be detained, or he may be on a journey, or perhaps he is asleep and will wake up." So they shouted louder, and gashed themselves with knives and spears, according to their practice, until the blood streamed over them. When noon passed, they kept raving until the hour of presenting the meal offering. Still there was no sound, and none who responded or heeded.

Then Elijah said to all the people, "Come closer to me"; and all the people came closer to him. He repaired the damaged altar of the Lord. Then Elijah took twelve stones, corresponding to the number of the tribes of the sons of Jacob—to whom the word of the Lord had come: "Israel shall be your name"—and with the stones he built an altar in the name of the Lord. Around the altar he made a trench large enough for two *seahs* of seed. He laid out the wood, and he cut up the bull and laid it on the wood. And he said, "Fill four jars with water and pour it over the burnt offering and the wood." Then he said, "Do it a second time"; and they did it a second time. "Do it a third time," he said; and they did it a third time. The water ran down around the altar, and even the trench was filled with water.

When it was time to present the meal offering, the prophet Elijah came forward and said, "O Lord, God of Abraham, Isaac, and Israel! Let it be known today that You are God in Israel and that I am Your servant, and that I have done all these things at Your bidding. Answer me, O Lord, answer me, that this people may know that You, O Lord, are God; for You have turned their hearts backward."

Then fire from the Lord descended and consumed the burnt offering, the wood, the stones, and the earth; and it licked up the water that was in the trench. When they saw this, all the people flung themselves on their faces and cried out: "The Lord alone is God, The Lord alone is God!"

Source: 1 Kings 16:29–33; 17:1; 18:1–2, 17–40, from *Tanakh: The Holy Scriptures*.

ISAIAH'S WARNING TO JUDAH

In 722 the northern kingdom fell to the Mesopotamian superpower of the time, Assyria. Although the southern kingdom of Judah survived Assyrian encroachment, it was embroiled in foreign political conflicts. The prophet Isaiah was an advisor to two kings of the southern kingdom at the time: Ahaz and his successor Hezekiah. Under the leadership of King Hezekiah, the Kingdom of Judah survived the Assyrian attack and continued for another 150 years. His advice to both kings was the same: Do not participate in anti-Assyrian conspiracies, but trust in God for deliverance. The Book of Isaiah is an anthology of prophetic writings from Isaiah's time through the Babylonian exile. Of the book's 66 chapters, Isaiah's own words are confined to Chapters 1–11 and 28–32. Chapter 1 below expresses Isaiah's indictment against the people of Judah: They have forsaken God and risk being purged. Chapter 6 is Isaiah's call to prophethood.

1. The prophecies of Isaiah son of Amoz, who prophesied concerning Judah and Jerusalem in the reigns of Uzziah, Jotham, Ahaz, and Hezekiah, kings of Judah.

   Hear, O heavens, and give ear, O earth,
   For the Lord has spoken:
   I reared children and brought them up—
   And they have rebelled against Me!
   An ox knows its owner,
   An ass its master's crib:
   Israel does not know,
   My people takes no thought.

Ah, sinful nation!
People laden with iniquity!
Brood of evildoers!
Depraved children!
They have forsaken the Lord,
Spurned the Holy One of Israel,
Turned their backs [on Him].

Why do you seek further beatings,
That you continue to offend?
Every head is ailing,
And every heart is sick.
From head to foot
No spot is sound:
All bruises, and welts,
And festering sores—
Not pressed out, not bound up,
Not softened with oil.
Your land is a waste,
Your cities burnt down;
Before your eyes, the yield of your soil
Is consumed by strangers—
A wasteland as overthrown by strangers!
Fair Zion is left
Like a booth in a vineyard,
Like a hut in a cucumber field,
Like a city beleaguered. Had not the Lord of Hosts
Left us some survivors,
We should be like Sodom,
Another Gomorrah. . . .

"Come, let us reach an understanding,—says the Lord.
Be your sins like crimson,
They can turn snow-white;
Be they red as died wool,
They can become like fleece."
If, then, you agree and give heed,
You will eat the good things of the earth;
But if you refuse and disobey,
You will be devoured [by] the sword.
For it was the Lord who spoke.

6. In the year that King Uzziah died, I beheld my Lord seated on a high and lofty throne; and the skirts of His robe filled the Temple. Seraphs stood in attendance on Him. Each of them had six wings: with two he covered his face, with two he covered his legs, and with two he would fly.

And one would call to the other,
"Holy, holy, holy!
The Lord of Hosts!
His presence fills all the earth!"

The doorposts would shake at the sound of the one who called, and the House kept filling with smoke. I cried,

"Woe is me; I am lost!
For I am a man of unclean lips
And I live among a people of unclean lips;
Yet my own eyes have beheld
The King Lord of Hosts."

Then one of the seraphs flew over to me with a live coal, which he had taken from the altar with a pair of tongs. He touched it to my lips and declared,

Now that this has touched your lips,
Your guilt shall depart
And your sin be purged away.

Then I heard the voice of my Lord saying, "Whom shall I send? Who will go for us?" And I said, "Here am I; send me." And He said, "Go say to that people:

'Hear, indeed, but do not understand;
See, indeed, but do not grasp'
Dull that people's mind,
Stop its ears,
And seal its eyes—
Lest, seeing with its eyes
And hearing with its ears,
It also grasp with its mind,
And repent and save itself."

I asked, "How long, my Lord?" And He replied:

"Till towns lie waste without inhabitants
And houses without people,
And the ground lies waste and desolate—
For the Lord will banish the population—
And deserted sites are many
In the midst of the land.
But while a tenth part yet remains in it,
it shall repent.
It shall be ravaged like the terebinth and the oak,
of which stumps are left
even when they are felled:
its stump shall be a holy seed."

Source: Isaiah 1:1–9, 18–21; 6, from *Tanakh: The Holy Scriptures.*

BABYLONIAN CONQUEST AND EXILE

Around 610 B.C.E., a group of Semites in Babylon, the Chaldeans, overthrew the Assyrians and formed a new Babylonian Empire. At first Judah's king paid tribute to the

Empire, but he later rebelled, thinking that Egypt would come to his defense if necessary. In retaliation, the Babylonian army marched into Judah, looted the temple and royal treasury, and exiled the royal family and upper-class Israelites to Babylon. The Babylonians appointed Zedekiah as a puppet king, but, when pressured by the Egyptians, he too rebelled. In 586 B.C.E., the Babylonian army again marched into Judah, this time destroying Jerusalem and the temple. The following recounts the tragedy of the exile.

24. . . . Jehoiachin was eighteen years old when he became king, and he reigned three months in Jerusalem; his mother's name was Nehushta daughter of Elnathan of Jerusalem. He did what was displeasing to the Lord, just as his father had done. At that time, the troops of King Nebuchadnezzar of Babylon marched against Jerusalem, and the city came under siege. King Nebuchadnezzar of Babylon advanced against the city while his troops were besieging it. Thereupon King Jehoiachin of Judah, along with his mother, and his courtiers, commanders, and officers, surrendered to the king of Babylon. The king of Babylon took him captive in the eighth year of his reign. He carried off from Jerusalem all the treasures of the House of the Lord and the treasures of the royal palace; he stripped off all the golden decorations in the Temple of the Lord—which King Solomon of Israel had made—as the Lord had warned. He exiled all of Jerusalem: all the commanders and all the warriors—ten thousand exiles—as well as all the craftsmen and smiths; only the poorest people in the land were left. He deported Jehoiachin to Babylon; and the king's mother and wives and officers and the notables of the land were brought as exiles from Jerusalem to Babylon. All the able men, to the number of seven thousand—all of them warriors, trained for battle—and a thousand craftsmen and smiths were brought to Babylon as exiles by the king of Babylon. And the king of Babylon appointed Mattaniah, Jehoiachin's uncle, king in his place, changing his name to Zedekiah.

    Zedekiah was twenty-one years old when he became king, and he reigned eleven years in Jerusalem; his mother's name was Hamutal daughter of Jeremiah of Libnah. He did what was displeasing to the Lord, just as Jehoiakim had done. Indeed, Jerusalem and Judah were a cause of anger for the Lord, so that He cast them out of His presence.

25. Zedekiah rebelled against the king of Babylon. And in the ninth year of his reign, on the tenth day of the tenth month, Nebuchadnezzar moved against Jerusalem with his whole army. He besieged it; and they built towers against it all around. The city continued in a state of siege until the eleventh year of King Zedekiah. By the ninth day [of the fourth month] the famine had become acute in the city; there was no food left for the common people.

    Then [the wall of] the city was breached. All the soldiers [left the city] by night through the gate between the double walls, which is near the king's garden—the Chaldeans were all around the city; and [the king] set out for the Arabah. But the Chaldean troops pursued the king, and they overtook him in the steppes of Jericho as his entire force left him and scattered. They captured the king and brought him before the king of Babylon at Riblah; and they put him on trial. They slaughtered Zedekiah's sons before his eyes; then Zedekiah's eyes were put out. He was chained in bronze fetters and he was brought to Babylon.

On the seventh day of the fifth month—that was the nineteenth year of King Nebuchadnezzar of Babylon—Nebuzaradan, the chief of the guards, an officer of the king of Babylon, came to Jerusalem. He burned the House of the Lord, the king's palace, and all the houses of Jerusalem; he burned down the house of every notable person. The entire Chaldean force that was with the chief of the guard tore down the walls of Jerusalem on every side. The remnant of the people that was left in the city, the defectors who had gone over to the king of Babylon—and the remnant of the population—were taken into exile by Nebuzaradan, the chief of the guards. But some of the poorest in the land were left by the chief of the guards, to be vinedressers and field hands.

The Chaldeans broke up the bronze columns of the House of the Lord, the stands, and the bronze tank that was in the House of the Lord; and they carried the bronze away to Babylon. They also took all the pails, scrapers, snuffers, ladles, and all the other bronze vessels used in the service. The chief of the guards took whatever was of gold and whatever was of silver: firepans and sprinkling bowls. The two columns, the one tank, and the stands that Solomon provided for the House of the Lord—all these objects contained bronze beyond weighing. The one column was eighteen cubits high. It had a bronze capital above it; the height of the capital was three cubits; and there was a meshwork [decorated] with pomegranates about the capital, all made of bronze. And the like was true of the other column with its meshwork.

Source: 2 Kings 24:8–20, 25:1–17, from *Tanakh: The Holy Scriptures.*

REMEMBERING ZION

Captive in Babylon, the psalmist in the following passage reflects nostalgically on the beauty of Zion, referring to the city of Jerusalem, possibly the Temple Mount.

By the rivers of Babylon,
there we sat,
sat and wept,
as we thought of Zion.
There on the poplars
we hung up our lyres,
for our captors asked us there for songs,
our tormentors, for amusement,
"Sing us one of the songs of Zion."
How can we sing a song of the Lord
on alien soil?
If I forget you, O Jerusalem,
let my right hand wither;
let my tongue stick to my palate
if I cease to think of you,

if I do not keep Jerusalem in memory
even at my happiest hour.
Remember, O Lord, against the Edomites
the day of Jerusalem's fall;
how they cried, "Strip her, strip her
to her very foundations!"
Fair Babylon, you predator,
a blessing on him who repays you in kind
what you have inflicted on us;
a blessing on him who seizes your babies
and dashes them against the rocks!

Source: Psalms 137, from *Tanakh: The Holy Scriptures.*

RETURN FROM EXILE AND RESTORATION

When Persian King Cyrus overthrew the Babylonian Empire in 539 B.C.E., he reversed the policy of exiling foreign captives as practiced by the Babylonians and, earlier, by the Assyrians. With his encouragement, 40,000 exiled Jews returned to their homeland. Cyrus encouraged the rebuilding of Jerusalem's temple and returned to the Jews the temple treasures that had been taken by the Babylonians.

1. In the first year of King Cyrus of Persia, when the word of the Lord spoken by Jeremiah was fulfilled, the Lord roused the spirit of King Cyrus of Persia to issue a proclamation throughout his realm by word of mouth and in writing as follows:

   "Thus said King Cyrus of Persia: The Lord God of Heaven has given me all the kingdoms of the earth and has charged me with building Him a house in Jerusalem, which is in Judah. Any one of you of all His people—may his God be with him, and let him go up to Jerusalem that is in Judah and build the House of the Lord God of Israel, the God that is in Jerusalem; and all who stay behind, wherever he may be living, let the people of his place assist him with silver, gold, goods, and livestock, besides the freewill offering to the House of God that is in Jerusalem."

   So the chiefs of the clans of Judah and Benjamin, and the priests and Levites, all whose spirit had been roused by God, got ready to go up to build the House of the Lord that is in Jerusalem. All their neighbors supported them with silver vessels, with gold, with goods, with livestock, and with precious objects, besides what had been given as a freewill offering. King Cyrus of Persia released the vessels of the Lord's house which Nebuchadnezzar had taken away from Jerusalem and had put in the house of his God. These King Cyrus of Persia released through the office of Mithredath the treasurer, who gave an inventory of them to Sheshbazzar the prince of Judah. This is the inventory: 30 gold basins, 1,000 silver basins, 29 knives, 30 gold bowls, 410 silver doubled bowls, 1,000 other vessels, in all, 5,400 gold and silver vessels. Sheshbazzar brought all these back when the exiles came back from Babylon to Jerusalem. . . .

3. When the seventh month arrived—the Israelites being settled in their towns—the entire people assembled as one man in Jerusalem. Then Jeshua son of Jozadak and his brother priests, and Zerubbabel son of Shealtiel and his brothers set to and built the altar of the God of Israel to offer burnt offerings upon it as is written in the Teaching of Moses, the man of God. They set up the Altar on its site because they were in fear of the peoples of the land, and they offered burnt offerings on it to the Lord, burnt offerings each morning and evening. Then they celebrated the festival of Tabernacles as is written, with its daily burnt offerings in the proper quantities, on each day as is prescribed for it, followed by the regular burnt offering and the offerings for the new moons and for all the sacred fixed times of the Lord, and whatever freewill offerings were made to the Lord. From the first day of the seventh month they began to make burnt offerings to the Lord, though the foundation of the Temple of the Lord had not been laid. They paid the hewers and craftsmen with money, and the Sidonians and Tyrians with food, drink, and oil to bring cedarwood from Lebanon by sea to Joppa, in accord with the authorization granted them by King Cyrus of Persia.

In the second year after their arrival at the House of God, at Jerusalem, in the second month, Zerubbabel son of Shealtiel and Jeshua son of Jozadak, and the rest of their brother priests and Levites, and all who had come from the captivity to Jerusalem, as their first step appointed Levites from the age of twenty and upward to supervise the work of the House of the Lord. Jeshua, his sons and brothers, Kadmiel and his sons, the sons of Judah, together were appointed in charge of those who did the work in the House of God; also the sons of Henadad, their sons and brother Levites.

When the builders had laid the foundation of the Temple of the Lord, priests in their vestments with trumpets, and Levites sons of Asaph with cymbals were stationed to give praise to the Lord, as King David of Israel had ordained. They sang songs extolling and praising the Lord, "For He is good, His steadfast love for Israel is eternal." All the people raised a great shout extolling the Lord because the foundation of the House of the Lord had been laid. Many of the priests and Levites and the chiefs of the clans, the old men who had seen the first house, wept loudly at the sight of the founding of this house. Many others shouted joyously at the top of their voices. The people could not distinguish the shouts of joy from the people's weeping, for the people raised a great shout, the sound of which could be heard from afar.

Source: Ezra 1, 3, from *Tanakh: The Holy Scriptures.*

ESTHER

The Book of Esther is one of two books of the Tanakh *focusing on the life of a Jewish heroine (the book of Ruth is the other). Esther is queen to Persian King Ahasuerus (Xerxes I), one of Cyrus's successors, reigning from 486 to 465 B.C.E. Unknown to the king, Esther is a Jew. When her cousin Mordecai refuses to bow to Haman, a member of the court, for religious reasons, Haman is incensed and plots to have Mordecai, along with the rest of the Jews in the region, executed. The king sanctions Haman's plan. When Mordecai pleads with Esther to speak to the king on behalf of the Jews, she plans a banquet for the king during which she reveals Haman's plot. Haman is hanged on the very gallows he had prepared for Mordecai. The Jews are granted the right to defend themselves against their anti-Jewish enemies. The story of Esther is the basis for the Jewish feast Purim.*

3. Some time afterward, King Ahasuerus promoted Haman son of Hammedatha the Agagite; he advanced him and seated him higher than any of his fellow officials. All the king's courtiers in the palace gate knelt and bowed low to Haman, for such was the king's order concerning him; but Mordecai would not kneel or bow low. Then the king's courtiers who were in the palace gate said to Mordecai, "Why do you disobey the king's order?" When they spoke to him day after day and he would not listen to them, they told Haman, in order to see whether Mordecai's resolve would prevail; for he had explained to them that he was a Jew. When Haman saw that Mordecai would not kneel or bow low to him, Haman was filled with rage. But he disdained to lay hands on Mordecai alone; having been told who Mordecai's people were, Haman plotted to do away with all the Jews, Mordecai's people, throughout the kingdom of Ahasuerus.

   In the first month, that is, the month of Nisan, in the twelfth year of King Ahasuerus, *pur*—which means "the lot"—was cast before Haman concerning every day and every month, [until it fell on] the twelfth month, that is, the month of Adar. Haman then said to King Ahasuerus, "There is a certain people, scattered and dispersed among the other peoples in all the provinces of your realm, whose laws are different from those of any other people and who do not obey the king's laws; and it is not in Your Majesty's interest to tolerate them. If it pleases Your Majesty, let an edict be drawn for their destruction, and I will pay ten thousand talents of silver to the stewards for deposit in the royal treasury." Thereupon the king removed his signet ring from his hand and gave it to Haman son of Hammedatha the Agagite, the foe of the Jews. And the king said, "The money and the people are yours to do with as you see fit.". . .

7. So the king and Haman came to feast with Queen Esther. On the second day, the king again asked Esther at the wine feast, "What is your wish, Queen Esther? It shall be granted you. And what is your request? Even to half the kingdom, it shall be fulfilled." Queen Esther replied: "If Your Majesty will do me the favor, and if it pleases Your Majesty, let my life be granted me as my wish, and my people as my request. For we have been sold, my people and I, to be destroyed, massacred, and exterminated. Had we only been sold as bondmen and bondwomen, I would have kept silent; for the adversary is not worthy of the king's trouble."

Thereupon King Ahasuerus demanded of Queen Esther, "Who is he and where is he who dared to do this?" "The adversary and enemy," replied Esther, "is this evil Haman!" And Haman cringed in terror before the king and the queen. The king, in his fury, left the wine feast for the palace garden, while Haman remained to plead with Queen Esther for his life; for he saw that the king was resolved to destroy him. When the king returned from the palace garden to the banquet room, Haman was lying prostrate on the couch on which Esther reclined. "Does he mean," cried the king, "to ravish the queen in my own palace?" No sooner did these words leave the king's lips than Haman's face was covered. Then Harbonah, one of the eunuchs in attendance on the king, said, "What is more, a stake is standing at Haman's house, fifty cubits high, which Haman made for Mordecai—the man whose words saved the king." "Impale him on it!" the king ordered. So they impaled Haman on the stake which he had put up for Mordecai, and the king's fury abated.

Source: Esther 3:7–11; 7, from *Tanakh: The Holy Scriptures.*

EZRA AND THE LAW

The concluding events of the Tanakh *focus on the activities of Ezra and Nehemiah, found in the books that bear their names. Ezra was a Babylonian-born Jewish priest devoted to the Law of Moses. In 458* B.C.E.*, he petitioned Artaxerxes, the reigning king of the Persian Empire, to lead another migration of Jews back to their homeland. Artaxerxes agreed and empowered him to make political and religious reforms as Ezra saw fit. On arrival, Ezra was distressed to see that the returning Jews before him had intermarried, and he proclaimed that 114 priests and laymen should have their marriages annulled. Thirteen years after Ezra's return, Nehemiah, a Jewish cupbearer to the Persian king, was granted permission by the king to rebuild the walls of Jerusalem, still in ruins from the Babylonian invasion. A gifted administrator, Nehemiah completed the project in fifty-two days, even in the face of opposition from neighboring provinces. Shortly after completion of the walls, the Jews celebrated a series of feasts, during which Ezra publicly read and interpreted the scrolls of Moses. The following recounts Ezra's reading of the scrolls.*

When the seventh month arrived—the Israelites being [settled] in their towns—the entire people assembled as one man in the square before the Water Gate, and they asked Ezra the scribe to bring the scroll of the Teaching of Moses with which the Lord had charged Israel. On the first day of the seventh month, Ezra the priest brought the Teaching before the congregation, men and women and all who could listen with understanding. He read from it, facing the square before the Water Gate, from the first light until midday, to the men and the women and those who could understand; the ears of all the people were given to the scroll of the Teaching.

Ezra the scribe stood upon a wooden tower made for the purpose, and beside him stood Mattithaih, Shema, Anaiah, Uriah, Hilkiah, and Maaseiah at his right, and at his left Pedaiah, Mishael, Malchijah, Hashum, Hashbaddanah, Zechariah, and Meshullam. Ezra opened the scroll in the sight of all the people, for he was above all the people; as he opened it, all the people stood up. Ezra blessed the Lord, the great God, and all the people answered, "Amen, Amen," with hands upraised. Then they bowed their heads and prostrated themselves before the Lord with their faces to the ground. Jeshua, Bani, Sherebiah, Jamin, Akkub, Shabbethai, Hodiah, Maaseiah, Kelita, Azariah, Jozabad, Hanan, Pelaiah, and the Levites explained the Teaching to the People, while the people stood in their places. They read from the scroll of the Teaching of God, translating it and giving the sense; so they understood the reading.

Nehemiah the Tirshatha, Ezra the priest and scribe, and the Levites who were explaining to the people said to all the people, "This day is holy to the Lord your God: you must not mourn or weep," for all the people were weeping as they listened to the words of the Teaching. He further said to them, "Go, eat choice foods and drink sweet drinks and send portions to whoever has nothing prepared, for the day is holy to our Lord. Do not be sad, for your rejoicing in the Lord is the source of your strength." The Levites were quieting the people, saying, "Hush, for the day is holy; do not be sad." Then all the people went to eat and drink and send portions and make great merriment, for they understood the things they were told.

On the second day, the heads of the clans of all the people and the priests and Levites gathered to Ezra the scribe to study the words of the Teaching. They found written in the Teaching that the Lord had commanded Moses that the Israelites must dwell in booths during the festival of the seventh month, and that they must announce and proclaim throughout all their towns and Jerusalem as follows: "Go out to the mountains and bring leafy branches of olive trees, pine trees, myrtles, palms and [other] leafy trees to make booths, as it is written." So the people went out and brought them, and made themselves booths on their roofs, in their courtyards, in the courtyards of the House of God, in the square of the Water Gate and in the square of the Ephraim Gate. The whole community that returned from the captivity made booths and dwelt in the booths—the Israelites had not done so from the days of Joshua son of Nun to that day—and there was very great rejoicing. He read from the scroll of the Teaching of God each day, from the first to the last day. They celebrated the festival seven days, and there was a solemn gathering on the eighth, as prescribed.

Source: Nehemiah 8, from *Tanakh: The Holy Scriptures.*

POST-EXILIC WRITINGS

GREEK RULE AND THE COMING OF THE MESSIAH

Although the final events reported in the Tanakh *take place around 430 B.C.E., the religious drama of the Jewish people continues in post-exilic writings, considered scriptural in many Jewish circles at the time. The extreme Hellenizing policies of the Selucid king Antiochus Epiphanes created a crisis for traditional Jews, further intensified by the advocacy of these policies by Jewish High Priests themselves. Loyal Jewish writers sought a divine explanation for this crisis, which threatened the Jews' very existence. They wrote apocalyptic texts reporting visionlike revelations about a messianic deliverer and a cataclysmic end to the empires of their oppressors, topped by final divine judgment. The Book of Daniel in the* Tanakh *is thought to be an apocalyptic work from this period. The following is from the First Book of Enoch, one of the best-known apocalyptic texts of the Pseudepigrapha. The work, written by several authors between 200* B.C.E. *and 100* C.E.*, reflects traditional apocalyptic themes.*

46. *The Son of Man.* There I saw one who was the Ancient of Days, and His head was white like wool. With Him was another being who had the appearance of a man; and his face was full of graciousness, like one of the holy angels. I asked the angel who went with me and showed me all the hidden things, concerning that Son of Man, who he was, from where he was, and why he went with the Ancient of Days. He answered and said to me: "This is the Son of Man who has righteousness, with whom dwells righteousness, and who reveals all the treasures of that which is hidden because the Lord of Spirits has chosen him, and whose lot has the preeminence before the Lord of Spirits in uprightness forever. This Son of Man whom you have seen will raise up the kings and the mighty from their seats, and the strong from their thrones. He will loosen the reins of the strong, and break the teeth of the sinners. He will put down the kings from their thrones and kingdoms because they do not extol and praise Him, nor humbly acknowledge from what source the kingdom was bestowed upon them. He will put down the countenance of the strong, and will fill them with shame. Darkness will be their dwelling, and worms will be their bed. They will have no hope of rising from their beds, because they do not extol the name of the Lord of Spirits, raise their hands against the Most High, and tread upon the earth and dwell upon it. All their deeds manifest unrighteousness and their power rests upon their riches. Their faith is in the gods that they have made with their hands. They deny the name of the Lord of Spirits, and they persecute the houses of His congregations and the faithful who hang upon the name of the Lord of Spirits."...
48. In that place I saw the fountain of righteousness which was inexhaustible. Around it were many fountains of wisdom: all the thirsty drank of them and were filled with wisdom. Their dwellings were with the righteous and holy and elect. At that hour that Son of Man was named in the presence of the Lord of Spirits, and his name before the Ancient of Days. Even before the sun and the signs were created, before the stars of the heavens were made, his name was named before the Lord of Spirits. He will be a staff to the righteous whereon to stay themselves and not fall. He will be the light of the Gentiles, and the hope of those who are troubled of heart. All who dwell on earth will fall down and worship before him, and will praise and bless and celebrate with song the Lord of Spirits. For this reason he has been chosen and hidden before Him, before the creation of the world and for evermore. And the

wisdom of the Lord of Spirits has revealed him to the holy and righteous. For he has preserved the lot of the righ-teous, because they have hated and despised this world of unrigh-teousness, and have hated all its works and ways in the name of the Lord of Spirits. For in his name they are saved, and according to his good pleasure it has been in regard to their life. In these days will the kings of the earth become shamed because of the works of their hands—the strong who possess the land. For on the day of their anguish and affliction they will not be able to save themselves. I will give them over into the hands of My elect. As straw in the fire, so will they burn before the face of the holy. As lead in the water, so will they sink before the face of the righteous, and no trace of them will any more be found. On the day of their affliction there will be rest on the earth, and before them they will fall and not rise again. There will be no one to take them with his hands and raise them. For they have denied the Lord of Spirits and His Messiah. The name of the Lord of Spirits be blessed. . . .

51. *Resurrection of the Dead.* In those days the earth will also give back that which has been entrusted to it. Sheol also will give back that which it has received, and hell will give back that which it owes. In those days the Elect One will arise, and he will choose the righteous and holy from among them [i.e., the risen dead]. The day has drawn near that they should be saved. The Elect One will in those days sit on My throne, and his mouth will pour forth all the secrets of wisdom and counsel. For the Lord of Spirits has given them to him and has glorified him. In those days the mountains will leap like rams, the hills will also skip like lambs satisfied with milk, and the faces of all the angels in heaven will be lighted up with joy. The earth will rejoice, the righteous will dwell upon it, and the elect will walk thereon. . . .

54. *Judgment.* I looked and turned to another part of the earth, and saw there a deep valley with burning fire. They brought the kings and the mighty, and began to throw them into this deep valley. There my eyes saw how they made instruments, iron chains of immeasurable weight. I asked the angel of peace who went with me, saying: "For whom are these chains being prepared?" He said to me: "These are being prepared for the hosts of [the demon] Azazel, so that they may take them and throw them into the abyss of complete condemnation, and they will cover their jaws with rough stones as the Lord of Spirits commanded. Michael, Gabriel, Raphael, and Phanuel will take hold of them on that great day, and throw them on that day into the burning furnace. The Lord of Spirits may then take vengeance on them for their unrighteousness in becoming subject to Satan and leading astray those who dwell on the earth." In those days will punishment come from the Lord of Spirits. He will open all the chambers of water that are above the heavens, and of the fountains which are beneath the earth. All the waters will be joined with the waters: that which is above the heavens is the masculine, and the water that is beneath the

earth is the feminine. They will destroy all who dwell on the earth and those who dwell under the ends of the heaven. When they have recognized their unrighteousness which they have created on the earth, then by these they will die.

Source: First Enoch, 46, 48, 51, 54, adapted from R. H. Charles, *The Apocrypha and Pseudepigrapha of the Old Testament* (Oxford: Clarendon Press, 1913).

MACCABEAN REVOLT

The Book of Maccabees chronicles the clash between Hellenistic and Jewish culture, culminating in the Maccabean revolt and rise to power. The Book of Maccabees, written about 100 B.C.E. and included in the Septuagint, is the primary source of information for this period of Jewish history. The following describes the Hellenizing policies of Antiochus Epiphanes and the initial revolt launched by Mattathias.

1. After Alexander the Macedonian, Philip's son, who came from the land of Kittim, had defeated Darius, king of the Persians and Medes, he became king in his place, having first ruled in Greece. He fought many campaigns, captured fortresses, and put kings to death. He advanced to the ends of the earth, gathering plunder from many nations; the earth fell silent before him, and his heart became proud and arrogant. He collected a very strong army and conquered provinces, nations, and rulers, and they became his tributaries. But after all this he took to his bed, realizing that he was going to die. He therefore summoned his officers, the nobles, who had been brought up with him from his youth, to divide his kingdom among them while he was still alive. Alexander had reigned twelve years when he died.

   So his officers took over his kingdom, each in his own territory, and after his death they all put on royal crowns, and so did their sons after them for many years, causing much distress over the earth.

   There sprang from these a sinful offshoot, Antiochus Epiphanes, son of King Antiochus, once a hostage at Rome. He became king in the year one hundred and thirty-seven of the kingdom of the Greeks.

   In those days there appeared in Israel men who were breakers of the law, and they seduced many people, saying: "Let us go and make an alliance with the Gentiles all around us; since we separated from them, many evils have come upon us." The proposal was agreeable; some from among the people promptly went to the king, and he authorized them to introduce the way of living of the Gentiles. Thereupon they built a gymnasium in Jerusalem according to the Gentile custom. They covered over the mark of their circumcision and abandoned the holy covenant; they allied themselves with the Gentiles and sold themselves to wrongdoing.

   When his kingdom seemed secure, Antiochus proposed to become king of Egypt, so as to rule over both kingdoms. He invaded

Egypt with a strong force, with chariots and elephants, and with a large fleet, to make war on Ptolemy, king of Egypt. Ptolemy was frightened at his presence and fled, leaving many casualties. The fortified cities in the land of Egypt were captured, and Antiochus plundered the land of Egypt.

After Antiochus had defeated Egypt in the year one hundred and forty-three, he returned and went up to Israel and to Jerusalem with a strong force. He insolently invaded the sanctuary and took away the golden altar, the lampstand for the light with all its fixtures, the offering table, the cups and the bowls, the golden censers, the curtain, the crowns, and the golden ornament on the facade of the temple. He stripped off everything, and took away the gold and silver and the precious vessels; he also took all the hidden treasures he could find. Taking all this, he went back to his own country, after he had spoken with great arrogance and shed much blood. . . .

Two years later, the king sent the Mysian commander to the cities of Judah, and he came to Jerusalem with a strong force. He spoke to them deceitfully in peaceful terms, and won their trust. Then he attacked the city suddenly, in a great onslaught, and destroyed many of the people in Israel. He plundered the city and set fire to it, demolished its houses and its surrounding walls, took captive the women and children, and seized the cattle. Then they built up the City of David with a high, massive wall and strong towers, and it became their citadel. There they installed a sinful race, perverse men, who fortified themselves inside it, storing up weapons and provisions, and depositing there the plunder they had collected from Jerusalem. And they became a great threat. . . .

Then the king wrote to his whole kingdom that all should be one people, each abandoning his particular customs. All the Gentiles conformed to the command of the king, and many Israelites were in favor of his religion; they sacrificed to idols and profaned the Sabbath.

The king sent messengers with letters to Jerusalem and to the cities of Judah, ordering them to follow customs foreign to their land: to prohibit holocausts, sacrifices, and libations in the sanctuary, to profane the sabbaths and feast days, to desecrate the sanctuary and the sacred ministers, to build pagan altars and temples and shrines, to sacrifice swine and unclean animals, to leave their sons uncircumcised, and to let themselves be defiled with every kind of impurity and abomination, so that they might forget the law and change all their observances. Whoever refused to act according to the command of the king should be put to death.

Such were the orders he published throughout his kingdom. He appointed inspectors over all the people, and he ordered the cities of Judah to offer sacrifices, each city in turn. Many of the people, those who abandoned the law, joined them and committed evil in the land. Israel was driven into hiding, wherever places of refuge could be found.

On the fifteenth day of the month Chislev, in the year one hundred and forty-five, the king erected the horrible abomination upon the altar of holocausts, and in the surrounding cities of Judah they built pagan altars. They also burnt incense at the doors of houses and in the streets. Any scrolls of the law which they found they tore up and burnt. Whoever was found with a scroll of the covenant, and whoever observed the law, was condemned to death by royal decree. So they used their power against Israel, against those who were caught, each month, in the cities. On the twenty-fifth day of each month they sacrificed on the altar erected over the altar of holocausts. Women who had had their children circumcised were put to death, in keeping with the decree, with the babies hung from their necks; their families also and those who had circumcised them were killed. But many in Israel were determined and resolved in their hearts not to eat anything unclean; they preferred to die rather than to be defiled with unclean food or to profane the holy covenant; and they did die. Terrible affliction was upon Israel.

2. In those days Mattathias, son of John, son of Simeon, a priest of the family of Joarib, left Jerusalem and settled in Modein. He had five sons: John, who was called Gaddi; Simon, who was called Thassi; Judas, who was called Maccabeus; Eleazar, who was called Avaran; and Jonathan, who was called Apphus. When he saw the sacrileges that were being committed in Judah and in Jerusalem, he said: "Woe is me! Why was I born to see the ruin of my people and the ruin of the holy city, and to sit idle while it is given into the hands of enemies, and the sanctuary into the hands of strangers? . . ."

Then Mattathias and his sons tore their garments, put on sackcloth, and mourned bitterly.

The officers of the king in charge of enforcing the apostasy came to the city of Modein to organize the sacrifices. Many of Israel joined them, but Mattathias and his sons gathered in a group apart. Then the officers of the king addressed Mattathias: "You are a leader, an honorable and great man in this city, supported by sons and kinsmen. Come now, be the first to obey the king's command, as all the Gentiles and the men of Judah and those who are left in Jerusalem have done. Then you and your sons shall be numbered among the King's Friends, and shall be enriched with silver and gold and many gifts." But Mattathias answered in a loud voice: "Although all the Gentiles in the king's realm obey him, so that each forsakes the religion of his fathers and consents to the king's orders, yet I and my sons and my kinsmen will keep to the covenant of our fathers. God forbid that we should forsake the law and the commandments. We will not obey the words of the king nor depart from our religion in the slightest degree."

As he finished saying these words, a certain Jew came forward in the sight of all to offer sacrifice on the altar in Modein according to the king's order. When Mattathias saw him, he was filled with zeal; his heart was moved and his just fury was aroused; he sprang forward and killed him upon the altar. At the same time, he also killed the messenger of the king who was forcing them to sacrifice, and he tore down the altar. Thus he showed his zeal for the law, just as Phinehas did with Zimri, son of Salu.

Then Mattathias went through the city shouting, "Let everyone who is zealous for the law and who stands by the covenant follow after me!" Thereupon he fled to the mountains with his sons, leaving behind in the city all their possessions.

Source: First Maccabees 1:1–24, 25–36, 41–64; 2:1–7, 12–28, from *The New American Bible* (Washington, DC: Confraternity of Christian Doctrine, 1970). Reprinted by permission.

QUMRAN *COMMUNITY RULE*

Isolating itself from despotic foreign rulers and politically driven religious leaders, the desert community of Qumran believed it was preparing for a final battle between good and evil. The following, from the Qumran's Community Rule, *describes our dual human nature as consisting of a spirit of truth and a spirit of error—the sources of proper and improper conduct, respectively. Reminiscent of Zoroastrianism, it records that God has "established the two spirits in equal measure until the last period." Followers of truth, the Sons of Light, will ultimately wage a victorious war over followers of error, the Sons of Darkness.*

The Master shall instruct all the sons of light and shall teach them the nature of all the children of men according to the kind of spirit which they possess, the signs identifying their works during their lifetime, their visitation for chastisement, and the time of their reward.

From the God of knowledge comes all that is and shall be. Before ever they existed He established their whole design, and when, as ordained for them, they come into being, it is in accord with His glorious design that they accomplish their task without change. The laws of all things are in His hand and He provides them with all their needs.

He has created man to govern the world, and has appointed for him two spirits in which to walk until the time of His visitation: the spirits of truth and falsehood. Those born of truth spring from a fountain of light, but those born of falsehood spring from a source of darkness. All the children of righteousness are ruled by the Prince of Light and walk in the ways of light, but all the children of falsehood are ruled by the Angel of Darkness and walk in the ways of darkness.

The Angel of Darkness leads all the children of righteousness astray, and until his end, all their sin, iniquities, wickedness, and all their unlawful deeds are caused by his dominion in accordance with the mysteries of God. Every one of their chastisements, and every one of the seasons of their distress, shall be brought about by the rule of his persecution; for all his allotted spirits seek the overthrow of the sons of light.

But the God of Israel and His Angel of Truth will succor all the sons of light. For it is He who created the spirits of Light and Darkness and founded every action upon them and established every deed [upon] their [ways]. And He loves the one everlastingly and delights in its works for ever; but the counsel of the other He loathes and for ever hates its ways.

These are their ways in the world for the enlightenment of the heart of man, and that all the paths of true righteousness may be made straight before him, and that the fear of the laws of God may be instilled in his heart: a spirit of humility, patience, abundant charity, unending goodness, understanding, and intelligence; (a spirit of) mighty wisdom which trusts in all the deeds of God and leans on His great loving kindness; a spirit of discernment in every purpose, of zeal for just laws, of holy intent with steadfastness of heart, of great charity towards all the sons of truth, of admirable purity which detests all unclean idols, of humble conduct sprung from an understanding of all things, and of faithful concealment of the mysteries of truth. These are the counsels of the spirit to the sons of truth in this world.

And as for the visitation of all who walk in this spirit, it shall be healing, great peace in a long life, and fruitfulness, together with every everlasting blessing and eternal joy in life without end, a crown of glory and a garment of majesty in unending light.

But the ways of the spirit of falsehood are these: greed, and slackness in the search for righteousness, wickedness and lies, haughtiness and pride, falseness and deceit, cruelty and abundant evil, ill-temper and much folly and brazen insolence, abominable deeds (committed) in a spirit of lust, and ways of lewdness in the service of uncleanness, a blaspheming tongue, blindness of eye and dullness of ear, stiffness of neck and heaviness of heart, so that man walks in all the ways of darkness and guile.

And the visitation of all who walk in the spirit shall be a multitude of plagues by the hand of all the destroying angels, everlasting damnation by the avenging wrath of the fury of God, eternal torment and endless disgrace together with shameful extinction in the fire of the dark regions. The times of all their generations shall be spent in sorrowful mourning and in bitter misery and in calamities of darkness until they are destroyed without remnant or survivor.

The nature of all the children of men is ruled by these (two spirits), and during their life all the hosts of men have a portion of their divisions and walk in (both) their ways. And the whole reward for their deeds shall be, for everlasting ages, according to whether each man's portion in their two divisions is great or small. For God has established the spirits in equal measure until the final age, and has set everlasting hatred between their divisions. Truth abhors the works of falsehood, and falsehood hates all the ways of truth. And their struggle is fierce in all their arguments for they do not walk together.

But in the mysteries of His understanding, and in His glorious wisdom, God has ordained an end for falsehood, and at the time of the visitation he will destroy it for ever. Then truth, which has wallowed in the ways of wickedness during the dominion of falsehood until the appointed time of judgment, shall arise in the world for ever. God will then purify every deed of man with his truth; He will refine for Himself the human frame by rooting out all spirit of falsehood from the bounds of his flesh. He will cleanse him of all wicked deeds with the spirit of holiness; like purifying waters He will shed upon him the spirit of truth (to cleanse him) of all abomination and falsehood. And he shall be plunged into the spirit of purification that he may instruct the upright in the knowledge of the Most High and teach the wisdom of the sons of heaven to the perfect of way. For God has chosen them for an everlasting Covenant and all the glory of Adam shall be theirs. There shall be no more lies and all the works of falsehood shall be put to shame.

Until now the spirits of truth and falsehood struggle in the hearts of men and they walk in both wisdom and folly. According to his portion of truth so does a man hate falsehood, and according to his inheritance in the realm of falsehood so is he wicked and so hates truth. For God has established the two spirits in equal measure until the determined end, and until the Renewal, and He knows the reward of their deeds from all eternity. He has allotted them to the children of men that they may know good [and evil, and] that the destiny of all the living may be according to the spirit within [them at the time] of the visitation.

Source: "The Community Rule," Cave 1 Copy, Column 3:13–4:26, from *The Dead Sea Scrolls in English,* 3d ed., tr. G. Vermes (New York: Penguin Books, 1987), pp. 64–67. Reprinted by permission.

RABBINIC WRITINGS

WISDOM OF THE FATHERS

The best-known section of the Mishnah *is* Abot *(literally, fathers), also called Wisdom of the Fathers. This section was considered so important that medieval copies of the* Talmud *have* Abot *as the conclusion of each of its six key divisions. The typical style of the* Mishnah *is a give-and-take legal debate between the* Tannaim. Abot *is different in that it is a collection of proverbs by the* Tannaim *that are not debated. The first two divisions of* Abot, *presented here, begin by listing the transmitters of the oral law from Moses to the* Tannaim *themselves.*

1. Moses received the Torah at Sinai. He conveyed it to Joshua; Joshua to the elders; the elders to the prophets; and the prophets transmitted it to the men of the Great Assembly. The latter emphasized three principles: Be deliberate in judgment; raise up many disciples; and make a fence to safeguard the Torah.
2. Simeon the Just was of the last survivors of the Great Assembly. He used to say: The world rests on three foundations: the Torah; the divine service; and the practices of loving kindness between man and man.
3. Antigonus of Soho received the tradition from him. He was accustomed to say: Be not like servants who serve their master because of

the expected reward, but be like those who serve a master without expecting a reward; and let the fear of God be upon you.

4. Yose ben Yoezer of Zeredah and Yose ben Yohanan of Jerusalem received the tradition from them. Yose ben Yoezer of Zeredah said: Let your house be a gathering place for wise men; sit attentively at their feet, and drink of their words of wisdom with eagerness.
5. Yose ben Yohanan of Jerusalem said: Let your home be a place of hospitality to strangers; and make the poor welcome in your household; and do not indulge in gossip with women. This applies even with one's own wife, and surely so with another man's wife. The sages generalized from this: He who engages in profuse gossiping with women causes evil for himself and neglects the study of the Torah, and he will bring upon himself retributions in the hereafter.
6. Joshua ben Perahya and Nittai the Arbelite received the tradition from them. Joshua ben Perahya said: Get yourself a teacher; and acquire for yourself a companion; and judge all people favorably.
7. Nittai the Arbelite said: Avoid an evil neighbor; do not associate with the wicked; and do not surrender your faith in divine retribution.
8. Judah ben Tabbai and Simeon ben Shatah received the traditions from them. Judah ben Tabbai said: Let not the judge play the part of the counselor; when they leave after submitting to the court's decree, regard them both as guiltless.
9. Simeon ben Shatah said: Search the witnesses thoroughly and be cautious with your own words lest you give them an opening to false testimony.
10. Shemaya and Abtalyon received the traditions from them. Shemaya said: love work; hate domineering over others; and do not seek the intimacy of public officials.
11. Abtalyon said: Sages, be precise in your teachings. You may suffer exile to a place where heresy is rampant, and your inexact language may lead your disciples astray, and they will lose their faith, thus leading to a desecration of the divine name.
12. Hillel and Shammai received the tradition from them. Hillel said: Be of the disciples of Aaron. Love peace and pursue peace; love your fellow creatures and bring them near to the Torah.
13. He also said: He who strives to exalt his name will in the end destroy his name; he who does not increase his knowledge decreases it; he who does not study has undermined his right to life; and he who makes unworthy use of the crown of the Torah will perish.
14. He also said: If I am not for myself who will be? But if I am for myself only, what am I? And if not now, when?
15. Shammai said: Set a fixed time for the study of the Torah; say little and do much; and greet every person with a cheerful countenance.
16. Rabban Gamaliel said: Provide yourself with a teacher, and extricate yourself from doubt; and do not habitually contribute your tithes by rough estimates.

17. Simeon his son said: All my life I was raised among scholars and I found that no virtue becomes a man more than silence; what is more essential is not study but practice; and in the wake of many words is sin.
18. Rabban Simeon ben Gamaliel said: The world rests on three foundations: truth, justice, and peace. As it is written (Zech 8:16): "You shall administer truth, justice and peace within your gates."

Source: *Mishnah, Abot*, ch. 1, from *The Talmud*, tr. Ben Zion Bokser (New York: Paulist Press, 1989), pp. 219–221. Reprinted by permission.

RABBINIC AUTHORITY

The chief theological paradox of the Talmud *is how collected opinions of early Rabbis can count as divine law. Although Judaism traces its oral law back to Moses, the* Mishnah *and* Talmud *are, quite obviously, only the collected sayings of the* Tannaim *and* Amoraim. *Early Rabbis themselves were aware of this paradox and provide an answer. In this selection from* Baba Mezia *(one of the most famous sections of the* Talmud*), they explain that the majority position held by the carriers of oral law in fact becomes the law. At that time, the sages of the* Talmud *were the carriers.*

MISHNA 8: As cheating is prohibited in buying or selling, so it is in words. (How so?) One must not ask the price of a thing when he does not intend to buy it. To a person who has repented one must not say, Remember your former acts. To a descendant from proselytes one must not say, Remember the acts of your parents. As it is written "And a stranger you shall not vex, nor shall you oppress him" (Exodus 22:20).

GEMARA: We studied in the Mishnah (Eduyot 7:7) that if a pottery stove was cut into tiles, and cemented over with sand placed between the tiles, R. Eliezer declared it unsusceptible to ritual uncleanliness, while the other Sages declared it susceptible. This was the Akhnai Stove.

Why was it called Akhnai? Said R. Judah in the name of Samuel: They surrounded it with arguments as a snake winds its body around an object, and declared it unclean. It has been taught: On that day R. Eliezer marshaled every conceivable argument, but they did not accept them. Then he said: If the law is according to my views, let this carob tree prove it. Thereupon the carob tree was thrust to a distance of a hundred cubits from its place, and some say four hundred. They replied to him: We adduce no evidence from a carob tree. Again he said to them: If the law is in accordance with my views, let the stream of water prove it, and at once the stream of water flowed in the opposite direction. But they said: We adduce no evidence from a stream of water. Again he said to them: If the law agrees with my views, let the walls of the academy prove it, and the walls of the academy began to bend and were about to fall. R. Joshua rebuked them, saying: If scholars argue on a point of law, what business is it of yours? The walls did not fall out of respect for R. Joshua, but they did not become straight again out of respect for R. Eliezer.

Thereupon he said: If the law is in accordance with my views, let them prove it from heaven. A heavenly voice came forth, saying: What have you against R. Eliezer? The law is as he propounds it in all instances. R. Joshua then stood up and quoted: "It is not in the heavens" (Dt 30:12). What did he mean by quoting: "It is not in the heavens"? Said R. Jeremiah: That the Torah has already been given at Sinai, and we pay no attention to heavenly voices, for You have written at Sinai in the Torah: "Incline after the majority" (Ex 23:2).

R. Nathan met the prophet Elijah and he asked him: What did the Holy One, praised be He, do at that time? He replied: He laughed, and He said: My children have won over me, my children have won over me!

Source: *Talmud, Baba Mezia* 59a–59b, from *The Talmud,* tr. Bokser, pp. 184–185.

RESURRECTION OF THE DEAD

The notion of resurrection of the dead is not readily present in the Tanakh. *The book of Job, for example, poetically pronounces against it: "As a cloud breaks up and disperses, so no one who goes down to Sheol ever comes back." The idea of resurrection took hold in post-exilic writings and by the time of the Rabbinic period had become an important tenet of Judaism. In this selection from the* Talmud, *several Rabbis debate the issues surrounding the resurrected.*

MISHNA I.: All Israel has a share in the world to come. As it reads: "And thy people—they will all be righteous, for ever will they possess the land, the sprout of my planting, the work of my hands, that I may glorify myself" (Isaiah 9:21). The following have no share in the world to come: He who says that there is no allusion in the Torah concerning resurrection, and he who says that the Torah was not given by Heaven. . . .

GEMARA: Is he who does not believe that the resurrection is hinted at in the Torah such a criminal that he loses his share in the world to come? It was taught: He denies resurrection therefore he will not have a share in it, as punishment corresponds to the deed; for all retributions of the Holy One are in correspondence with man's doing. . . .

Queen Cleopatra questioned Rabbi Mair thus: I am aware that the dead will be restored. As it reads: "And men will blossom out of the city like herbs of the earth" (Psalms 72:16). My question, however, is this: When they will be restored, will they be naked or dressed? And he answered: This may be drawn by an *a fortiori* conclusion from wheat. A grain of wheat which is buried naked comes out dressed in so many garments: the upright, who are buried in their dress, so much the more will they come out dressed in many garments. . . .

Cæsar questioned Rabbon Gamaliel: You say that the dead will be restored. Does not the corpse become dust? How, then, can dust be restored? And the daughter of Cæsar said to Rabbi Gamaliel: Leave the question to me and I myself will answer it. And she said to her father: If there were two potters in our city, of whom one should make a pot from water and the other from clay, to which of them would you give preference? And he said: Certainly to him who creates from water; for if he is able to create from water, he is undoubtedly able to create from clay. And she said: This is an answer to your question.

The school of Rabbi Ismael taught: One may learn it from glass-wares, which are made by human beings, and if they break there is a remedy for them, as they can be renewed: human beings, who are created by the spirit of the Lord, so much the more will they be restored. . . .

Antoninus said to Rabbi: The body and the soul of a human may free themselves on the day of judgment by Heaven. How so? The body may say: The soul has sinned; for since she has departed I lie in the grave like a stone. And the soul may say: The body has sinned; for since I am separated from it, I fly in the air like a bird. And he answered: I will give you a parable to which this is similar: A human king, who had an excellent garden which contained very fine figs, appointed two watchmen for it—one of whom was blind, and the other had no feet. He who was without feet said to the one who was blind: I see in the garden fine figs. Take me on your shoulders, and I shall get them, and we shall consume them. He did so, and while on his shoulders he took them off, and both consumed them. And when the owner of the garden came and did not find the figs, and questioned them what became of them, the blind one answered: Have I, then, eyes to see them, that you should suspect my taking them? And the lame one answered: Have I, then, feet to go there? The owner then put the lame one on the shoulders of the one who was blind, and punished them together. So also the Holy One puts the soul in the body and punishes them together. As it reads: "He will call to the heavens above, and to the earth beneath, to judge his people" (Psalms 1:4). "To the heavens above" means the soul, and, "to the earth beneath" means the body.

Source: Sanhedrin 11, from *New Edition of the Babylonian Talmud* (Boston: The Talmud Society, 1918).

COMING OF THE MESSIAH

During the Babylonian exile, the Jews lost hope in the ability of any present leader to return Israel to its former glory and so they placed their hopes in a future Messiah, or anointed one. The notion gained momentum and complexity during post-exilic times, and by the Rabbinic period the coming of the Messiah was linked to the culmination of human history and the establishment of God's kingdom on earth. In the following selections from the Talmud, *several Rabbis debate about the events leading up to the Messiah's arrival.*

The rabbis taught: In this Sabbatic period in which the son of David will appear in the first year there will be fulfilled what is written: "And I caused it to rain upon one city, and upon another city I caused it not to rain" (Amos 4:7). In the second year, arrows of famine will be sent. In the third, a great famine, from which men, women, and children, pious men and men of good deeds will die, and the Torah will be forgotten by their scholars. In the fourth there will be abundance, and not abundance. In the fifth there will be great abundance, and the people will eat, drink, and enjoy themselves, and the Torah will return to her scholars. In the sixth, voices will be heard saying that the Messiah is near. In the seventh, war will be, and at the end of the seventh, the son of David will come. Said Rabbi Joseph: Were there not many Sabbatical periods which were like this, but still he did not come? Said Abayi: Were then the above-mentioned voices heard in the sixth? And was there in the seventh war? And secondly, has it then happened in the same order as said above? . . .

Rabbi Jehudah said: The generation in which the son of David will come, the houses of assembly will be converted into houses of prostitution. Galilee will be destroyed. The place called Gablan will be astonished. Men of the borders of Palestine will travel from one city to another, but will find no favor. The wisdom of the scribes will be corrupted. Men fearing sin will be hated. The leaders of that generation will have the nature of dogs. . . .

Rabbi Nehuraia taught: The generation in which the son of David will come, young men will make pale the faces of the old, old men will rise before youth, a daughter will rebel against her mother, a daughter-in-law against her mother-in-law, the leaders of the generation will have the nature of dogs, and a son will not be ashamed when his father reproaches him.

Rabbi Nehemiah said: The generation in which the son of David will come, insolence will increase, an evil man will be honored, respect will be missed, the vine will give forth its fruit abundantly; wine, however, will be dear, and all the governments will be turned over to heretics (will embrace the religion of the heretics), and no preaching will avail. And this is as to Rabbi Itz'hak, who said that the son of David will not come unless all governments will be turned over to heretics. Where is to be found a hint to this in the Scripture? (Leviticus 13:13): "It is all turned white, he is clean."

Source: Sanhedrin 11, from *New Edition of the Babylonian Talmud.*

UNITY OF THE TEN COMMANDMENTS

In addition to debates on fine points of law and theology, Rabbis and other Jewish writers for hundreds of years had developed legends and embellishments surrounding the historical narrative in the Tanakh*—from creation to the restoration. The stories are scattered throughout the Apocrypha, Pseudepigrapha,* Talmud, *and* Midrash *and are even found in early Christian writings. The following is one such legend explaining how the Ten Commandments are woven into a unified whole.*

The Ten Commandments are so closely interwoven, that the breaking of one leads to the breaking of another. But there is a particularly strong bond of union between the first five commandments, which are written on one table, and the last five, which were on the other table. The first commandment: "I am the Lord, thy God," corresponds to the sixth: "Thou shalt not kill," for the murderer slays the image of God. The second: "Thou shalt have no strange gods before me," corresponds to the seventh: "Thou shalt not commit adultery," for conjugal faithlessness is as grave a sin as idolatry, which is faithlessness to God. The third commandment: "Thou shalt not take the name of the Lord in vain," corresponds to the eighth: "Thou shalt not steal," for theft leads to false oath. The fourth commandment: "Remember the Sabbath day, to keep it holy," corresponds to the ninth: "Thou shalt not bear false witness against thy neighbor," for he who bears false witness against his neighbor commits as grave a sin as if he had borne false witness against God, saying that He had not created the world in six days and rested on the seventh, the Sabbath. The fifth commandment: "Honor thy father and thy mother," corresponds to the tenth: "Covet not thy neighbor's wife," for one who indulges this lust produces children who will not honor their true father, but will consider a stranger their father.

The Ten Commandments, which God first revealed on Mount Sinai, correspond in their character to the ten words of which He had made use at the creation of the world. The first commandment: "I am the Lord, thy God," corresponds to the first word at the creation: "Let there be light," for God is the eternal light. The second commandment: "Thou shalt have no strange gods before me," corresponds to the second word: "Let there be a firmament in the midst of the waters, and let it divide the waters from the waters." For God said: "Choose between Me and the idols; between Me, the fountain of living waters, and the idols, the stagnant waters." The third commandment: "Thou shalt not take the name of thy God in vain," corresponds to the word: "Let the waters be gathered together," for as little as water can be gathered in a cracked vessel, so can a man maintain his possession which he has obtained through false oaths. The fourth commandment: "Remember to keep the Sabbath holy," corresponds to the word: "Let the earth bring forth grass," for he who truly observes the Sabbath will receive good things from God without having to labor for them, just as the earth produces grass that need not be sown. For at the creation of man it was God's intention that he be free from sin, immortal, and capable of supporting himself by the products of the soil without toil. The fifth commandment: "Honor thy father and thy mother," corresponds to the word: "Let there be lights in the firmament of the heaven," for God said to man: "I gave thee two lights, thy father and thy mother, treat them with care." The sixth commandment: "Thou shalt not kill," corresponds to the word: "Let the waters bring forth abundantly the moving creature," for God said: "Be not like the fish, among whom the great swallow the small." The seventh commandment: "Thou shalt not commit adultery," corresponds to the word: "Let the earth bring forth the living creature after his kind," for God said: "I chose for thee a spouse, abide with her." The eighth commandment: "Thou shalt not steal," corresponds to the word: "Behold, I have given you every herb-bearing seed," for none, said God, should touch his neighbor's goods, but only that which grows free as the grass, which is the common property of all. The ninth commandment: "Thou shalt not bear false witness against thy neighbor," corresponds to the word: "Let us make man in our image." Thou, like thy neighbor, art made in My image, hence bear not false witness against thy neighbor. The tenth commandment: "Thou shalt not covet the wife of thy neighbor," corresponds to the tenth word of the creation: "It is not good for man to be alone," for God said: "I created thee a spouse, and let not one among ye covet his neighbor's wife."

Source: Louis Ginzberg, *The Legends of the Jews,* vol. 3, ch. 2 (Philadelphia: The Jewish Publication Society of America, 1909).

MEDIEVAL JUDAISM

THIRTEEN PRINCIPLES OF FAITH: MAIMONIDES

Judaism has resisted the formulation of creeds or other statements of belief, perhaps in part because of the dialogical nature of the Talmud *and its other principal theological works. Nevertheless, the medieval Jewish philosopher Maimonides (1135–1204) developed a list of thirteen principles of Jewish faith, which was embraced by Judaism and, in much abbreviated form, appears in most Jewish prayer books today. The following is from Maimonides' original discussion of the principles.*

The First Foundation is to believe in the existence of the Creator, blessed be He. This means that there exists a Being that is complete in all ways and He is the cause of all else that exists. He is what sustains their existence and the existence of all that sustains them. It is inconceivable that He would not exist, for if He would not exist then all else would cease to exist as well, nothing would remain. And if we would imagine that everything other than He would cease to exist, this would not cause His, God's, blessed be He, existence to cease or be diminished. Independence and mastery is to Him alone, God, blessed be His Name, for He needs nothing else and is sufficient unto himself. He does not need the existence of anything else. All that exists apart from Him, the angels, the universe and all that is within it, all these things are dependent on Him for their existence. . . .

The Second Foundation is the unity of God, Blessed be His Name. In other words, to believe that this being, which is the cause of all, is one. This does not mean one as in one of a pair nor one like a species [which encompasses many individuals] nor one as in one object that is made up of many elements nor as a single simple object which is infinitely divisible. Rather, He, God, Blessed be His Name, is a unity unlike any other possible unity. . . .

The Third Foundation is that He is not physical. This means to believe that the One whom we have mentioned is not a body and His powers are not physical. The concepts of physical bodies such as movement, rest, or existence in a particular place cannot be applied to Him. Such things cannot be part of His nature nor can they happen to Him. Therefore the Sages of blessed memory stated that the concepts of combination and separation do not apply to Him and they said, "Above there is no sitting nor standing, no separation nor combination." The prophet says, *"To whom can you compare Me? To what am I equal? Says the Holy One"* (Isaiah 40:25). If He would be a physical body He would be comparable to physical bodies. . . .

The Fourth Foundation is that He is first. This means to believe that the One was the absolute first and everything else in existence is not first relative to Him. There are many proofs to this in the Holy Scriptures. . . .

The Fifth Foundation is that it is proper to serve Him, blessed be He, to ascribe to Him greatness, to make known His greatness, and to fulfill His commandments. We may not do this to any lesser being, whether it be one of the angels, the stars, the celestial spheres, the elements, or anything formed from them. For all these things have predetermined natures and have no authority or control over their actions. Rather, such authority and control is God's. Similarly, it is not proper to serve them as intermediaries in order that they should bring us closer to God. Rather, to God Himself we must direct our thoughts, and abandon anything else. . . .

The Sixth Foundation is prophecy. That is, that a person must know that there exist amongst mankind individuals who have very lofty qualities and great perfection; whose souls are prepared until their minds receive perfect intellect. After this, their human intellect can then become attached to the Active Intellect [i.e., the "mind," so to speak, of God] and have bestowed upon them an exalted state. These are the prophets and this is prophecy. . . .

The Seventh Foundation is the prophecy of Moses our Teacher, may he rest in peace. This means to believe that he is the father of all the prophets, both those that preceded him and those who arose after him; all of them were below his level. He was the chosen one from all of Mankind, for he attained a greater knowledge of the Blessed One, more than any other man ever attained or ever will attain. For he, may he rest in peace, rose up from the level of man to the level of the angels and gained the exalted status of an angel. There did not remain any screen that he did not tear and penetrate; nothing physical held him back. He was devoid of any flaw, big or small. His powers of imagination, the senses, and the perceptions were nullified; the power of desire was separated from him leaving him with pure intellect. It is for this reason that it is said of him that he could speak to God, blessed be He, without the intermediary of angels. . . .

The Eighth Foundation is that the Torah is from Heaven. This means that we must believe that this entire Torah, which was given to us from Moses our Teacher, may he rest in peace, is entirely from the mouth of the Almighty. In other words, that it all was conveyed to him from God, blessed be He, in the manner which is called, for lack of a better term, "speech." It is not known how it was conveyed to him, except to [Moses], may he rest in peace, to whom it was given, and he was like a scribe writing from dictation, and he wrote all the incidents, the stories, and the commandments. Therefore [Moses] is called "scribe" (Numbers 21:18). . . .

The Ninth Foundation is the transcription, meaning that this Torah, and no other, was transcribed from the Creator and we may not add to it or remove from it, not in the Written Torah or in the Oral Torah, as it says, "*. . . you will not add to it, nor diminish from it*" (Deuteronomy 13:1). . . .

The Tenth Foundation is that God, blessed be He, knows the actions of mankind and does not turn His eyes from them. . . .

The Eleventh Foundation is that God, blessed be He, gives reward to one who obeys the commandments of the Torah and punishes one who violates its prohibitions. The greatest reward is the World to Come, and the greatest punishment is spiritual excision. . . .

The Twelfth Foundation is the time of the *Messiah*. This means to believe and be certain that he will come, and not to think that he is late in coming, *"if it seems slow, wait for it; [because it will surely come, it will not come late]"* (Chabakuk 2:3). You should not set a time for him, and you should not make calculations in Scripture to determine the time of his coming. The Sages say, *"Let despair come upon those who calculate endtimes."* [This foundation further includes] to believe that he [*Messiah*] will possess advantages, superiority, and honor to a greater degree than all the kings that have ever existed, as was prophesied regarding him by all the prophets, from Moses, peace be upon him, till Malachi, peace be upon him. One who doubts this or who minimizes his greatness denies the Torah that testifies explicitly to [the coming of Messiah] in the account of Balaam (Numbers 24) and in the portion of *Netzavim* (Deuteronomy 30:3–5). Included in this principle is that there is no king to the Jewish people except from the House of David and the seed of Solomon alone. Anyone who disagrees with [the status of] this family denies God and His prophets. . . .

The Thirteenth Foundation is the resurrection of the dead. . . .

Source: Maimonides, *Commentary on the Mishnah,* Sanhedrin, ch. 10, tr. Eliezer C. Abrahamson. Reprinted by permission.

KABBALA: CREATION

Since the twelfth century, the most dominant school of Jewish mysticism has been Kabbala, the classic statement of which is the Book of Splendor (Sefer ha-Zohar), *written between 1280 and 1286 by Moses de Leon, a Spanish Jew from Guadalajara. The work emphasizes ten emanations—or* Sefirot*—of God's personality. These attributes of the divinity permeate all of creation, including our personal lives. De Leon does not systematically discuss the emanations and typically does not refer to them by their formal names. Instead, he relies heavily on metaphors, leaving it to the reader to make the association. The following is de Leon's account of creation, presented as a commentary on the first phrase of the Book of Genesis, that is, "In the beginning." He describes how God* (Eyn Sof, *or the Infinite) created two primary emanations. The first is Hokhmah (wisdom), described below as "point" and "beginning," which is the primal point of God's emanation. The second is Binah (derivative wisdom), described below as "palace," which is the prime mother who receives seed from Hokhmah and gives birth to seven lower emanations.*

"In the beginning" [Gen. 1:1]—when the will of the King began to take effect, he engraved signs into the heavenly sphere [that surrounded him]. Within the most hidden recess a dark flame issued from the mystery of *eyn sof,* the Infinite, like a fog forming in the unformed—enclosed in the ring of that sphere, neither white nor black, neither red nor green, of no color whatever. Only after this flame began to assume size and dimension, did it produce radiant colors. From the innermost center of the flame sprang forth a well out of which colors issued and spread upon everything beneath, hidden in the mysterious hiddenness of *eyn sof.*

The well broke through and yet did not break through the ether [of the sphere]. It could not be recognized at all until a hidden, supernatural point shone forth under the impact of the final breaking through.

Beyond this point nothing can be known. Therefore it is called *reshit,* beginning—the first word [out of the ten] by means of which the universe has been created. When King Solomon "penetrated into the depths of the nut garden," as it is written, "I descended into the garden of nuts" [Cant. 6:11], he took up a nut shell and studying it, he saw an analogy in its layers with the spirits which motivate the sensual desires of humans, as it is written, "and the delights of the sons of men [are from] male and female demons" [Eccles. 2:8].

The Holy One, be blessed, saw that it was necessary to put into the world all of these things so as to make sure of permanence, and of having, so to speak, a brain surrounded by numerous membranes. The whole world, upper and lower, is organized on this principle, from the primary mystic center to the very outermost of all the layers. All are coverings, the one to the other, brain within brain, spirit inside of spirit, shell within shell.

The primal center is the innermost light, of translucence, subtlety, and purity beyond comprehension. That inner point extended becomes a "palace" which acts as an enclosure for the center, and is also of a radiance translucent beyond the power to know it.

The "palace" vestment for the incognizable inner point, while it is an unknowable radiance in itself, is nevertheless of a lesser subtlety and translucency than the primal point. The "palace" extends into a vestment for itself, the primal light. From then outward, there is extension upon extension, each constituting a vesture to the one before, as a membrane to the brain. Though membrane first, each extension becomes brain to the next extension.

Likewise does the process go on below; and after this design, man in the world combines brain and membrane, spirit and body, all to the more perfect ordering of the world. When the moon was conjoined with the sun, she was luminous, but when she went apart from the sun and was given governance of her own hosts, her status and her light were reduced, and shell after shell as fashioned for investing the brain, and all was for its good.

Source: Zohar, 1:49b, from *Zohar, The Book of Splendor,* ed. Gershom Scholem (New York: Schocken Books, 1949). Reprinted by permission.

RECENT MOVEMENTS

HASIDISM: THE SEVEN BEGGARS

The Hasidic movement was founded by Baal Shem Tov (1700–1760) as a mystical response to disillusionment with both messianic hope (brought on by messianic pretenders of the previous century) and rabbinic legalism. Followers of Baal Shem Tov were preachers, rather than theologians, and thus communicated orally rather than in writing. Their homilies eventually were put in writing by their sons or disciples. The Hasids describe God pantheistically and maintain that God can be directly accessed.

Another genre of writing also emerged from the Hasidic movement: the tale. These parable-like stories draw from events in peasant life and describe God more anthropomorphically than pantheistically. The most distinguished of these are by Ukrainian Rabbi Nahman of Bratslav (1772–1810). The following selection is from his best-known and most cryptic tale, "The Seven Beggars." The story surrounds a wedding ceremony that is attended by six deformed beggars, each of whom presents tales explaining his respective deformity (a seventh beggar remained in the forest). Their stories emphasize the illusory nature of the world in which we live.

. . . Today I present you a wedding gift that you should be as I am. Do you think my neck is twisted? My neck is not twisted at all. In fact, I have a straight neck, a very handsome neck. Only that there are worldly vanities (empty breaths) which are so numerous that I do not want to exhale the last breath. . . . But I really have a handsome neck, a wonderful neck because I have such a wonderful voice. I can imitate with my voice every speechless sound. . . . And I have an affidavit to that effect from a certain country.

For there is a country where everyone is skilled in the art of music. Everyone practices these arts, even little children. . . . The youngest in that country would be the wisest in another country in the art of music. And the wise men, and the king of that country and the musicians are experts in the art of music.

Once, the country's wise men sat and boasted of their expertise in the art of music. One boasted that he could play on one instrument; another, on another; and still another, on all instruments. This one boasted that he could imitate with his voice the sound of one instrument, and another boasted that he could imitate with his voice yet another instrument. . . . Another one boasted that with his voice he could make the sound of cannon firing.

I, too, was there, so I declared saying, "My Voice is better than all of yours. And here is the proof. If you are such wise men in music, see if you can save these two countries. There are two countries one thousand miles apart from each other where no one can sleep when night falls. As soon as night falls, everyone begins to wail with such anguish—men, women, and children—because they hear a certain wailing sound of mourning. Stones would melt because of this wail. . . . So if you are all so very wise in music, let us see if you can save these two countries, or at least imitate the sounds of the laments heard there."

And they all arose to go there. They left and reached one of those two countries. When they arrived, and night fell, as usual, everyone began to wail and the wise men also wailed. And so they saw that they were of no help at all to the two countries. And I said to the wise men: "Can you, at least, tell me where the sound of the wailing comes from?" They asked: "Do you know?" And I answered: "Of course I know. There are two birds, a male and a female. There was only one pair of these species on earth. The female was lost and the male roamed about seeking her. She was also seeking him. They searched for each other for such a long time that they lost their ways and realized they could no longer find one another. They remained where they were and made nests. . . . And when night fell, each one of this pair of birds began to lament with a very great wail. Each wailed for its mate. This is the wailing that is heard in these two countries, and because of the sound, everyone must wail and no one can sleep." . . .

The wise man said to me: "and you set it right?" I answered: "Yes, I can set it right, since I can imitate all the sounds of the world. I can also throw my voice, so that in the place from where I throw my voice, nobody hears, but it is heard far, far away. . . ."

But who could believe me? So I led them into a forest. They heard somebody open a door, and shut it, and lock it with a bolt. Then I shot a gun and sent my dog to retrieve what I had shot. And the dog struggled in the snow. These wise men heard it all and looked around, but they saw absolutely nothing. They heard no sound from me . . . so they understood that I could imitate all the sounds and could throw my voice and thus could set everything right.

Source: Selections from "The Seven Beggars," from *Nahman of Bratslav: The Tales* (New York: Paulist Press, 1978), pp. 274–277. Reprinted by permission.

ORTHODOX JUDAISM: SERVICE PRAYER FOR THE DAY OF ATONEMENT

The term Orthodox Judaism *was first used in the late seventeenth century to distinguish traditional Judaism from the Reform Judaism movement that modernized many aspects of Jewish theology and ritual. Today Orthodox Judaism is diverse in its belief and practices, and contains divisions such as between modernists and centrists. A common theme within this diversity, though, is adherence to the traditional view that God is the source of the Torah and that the oral law is authoritative. The selection below is from a Jewish prayer book that gained wide acceptance in English-speaking Orthodox Jewish communities. The prayer is specifically earmarked for one of Judaism's most sacred days, Yom Kippur—that is, the Day of Atonement—during which time Jewish people seek God's forgiveness for the wrongs they have committed. Accordingly, the Yom Kippur service prayer enumerates a range of possible sins, requesting God's forgiveness for the commission of each.*

May it then be thy will, O Lord our God and God of our fathers, to forgive us for all our sins, to pardon us for all our iniquities, and to grant us remission for all our transgressions.

For the sin which we have committed before thee under compulsion, or of our own will;

And for the sin which we have committed before thee in hardening of the heart;

For the sin which we have committed before thee unknowingly;

And for the sin which we have committed before thee with utterance of the lips;

For the sin which we have committed before thee by unchastity;

And for the sin which we have committed before thee openly and secretly;

For the sin which we have committed before thee knowingly and deceitfully;

And for the sin which we have committed before thee in speech;

For the sin which we have committed before thee by wronging our neighbor;

And for the sin which we have committed before thee by the sinful meditating of the heart;

For the sin which we have committed before thee by association with impurity;

And for the sin which we have committed before thee by confession with the mouth alone;

For the sin which we have committed before thee by despising parents and teachers;

And for the sin which we have committed before thee in presumption or in error;

For the sin which we have committed before thee by violence;

And for the sin which we have committed before thee by the profanation of the divine Name;

For the sin which we have committed before thee by unclean lips;

And for the sin which we have committed before thee by folly of the mouth;

For the sin which we have committed before thee by the evil inclination;

And for the sin which we have committed before thee wittingly or unwittingly;

For all these, O God of forgiveness, forgive us, pardon us, grant us remission.

For the sin which we have committed before thee by denying and lying;

And for the sin which we have committed before thee by taking of bribes;

For the sin which we have committed before thee by scoffing;

And for the sin which we have committed before thee by slander;

For the sin which we have committed before thee in business;

And for the sin which we have committed before thee in eating and drinking;

For the sin which we have committed before thee by usury and interest;

And for the sin which we have committed before thee by the stretched forth neck of pride;

For the sin which we have committed before thee by the conversation of our lips;

And for the sin which we have committed before thee with wanton looks;

For the sin which we have committed before thee with haughty eyes;

And for the sin which we have committed before thee by effrontery;

For all these, O God of forgiveness, forgive us, pardon us, grant us remission.

For the sin which we have committed before thee by breaking off the yoke of thy commandments;

And for the sin which we have committed before thee by contentiousness;

For the sin which we have committed before thee by ensnaring our neighbor;

And for the sin which we have committed before thee by envy;

For the sin which we have committed before thee by levity;

And for the sin which we have committed before thee by being stiff-necked;

For the sin which we have committed before thee by running to do evil;

And for the sin which we have committed before thee by tale-bearing;

For the sin which we have committed before thee by vain oaths;

And for the sin which we have committed before thee by causeless hatred;

For the sin which we have committed before thee by breach of trust;

And for the sin which we have committed before thee with confusion of mind;

For all these, O God of forgiveness, forgive us, pardon us, grant us remission.

And also for the sins for which we owe a burnt offering;

And for the sins for which we owe a sin offering;

And for the sins for which we owe an offering, varying according to our means;

And for the sins for which we owe an offering, whether for certain or for doubtful trespass;

And for the sins for which we are liable to the penalty of chastisement;

And for the sins for which we are liable to the penalty of forty stripes;

And for the sins for which we are liable to the penalty of death by the hand of heaven;

And for the sins for which we are liable to the penalty of excision and childlessness;

For all these, O God of forgiveness, forgive us, pardon us, grant us remission.

Source: *The Standard Prayer Book*, tr. Simeon Singer (New York: Bloch Publishing Company, 1915).

REFORM JUDAISM: DECLARATION OF PRINCIPLES

The eighteenth-century Enlightenment and its emphasis on political rights sparked a movement among Jews in Germany to reform their religious practices. Initial efforts focused on revamping the liturgy: modernizing music and integrating some components of Christian practice. This was followed by a more "scientific" approach to Judaism advocated by Abraham Geiger (1810–1875), who was influenced by the critical methodology taught at German universities. Geiger believed that the Jewish Torah was fluid, adaptable to different historical contexts. Reform Judaism was brought to the United States with the immigration of German Jews, and in 1885 a conference of Rabbis was held in Pittsburgh, Pennsylvania, that explored the direction of that denomination. The outcome was the following Declaration of Principles—or the Pittsburgh Platform, as it is often called. Although the statement was modified at later conferences, Reform Judaism today still holds to these basic tenets.

1. We recognize in every religion an attempt to grasp the Infinite, and in every mode, source or book of revelation held sacred in any religious system the consciousness of the indwelling of God in man. We hold that Judaism presents the highest conception of the God-idea as taught in our Holy Scriptures and developed and spiritualized by the Jewish teachers, in accordance with the moral and philosophical progress of their respective ages. We maintain that Judaism preserved and defended midst continual struggles and trials and under enforced isolation, this God-idea as the central religious truth for the human race.
2. We recognize in the Bible the record of the consecration of the Jewish people to its mission as the priest of the one God, and value it as the most potent instrument of religious and moral instruction. We hold that the modern discoveries of scientific researches in the domain of nature and history are not antagonistic to the doctrines of Judaism, the Bible reflecting the primitive ideas of its own age, and at times clothing its conception of divine Providence and Justice dealing with men in miraculous narratives.
3. We recognize in the Mosaic legislation a system of training the Jewish people for its mission during its national life in Palestine, and today we accept as binding only its moral laws, and maintain only such ceremonies as elevate and sanctify our lives, but reject all such as are not adapted to the views and habits of modern civilization.
4. We hold that all such Mosaic and rabbinical laws as regulate diet, priestly purity, and dress originated in ages and under the influence

of ideas entirely foreign to our present mental and spiritual state. They fail to impress the modern Jew with a spirit of priestly holiness; their observance in our days is apt rather to obstruct than to further modern spiritual elevation.

5. We recognize, in the modern era of universal culture of heart and intellect, the approaching of the realization of Israel's great messianic hope for the establishment of the kingdom of truth, justice, and peace among all men. We consider ourselves no longer a nation, but a religious community, and therefore expect neither a return to Palestine, nor a sacrificial worship under the sons of Aaron, nor the restoration of any of the laws concerning the Jewish state.
6. We recognize in Judaism a progressive religion, ever striving to be in accord with the postulates of reason. We are convinced of the utmost necessity of preserving the historical identity with our great past. Christianity and Islam, being daughter religions of Judaism, we appreciate their providential mission, to aid in the spreading of monotheistic and moral truth. We acknowledge that the spirit of broad humanity of our age is our ally in the fulfillment of our mission, and therefore we extend the hand of fellowship to all who cooperate with us in the establishment of the reign of truth and righteousness among men.
7. We reassert the doctrine of Judaism that the soul is immortal, grounding the belief on the divine nature of human spirit, which forever finds bliss in righteousness and misery in wickedness. We reject as ideas not rooted in Judaism, the beliefs both in bodily resurrection and in Gehenna and Eden (Hell and Paradise) as abodes for everlasting punishment and reward.
8. In full accordance with the spirit of the Mosaic legislation, which strives to regulate the relations between rich and poor, we deem it our duty to participate in the great task of modern times, to solve, on the basis of justice and righteousness, the problems presented by the contrasts and evils of the present organization of society.

Source: *Proceedings of the Pittsburg Rabbinical Conference, November 16, 17, 18, 1885* (Richmond, VA: Old Dominion Press, 1923).

ZIONISM: THEODOR HERZL

Zion *in Jewish tradition refers variously to the Temple Mount in Jerusalem, the city of Jerusalem itself, or the larger territory of Judea. Since the days of the Babylonian exile, it has been the focal point in the desires of dispersed Jews to return to their native land. In the 1890s, Hungarian-born Theodor Herzl (1860–1904) founded the modern Zionist movement, which, in response to rampant anti-Semitism throughout Europe, aimed to reunite Jews in a homeland. Herzl's movement continued after his death and, in the aftermath of the Nazi Holocaust, succeeded in creating the modern country of Israel. The following is from Herzl's seminal book,* The Jewish State, *in which he argues that Palestine, rather than Argentina, is the most suitable location for Jewish repatriation.*

No one can deny the gravity of the situation of the Jews. Wherever they live in perceptible numbers, they are more or less persecuted. Their equality before the law, granted by statute, has become practically a dead letter. They are debarred from filling even moderately high positions, either in the army, or in any public or private capacity. And attempts are made to thrust them out of business also: "Don't buy from Jews!"

Attacks in Parliaments, in assemblies, in the press, in the pulpit, in the street, on journeys—for example, their exclusion from certain hotels—even in places of recreation, become daily more numerous. The forms of persecution vary according to the countries and social circles in which they occur. In Russia, imposts are levied on Jewish villages; in Rumania, a few persons are put to death; in Germany, they get a good beating occasionally; in Austria, Anti-Semites exercise terrorism over all public life; in Algeria, there are traveling agitators; in Paris, the Jews are shut out of the so-called best social circles and excluded from clubs. Shades of anti-Jewish feeling are innumerable. But this is not to be an attempt to make out a doleful category of Jewish hardships. . . .

The whole plan is in its essence perfectly simple, as it must necessarily be if it is to come within the comprehension of all.

Let the sovereignty be granted us over a portion of the globe large enough to satisfy the rightful requirements of a nation; the rest we shall manage for ourselves.

The creation of a new State is neither ridiculous nor impossible. We have in our day witnessed the process in connection with nations which were not largely members of the middle class, but poorer, less educated, and consequently weaker than ourselves. The Governments of all countries scourged by Anti-Semitism will be keenly interested in assisting us to obtain the sovereignty we want.

The plan, simple in design, but complicated in execution, will be carried out by two agencies: The Society of Jews and the Jewish Company. . . .

Shall we choose Palestine or Argentine? We shall take what is given us, and what is selected by Jewish public opinion. The Society will determine both these points.

Argentine is one of the most fertile countries in the world, extends over a vast area, has a sparse population and a mild climate. The Argentine Republic would derive considerable profit from the cession of a portion of its territory to us. The present infiltration of Jews has certainly produced some discontent, and it would be necessary to enlighten the Republic on the intrinsic difference of our new movement.

Palestine is our ever-memorable historic home. The very name of Palestine would attract our people with a force of marvelous potency. If his Majesty the Sultan were to give us Palestine, we could in return undertake to regulate the whole finances of Turkey.

Source: Theodor Herzl, *The Jewish State,* tr. Sylvie d' Avigdor (London: D. Nutt, 1896), ch. 2, "The Jewish Question."

RECONSTRUCTIONIST JUDAISM: PRAYER OF THIRTEEN WANTS

In 1926, a dedication ceremony took place for the new headquarters of the Society for the Advancement of Judaism, an organization associated with Reconstructionist Judaism. On that occasion Rabbi Mordecai Kaplan offered the following "Prayer of Thirteen Wants," which subsequently was included in the Reconstructionist Sabbath Prayer Book. *The eighth and tenth of these "wants" especially reflect the progressive Reconstructionist ideal of integrating traditional Judaism with contemporary life.*

1. We want Judaism to help us overcome temptation, doubt and discouragement.
2. We want Judaism to imbue us with a sense of responsibility for the righteous use of the blessings wherewith God endows us.
3. We want the Jew so to be trusted that his yea will be taken as yea, and his nay as nay.
4. We want to learn how to utilize our leisure to best advantage, physically, intellectually, and spiritually.
5. We want the Jewish home to live up to its traditional standards of virtue and piety.
6. We want the Jewish upbringing of our children to further their moral and spiritual growth, and to enable them to accept with joy their heritage as Jews.
7. We want the synagogue to enable us to worship God in sincerity and in truth.
8. We want our religious traditions to be interpreted in terms of understandable experience and to be made relevant to our present-day needs.
9. We want to participate in the upbuilding of Eretz Yisrael as a means to the renaissance of the Jewish spirit.
10. We want Judaism to find rich, manifold and ever new expression in philosophy, letters and the arts.
11. We want all forms of Jewish organization to make for spiritual purpose and ethical endeavor.
12. We want the unity of Israel throughout the world to be fostered through mutual help in time of need, and through cooperation in the furtherance of Judaism at all time.
13. We want Judaism to function as a potent influence for justice, freedom and peace in the life of men and nations.

Source: Mordecai Kaplan, "Criteria of Jewish Loyalty," *Sabbath Prayer Book* (New York: Jewish Reconstructionist Foundation, 1945).

Christianity

Christianity

INTRODUCTION

Christianity is founded on the life and teachings of Jesus, a first century C.E. Jew who was executed by the Roman authorities for subversion. During its first few decades, Christianity was a sect within Judaism, but it quickly expanded beyond its Palestinian borders and Jewish framework, becoming an independent religion. Two elements of Christian doctrine are essentially Jewish. First, Jesus is the Messiah, or anointed king, who is spoken of in Jewish prophetic writings. The term *christ* is a Greek translation of the Hebrew word *messiah,* so Jesus is referred to as the Christ. Second, the message of Jesus is the kingdom of God. Keeping with Jewish apocalyptic notions of the Messiah, early Christians expected that the kingdom would be established by cataclysmic events. A third element of Christianity departs from its Jewish heritage, namely, the belief that Jesus is God in human form. Building on this, a fourth element is that, by his work, teachings, death, and resurrection, Jesus became the savior of the world.

The Life of Jesus

Jesus left no writings, and our knowledge of his life and teachings comes almost exclusively from the Gospels of Matthew, Mark, and Luke. These narratives are traditionally ascribed to his disciples, but they probably were written and compiled anonymously between forty and sixty years after his death. They also were written by believers for believers, blending historical memories with early Church teaching. Reconstructing an accurate picture of Jesus, then, is difficult—according to some theologians, impossible.

Jesus was born about 4 B.C.E. and raised in Nazareth, a small agricultural city in the Galilee region. Little is known about Jesus until he began his ministry at about age 30. Jewish territories at that time were under especially oppressive Roman rule, which caused widespread unrest. Since the times of the independent Jewish monarchies hundreds of years earlier, 90 percent of the Jewish population had consisted of agrarian peasants who supported the ruling priestly elite through taxes on their harvest. Additional taxes were imposed by the Romans, and still more were collected to support local building projects, such as those of King Herod. By the time of Jesus, peasant taxes totaled about 40 percent of the harvest, forcing many into debt or sale of family land. Unemployment was also high. As the Romans reduced the size of

Jewish territories, Jews from surrounding areas flooded into Judea and Galilee, the two principal territories of Jewish settlement. Occasional famine made economic times worse and intensified the rift between peasants and the ruling class, which supported the Romans.

Desperate peasants rallied around charismatic leaders who offered hope. Some supported social bandits who systematically robbed rich Jewish landowners and shared the wealth with the peasants. Others found comfort in the company of prophets who, in the tradition of the old Jewish prophets, pronounced apocalyptic judgment against the Romans and called the people to repentance. Still others took refuge in the leadership of messiahs, that is, anointed kings. The concept of a Messiah in Jewish literature did not become fixed until rabbinic discussions after the revolt of 66 C.E. Prior to that time, written discussions refer to a Davidic king, a prophet like Moses or a perfect priest; the actual term *Messiah* is rarely used. The notion of Messiah in the minds of the illiterate peasants was somewhat different from that which appeared in the writings of the ruling elite. Although the peasants retained the idea of kingship, they saw the anointing of this king as a revolutionary act of popular election. The Messiah was to be a flesh-and-blood military leader, not simply an apocalyptic figure waging spiritual war.

Jesus began his ministry during his association with John the Baptizer, an apocalyptic prophet who proclaimed impending doom. John baptized Jesus and shortly afterward was executed by the ruler of Galilee, who feared that John's enthusiastic followers might provoke a rebellion. Jesus attracted his own followers in Galilee, who initially saw him as a popular prophet, rather more like John the Baptizer than a political Messiah. Of his large following of both men and women, later Christian tradition honored twelve as having special authority (although there is disagreement over who exactly the twelve were). With his disciples, Jesus traveled around Galilee teaching, befriending outcasts, healing people, and performing exorcisms. He taught to both small gatherings in synagogues and large peasant crowds in open-air places. His ministry lasted only a couple of years until he was executed on a Roman cross. The precise reasons for his execution may never be known. For John the Baptizer, attracting large crowds in a revolutionary environment was enough to cost him his life. To the extent that Jesus appeared to be another popular prophet, Jewish and Roman leaders had reason for concern.

The Teaching of Jesus

Like the events of his life, Jesus' teachings in the Gospels blend his words with early Church doctrine. Some scholars argue that fewer than 20 percent of the sayings attributed to Jesus in the Gospels were spoken by him. The dominant message that emerges, though, is the kingdom of God. The "kingdom," never actually defined, is the final state of affairs in which the world runs according to God's will. Paradoxically, some teachings proclaim that the kingdom will arrive in the near future, while others maintain that the kingdom has already begun. Although the concepts of both a future and a present kingdom of God can be found in Jewish apocalyptic literature, Jesus is unique in making the doctrine of the kingdom the basis of ethical behavior. Moral acts of repentance, love, charity, and nonviolence are God's requirements for acceptance into the kingdom. Because of the urgency in preparing for the kingdom, uncompromising behavior is required. Jesus did not see himself as the messianic ruler of the kingdom he proclaimed, especially in view of the military implications of the popular messiahs.

Along with its content, the style of Jesus' teaching—the parable—is also important. Most broadly, a parable is a statement, story, or dialog that has a metaphorical or figurative meaning. It can be as short as a single sentence, such as "It is easier for a camel to pass through the eye of a needle than for a rich man to enter the kingdom of God" (Mark 10:25), or paragraphs long. Understood this way, almost everything attributed to Jesus in the Gospels of Matthew, Mark, and Luke is in the form of a parable. More narrowly, parables are extended metaphorical narratives, or figurative stories, about thirty of which appear in these first three Gospels and the Gospel of Thomas (see following). In view of their figurative nature, the parables require interpretation, and sometimes an early Christian explanation is presented within the Gospel text itself. The interpretation of virtually all the parables, though, relates to some challenging aspect of the kingdom. Like much of Old Testament literature, Jesus' parables follow specific literary structures. For example, Luke 11:9–10 follows step parallelism:

A Ask, and it will be given you
  B Seek, and you will find
    C Knock, and it will be opened to you

A′ For everyone who asks receives
  B′ And he who seeks finds
    C′ And to him who knocks it will be opened

Even the longest narrative parables use a combination of various parallel structures.

The Early Church

After Jesus' execution, strong leaders and apostles emerged within the Jesus movement, keeping its spirit alive and recruiting even more followers. Jesus was quickly seen as the crucified and risen Messiah who would return from heaven at any moment and begin an apocalyptic (as opposed to military) reign. Old Testament messianic prophecies were applied to him, bolstering the interpretation that Jesus was the Christ. Some followers sold their possessions and awaited his arrival. Others, such as Paul, a former Pharisee, effectively recruited believers from among non-Jews. Early interpretations of Jesus and his message varied greatly among the new followers, and the Christian tradition we inherit was defined in reaction to and in competition with early alternatives. The New Testament canon and early Church hierarchy are products of the winning tradition, whereas the losing traditions were branded as heresies along the way. An early losing interpretation was that of Judaizers who believed that Christianity was the messianic fulfillment of Judaism, and not a different religion. Thus, Christians were still bound by traditional Jewish laws, such as circumcision and food rituals. However, the Judaizers' narrow notion of Christianity did not fit the broader vision of other early Church leaders.

Another unsuccessful early interpretation of Christianity was offered by Gnosticism, a diverse religious movement that flourished throughout the Near East from 100 to 400 C.E. The aim of the Gnostic religion in general was to free one's spirit from the illusions of the evil, material world and reascend to heaven. Release was to be accomplished by acquiring special knowledge *(gnosis).* In Christian Gnosticism, the material world was created by an evil demigod, and Jesus' teachings provide the knowledge that redeems us from worldly illusion. Church leaders reacted vehemently to the Gnostic interpretation, penning many polemics against it.

While theologians battled over doctrine, churches were established throughout the Roman Empire, and bishops—successors of the original Apostles—officiated in key regions. At first, Roman rulers did not distinguish between Christians and Jews. But the rapid advance of Christianity soon made the distinction apparent and, from their perspective, threatened the unity of the Empire. Christianity was outlawed and, throughout the first three centuries C.E., several emperors systematically persecuted Christians, some bent on their extinction. A decisive turning point came when Emperor Constantine took the throne. In 313 C.E. he proclaimed complete religious liberty for Christians. He sponsored a world Church council, at Nicea, which determined that Christ was not subordinate to God but was substantively identical with God. The council also established the bishops of Rome, Antioch, and Alexandria as the primary officiators of the Church; later the bishop of Constantinople was added to the list. In 392 C.E. Emperor Theodosius declared Christianity the only allowable religion throughout the empire.

Christian Denominations

During the fourth century C.E., the vast Roman Empire became too difficult to manage from a single location, so it was regionally divided, with the western territory governed by Rome and the eastern territory governed by Constantinople. Now inseparably tied to empire politics, the Church too established parallel jurisdictions. The western jurisdiction, later designated *Catholic,* was led by Rome's bishop, or *Pope,* and the eastern (or *Orthodox*) jurisdiction looked, less formally, to Constantinople's bishop, or *Patriarch.* Differences of worship and authority further divided the regions, such as the east's use of icons, rejection of papal authority, and emphasis on Christ's divinity above his humanity. The rift was complete in 1054 when Rome's Pope Leo IX and Constantinople's Patriarch Michael Cerularius mutually excommunicated each other. Since the great Catholic-Orthodox schism, the three original eastern church jurisdictions (Antioch, Alexandria, and Constantinople) have multiplied to more than twenty, each with its own Patriarch. Although the Orthodox jurisdictions govern independently, they are unified by shared liturgy and doctrine.

After the fall of the western Roman empire to barbarian invasions in the fifth century, missionary journeys spread Christianity throughout northern Europe. The Pope was on a par with emperors of new and primitive European states, and Christian monasteries were the default centers of learning. By the sixteenth century, growing discontentment with Catholic hierarchy erupted in the Protestant Reformation, led by the German priest Martin Luther. Luther stressed that the Bible, not the Pope and not Church traditions, is Christianity's exclusive authority. Salvation, Luther declared, is achieved through God's grace, not through human achievement, and is available to all who ask. Luther was particularly successful in convincing German nobility of the benefits of breaking ties with Rome. As surrounding European countries soon followed the reformer's lead, Luther believed that the protesters would remain theologically unified because God would guide each person toward the same interpretation of the Bible. This was not to be, and five centuries later hundreds of Protestant denominations have emerged from disputes over doctrine. The largest Protestant denominations are the Lutherans, Baptists, Presbyterians, Methodists, and Episcopalians. The large denominations are often doctrinally divided among themselves; the more conservative emphasize evangelism and biblical inerrency, whereas the more liberal stress social concerns and metaphorical interpretations of the Bible. Pentecostal churches are part of a movement, rather than a single denomination, and stress spiritual gifts such as prophecy and speaking in tongues.

The Bible

The primary body of scriptures in the Christian tradition is the Bible, which consists of an Old and a New Testament. The Old Testament is the Jewish *Tanakh,* which makes the Christian Bible unique among world scriptures in including the canon of a different religion. The Christian Old Testament initially was based on the Septuagint, the Greek translation of the Jewish canon from 100 B.C.E. Accordingly, the Old Testament retains the book arrangement of the Septuagint. Catholic and Orthodox Christians also accept the apocryphal books from the Septuagint, although Protestants reject these, opting for what they believe are the older books as they appear in the Jewish *Tanakh.* The term *Old Testament* was coined by Paul, who used it in reference to the writings of the Mosaic covenant (2 Cor. 3:14).

By the fourth century C.E., the term *New Testament* was commonly used to refer to a collection of twenty-seven early Christian texts composed in Greek. Traditionally they are thought to have been written by the original Apostles who were Jesus' followers. Historically, though, the texts appear to have been written by second- and third-generation Christians from 50 to 150 C.E. For the first few centuries, there was no fixed New Testament canon, and manuscripts of hundreds of individual Christian texts circulated independently among the early churches. Early Church Fathers made recommendations as to which of these were authoritative. The first known list containing the present twenty-seven books appears as a side comment in St. Athanasius's Easter letter of 367 C.E.

As Latin became the spoken language of the Roman Empire, Latin translations of the Old Testament and various Christian texts circulated. In 382, the Pope commissioned Jerome, a priest and scholar, to bring order to the chaotic collection of Latin texts. Returning to Hebrew and Greek language texts, Jerome produced a new Latin translation of the Old and New Testaments, referred to as the Vulgate, which after some resistance was accepted as definitive. Even with a more fixed canon, early theologians questioned the authority of several Old and New Testament texts and introduced a distinction between protocanonical and deuterocanonical texts: canonical writings with either primary or secondary status. In the thirteenth century, the traditional chapter divisions were added to each book of the Bible by a cardinal who was preparing a biblical index. The Vulgate continued to be the official text of the Bible until the Protestant Reformation, when several modern-language translations appeared, many of which removed the books of the Old Testament Apocrypha, or at least relegated them to an appendix. Verse divisions also were added at this time. As scholars today discover older manuscript copies of biblical books, passages are revised or deleted to reflect the earliest sources. For example, the well-known story from John 9 of the stoning of the adulterous woman ("Let him who is without sin cast the first stone") is now removed from many modern editions of the Bible.

The texts of the New Testament fall into five categories:

Gospels: Matthew, Mark, Luke, John

Book of Acts

Letters of Paul: Romans, 1 and 2 Corinthians, Galatians, Ephesians, Philippians, Colossians, 1 and 2 Thessalonians, 1 and 2 Timothy, Titus, Philemon, Hebrews

General letters: Letter of James; 1 and 2 Letters of Peter; 1, 2, and 3 Letters of John; Letter of Jude

Book of Revelation

The Gospels, which contain accounts of Jesus, have always been considered the most primary of all Christian texts. Scholars believe that for a few decades after Jesus' execution, the recollections of his immediate followers were transmitted orally. The first written accounts, from perhaps 50 C.E., were simply lists of his sayings with no stories. None of these have survived intact. The book of Mark appeared around 70 C.E., based on oral traditions of Jesus' life and teachings. Matthew and Luke appeared around 85 C.E., both using information from Mark and an earlier lost list of sayings called *Quelle* (German for *source*). Matthew and Luke also contain unique stories and sayings, based on either oral traditions or earlier lost lists of sayings. Mark, Matthew, and Luke are referred to as the *synoptic gospels,* because they give very similar accounts of Jesus' life and teachings. Finally, the Gospel of John appeared in 90 C.E. Initially considered heretical by some early Church Fathers, it presents an account that is 90 percent different in content from the synoptic Gospels.

All four Gospels first circulated anonymously and were not ascribed to the apostles until the middle of the second century.

The Book of Acts is a continuation of Luke, penned by the same author, and discusses the spread of early Christianity immediately after Jesus. Of particular concern is the relationship of Christianity to Judaism in view of the large numbers of non-Jewish converts. More than half of Acts chronicles the conversion and missionary journeys of Paul. Of the fourteen letters ascribed to Paul, only seven are confidently traced to him (Romans, 1 and 2 Corinthians, Galatians, Philippians, 1 Thessalonians, and Philemon). His letters, composed between 50 and 60 C.E., contain encouragement and instructions to the churches he helped establish, but they did not gain a wide readership until the end of the first century. The general letters were written at the close of the first century as tracts or sermons addressing problems in early Church communities. Finally, the Book of Revelation, also written at the close of the first century, describes a series of apocalyptic visions that contain instructions for Christians to remain faithful in the face of Roman persecution.

Non-Biblical Sacred Writings

Early noncanonical Christian texts are extraordinarily varied and include gospels, creeds, and writings of the Church Fathers. Some collections of early sacred texts have special designations. The term *Apostolic Fathers* was coined in the seventeenth century in reference to a collection of works attributed to followers of the original apostles. The fourteen texts now included under this label were popular in the early Church and were even included in scripture lists by early Church Fathers. Of particular interest in this collection is the *Didache,* or Teaching of the Twelve, which gives instructions on baptism, fasting, prayer, and the Eucharist. The expression *New Testament Apocrypha* is applied loosely to a range of early Christian texts, mostly from the second century, that are not included in the New Testament. Many of these were considered sacred by early churches and are the source of Christian beliefs, such as the assumption of Mary. Frequently they aim to fill gaps in the chronologies of Jesus' life and the early Church. Paralleling the genres of New Testament texts, the writings fall into the categories of gospels, acts, epistles, and apocalypses. They are of particular value as a possible source of stray sayings of Jesus that continued to circulate into the second century.

One collection of early writings that has recently attracted scholarly attention is the Gnostic texts discovered in 1945 in Nag Hammadi, Egypt. The forty-five texts are fourth- and fifth-century Coptic translations of Greek manuscripts, although the originals go back much farther. Representing both Christian and non-Christian Gnostic ideas, they are thought to be the library of an early Gnostic Christian monastery that buried the documents in containers for protection. The texts suggest that early Christianity was more theologically diverse than initially believed. Some texts, for instance, emphasize a divine Mother. Most important among the writings is the Gnostic Gospel of Thomas, a list of 114 sayings of Jesus. Some scholars believe that this list is based on an earlier compilation of sayings, predating the New Testament Gospels, and thus, like Q, represents the earliest stratum of sayings attributed to Jesus.

Many early Christian creeds were the outcome of theological disputes and represent official positions arrived at in early Church councils. They are typically short and list the principal propositions of the official Church. The most famous of the early ones are the Apostles' Creed, Nicene Creed, and Chalcedon Creed, which even today are incorporated into worship services in many Christian traditions.

From as early as the first century, another inspirational source of Christian literature was the voluminous writings of early Church Fathers, saints, and mystics. The purposes and genres of these texts are quite varied and include defenses of Christianity against heretics and pagans, stories of martyred Christians, commentaries on books of the Bible, sermons, letters, and theological treatises. Perhaps the most influential of these are the writings of St. Augustine (354–430), Bishop of the North African city of Hippo. The Orthodox, Catholic, and later Protestant traditions have a long and continuous history of mystical writings, which emphasize the importance of spiritual union with God. One such mystical work from a later period of Catholic thought is *Interior Castle,* by Spanish Carmelite nun Teresa of Avila (1515–1582).

Since the Protestant Reformation, denominations have formed specific statements of faith, and some movements have their own special sacred texts in addition to the Bible. Protestant denominations tend to hold that the Bible is the principal, if not the exclusive, scripture of Christianity. Nevertheless, almost every Protestant group has formed some statement of faith that defines its views and distinguishes it from other denominations. In keeping with the religious freedom and pioneering spirit of nineteenth-century America, some Christian movements gave rise to new sacred texts. The distinct beliefs of the Church of Latter-Day Saints are founded on the *Book of Mormon,* a text produced by founder Joseph Smith (1805–1844). The Christian Science movement reveres *Science and Health* (1875), by founder Mary Baker Eddy (1821–1910), which emphasizes the healing aspect of Christianity. Associated with the New Age movement, American pastor Levi H. Dowling (1844–1911) produced the *Aquarian Gospel* in 1907, which recounts eighteen lost years of Jesus' life as he traveled to India, Tibet, Egypt, Persia, and Greece.

HOLIDAYS

Sunday Weekly day of worship that commemorates God's day of rest and Jesus' resurrection.

Advent (four weeks beginning four Sundays before Christmas) Commemorates the coming of Jesus.

Christmas (December 25) Commemorates the birth of Jesus and begins the Christmas season.

(Continued)

Epiphany (January 6) Commemorates the manifestation of Jesus to the Gentiles and closes the Christmas season.

Lent (forty days prior to Easter) Period of penance.

Holy Week (last seven days of Lent) Commemorates Jesus' final arrival in Jerusalem and his suffering and death; includes Palm Sunday and Good Friday.

Easter (usually April) Commemorates Jesus' rising from the dead and the beginning of the fifty-day Easter season.

Pentecost Commemorates the appearance of the Holy Spirit to the Christian community and concludes the Easter season.

TIMELINE

4 B.C.E.	Jesus born
29 C.E.	Jesus executed
70	First Gospels written
150	Gnostic controversy and the Apostle's Creed
313	Constantine's Edict of Milan
325	Arian controversy and Council of Nicaea
382	Jerome commissioned to produce the Vulgate
550	Five Patriarchates established
1054	Catholic/Orthodox schism
1204	Roman Crusaders invade Constantinople
1517	Martin Luther posts the Ninety-Five Theses
1545	Catholic Council of Trent
1549	English *Book of Common Prayer* published
1589	Russian Patriarchate founded
1608	Baptists founded by John Smyth
1784	Methodists founded by John Wesley
1830	*Book of Mormon* published by Joseph Smith
1914	Assemblies of God founded
1948	World Council of Churches founded
1962	Second Vatican Council

GLOSSARY

Apostles Early followers of Jesus commissioned to lead the Church after his death.

Bible Fundamental Christian scripture consisting of the Old and New Testaments.

Catholic The largest Christian denomination, which follows a Church hierarchy led by the bishop of Rome (i.e., the Pope).

Disciples Jesus' followers.

Eastern Orthodox The church diocese originally of the eastern Roman Empire that rejects the supreme authority of the bishop of Rome.

Gnosticism The Near Eastern religious movement from 100 to 400 C.E, which aims to free one's spirit from the evil material world by acquiring special knowledge (gnosis).

Holy Spirit Divine presence and agent of guidance for Christians. One person of the Trinity, along with the Father and Son.

Judaizers First-century Jewish Christians who maintained that Christians were still bound by traditional Jewish laws.

Messiah Hebrew term for "anointed one" or "king," indicating that someone is set aside for a divinely appointed office, either in a religious, apocalyptic sense or in a political, revolutionary sense.

New Age Contemporary religious movement based on the astrological view that the present Piscean age is ending and will be succeeded by a new age of Aquarius.

Pentecostal Protestant religious movement emphasizing baptism of the Holy Spirit and speaking in tongues.

Pope Head of the Church and successor to the Apostle Peter according to the Roman Catholic tradition.

Protestant Christian denominations whose lineages derive from the sixteenth-century Protestant Reformation.

Quelle (or Q) A written sayings list, no longer extant, that Matthew and Luke used as a source for Jesus' teachings.

Synoptic Gospels Gospels of Mark, Matthew, and Luke, which are similar in content, in contrast to the Gospel of John, which vastly differs from all three.

Trinity Doctrine that God is a unity of three persons: the Father, Son, and Holy Spirit.

FURTHER READINGS

BAINTON, ROLAND HERBERT. *The Reformation of the Sixteenth Century*. Boston: Beacon Press, 1952.

BORG, MARCUS J. *Jesus in Contemporary Scholarship*. Valley Forge, PA: Trinity, 1994.

BOWDEN, JOHN. *Encyclopedia of Christianity*. New York: Oxford University Press, 2005.

CHADWICK, OWEN (ed.). *The Pelican History of the Church*. 5 vols. London: Penguin, 1960–1970.

CHIDESTER, DAVID. *Christianity: A Global History*. San Francisco: HarperCollins, 2004.

CROSSAN, JOHN DOMINIC. *Jesus: A Revolutionary Biography*. San Francisco: HarperCollins, 1994.

HACKEL, SERGEI. *The Orthodox Church*. London: Ward Lock Educational, 1971.

HUGHES, PHILIP. *A Short History of the Catholic Church*. London: Burns and Oates, 1978.

LATOURETTE, KENNETH S. *A History of Christianity*. 2 vols. San Francisco: HarperCollins, 1975.
MCMANNERS, JOHN. *The Oxford Illustrated History of Christianity*. New York: Oxford University Press, 2002.
PELIKAN, JAROSLAV. *The Christian Tradition: A History of the Development of Doctrine*. 4 vols. Chicago: University of Chicago Press, 1971–1983.
WHITE, MICHAEL. *From Jesus to Christianity*. San Francisco: HarperCollins, 2004.
WOODHEAD, LINDA. *Christianity: A Very Short Introduction*. Cambridge: Cambridge University Press, 2005.

JESUS' BIRTH AND MINISTRY

PRINCE OF PEACE AND SUFFERING SERVANT

The principal value of the Old Testament for Christianity is that Christ is the ultimate fulfillment of its covenants and messianic prophecies. Nowhere is that seen more clearly than in the following two selections from Isaiah on the birth of the prince of peace and the suffering servant. For Christians, these are allusions to Jesus' birth and his suffering on the cross.

9.

For to us a child is born, to us a son is given, and the government will be on his shoulders. And he will be called Wonderful Counselor, Mighty God, Everlasting Father, Prince of Peace. Of the increase of his government and peace there will be no end. He will reign on David's throne and over his kingdom, establishing and upholding it with justice and righteousness from that time on and forever. The zeal of the Lord Almighty will accomplish this.

53.

He grew up before him like a tender shoot, and like a root out of dry ground. He had no beauty or majesty to attract us to him, nothing in his appearance that we should desire him. He was despised and rejected by men, a man of sorrows, and familiar with suffering. Like one from whom men hide their faces he was despised, and we esteemed him not. Surely he took up our infirmities and carried our sorrows, yet we considered him stricken by God, smitten by him, and afflicted. But he was pierced for our transgressions, he was crushed for our iniquities; the punishment that brought us peace was upon him, and by his wounds we are healed. We all, like sheep, have gone astray, each of us has turned to his own way; and the Lord has laid on him the iniquity of us all.

He was oppressed and afflicted, yet he did not open his mouth; he was led like a lamb to the slaughter, and as a sheep before her shearers is silent, so he did not open his mouth. By oppression and judgment he was taken away. And who can speak of his descendants? For he was cut off from the land of the living; for the transgression of my people he was stricken. He was assigned a grave with the wicked, and with the rich in his death, though he had done no violence, nor was any deceit in his mouth.

Yet it was the Lord's will to crush him and cause him to suffer, and though the Lord makes his life a guilt offering, he will see his offspring and prolong his days, and the will of the Lord will prosper in his hand. After the suffering of his soul, he will see the light (of life) and be satisfied; by his knowledge my righteous servant will justify many, and he will bear their iniquities.

Source: Isaiah 9:6–7, 53:2–11, from *The Holy Bible, New International Version* (International Bible Society, 1984). Reprinted by permission.

BIRTH OF JESUS

Two of the four canonical Gospels give accounts of the birth of Jesus, each slightly different. The following is Luke's version. The author of Luke was an educated non-Jewish Christian and thus his Gospel reflects the broader non-Jewish implications of both Jesus' life and the Christian Church. Unlike Matthew, Luke begins by placing the birth story in the context of Roman emperor Augustus' reign.

In those days it so happened that a decree was issued by Emperor Augustus that a census be taken of the whole civilized world. This first census was taken while Quirinius was governor of Syria. Everybody had to travel to their ancestral city to be counted in the census. So Joseph too went up from Galilee, from the town of Nazareth, to Judea, to the town of David called Bethlehem, because he was a descendant of David, to be counted in the census with Mary, to whom he was engaged; Mary was pregnant. It so happened while they were there that the time came for her to give birth; and she gave birth to a son, her firstborn. She wrapped him in strips of cloth and laid him in a feeding trough, because the travelers' shelter was no place for that.

Now in the same area there were shepherds living outdoors. They were keeping watch over their sheep at night, when a messenger of the Lord stood near them and the glory of the Lord shone around them. They became terrified. But the messenger said to them, "Don't be afraid: I bring you good news of a great joy, which is to benefit the whole nation; today in the city of David, the Savior was born to you—he is the Anointed, the Lord. And this will be a sign for you: you will find a baby wrapped in strips of cloth and lying in a feeding trough."

And suddenly there appeared with the messenger a whole troop of the heavenly army praising God:

> Glory to God in the highest,
> and on earth peace to people whom he has favored!

It so happened when the messengers left and returned to heaven that the shepherds said to one another, "Come on! Let's go over to Bethlehem and see what has happened, the event the Lord has told us about." And they hurried away, and found Mary, Joseph, and the baby lying in a feeding trough. And when they saw it they reported what they had been told about this child. Everyone who listened was astonished at what the shepherds told them. But Mary took all this in and reflected on it. And the shepherds returned, glorifying and praising God for all they had heard and seen; everything turned out just as they had been told.

Now eight days later, when the time came to circumcise him, they gave him the name Jesus, the name assigned him by the heavenly messenger before he was conceived in the womb.

Now when the time came for their purification according to the Law of Moses, they brought him up to Jerusalem to present him to the Lord—as it is written in the Law of the Lord, "Every male that opens the womb is to be considered holy to the Lord"—and to offer sacrifice according to what is dictated in the Law of the Lord: "A pair of turtledoves or two young pigeons." . . .

And when they had carried out everything required by the Law of the Lord, they returned to Galilee, to Nazareth, their own city. And the boy grew up and became strong, and was filled with wisdom; and God regarded him favorably.

Source: Luke, 2:1–24, 39, 40, from *The Complete Gospels: Annotated Scholars Version*, ed. Robert J. Miller (Polebridge Press, Harper San Francisco, 1994). Reprinted by permission.

JESUS' BAPTISM, TEMPTATION, AND FIRST DISCIPLES

The first canonical Gospel to appear was Mark. Mark focuses more on activities in the life of Jesus than on teachings. His narrative is concise, matter-of-fact, and probably written for a non-Jewish audience in Rome about 70 C.E. *Because virtually the entire content of Mark's account is included in the longer Gospels of Matthew and Luke (which use Mark as one of several sources), Mark's Gospel was typically not the most popular. However, as modern scholars try to identify the earliest recorded accounts of Jesus, preference is now given to Mark's narrative. The following selection, from the opening chapter of Mark, describes Jesus' baptism by John the Baptizer. This initiated his ministry, his temptation in the desert where he confronted Satan, and his acquiring of his first followers. Some scholars believe that after Jesus' death early Christians had to explain why the Jewish populace did not recognize Jesus as the Messiah. Mark has an explanation that both Matthew and Luke adopt: Jesus purposefully kept word of his messiahship from circulating in order to minimize conflict with officials. Referred to as the* messianic secret, *this explanation appears twice in the following passage.*

The good news of Jesus the Anointed begins with something Isaiah the prophet wrote:

Here is my messenger,
whom I send on ahead of you
to prepare your way!
A voice of someone shouting in the wilderness:
"Make ready the way of the Lord,
make his paths straight."

So, John the Baptizer appeared in the wilderness calling for baptism and a change of heart that led to forgiveness of sins. And everyone from the Judean countryside and all the residents of Jerusalem streamed out to him and got baptized by him in the Jordan river, admitting their sins. And John wore a mantel made of camel hair and had a leather belt around his waist and lived on locust and raw honey. And he began his proclamation by saying:

"Someone more powerful than I will succeed me, whose sandal straps I am not fit to bend down and untie. I have been baptizing you with water, but he'll baptize you with holy spirit."

During the same period Jesus came from Nazareth, Galilee, and was baptized in the Jordan by John. And just as he got up out of the water, he saw the skies torn open and the spirit coming down toward him like a dove. There was also a voice from the skies: "You are my favored son—I fully approve of you."

And right away the spirit drives him out into the wilderness, where he remained for forty days, being put to the test by Satan. While he was living there among the wild animals, the heavenly messengers looked after him.

After John was locked up, Jesus came to Galilee proclaiming God's good news. His message went:

"The time is up: God's imperial rule is closing in. Change your ways, and put your trust in the good news!"

As he was walking alone by the Sea of Galilee, he spotted Simon and Andrew, Simon's brother, casting [their nets] into the sea—since they were fishermen—and Jesus said to them: "Become my followers and I'll have you fishing for people!"

And right then and there they abandoned their nets and followed him.

When he had gone a little farther, he caught sight of James, son of Zebedee, and his brother John mending their nets in the boat. Right then and there he called out to them as well, and they left their father Zebedee behind in the boat with the hired hands and accompanied him.

Then they come to Capernaum, and on the sabbath day he went right to the synagogue and started teaching. They were astonished at his teaching, since he would teach them on his own authority, unlike the scholars.

Now right there in their synagogue was a person possessed by an unclean spirit, which shouted, "Jesus! What do you want with us, you Nazarene? Have you come to get rid of us? I know you, who you are: God's holy man!"

But Jesus yelled at it, "Shut up and get out of him!"

Then the unclean spirit threw the man into convulsions, and letting out a loud shriek it came out of him. And they were all so amazed that they asked themselves, "What's this? A new kind of teaching backed by authority! He gives orders even to unclean spirits and they obey him!"

So his fame spread rapidly everywhere throughout Galilee and even beyond.

They left the synagogue right away and entered the house of Simon and Andrew along with James and John. Simon's mother-in-law was in bed with a fever, and they told him about her right away. He went up to her, took hold of her hand, raised her up, and the fever disappeared. Then she started looking after them.

In the evening, at sundown, they would bring all the sick and demon possessed to him. And the whole town would crowd around the door. On such occasions he cured many people afflicted with various diseases and drove out many demons. He would never let the demons speak, because they realized who he was.

And rising early, while it was still very dark, he went outside and stole away to an isolated place, where he started praying. Then Simon and those with him hunted him down. When they had found him they say to him, "They're all looking for you."

But he replies: "Let's go somewhere else, to the neighboring villages, so I can speak there too, since that's what I came for."

So he went all around Galilee speaking in their synagogues and driving out demons.

Then a leper comes up to him, pleads with him, falls down on his knees, and says to him, "If you want to, you can make me clean."

Although Jesus was indignant, he stretched out his hand, touched him, and says to him, "Okay—you're clean!"

And right away the leprosy disappeared, and he was made clean. And Jesus snapped at him, and dismissed him curtly with this warning: "See that you don't tell anyone anything, but go, have a priest examine [your skin]. Then offer for your cleansing what Moses commanded, as evidence [of your cure]."

But after he went out, he started telling everyone and spreading the story, so that [Jesus] could no longer enter a town openly, but had to stay out in the countryside. Yet they continued to come to him from everywhere.

Source: Mark 1, from *The Complete Gospels.*

SERMON ON THE MOUNT

Matthew's Gospel was written for a Jewish audience, and it continually draws parallels from the Old Testament. He incorporates Jesus' sayings into five distinct discourses—possibly representing the five books of Moses, to symbolize a new Torah. The Sermon on the Mount is the first of these; again, the mountain motif here parallels the story of Moses receiving the Law at Mount Sinai. Many of the teachings in Matthew overlap those in Luke, suggesting that they independently drew their information from a third source (called Q by contemporary scholars). Some sayings in the Sermon on the Mount also appear in Luke in a section often called the Sermon on the Plain (6:20–49). Matthew's discourse opens with a description of how the kingdom of God will involve a dramatic reversal of conditions for the oppressed and faithful. Citizens of the kingdom must distinguish themselves through obedience to a new law, principally one of love for others, forgiveness, and trust in God.

5. Taking note of the crowds, he climbed up the mountain, and when he had sat down, his disciples came to him. He then began to speak, and this is what he would teach them:

    Congratulations to the poor in spirit!
    Heaven's domain belongs to them.
    Congratulations to those who grieve!
    They will be consoled.
    Congratulations to the gentle!
    They will inherit the earth.
    Congratulations to those who hunger and thirst for justice!
    They will have a feast.
    Congratulations to the merciful!
    They will receive mercy.
    Congratulations to those with undefiled hearts!
    They will see God.
    Congratulations to those who work for peace!
    They will be known as God's children.
    Congratulations to those who have suffered persecution for the sake of justice!
    Heaven's domain belongs to them.

"Congratulations to you when they denounce you and persecute you and spread malicious gossip about you because of me. Rejoice and be glad! In heaven you will be more than compensated. Remember, this is how they persecuted the prophets who preceded you.

"You are the salt of the earth. But if salt loses its zing, how will it be made salty? It then has no further use than to be thrown out and stomped on. You are the light of the world. A city sitting on top of a mountain can't be concealed. Nor do people light a lamp and put it under a bushel basket but rather on a lampstand, where it sheds light for everyone in the house. That's how your light is to shine in the presence of others, so they can see your good deeds and acclaim your Father in the heavens.

"Don't imagine that I have come to annul the Law or the Prophets. I have come not to annul but to fulfill. I swear to you, before the world disappears, not one iota, not one serif, will disappear from the Law, until that happens. Whoever ignores one of the most trivial of these regulations, and teaches others to do so, will be called trivial in Heaven's domain. But whoever acts on [these regulations] and teaches [others to do so], will be called great in Heaven's domain. Let me tell you: unless your religion goes beyond that of the scholars and Pharisees, you won't set foot in Heaven's domain.

"As you know, our ancestors were told, 'You must not kill' and 'Whoever kills will be subject to judgment.' But I tell you: those who are angry with a companion will be brought before a tribunal. And those who say to a companion, 'You moron,' will be subject to the sentence of the court. And whoever says, 'You idiot,' deserves the fires of Gehenna. So, even if you happen to be offering your gift at the altar and recall that your friend has some claim against you, leave your gift there at the altar. First go and be reconciled with your friend, and only then return and offer your gift. You should come to terms quickly with your opponent while you are both on the way [to court], or else your opponent will hand you over to the judge, and the judge [will turn you over] to the bailiff, and you are thrown in jail. I swear to you, you'll never get out of there until you've paid the last dime.

"As you know, we once were told, 'You are not to commit adultery.' But I tell you: Those who leer at a woman and desire her have already committed adultery with her in their hearts. And if your right eye gets you into trouble, rip it out and throw it away! You would be better off to lose a part of your body, than to have your whole body thrown into Gehenna. And if your right hand gets you into trouble, cut it off and throw it away! You would be better off to lose a part of your body, than to have your whole body wind up in Gehenna.

"We once were told, 'Whoever divorces his wife should give her a bill of divorce.' But I tell you: Everyone who divorces his wife (except in the case of infidelity) makes her the victim of adultery; and whoever marries a divorced woman commits adultery.

"Again, as you know, our ancestors were told, 'You must not break an oath,' and 'Oaths sworn in the name of God must be kept.' But I tell you: Don't swear at all. Don't invoke heaven, because it is the throne of God, and don't invoke earth, because it is God's footstool, and don't invoke Jerusalem, because it is the city of the great king. You shouldn't swear by your head either, since you aren't able to turn a single hair either white or black. Rather, your responses should be simply 'Yes' and 'No.' Anything that goes beyond this is inspired by the evil one.

"As you know, we once were told, 'An eye for an eye' and 'A tooth for a tooth.' But I tell you: Don't react violently against the one who is evil: when someone slaps you on the right cheek, turn the other as well. If someone is determined to sue you for your shirt, let that person have your coat along with it. Further, when anyone conscripts you for one mile, go along an extra mile. Give to the one who begs from you; and don't turn away the one who tries to borrow from you.

"As you know, we once were told, 'You are to love your neighbor' and 'You are to hate your enemy.' But I tell you: Love your enemies and pray for your persecutors. You'll then become children of your Father in the heavens. [God] causes the sun to rise on both the bad and the good, and sends rain on both the just and the unjust. Tell me, if you love those who love you, why should you be commended for that? Even the toll collectors do as much, don't they? And if you greet only your friends, what have you done that is exceptional! Even the pagans do as much, don't they? To sum up, you are to be as liberal in your love as your heavenly Father is."

6. "Take care that you don't flaunt your religion in public to be noticed by others. Otherwise, you will have no recognition from your Father in the heavens. For example, when you give to charity, don't bother to toot your own horn as some phony pietists do in houses of worship and on the street. They are seeking human recognition. I swear to you, their grandstanding is its own reward. Instead, when you give to charity, don't let your left hand in on what your right hand is up to, so your acts of charity may remain hidden. And your Father, who has an eye for the hidden, will applaud you.

"And when you pray, don't act like phonies. They love to stand up and pray in houses of worship and on street corners, so they can show off in public. I swear to you, their prayers have been answered! When you pray, go into a room by yourself and shut the door behind you. Then pray to your Father, the hidden one. And your Father, with his eye for the hidden, will applaud you. And when you pray, you should not babble on as the pagans do. They imagine that the length of their prayers will command attention. So don't imitate them. After all, your Father knows what you need before you ask. Instead, you should pray like this:

> Our Father in the heavens,
> your name be revered.
> Impose your imperial rule,
> enact your will on earth as you have in heaven.
> Provide us with the bread we need for the day.
> Forgive our debts
> to the extent that we have forgiven those in debt to us.
> And please don't subject us to test after test,
> but rescue us from the evil one.

For if you forgive others their failures and offenses, your heavenly Father will also forgive yours. And if you don't forgive the failures and mistakes of others, your Father won't forgive yours.

"When you fast, don't make a spectacle of your remorse as the pretenders do. As you know, they make their faces unrecognizable so their fasting may be publicly recognized. I swear to you, they have been paid in full. When you fast, comb your hair and wash your face, so your fasting may go unrecognized in public. But it will be recognized by your Father, the hidden one, and your Father, who has an eye for the hidden, will applaud you.

"Don't acquire possessions here on earth, where moths and insects eat away and where robbers break in and steal. Instead, gather your nest egg in heaven, where neither moths nor insects eat away and where no robbers break in or steal. As you know, what you treasure is your heart's true measure.

"The eye is the body's lamp. If follows that if your eye is clear, your whole body will be flooded with light. If your eye is clouded, your whole body will be shrouded in darkness. If, then, the light within you is darkness, how dark that can be!

"No one can be a slave to two masters. No doubt that slave will either hate one and love the other, or be devoted to one and disdain the other. You can't be enslaved to both God and a bank account!

"That's why I tell you: Don't fret about your life—what you're going to eat and drink—or about your body—what you're going to wear. There is more to living than food and clothing, isn't there? Take a look at the birds of the sky: they don't plant or harvest, or gather into barns. Yet your heavenly Father feeds them. You're worth more than they, aren't you? Can any of you add one hour to life by fretting about it? Why worry about clothes? Notice how the wild lilies grow: they don't slave and they never spin. Yet let me tell you, even Solomon at the height of his glory was never decked out like one of them. If God dresses up the grass in the field, which is here today and tomorrow is thrown into an oven, won't [God care for] you even more, you who don't take anything for granted? So don't fret. Don't say, 'What am I going to eat?' or 'What am I going to drink?' or 'What am I going to wear?' These are all things pagans seek. After all, our heavenly Father is aware that you need them. You are to seek [God's] domain, and his justice first, and all these things will come to you as a bonus. So don't fret about tomorrow. Let tomorrow fret about itself. The troubles that the day brings are enough."

7. "Don't pass judgment, so you won't be judged. Don't forget, the judgment you hand out will be the judgment you get back. And the standard you apply will be the standard applied to you. Why do you notice the sliver in your friend's eye, but overlook the timber in your own? How can you say to your friend, 'Let me get the sliver out of your eye,' when there is that timber in your own? You phony, first take the timber out of your own eye and then you'll see well enough to remove the sliver from your friend's eye.

"Don't offer to dogs what is sacred, and don't throw your pearls to pigs, or they'll trample them underfoot and turn and tear you to shreds.

"Ask—it'll be given to you; seek—you'll find; knock—it'll be opened for you. Rest assured: everyone who asks receives; everyone who seeks finds; and for the one who knocks it is opened. Who among you would hand a son a stone when it's bread he's asking for? Again, who would hand him a snake when it's fish he's asking for? Of course no one would! So if you, worthless as you are, know how to give your children good gifts, isn't it much more likely that your Father in the heavens will give good things to those who ask him?

"Consider this: Treat people in ways you want them to treat you. This sums up the whole of the Law and the Prophets.

"Try to get in through the narrow gate. Wide and smooth is the road that leads to destruction. The majority are taking that route. Narrow and rough is the road that leads to life. Only a minority discover it.

"Be on the lookout for phony prophets, who make their pitch disguised as sheep; inside they are really voracious wolves. You'll know who they are by what they produce. Since when do people pick grapes from thorns or figs from thistles? Every healthy tree produces choice fruit, but the rotten tree produces spoiled fruit. A healthy tree cannot produce spoiled fruit, any more than a rotten tree can produce choice fruit. Every tree that does not produce choice fruit gets cut down and tossed on the fire. Remember, you'll know who they are by what they produce.

"Not everyone who addresses me as 'Master, master,' will get into Heaven's domain—only those who carry out the will of my Father in heaven. On that day many will address me: 'Master, master, didn't we use your name when we prophesied? Didn't we use your name when we exorcised demons? Didn't we use your name when we performed all those miracles?' Then I will tell them honestly: 'I never knew you; get away from me, you subverters of the Law!'

"Everyone who pays attention to these words of mine and acts on them will be like a shrewd builder who erected a house on bedrock. Later the rain fell, and the torrents came, and the winds blew and pounded that house, yet it did not collapse, since its foundation rested on bedrock. Everyone who listens to these words of mine and doesn't act on them will be like a careless builder, who erected a house on the sand. When the rain fell, and the torrents came, and the winds blew and pounded that house, it collapsed. Its collapse was colossal."

And so, when Jesus had finished this discourse, the crowds were astonished at his teaching, since he had been teaching them on his own authority, unlike their [own] scholars.

Source: Matthew 5–7, from *The Complete Gospels*.

GOOD SAMARITAN AND PRODIGAL SON

Of the approximately thirty parables of Jesus, the two most famous appear only in Luke: the good Samaritan and the prodigal son. Luke sets both parables in a larger narrative context. The good Samaritan parable is introduced in a dialog between Jesus and a lawyer (adapted from Mark 12:28–34) on loving one's neighbor. Jesus then explains that the notion of one's neighbor crosses religious and social boundaries, just as a Samaritan aids a battered Jew in spite of enmity between their two ethnic groups. The prodigal son parable is one of three that Jesus gives in response to criticisms that he associates with sinners. The parable's message is one of forgiveness. The father (representing God) forgives the younger son (representing non-Jews) who squanders his inheritance, while the dutiful older brother (representing Jews) protests.

10. On one occasion, a legal expert stood up to put him to the test with a question: "Teacher, what do I have to do to inherit eternal life?"

He said to him, "How do you read what is written in the Law?"

And he answered, "You are to love the Lord your God with all your heart, with all your soul, with all your energy, and with all your mind; and your neighbor as yourself."

Jesus said to him, "You have given the correct answer; do this and you will have life."

But with a view to justifying himself, he said to Jesus, "But who is my neighbor?"

Jesus replied:

> This fellow was on his way from Jerusalem down to Jericho when he fell into the hands of robbers. They stripped him, beat him up, and went off, leaving him half dead. Now by coincidence a priest was going down that road; when he caught sight of him, he went out of his way to avoid him. In the same way, when a Levite came to the place, he took one look at him and crossed the road to avoid him. But this Samaritan who was traveling that way came to where he was and was moved to pity at the sight of him. He went up to him and bandaged his wounds, pouring olive oil and wine on them. He hoisted him onto his own animal, brought him to an inn, and looked after him. The next day he took out two silver coins, which he gave to the innkeeper, and said, "Look after him, and on my way back I'll reimburse you for any extra expenses you have had."

"Which of these three, in your opinion, acted like a neighbor to the man who fell into the hands of the robbers?"

He said, "The one who showed him compassion."

Jesus said to him, "Then go and do the same yourself."

15. Now the toll collectors and sinners kept crowding around Jesus so they could hear him. But the Pharisees and the scholars would complain to each other: "This fellow welcomes sinners and eats with them."

So he told them this parable: . . .

> Once there was this man who had two sons. The younger of them said to his father, "Father, give me the share of the property that's coming to me." So he divided his resources between them.
>
> Not too many days later, the younger son got all his things together and left home for a faraway country, where he squandered his property by living extravagantly. Just when he had spent it all, a serious famine swept through that country, and he began to do without. So he went and hired himself out to one of the citizens of that country, who sent him out to his farm to feed the pigs. He longed to satisfy his hunger with the carob pods, which the pigs usually ate; but no one offered him anything. Coming to his senses he said, "Lots of my father's hired hands have more than enough to eat, while here I am dying of starvation! I'll get up and go to my father and I'll say to him, 'Father, I have sinned against heaven and affronted you; I don't deserve to be called a son of yours any longer; treat me like one of your hired hands.'" And he got up and returned to his father.
>
> But while he was still a long way off, his father caught sight of him and was moved to compassion. He went running out to him, threw his arms around his neck, and kissed him. And the son said to him, "Father, I have sinned against heaven and affronted you; I don't deserve to be called a son of yours any longer."

0

But the father said to his slaves, "Quick! Bring out the finest robe and put it on him; put a ring on his finger and sandals on his feet. Fetch the fat calf and slaughter it; let's have a feast and celebrate, because this son of mine was dead and has come back to life; he was lost and now is found." And they started celebrating.

Now his elder son was out in the field; and as he got closer to the house, he heard music and dancing. He called one of the servant-boys over and asked what was going on.

He said to him, "Your brother has come home and your father has slaughtered the fat calf, because he has him back safe and sound."

But he was angry and refused to go in. So his father came out and began to plead with him. But he answered his father, "See here, all these years I have slaved for you. I never once disobeyed any of your orders; yet you never once provided me with a kid goat so I could celebrate with my friends. But when this son of yours shows up, the one who has squandered your estate with prostitutes—for him you slaughter the fat calf."

But [the father] said to him, "My child, you are always at my side. Everything that's mine is yours. But we just had to celebrate and rejoice, because this brother of yours was dead, and has come back to life; he was lost, and now is found."

Source: Luke 10:25–37; 15:1–3, 11–32, from *The Complete Gospels.*

PETER RECEIVES THE KEYS

Early Christian traditions typically traced their lineage back to an original follower of Jesus. Early Gnostics viewed Jesus' brothers, James and Thomas, as their founders. For Ethiopians, the founder is the eunuch of Acts 8. For the Orthodox of Constantinople, he is Andrew the Apostle. The Catholic Church, though, considers its foundation to be Peter, the first supreme Pope. The concept of the Petrine Papacy is based on two doctrines. First, the doctrine of apostolic succession maintains that the original Apostles had authority over specific regional churches, which they passed on to their successors. Peter established the Church of Rome, and at his death authority was passed to Linus. Second, the doctrine of the primacy of Peter, forged in the third through fifth centuries, maintains that Peter was given supreme authority over all Church congregations. The argument for this latter claim is based on the following passage from Matthew. Drawing from a scene in Mark 8:27 in which Peter identifies Jesus as the Messiah, Matthew then recounts that Jesus rewarded Peter with keys to the kingdom of God. Although the language is metaphorical, Peter is clearly given sweeping authority, indicating Matthew's allegiance to the Petrine tradition. Matthew continues by foreshadowing Jesus' fate.

When Jesus came to the region of Caesarea Philippi, he started questioning his disciples, asking, "What are people saying about the son of Adam?"

They said, "Some [say, 'He is] John the Baptist,' but others, 'Elijah,' and others, 'Jeremiah or one of the prophets.'"

He says to them, "What about you, who do you say I am?"

And Simon Peter responded, "You are the Anointed, the son of the living God!"

And in response Jesus said to him, "You are to be congratulated, Simon son of Jonah, because flesh and blood did not reveal this to you but my Father who is in heaven. Let me tell you, you are Peter, 'the Rock,' and on this very rock I will build my congregation, and the gates of Hades will not be able to overpower it. I shall give you the keys of Heaven's domain, and whatever you bind on earth will be considered bound in heaven, and whatever you release on earth will be considered released in heaven."

Then he ordered the disciples to tell no one that he was the Anointed.

From that time on Jesus started to make it clear to his disciples that he was destined to go to Jerusalem, and suffer a great deal at the hands of the elders and ranking priests and scholars, and be killed and, on the third day, be raised.

And Peter took him aside and began to lecture him, saying, "May God spare you, master; this surely can't happen to you."

But he turned and said to Peter, "Get out of my sight, you Satan, you. You are dangerous to me because you are not thinking in God's terms, but in human terms."

Then Jesus said to his disciples, "If any of you wants to come after me you should deny yourself, pick up your cross, and follow me!

"Remember, by trying to save your own life, you are going to lose it, but by losing your own life for my sake, you are going to find it. After all, what good will it do if you acquire the whole world but forfeit your life? Or what will you give in exchange for your life?

"Remember, the son of Adam is going to come in the glory of his father with his messengers, and then he will reward everyone according to their deeds. I swear to you: Some of those standing here won't ever taste death before they see the son of Adam's imperial rule arriving."

Source: Matthew 16:13–28, from *The Complete Gospels.*

LAZARUS RAISED FROM THE DEAD

The Gospel of John presents an account of Jesus that is almost entirely different from that of the synoptic Gospels. In John, Jesus' ministry is three years, as opposed to one year; the subject of eternal life is emphasized, and not the kingdom of God; Jesus performs no exorcisms, refers to himself as the son of God, is the subject of his own teachings, and says little about the poor. Although Jesus performs miracles in both John and the synoptics, the purpose is different. In John, they are intentionally performed as signs indicating his divine role, whereas in the synoptics such signs are shunned and miracles are depicted mainly as acts of compassion. In the following passage, Jesus performs his most dramatic miracle by raising a dead man to life. For John, as well as the synoptics, Jesus' supernatural powers were seen by the Jewish leaders as a threat to social and religious stability, inciting them to plot against him.

Now someone named Lazarus had fallen ill; he was from Bethany, the village of Mary and her sister Martha. (This was the Mary who anointed the Master with oil and wiped his feet with her hair; it was her brother

Lazarus who was sick.) So the sisters sent for [Jesus]: "Master, the one you love is sick."

But when Jesus heard this he said, "This illness is not fatal; it is to show God's majesty, so God's son also will be honored by it."

Jesus loved Martha and her sister and Lazarus. When he heard that [Lazarus] was sick, he lingered two more days where he was; then he says to the disciples, "Let's go to Judea again."

The disciples say to him, "Rabbi, just now the Judeans were looking for the opportunity to stone you; are you really going back there?"

"Aren't there twelve hours in the day?" Jesus responded. "Those who walk during the day won't stumble; they can see by this world's light. But those who walk at night are going to stumble, because they have no light to go by."

He made these remarks, and then he tells them, "Our friend Lazarus has fallen asleep, but I am going to wake him up."

"Master, if he's only fallen asleep," said the disciples, "he'll revive." (Jesus had been speaking of death but they thought that he meant [he was] only asleep.)

Then Jesus told them plainly, "Lazarus is dead; and I'm happy for you that I wasn't there, so you can believe. Now let's go to him."

Then Thomas, called "the Twin," said to his fellow disciples, "Let's go along too, so we can die with him."

When Jesus arrived, he found that [Lazarus] had been buried four days earlier. Bethany was near Jerusalem, about two miles away, and many of the Judeans had come to Martha and Mary to console them about their brother. When Martha heard that Jesus was coming, she went to meet him; Mary stayed at home. "Master," said Martha, "if you'd been here, my brother wouldn't have died. Still I know that whatever you ask of God, God will grant you."

Jesus says to her, "Your brother will be resurrected."

Martha responds, "I know he'll be raised in the resurrection on the last day."

Jesus said to her, "I am resurrection and life; those who believe in me, even if they die, will live; but everyone who is alive and believes in me will never die. Do you believe this?"

"Yes, Master," she says, "I believe that you are the Anointed, God's son, who is to come to earth."

At this point she went to call her sister Mary, telling her privately, "The Teacher is here and is asking for you." When she heard that, she got up quickly and went to him.

Jesus hadn't yet arrived at the village; he was still where Martha had met him.

When the Judeans, who hovered about her in the house to console her, saw Mary get up and go out quickly, they followed her, thinking she was going to the tomb to grieve there. When Mary got to where Jesus was and saw him, she fell down at his feet. "Master," she said, "if you'd been here, my brother wouldn't have died."

When Jesus saw her crying, and the Judeans who accompanied her crying too, he was agitated and deeply disturbed; he said, "Where have you put him?"

"Master," they say, "come and see."

Then Jesus cried.

So the Judeans observed, "Look how much he loved him." But some wondered: "He opened the blind man's eyes; couldn't he have kept this man from dying?"

Again greatly agitated, Jesus arrives at the tomb; it was a cave, and a stone lay up against the opening. Jesus says, "Take the stone away."

Martha, sister of the dead man, replies, "But Master, by this time the body will stink; it's been four days."

Jesus says to her, "Didn't I tell you, if you believed you'll see God's majesty?" So they took the stone away, and Jesus looked upwards and said, "Father, thank you for hearing me. I know you always hear me, but I say this because of the people standing here, so they'll believe that you sent me." Then he shouted at the top of his voice, "Lazarus, come out!" The dead man came out, his hands and feet bound in strips of burying cloth, and his face covered with a cloth. Jesus says to them, "Free him [from the burying cloth] and let him go."

As a result, many of the Judeans who had come to Mary and observed what Jesus had done came to believe in him. But some of them went to the Pharisees and reported what Jesus had done.

So the ranking priests and Pharisees called the Council together and posed this question to them: "What are we going to do now that this fellow performs many miracles? If we let him go on like this, everybody will come to believe in him. Then the Romans will come and destroy our [holy] place and our nation."

Then one of them, Caiaphas, that year's high priest, addressed them as follows: "Don't you know anything? Don't you realize that it's to your advantage to have one person die for the people and not have the whole nation wiped out?"

(He didn't say this on his own authority, but since he was that year's high priest he could foresee that Jesus would die for the nation. In fact, [he would die] not only for the nation, but to gather together all God's dispersed children and make them one [people].)

Source: John 11:1–54, from *The Complete Gospels.*

JESUS' DEATH

LAST SUPPER

Jesus' final days took place in Jerusalem during the Jewish holiday of Passover. The four Gospels depict Jesus and his disciples gathering for a meal, known as the "Last Supper" (Luke describes this as the traditional meal of the Passover festival). At this meal, according to the synoptic Gospels, Jesus performed ritual acts with the bread and wine.

This event is the basis of the Christian sacrament of the Eucharist. In Christian doctrine, a sacrament is a visible religious rite that confers special grace. The number of sacraments has varied throughout Christian history; twelfth-century theologian Hugo of St. Victor listed thirty. Baptism and the Eucharist have always been the most important.

Now it was two days until Passover and the feast of Unleavened Bread. And the ranking priests and the scholars were looking for some way to arrest him by trickery and kill him. For their slogan was "Not during the festival, otherwise the people will riot."

When he was in Bethany at the house of Simon the leper, he was just reclining there, and a woman came in carrying an alabaster jar of myrrh, of pure and expensive nard. She broke the jar and poured [the myrrh] on his head.

Now some were annoyed [and thought] to themselves: "What good purpose is served by this waste of myrrh? For she could have sold the myrrh for more than three hundred silver coins and given [the money] to the poor." And they were angry with her.

Then Jesus said, "Let her alone! Why are you bothering her? She has done me a courtesy. Remember, there will always be poor around, and whenever you want you can do good for them, but I won't always be around. She did what she could—she anticipates in anointing my body for burial. So help me, wherever the good news is announced in all the world, what she has done will also be told in memory of her!"

And Judas Iscariot, one of the twelve, went off to the ranking priests to turn him over to them. When they heard, they were delighted, and promised to pay him in silver. And he started looking for some way to turn him in at the right moment.

On the first day of Unleavened Bread, when they would sacrifice the Passover lamb, his disciples say to him, "Where do you want us to go and get things ready for you to celebrate Passover?"

He sends two of his disciples and says to them, "Go into the city, and someone carrying a waterpot will meet you. Follow him, and whatever place he enters say to the head of the house, 'The teacher asks, "Where is my guest room where I can celebrate Passover with my disciples?"' And he'll show you a large upstairs room that has been arranged. That's the place you're to get ready for us."

And the disciples left, went into the city, and found it exactly as he had told them; and they got things ready for Passover.

When evening comes, he arrives with the twelve. And as they reclined at tables and were eating, Jesus said, "So help me, one of you eating with me is going to turn me in!"

They began to fret and to say to him one after another, "I'm not the one, am I?"

But he said to them, "It's one of the twelve, the one who is dipping into the bowl with me. The son of Adam departs just as the scriptures predict, but damn the one responsible for turning the son of Adam in! It would be better for that man had he never been born!"

And as they were eating, he took a loaf, gave a blessing, broke it into pieces and offered it to them. And he said, "Take some; this is my body!" He also took a cup, gave thanks and offered it to them, and they all drank from it. And he said to them: "This is my blood of the covenant, which has been poured out for many! So help me, I certainly won't drink any of the fruit of the vine again until that day when I drink it for the first time in God's domain!"

Source: Mark 14:1–25, from *The Complete Gospels.*

FATHER, SON, AND HOLY SPIRIT

In John's account of the Last Supper, Jesus gives a farewell discourse, presented here. Unlike the synoptic Gospels, in which Jesus speaks in short, crisp sayings and parables, in John Jesus speaks in extended discourses. The discourse topic here is the relation between God the Father and Jesus the Son. The doctrine of the Trinity, central to Christianity, holds that God is a unity of three persons: the Father, Son, and Holy Spirit. Although the term "Trinity" and its technical meaning were developed by early Church Fathers, passages that associate the Father, Son, and Holy Spirit are the scriptural basis of the doctrine. The following account is particularly important in this regard. The Holy Spirit is only briefly mentioned at the end of this passage. In the Old Testament occasional references are made to a spirit of God, but John and other New Testament writers expand on this notion and see the Holy Spirit both as a divine presence and as an agent of guidance for the Church.

"Don't give in to your distress. You believe in God, then believe in me too. There are plenty of places to stay in my Father's house. If it weren't true, I would have told you; I'm on my way to make a place ready for you. And if I go to make a place ready for you, I'll return and embrace you. So where I am you can be too. You know where I'm going and you know the way."

Thomas says to him, "Master, we don't know where you're going. How can we possibly know the way?"

"I am the way, and I am truth, and I am life," replies Jesus. "No one gets to the Father unless it is through me. If you do recognize me, you will recognize my Father also. From this moment on you know him and you've even seen him."

"Let us see the Father," Philip says to him, "and we'll be satisfied."

"I've been around you all this time," Jesus replies, "and you still don't know me, do you, Philip? Anyone who has seen me has seen the Father. So how can you say, 'Let us see the Father'? Don't you believe that I'm in the Father and the Father is in me? I don't say what I say on my own. The Father is with me constantly, and I perform his labors. You ought to believe that I'm in the Father and the Father is in me. If not, at least you ought to believe these labors in and of themselves. I swear to God, anyone who believes in me will perform the works I perform and will be able to perform even greater feats, because I'm on my way to the Father. In addition, I'll do whatever you request in my name, so the Father can be honored by means of the son. If you request anything using my name, I'll do it.

"If you love me, you'll obey my instructions. At my request the Father will provide you with yet another advocate, the authentic spirit, who will be with you forever. The world is unable to accept [this spirit] because it neither perceives nor recognizes it. You recognize it because it dwells in you and will remain in you.

"I won't abandon you as orphans; I'll come to you. In a little while the world won't see me any longer, but you'll see me because I'm alive as you will be alive. At the time you will come to know that I'm in my Father and that you're in me and I'm in you. Those who accept my instructions and obey them—they love me. And those who love me will be loved by my Father; moreover, I will love them and make myself known to them."

Judas (not Iscariot) says to him, "Master, what has happened that you are about to make yourself known to us but not to the world?"

Jesus replied to him, "Those who love me will heed what I tell them, and my Father will love them, and we'll come to them and make our home there. Those who don't love me won't follow my instructions. Of course, the things you heard me say are not mine but come from the Father who sent me.

"I have told you these things while I am still here with you. Yet the advocate, the holy spirit the Father will send in my stead, will teach you everything and remind you of everything I told you. Peace is what I leave behind for you; my peace is what I give you. What I give you is not a worldly gift. Don't give in to your distress or be overcome by terror. You heard me tell you, 'I'm going away and I'm going to return to you.' If you loved me, you'd be glad that I'm going to the Father, because the Father is greater than I am. So I have now told you all this ahead of time so you will believe when it happens.

"Time does not permit me to tell you much more; you see, the ruler of this world is already on the way. However, so the world may know I love the Father, I act exactly as my Father instructed me. Come on, let's get out of here."

Source: John 14:1–26, from *The Complete Gospels*.

TRIAL, CRUCIFIXION, RESURRECTION

After the Last Supper, Jesus went with his disciples to a hillside graveyard to pray. There he was arrested, brought before the Jewish legal council, and accused of blasphemy. Not empowered to perform criminal executions, the council brought Jesus to the Roman governor Pilate, where they made a case for treason based on Jesus' messianic claims. Pilate pronounced the desired verdict and sentence. All four Gospels place responsibility on the Jews, first the priests and then an angry mob, although the ultimate decision rested with the governor. Jesus was then executed on a cross, in classic Roman fashion, and placed in the rock-hewn tomb of a wealthy follower. Mark's Gospel reports that after a few days the tomb was found empty, and a young man present at the tomb announced that Jesus was resurrected. The other Gospels report appearances of the resurrected Jesus.

14. And right away, while he was still speaking, Judas, one of the twelve, shows up, and with him a crowd, dispatched by the ranking priests and the scholars and the elders, wielding swords and clubs. Now the one who was to turn him in had arranged a signal with them, saying, "The one I'm going to kiss is the one you want. Arrest him and escort him safely away!" And right away he arrives, comes up to him, and says, "Rabbi," and kisses him.

And they seized him and held him fast. One of those standing around drew his sword and struck the high priest's slave and cut off his ear. In response Jesus said to them, "Have you come out to take me with swords and clubs as though you were apprehending a rebel? I was with you in the temple area day after day teaching and you didn't lift a hand against me. But the scriptures must come true!"

And they all deserted him and ran away. And a young man was following him, wearing a shroud over his nude body, and they grab him. But he dropped the shroud and ran away naked.

And they brought Jesus before the high priest, and all the ranking priests and elders and scholars assemble.

Peter followed him at a distance until he was inside the courtyard of the high priest, and was sitting with the attendants and keeping warm by the fire.

The ranking priests and the whole Council were looking for evidence against Jesus in order to issue a death sentence, but they couldn't find any. Although many gave false evidence against him, their stories didn't agree. And some people stood up and testified falsely against him: "We have heard him saying, 'I'll destroy this temple made with hands and in three days I'll build another, not made with hands!'" Yet even then their stories did not agree.

And the high priest got up and questioned Jesus: "Don't you have some answer to give? Why do these people testify against you?"

But he was silent and refused to answer.

Once again the high priest questioned him and says to him, "Are you the Anointed, the son of the Blessed One?"

Jesus replied, "I am! And you will see the son of Adam sitting at the right hand of Power and coming with the clouds of the sky!"

Then the high priest tore his vestments and says, "Why do we still need witnesses? You have heard the blasphemy! What do you think?" And they all concurred in the death penalty.

And some began to spit on him, and to put a blindfold on him, and punch him, and say to him, "Prophesy!" And the guards abused him as they took him into custody.

And while Peter was below in the courtyard, one of the high priest's slave women comes over, and sees Peter warming himself; she looks at him closely, then speaks up: "You too were with that Nazarene, Jesus!"

But he denied it, saying, "I haven't the slightest idea what you're talking about!" And he went outside into the forecourt.

And when the slave woman saw him, she once again began to say to those standing nearby, "This fellow is one of them!"

But once again he denied it.

And a little later, those standing nearby would again say to Peter, "You really are one of them, since you also are a Galilean!"

But he began to curse and swear, "I don't know the fellow you're talking about!" And just then a rooster crowed a second time, and Peter remembered what Jesus had told him: "Before a rooster crows twice you will disown me three times!" And he broke down and started to cry.

15. And right away, at daybreak, the ranking priests, after consulting with the elders and scholars and the whole Council, bound Jesus and led him away and turned him over to Pilate. And Pilate questioned him: "*You* are 'the King of the Judeans'?"

And in response he says to him, "If you say so."

And the ranking priests started a long list of accusations against him. Again Pilate tried questioning him: "Don't you have some answer to give? You see what a long list of charges they bring against you!"

But Jesus still did not respond, so Pilate was baffled.

At each festival it was the custom for him to set one prisoner free for them, whichever one they requested. And one called Barabbas was being held with the insurgents who had committed murder during the uprising. And when the crowd arrived, they began to demand that he do what he usually did for them.

And in response Pilate said to them, "Do you want me to set 'the King of the Judeans' free for you?" After all, he realized that the ranking priests had turned him over out of envy.

But the ranking priests incited the crowd to get Barabbas set free for them instead.

But in response [to their request] Pilate would again say to them, "What do you want me to do with the fellow you call 'the King of the Judeans'?"

And they in turn shouted, "Crucify him!"

Pilate kept saying to them, "Why? What has he done wrong?"

But they shouted all the louder, "Crucify him!" And because Pilate was always looking to satisfy the crowd, he set Barabbas free for them, had Jesus flogged, and then turned him over to be crucified.

And the soldiers led him away to the courtyard of the governor's residence, and they called the whole company together. And they dressed him in purple and crowned him with a garland woven of thorns.

And they began to salute him: "Greetings, 'King of the Judeans'!" And they kept striking him on the head with a staff, and spitting on him; and they would get down on their knees and bow down to him. And when they had made fun of him, they stripped off the purple and put his own clothes back on him. And they led him out to crucify him.

And they conscript someone named Simon of Cyrene, who was coming in from the country, the father of Alexander and Rufus, to carry his cross.

And they bring him to the place Golgotha (which means "Place of the Skull"). And they tried to give him wine mixed with myrrh, but he didn't take it. And they crucify him, and they divide up his garments, casting lots to see who would get what. It was 9 o'clock in the morning when they crucified him. And the inscription, which identified his crime, read, "The King of the Judeans." And with him they crucify two rebels, one on his right and one on his left.

Those passing by kept taunting him, wagging their heads, and saying, "Ha! You who would destroy the temple and rebuild it in three days, save yourself and come down from the cross!"

Likewise the ranking priests had made fun of him to one another, along with the scholars; they would say, "He saved others, but he can't save himself! 'The Anointed,' 'the King of Israel,' should come down from the cross here and now, so that we can see and trust for ourselves!"

Even those being crucified along with him would abuse him.

And when noon came, darkness blanketed the whole land until mid-afternoon. And at 3 o'clock in the afternoon Jesus shouted at the top of his voice, "*Eloi, Eloi, lema sabachthani*" (which means "My God, my God, why did you abandon me?").

And when some of those standing nearby heard, they would say, "Listen, he's calling Elijah!" And someone ran and filled a sponge with sour wine, stuck it on a pole, and offered him a drink, saying, "Let's see if Elijah comes to rescue him!"

But Jesus let out a great shout and breathed his last.

And the curtain of the temple was torn in two from top to bottom! When the Roman officer standing opposite him saw that he had died like this, he said, "This man really was God's son!"

Now some women were observing this from a distance, among whom were Mary of Magdala, and Mary the mother of James the younger and Joses, and Salome. [These women] had regularly followed and assisted him when he was in Galilee, along with many other women who had come up to Jerusalem in his company.

And when it had already grown dark, since it was preparation day (the day before the sabbath), Joseph of Arimathea, a respected council member, who himself was anticipating God's imperial rule, appeared on the scene, and dared to go to Pilate to request the body of Jesus.

And Pilate was surprised that he had died so soon. He summoned the Roman officer and asked him whether he had been dead for long. And when he had been briefed by the Roman officer, he granted the body to Joseph. And he brought a shroud and took him down and wrapped him in the shroud, and placed him in a tomb that had been hewn out of rock, and rolled a stone up against the opening of the tomb. And Mary of Magdala and Mary the mother of Joses noted where he had been laid to rest.

16. And when the sabbath day was over, Mary of Magdala and Mary the mother of James and Salome brought spices so they could go and embalm him. And very early on Sunday they got to the tomb just as the sun was coming up. And they had been asking themselves, "Who will help us roll the stone away from the opening of the tomb?" Then they look up and discover that the stone has been rolled away! (For in fact the stone was very large.)

    And when they went into the tomb, they saw a young man sitting on the right, wearing a white robe, and they grew apprehensive.

    He says to them, "Don't be alarmed! You are looking for Jesus the Nazarene who was crucified. He was raised, he is not here! Look at the spot where they put him! But go and tell his disciples, including 'Rock,' "He is going ahead of you to Galilee! There you will see him, just as he told you."

    And once they got outside, they ran away from the tomb, because great fear and excitement got the better of them. And they didn't breathe a word of it to anyone: talk about terrified. . . .

Source: Mark 14:43–16:8, from *The Complete Gospels.*

NEW TESTAMENT CHURCH

ASCENSION, PENTECOST

The book of the Acts of the Apostles, written about 85 C.E., chronicles the events of the early Church after Jesus' resurrection. The book is sometimes termed the Gospel of the Holy Spirit, because the author depicts the expansion of the early Church as being guided by the Holy Spirit. The opening of Acts, presented here, recounts Jesus' ascension into heaven and the arrival of the Holy Spirit a few days later, during the Jewish agricultural festival of Pentecost. The believers are directly affected by the presence of the Holy Spirit, as evidenced by their speaking in foreign tongues. Peter emerges as the leader of the Church, and thousands of believers are baptized.

1. After his suffering, he showed himself to these men [i.e., the Apostles] and gave many convincing proofs that he was alive. He appeared to them over a period of forty days and spoke about the kingdom of God. On one occasion, while he was eating with them, he gave them this command: "Do not leave Jerusalem, but wait for the gift my Father

promised, which you have heard me speak about. For John baptized with water, but in a few days you will be baptized with the Holy Spirit."

So when they met together, they asked him, "Lord, are you at this time going to restore the kingdom to Israel?"

He said to them: "It is not for you to know the times or dates the Father has set by his own authority. But you will receive power when the Holy Spirit comes on you; and you will be my witnesses in Jerusalem, and in all Judea and Samaria, and to the ends of the earth."

After he said this, he was taken up before their very eyes, and a cloud hid him from their sight.

They were looking intently up into the sky as he was going, when suddenly two men dressed in white stood beside them. "Men of Galilee," they said, "why do you stand here looking into the sky? This same Jesus, who has been taken from you into heaven, will come back in the same way you have seen him go into heaven."

2. When the day of Pentecost came, they were all together in one place. Suddenly a sound like the blowing of a violent wind came from heaven and filled the whole house where they were sitting. They saw what seemed to be tongues of fire that separated and came to rest on each of them. All of them were filled with the Holy Spirit and began to speak in other tongues as the Spirit enabled them.

Now there were staying in Jerusalem God-fearing Jews from every nation under heaven. When they heard this sound, a crowd came together in bewilderment, because each one heard them speaking in his own language. Utterly amazed, they asked: "Are not all these men who are speaking Galileans? Then how is it that each of us hears them in his own native language? Parthians, Medes and Elamites; residents of Mesopotamia, Judea and Cappadocia, Pontus and Asia, Phrygia and Pamphylia, Egypt and the parts of Libya near Cyrene; visitors from Rome (both Jews and converts to Judaism); Cretans and Arabs—we hear them declaring the wonders of God in our own tongues!" Amazed and perplexed, they asked one another, "What does this mean?"

Some, however, made fun of them and said, "They have had too much wine."

Then Peter stood up with the Eleven, raised his voice and addressed the crowd: "Fellow Jews and all of you who live in Jerusalem, let me explain this to you; listen carefully to what I say. These men are not drunk, as you suppose. It's only nine in the morning! No, this is what was spoken by the prophet Joel:

> In the last days, God says, I will pour out my Spirit on all people. Your sons and daughters will prophesy, your young men will see visions, your old men will dream dreams. Even on my servants, both men and women, I will pour out my Spirit in those days, and they will prophesy. I will show wonders in the heaven above and signs on the earth below, blood and fire and billows of smoke. The sun will be

turned to darkness and the moon to blood before the coming of the great and glorious day of the Lord. And everyone who calls on the name of the Lord will be saved.

"Men of Israel, listen to this: Jesus of Nazareth was a man accredited by God to you by miracles, wonders, and signs, which God did among you through him, as you yourselves know. This man was handed over to you by God's set purpose and foreknowledge; and you, with the help of wicked men, put him to death by nailing him to the cross. But God raised him from the dead, freeing him from the agony of death, because it was impossible for death to keep its hold on him. . . ."

With many other words he warned them; and he pleaded with them, "Save yourselves from this corrupt generation." Those who accepted his message were baptized, and about three thousand were added to their number that day.

They devoted themselves to the apostles' teaching and to the fellowship, to the breaking of bread and to prayer. Everyone was filled with awe, and many wonders and miraculous signs were done by the apostles. All the believers were together and had everything in common. Selling their possessions and goods, they gave to anyone as he had need. Every day they continued to meet together in the temple courts. They broke bread in their homes and ate together with glad and sincere hearts, praising God and enjoying the favor of all the people. And the Lord added to their number daily those who were being saved.

Source: Acts 1:3–11, 2:1–24, 40–47, from *The Holy Bible, New International Version.* Reprinted by permission.

PAUL ON THE DISTINCTION BETWEEN CHRISTIANITY AND JUDAISM

After a dramatic conversion experience and a period of indoctrination, Paul soon rose in the leadership to the status of an Apostle. During three missionary journeys in non-Jewish territories throughout the Mediterranean region, he established dozens of churches and corresponded with many of them. Written about 55 C.E., Paul's letter to the Church of Galatia is a pivotal text in the development of early Christianity. Shortly after his visit, Church members in Galatia were persuaded by Christian Judaizers that adherence to Jewish law was a prerequisite for becoming a Christian. Paul argues vehemently that obedience to Jewish law will not absolve our sins. Righteousness comes about only through faith in Christ, and this is open to Jews and non-Jews alike. The larger issue in the debate was whether Christianity was merely a Jewish sect or a distinct religion; in the first two chapters presented here, Paul describes his efforts to set Christianity apart from its Jewish framework. His account is important for its autobiographical content, and also because it is the earliest written discussion of first-century Church politics.

1. I am astonished that you are so quickly deserting the one who called you by the grace of Christ and are turning to a different gospel—which is really no gospel at all. Evidently some people are throwing you into confusion and are trying to pervert the gospel of Christ. But even if we or an angel from heaven should preach a gospel other than the one we preached to you, let him be eternally condemned! As we have already said, so now I say again: If anybody is preaching to you a gospel other than what you accepted, let him be eternally condemned!

   Am I now trying to win the approval of men, or of God? Or am I trying to please men? If I were still trying to please men, I would not be a servant of Christ.

   I want you to know, brothers, that the gospel I preached is not something that man made up. I did not receive it from any man, nor was I taught it; rather, I received it by revelation from Jesus Christ.

   For you have heard of my previous way of life in Judaism, how intensely I persecuted the church of God and tried to destroy it. I was advancing in Judaism beyond many Jews of my own age and was extremely zealous for the traditions of my fathers. But when God, who set me apart from birth and called me by his grace, was pleased to reveal his Son in me so that I might preach him among the Gentiles, I did not consult any man, nor did I go up to Jerusalem to see those who were apostles before I was, but I went immediately into Arabia and later returned to Damascus.

   Then after three years, I went up to Jerusalem to get acquainted with Peter and stayed with him fifteen days. I saw none of the other apostles—only James, the Lord's brother. I assure you before God that what I am writing you is no lie. Later I went to Syria and Cilicia. I was personally unknown to the churches of Judea that are in Christ. They only heard the report: "The man who formerly persecuted us is now preaching the faith he once tried to destroy."
2. Fourteen years later I went up again to Jerusalem, this time with Barnabas. I took Titus along also. I went in response to a revelation and set before them the gospel that I preach among the Gentiles. But I did this privately to those who seemed to be leaders, for fear that I was running or had run my race in vain. Yet not even Titus, who was with me, was compelled to be circumcised, even though he was a Greek. [This matter arose] because some false brothers had infiltrated our ranks to spy on the freedom we have in Christ Jesus and to make us slaves. We did not give in to them for a moment, so that the truth of the gospel might remain with you.

   As for those who seemed to be important—whatever they were makes no difference to me; God does not judge by external appearance—those men added nothing to my message. On the contrary, they saw that I had been entrusted with the task of preaching the gospel to the Gentiles, just as Peter had been to the Jews. For God, who was at work in the ministry of Peter as an apostle to the Jews, was also at work in my ministry as an apostle to the Gentiles. James, Peter and John, those reputed to be pillars, gave me and Barnabas the right hand of fellowship when they recognized the grace given to me. They agreed that we should go to the Gentiles, and they to the Jews. All they asked was that we should continue to remember the poor, the very thing I was eager to do.

When Peter came to Antioch, I opposed him to his face, because he was clearly in the wrong. Before certain men came from James, he used to eat with the Gentiles. But when they arrived, he began to draw back and separate himself from the Gentiles because he was afraid of those who belonged to the circumcision group. The other Jews joined him in his hypocrisy, so that by their hypocrisy even Barnabas was led astray.

When I saw that they were not acting in line with the truth of the gospel, I said to Peter in front of them all, "You are a Jew, yet you live like a Gentile and not like a Jew. How is it, then, that you force Gentiles to follow Jewish customs?

"We who are Jews by birth and not 'Gentile sinners' know that a man is not justified by observing the law, but by faith in Jesus Christ. So we, too, have put our faith in Christ Jesus that we may be justified by faith in Christ and not by observing the law, because by observing the law no one will be justified.

"If, while we seek to be justified in Christ, it becomes evident that we ourselves are sinners, does that mean that Christ promotes sin? Absolutely not! If I rebuild what I destroyed, I prove that I am a lawbreaker. For through the law I died to the law so that I might live for God. I have been crucified with Christ and I no longer live, but Christ lives in me. The life I live in the body, I live by faith in the Son of God, who loved me and gave himself for me. I do not set aside the grace of God, for if righteousness could be gained through the law, Christ died for nothing!"

Source: Galatians 1:6–23, 2:1–21, from *The Holy Bible, New International Version.*

PAUL ON LIFE AFTER DEATH

An immediate theological difficulty faced by Paul was the question of how Jesus could be divine despite his criminal execution. Paul's solution was to see Jesus' death on the cross and subsequent resurrection as the end of the old Jewish law and the beginning of a new era of divine grace. Through baptism, Christians symbolically participate in the cross by dying to their old lives and reemerging anew. The crucifixion and resurrection are so central to Paul's teaching that they are the only features of the life of Jesus with which he is concerned. In the following discussion from Paul's first letter to the church of Corinth, written about 55 C.E., life after death is also linked to the resurrection: Because Christ resurrected, we are assured that we too will be. Unlike Greek writers, who construe life after death as the continuation of a bodiless, immortal soul, Christian doctrine holds to the bodily resurrection of the dead as found in post-exilic Jewish writings. Paul teaches that our new bodies will be heavenly and imperishable in nature, rather than earthly and perishable, and that all those who belong to Christ will be simultaneously resurrected when he returns.

15. But if it is preached that Christ has been raised from the dead, how can some of you say that there is no resurrection of the dead? If there is no resurrection of the dead, then not even Christ has been raised. And if Christ has not been raised, our preaching is useless and so is your faith. More than that, we are then found to be false witnesses about God, for we have testified about God that he raised Christ from the dead. But he did not raise him if in fact the dead are not raised. For if the dead are not raised, then Christ has not been raised either. And if Christ has not been raised, your faith is futile; you are still in your sins. Then those also who have fallen asleep in Christ are lost. If only for this life we have hope in Christ, we are to be pitied more than all men.

But Christ has indeed been raised from the dead, the firstfruits of those who have fallen asleep. For since death came through a man, the resurrection of the dead comes also through a man. For as in Adam all die, so in Christ all will be made alive. But each in his own turn: Christ, the firstfruits; then, when he comes, those who belong to him. Then the end will come, when he hands over the kingdom to God the Father after he has destroyed all dominion, authority and power. For he must reign until he has put all his enemies under his feet. The last enemy to be destroyed is death. For he "has put everything under his feet." Now when it says that "everything" has been put under him, it is clear that this does not include God himself, who put everything under Christ. When he has done this, then the Son himself will be made subject to him who put everything under him, so that God may be all in all. . . .

But someone may ask, "How are the dead raised? With what kind of body will they come?" How foolish! What you sow does not come to life unless it dies. When you sow, you do not plant the body that will be, but just a seed, perhaps of wheat or of something else. But God gives it a body as he has determined, and to each kind of seed he gives its own body. All flesh is not the same: Men have one kind of flesh, animals have another, birds another and fish another. There are also heavenly bodies and there are earthly bodies; but the splendor of the heavenly bodies is one kind, and the splendor of the earthly bodies is another. The sun has one kind of splendor, the moon another and the star another; and star differs from star in splendor.

So will it be with the resurrection of the dead. The body that is sown is perishable, it is raised imperishable; it is sown in dishonor, it is raised in glory; it is sown in weakness, it is raised in power; it is sown a natural body, it is raised a spiritual body. If there is a natural body, there is also a spiritual body.

So it is written: "The first man Adam became a living being"; the last Adam, a life-giving spirit. The spiritual did not come first, but the natural, and after that the spiritual. The first man was of the dust of the earth, the second man from heaven. As was the earthly man, so are those who are of the earth; and as is the man from heaven, so also are those who are of heaven. And just as we have borne the likeness of the earthly man, so shall we bear the likeness of the man from heaven.

I declare to you, brothers, that flesh and blood cannot inherit the kingdom of God, nor does the perishable inherit the imperishable. Listen, I tell you a mystery: We will not all sleep, but we will all be changed—in a flash, in the twinkling of an eye, at the last trumpet. For the trumpet will sound, the dead will be raised imperishable, and we will be changed. For the perishable must clothe itself with the imperishable, and the mortal with immortality. When the perishable has been clothed with the imperishable, and the mortal with immortality, then the saying that is written will come true: "Death has been swallowed up in victory."

"Where, O death, is your victory?
"Where, O death, is your sting?"

The sting of death is sin, and the power of sin is the law. But thanks to God! He gives us the victory through our Lord Jesus Christ.

Source: 1 Corinthians 15:12–28, 35–57, from *The Holy Bible, New International Version.*

NONCANONICAL GOSPELS

INFANCY GOSPEL OF JAMES

Early Christians were interested in accounts of Jesus' childhood, which filled the gaps in the four Gospel narratives. Many childhood gospels circulated, but most of the information in these derive from two texts written about 150 C.E.: the Infancy Gospel of James and the Infancy Gospel of Thomas. The Infancy Gospel of James, also called the Protoevangelium, *or first gospel, is pseudonomously ascribed to James, the brother of Jesus, and scholars believe that its author was a non-Jewish Christian from outside Palestine. The text presents the oldest account of the early life of Mary, including her espousal to Joseph, and describes the virgin birth of Jesus. The tradition of Mary's lifelong virginity runs counter to statements in the gospels referring to Jesus' brothers. The Infancy Gospel of James reconciles these two traditions by presenting Joseph as a widower with children from his previous marriage. The feast of Mary's presentation in the temple (November 21) in Catholic* and *Orthodox traditions is based on events in the following selection.*

7. Many months passed, but when the child reached two years of age, Joachim said, "Let's take her up to the temple of the Lord, so that we can keep the promise we made, or else the Lord will be angry with us and our gift will be unacceptable."

And Anna said, "Let's wait until she is three, so she won't miss her father or mother."

And Joachim agreed: "Let's wait."

When the child turned three years of age, Joachim said, "Let's send for the undefiled Hebrew daughters. Let them each take a lamp and light it, so the child won't turn back and have her heart captivated by things outside the Lord's temple." And this is what they did until the time they ascended to the Lord's temple.

The priest welcomed her, kissed her, and blessed her: "The Lord God has exalted your name among all generations. In you the Lord will disclose his redemption to the people of Israel during the last days."

And he sat her down on the third step of the altar, and the Lord showered favor on her. And she danced, and the whole house of Israel loved her.

8. Her parents left for home marveling and praising and glorifying the Lord God because the child did not look back at them. And Mary lived in the temple of the Lord. She was fed there like a dove, receiving her food from the hand of a heavenly messenger.

   When she turned twelve, however, there was a meeting of the priests. "Look," they said, "Mary has turned twelve in the temple of the Lord. What should we do with her so she won't pollute the sanctuary of the Lord our God?" And they said to the high priest, "You stand at the altar of the Lord. Enter and pray about her, and we'll do whatever the Lord God discloses to you."

   And so the high priest took the vestment with the twelve bells, entered the Holy of Holies, and began to pray about her. And suddenly a messenger of the Lord appeared: "Zechariah, Zechariah, go out and assemble the widowers of the people and have them each bring a staff. She will become the wife of the one to whom the Lord God shows a sign." And so heralds covered the surrounding territory of Judea. The trumpet of the Lord sounded and all the widowers came running.

9. And Joseph, too, threw down his carpenter's axe and left for the meeting. When they had all gathered, they went to the high priest with their staffs. After the high priest had collected everyone's staff, he entered the temple and began to pray. When he had finished his prayer, he took the staffs and went out and began to give them back to each man. But there was no sign of any of them. Joseph got the last staff. Suddenly a dove came out of this staff and perched on Joseph's head. "Joseph, Joseph," the high priest said, "you've been chosen by lot to take the virgin of the Lord into your care and protection."

   But Joseph objected: "I already have sons and I'm an old man; she's only a young woman. I'm afraid that I'll become the butt of jokes among the people of Israel." . . .

13. She was in her sixth month when one day Joseph came home from his building projects, entered the house, and found her pregnant. He struck himself in the face, threw himself to the ground on sackcloth, and began to cry bitterly: "What sort of face should I present to the

Lord God? What prayer can I say on her behalf since I received her as a virgin from the temple of the Lord God and didn't protect her? Who has set this trap for me? Who has done this evil deed in my house? Who has lured this virgin away from me and violated her? The story of Adam has been repeated in my case, hasn't it? For just as Adam was praying when the serpent came and found Eve alone, deceived her, and corrupted her, so the same thing has happened to me."

So Joseph got up from the sackcloth and summoned Mary and said to her, "God has taken a special interest in you—how could you have done this? Have you forgotten the Lord your God? Why have you brought shame on yourself, you who were raised in the Holy of Holies and fed by a heavenly messenger?"

But she began to cry bitter tears: "I'm innocent. I haven't had sex with any man."

And Joseph said to her, "Then where did the child you're carrying come from?"

And she replied, "As the Lord my God lives, I don't know where it came from."

14. And Joseph became very frightened and no longer spoke with her as he pondered what he was going to do with her. And Joseph said to himself, "If I try to cover up her sin, I'll end up going against the law of the Lord. And if I disclose her condition to the people of Israel, I'm afraid that the child inside her might be heaven-sent and I'll end up handing innocent blood over to a death sentence. So what should I do with her? [I know,] I'll divorce her quietly."

But when night came a messenger of the Lord suddenly appeared to him in a dream and said: "Don't be afraid of this girl, because the child in her is the holy spirit's doing. She will have a son and you will name him Jesus—the name means 'he will save his people from their sins.'" And Joseph got up from his sleep and praised the God of Israel, who had given him this favor. And so he began to protect the girl.

15. Then Annas the scholar came to him and said to him, "Joseph, why haven't you attended our assembly?"

And he replied to him, "Because I was worn out from the trip and rested my first day home."

Then Annas turned and saw that Mary was pregnant.

He left in a hurry for the high priest and said to him, "You remember Joseph, don't you—the man you yourself vouched for? Well, he has committed a serious offense."

And the high priest asked, "In what way?"

"Joseph has violated the virgin he received from the temple of the Lord," he replied. "He had his way with her and hasn't disclosed his action to the people of Israel."

And the high priest asked him, "Has Joseph really done this?"

And he replied, "Send temple assistants and you'll find the virgin pregnant."

And so the temple assistants went and found her just as Annas had reported, and then they brought her, along with Joseph, to the court.

"Mary, why have you done this?" the high priest asked her. "Why have you humiliated yourself? Have you forgotten the Lord your God, you who were raised in the Holy of Holies and were fed by heavenly messengers? You of all people, who heard their hymns and danced for them—why have you done this?"

And she wept bitterly: "As the Lord God lives, I stand innocent before him. Believe me, I've not had sex with any man."

And the high priest said, "Joseph, why have you done this?"

And Joseph said, "As the Lord lives, I am innocent where she is concerned."

And the high priest said, "Don't perjure yourself, but tell the truth. You've had your way with her and haven't disclosed this action to the people of Israel. And you haven't humbled yourself under God's mighty hand, so that your offspring might be blessed."

But Joseph was silent.

16. Then the high priest said, "Return the virgin you received from the temple of the Lord."

And Joseph, bursting into tears . . . [said nothing].

And the high priest said, "I'm going to give you the Lord's drink test, and it will disclose your sin clearly to both of you."

And the high priest took the water and made Joseph drink it and sent him into the wilderness, but he returned unharmed. And he made the girl drink it, too, and sent her into the wilderness. She also came back unharmed. And everybody was surprised because their sin had not been revealed. And so the high priest said, "If the Lord God has not exposed your sin, then neither do I condemn you." And he dismissed them. Joseph took Mary and returned home celebrating and praising the God of Israel.

Source: Infancy Gospel of James 7–9, 13–16, from *The Complete Gospels.*

INFANCY GOSPEL OF THOMAS

Written about 150 C.E., the Infancy Gospel of Thomas was among the most popular apocryphal writings in the early Church. The text deals with Jesus' childhood up to his twelfth year. The youthful Jesus is presented as having deadly divine powers, which he angrily uses to get his way. As he grows, though, his sense of moral responsibility progressively develops, and he uses his powers to heal rather than harm. The story provides an interesting commentary on the divine and human natures of Jesus: His power and knowledge are fully divine, but his conscience and emotions are human and require maturing. The text is reconstructed from several surviving manuscripts that vary greatly; some scholars believe that the original included sayings, although only the story lines are preserved.

1. I, Thomas the Israelite, am reporting to you, all my non-Jewish brothers and sisters, to make known the extraordinary childhood deeds of our Lord Jesus Christ—what he did after his birth in my region. This is how it all started:
2. When this boy, Jesus, was five years old, he was playing at the ford of a rushing stream. He was collecting the flowing water into ponds and made the water instantly pure. He did this with a single command. He then made soft clay and shaped it into twelve sparrows. He did this on the sabbath day, and many other boys were playing with him.

   But when a Jew saw what Jesus was doing while playing on the sabbath day, he immediately went off and told Joseph, Jesus' father: "See here, your boy is at the ford and has taken mud and fashioned twelve birds with it, and so has violated the sabbath."

   So Joseph went there, and as soon as he spotted him he shouted, "Why are you doing what's not permitted on the sabbath?"

   But Jesus simply clapped his hands and shouted to the sparrows: "Be off, fly away, and remember me, you who are now alive!" And the sparrows took off and flew away noisily.

   The Jews watched with amazement, then left the scene to report to their leaders what they had seen Jesus doing.
3. The son of Annas the scholar, standing there with Jesus, took a willow branch and drained the water Jesus had collected. Jesus, however, saw what had happened and became angry, saying to him, "Damn you, you irreverent fool! What harm did the ponds of water do to you? From this moment you, too, will dry up like a tree, and you'll never produce leaves or root to bear fruit."

   In an instant the boy had completely withered away. Then Jesus departed and left for the house of Joseph. The parents of the boy who had withered away picked him up and were carrying him out, sad because he was so young. And they came to Joseph and accused him: "It's your fault—your boy did all this."
4. Later he was going through the village again when a boy ran by and bumped him on the shoulder. Jesus got angry and said to him, "You won't continue your journey." And all of a sudden he fell down and died.

   Some people saw what had happened and said, "Where has this boy come from? Everything he says happens instantly!"

   The parents of the dead boy came to Joseph and blamed him, saying, "Because you have such a boy, you can't live with us in the village, or else teach him to bless and not curse. He's killing our children!" . . .

14. When Joseph saw the child's aptitude, and his great intelligence for his age, he again resolved that Jesus should not remain illiterate. So he took him and handed him over to another teacher. The teacher said to Joseph, "First I'll teach him Greek, then Hebrew." This teacher, of course, knew of the child's previous experience [with a teacher] and was afraid of him. Still, he wrote out the alphabet and instructed him for quite a while, though Jesus was unresponsive.

0

Then Jesus spoke: "If you're really a teacher, and if you know the letters well, tell me the meaning of the letter alpha, and I'll tell you the meaning of beta."

The teacher became exasperated and hit him on the head. Jesus got angry and cursed him, and the teacher immediately lost consciousness and fell face down on the ground.

The child returned to Joseph's house. But Joseph was upset and gave this instruction to his mother: "Don't let him go outside, because those who annoy him end up dead."

15. After some time another teacher, a close friend of Joseph, said to him, "Send the child to my schoolroom. Perhaps with some flattery I can teach him his letters."

Joseph replied, "If you can muster the courage, brother, take him with you." And so he took him along with much fear and trepidation, but the child was happy to go.

Jesus strode boldly into the schoolroom and found a book lying on the desk. He took the book but did not read the letters in it. Rather, he opened his mouth and spoke by [the power of] the holy spirit and taught the law to those standing there.

A large crowd gathered and stood listening to him, and they marveled at the maturity of his teaching and his readiness of speech—a mere child able to say such things.

When Joseph heard about this he feared the worst and ran to the schoolroom, imagining that his teacher was having trouble with Jesus.

But the teacher said to Joseph, "Brother, please know that I accepted this child as a student, but already he's full of grace and wisdom. So I'm asking you, brother, to take him back home."

When the child heard this, he immediately smiled at him and said, "Because you have spoken and testified rightly, that other teacher who was struck down will be healed." And right away he was. Joseph took his child and went home.

16. Joseph sent his son James to tie up some wood and carry it back to the house, and the child Jesus followed. While James was gathering the firewood, a viper bit his hand. And as he lay sprawled out on the ground, dying, Jesus came and blew on the bite. Immediately the pain stopped, the animal burst apart, and James got better on the spot.

17. After this incident an infant in Joseph's neighborhood became sick and died, and his mother grieved terribly. Jesus heard the loud wailing and the uproar that was going on and quickly ran there.

When he found the child dead, he touched its chest and said, "I say to you, infant, don't die but live, and be with your mother."

And immediately the infant looked up and laughed. Jesus then said to the woman, "Take it, give it your breast, and remember me."

The crowd of onlookers marveled at this: "Truly this child was a god or a heavenly messenger of God—whatever he says instantly happens." But Jesus left and went on playing with the other children.

18. A year later, while a building was under construction, a man fell from the top of it and died. There was quite a commotion, so Jesus got up and went there. When he saw the man lying dead, he took his hand and said, "I say to you, sir, get up and go back to work." And he immediately got up and worshipped him.

    The crowd saw this and marveled: "This child's from heaven—he must be, because he has saved many souls from death, and he can go on saving all his life."

Source: Infancy Gospel of Thomas 1–4, 14–18, from *The Complete Gospels*.

GNOSTIC GOSPEL OF THOMAS

The 1945 discovery of several dozen Gnostic texts has redefined the study of early Christianity. The jewel in the crown of these texts is the Gospel of Thomas, which broadens our understanding of the historical Jesus. The text is a sayings gospel insofar as it contains no story line and little dialog. The 114 sayings are organized around particular catchwords but do not systematically develop themes. Although the text was ultimately compiled in the second century, it may be based on an original core of short sayings as early as those in any other Gospel. These, in turn, come from orally transmitted accounts of Jesus' teachings. The challenge for scholars is to identify that core amid embellishments penned by later writers. A Gnostic component of the text suggests that these are secret teachings of Jesus, knowledge of which will free one's spirit from the material world. Many of the sayings parallel those found in the four canonical Gospels. Some of the parables in Thomas are more concise and thus, perhaps, earlier than their canonical counterparts (8, 9, 57, 63, 64, 65). A large group of sayings is unique to this text, although it probably did not originate with Jesus (15, 17, 18, 19). Most interesting, however, are two sayings that scholars believe originated with Jesus but that are absent from the canonical Gospels (97, 98).

Prologue. These are the secret sayings that the living Jesus spoke and Didymos Judas Thomas recorded.

1. And he said, "Whoever discovers the interpretation of these sayings will not taste death."
2. Jesus said, "Those who seek should not stop seeking until they find. When they find, they will be disturbed. When they are disturbed, they will marvel, and will rule overall."
3. Jesus said, "If your leaders say to you, 'Look, the [Father's] imperial rule is in the sky,' then the birds of the sky will precede you. If they say to you, 'It is in the sea,' then the fish will precede you. Rather, the [Father's] imperial rule is inside you and outside you. When you know yourselves, then you will be known, and you will understand that you are children of the living Father. But if you do not know yourselves, then you live in poverty, and you are the poverty."
4. Jesus said, "The person old in days won't hesitate to ask a little child seven days old about the place of life, and that person will live. For many of the first will be last, and will become a single one."

5. Jesus said, "Know what is in front of your face, and what is hidden from you will be disclosed to you. For there is nothing hidden that won't be revealed."
6. His disciples asked him and said to him, "Do you want us to fast? How should we pray? Should we give to charity? What diet should we observe?"

   Jesus said, "Don't lie, and don't do what you hate, because all things are disclosed before heaven. After all, there is nothing hidden that won't be revealed, and there is nothing covered up that will remain undisclosed."
7. Jesus said, "Lucky is the lion that the human will eat, so that the lion becomes human. And foul is the human that the lion will eat, and the lion still will become human."
8. And he said, "The human one is like a wise fisherman who cast his net into the sea and drew it up from the sea full of little fish. Among them the wise fisherman discovered a fine large fish. He threw all the little fish back into the sea, and easily chose the large fish. Anyone here with two good ears had better listen!"
9. Jesus said,

   > Look, the sower went out, took a handful (of seeds), and scattered (them). Some fell on the road, and the birds came and gathered them. Others fell on rock, and they didn't take root in the soil and didn't produce heads of grain. Others fell on thorns, and they choked the seeds and worms ate them. And others fell on good soil, and it produced a good crop: it yielded sixty per measure and one hundred twenty per measure.

10. Jesus said, "I have cast fire upon the world, and look, I'm guarding it until it blazes."
11. Jesus said, "This heaven will pass away, and the one above it will pass away. The dead are not alive, and the living will not die. During the days when you ate what is dead, you made it come alive. When you are in the light, what will you do? On the day when you were one, you became two. But when you become two, what will you do?"
12. The disciples said to Jesus, "We know that you are going to leave us. Who will be our leader?"

    Jesus said to them, "No matter where you are, you are to go to James the Just, for whose sake heaven and earth came into being."
13. Jesus said to his disciples, "Compare me to something and tell me what I am like."

    Simon Peter said to him, "You are like a just angel."

    Matthew said to him, "You are like a wise philosopher."

    Thomas said to him, "Teacher, my mouth is utterly unable to say what you are like."

    Jesus said, "I am not your teacher. Because you have drunk, you have become intoxicated from the bubbling spring that I have tended."

And he took him, and withdrew, and spoke three sayings to him.

When Thomas came back to his friends, they asked him, "What did Jesus say to you?"

Thomas said to them, "If I tell you one of the sayings he spoke to me, you will pick up rocks and stone me, and fire will come from the rocks and devour you."

14. Jesus said to them, "If you fast, you will bring sin upon yourselves, and if you pray, you will be condemned, and if you give to charity, you will harm your spirits. When you go into any region and walk about in the countryside, when people take you in, eat what they serve you and heal the sick among them. After all, what goes into your mouth won't defile you; what comes out of your mouth will."
15. Jesus said, "When you see one who was not born of woman, fall on your faces and worship. That one is your Father."
16. Jesus said, "Perhaps people think that I have come to cast peace upon the world. They do not know that I have come to cast conflicts upon the earth: fire, sword, war. For there will be five in a house: there'll be three against two and two against three, father against son and son against father, and they will stand alone."
17. Jesus said, "I will give you what no eye has seen, what no ear has heard, what no hand has touched, what has not arisen in the human heart."
18. The disciples said to Jesus, "Tell us, how will our end come?"

    Jesus said, "Have you found the beginning, then, that you are looking for the end? You see, the end will be where the beginning is. Congratulations to the one who stands at the beginning: that one will know the end and will not taste death."
19. Jesus said, "Congratulations to the one who came into being before coming into being. If you become my disciples and pay attention to my sayings, these stones will serve you. For there are five trees in Paradise for you; they do not change, summer or winter, and their leaves do not fall. Whoever knows them will not taste death."
20. The disciples said to Jesus, "Tell us what Heaven's imperial rule is like."

    He said to them,

    > It's like a mustard seed. [It's] the smallest of all seeds, but when it falls on prepared soil, it produces a large branch and becomes a shelter for birds of the sky. . . .

57. Jesus said,

    > The Father's imperial rule is like a person who had [good] seed. His enemy came during the night and sowed weeds among the good seed. The person did not let the workers pull up the weeds, but said to them, "No, otherwise you might go to pull up the weeds and pull up the wheat along with them." For on the day of the harvest the weeds will be conspicuous, and will be pulled up and burned. . . .

63. Jesus said,

There was a rich man who had a great deal of money. He said, "I shall invest my money so that I may sow, reap, plant, and fill my storehouses with produce, that I may lack nothing." These were the things he was thinking in his heart, but that very night he died. Anyone here with two ears had better listen!

64. Jesus said,

Someone was receiving guests. When he had prepared the dinner, he sent his slave to invite the guests. The slave went to the first and said, "My master invites you." The first replied, "Some merchants owe me money; they are coming to me tonight. I have to go and give them instructions. Please excuse me for dinner." The slave went to another and said, "My master has invited you." The second said to the slave, "I have bought a house, and I have been called away for a day. I shall have no time." The slave went to another and said, "My master invites you." The third said to the slave, "My friend is to be married, and I am to arrange the banquet. I shall not be able to come. Please excuse me from dinner." The slave went to another and said, "My master invites you." The fourth said to the slave, "I have bought an estate, and I am going to collect the rent. I shall not be able to come. Please excuse me." The slave returned and said to his master, "Those whom you invited to dinner have asked to be excused." The master said to his slave, " Go out on the streets and bring back whomever you find to have dinner."

Buyers and merchants [will] not enter the places of my Father.

65. He said,

A person owned a vineyard and rented it to some farmers, so they could work it and he could collect its crops from them. He sent his slave so the farmers would give him the vineyard's crop. They grabbed him, beat him, and almost killed him, and the slave returned and told his master. His master said, "Perhaps he didn't know them." He sent another slave, and the farmers beat that one as well. Then the master sent his son and said, "Perhaps they'll show my son some respect." Because the farmers knew that he was the heir to the vineyard, they grabbed him and killed him. Anyone here with two ears had better listen! . . .

97. Jesus said,

The [Father's] imperial rule is like a woman who was carrying a [jar] full of meal. While she was walking along [a] distant road, the handle of the jar broke and the meal spilled behind her [along] the road. She didn't know it; she hadn't noticed a problem. When she reached her house, she put the jar down and discovered that it was empty.

98. Jesus said,

The Father's imperial rule is like a person who wanted to kill someone powerful. While still at home he drew his sword and thrust it

> into the wall to find out whether his hand would go in. Then he killed the powerful one.

Source: Gospel of Thomas 1–20, 57, 63–65, 97, 98, from *The Complete Gospels.*

GNOSTIC GOSPEL OF MARY

Gnostic writings contained feminine imagery typical of ancient mythology, which was ultimately removed from mainstream Christianity. Much of this imagery is cosmological, and it involves various layers of God's being and creative activity. Some Gnostic texts portray God as having both a male and a female quality: God is the primal father and the mother of all things. Others describe God as radiating divine beings or personalities, one of which is the female spirit of wisdom, the womb of everything. Finally, and most interestingly, several texts depict the divine Trinity as the father, mother, and son. In addition to their feminine theological themes, Gnostic texts defend the role of women as teachers of divine knowledge. This is most evident in the Gospel of Mary (named after Mary Magdalene), where, after Mary presents some private teachings of Jesus, her authority is first challenged by Peter and then defended by Levi. Much of the Gospel of Mary is lost; the surviving sections are presented below.

1. [Six manuscript pages are missing.]
2. [Jesus said] ". . . Will matter then be utterly destroyed or not?"

   The Savior replied, "Every nature, every modeled form, every creature, exists in and with each other. They will dissolve again into their own proper root. For the nature of matter is dissolved into what belongs to its nature. Anyone with two ears capable of hearing should listen!"
3. Then Peter said to him, "You have been expounding every topic to us; tell us one further thing. What is the sin of the world?"

   The Savior replied, "There is no such thing as sin; rather, you yourselves are what produces sin when you act according to the nature of adultery, which is called 'sin.' For this reason, the Good came among you approaching what belongs to every nature. It will set it within its root."

   Then he continued. He said, "This is why you get sick and die, for [you love] what de[c]ei[ve]s you. Anyone with a mind should use it to think!

   [Ma]tter gav[e bi]rth to a passion which has no [true] image because it derives from what is contrary to nature. Then a disturbing confusion occurred in the whole body. This is why I told you, 'Be content of heart.' And do not conform [to the body], but form yourselves in the presence of that other image of nature. Anyone with two ears capable of hearing should listen!"
4. When the Blessed One had said this, he greeted them all. "Peace be with you!" he said. "Acquire my peace within yourselves!

   "Be on your guard so that no one deceives you by saying, 'Look over here!' or 'Look over there!' For the seed of true humanity exists within you. Follow it! Those who search for it will find it.

"Go then, preach the good news of the domain. Do not lay down any rule beyond what I ordained for you, nor promulgate law like the lawgiver, or else it will dominate you."

After he said these things, he left them.

5. But they were distressed and wept greatly. "How are we going to go out to the rest of the world to preach the good news, about the domain of the seed of true humanity?" they said. "If they didn't spare him, how will they spare us?"

Then Mary stood up. She greeted them all and addressed her brothers: "Do not weep and be distressed nor let your hearts be irresolute. For his grace will be with you all and will shelter you. Rather we should praise his greatness, for he has joined us together and made us true human beings."

When Mary said these things, she turned their minds [to]ward the Good, and they began to [as]k about the wor[d]s of the Savi[or].

6. Peter said to Mary, "Sister, we know that the Savior loved you more than any other woman. Tell us the words of the Savior that you know, but which we haven't heard."

Mary responded, "I will rep[ort to you as much as] I remember that you don't know." And she began to speak these words to them.

7. She said, "I saw the Lord in a vision and I said to him, 'Lord, I saw you today in a vision.'

"He said to me, 'Congratulations to you for not wavering at seeing me. For where the mind is, there is the treasure.'

"I said to him, 'Lord, how does a person who sees a vision see it—[with] the soul [or] with the spirit?'

"The Savior answered, 'The [visionary] does not see with the soul or with the spirit, but with the mind which exists between these two—that is [what] sees the vision and that is w[hat . . .]'"

8. [Four manuscript pages are missing.]

9. . . ."And Desire said, 'I did not see you go down, yet now I see you go up. So why do you lie since you belong to me?'

"The soul answered, 'I saw you. You did not see me nor did you know me. You [mis]took the garment [I wore] for my [true] self. And you did not recognize me.'

"After it had said these things, [the soul] left rejoicing greatly.

"Again, it came to the third Power, which is called 'Ignorance.' [It] examined the soul closely, saying, 'Where are you going? You are bound by fornication. Indeed you are bound! Do not pass judgment!'

"And the soul said, 'Why do you judge me, since I have not passed judgment? I am bound, but I have not bound. They did not recognize me, but I have recognized that the universe is to be dissolved, both the things of earth and those of heaven.'

"When the soul had overcome the third Power, it went upward and it saw the fourth Power. It had seven forms. The first form is Darkness; the second, Desire; the third, Ignorance; the fourth, Zeal of

Death; the fifth, the Domain of the Flesh; the sixth, the Foolish Wisdom of the Flesh, and seventh is the Wisdom of the Wrathful Person. These are seven Powers of Wrath.

"They interrogated the soul, 'Where are you coming from, human-killer, and where are you going, space-conqueror?'

"The soul replied, 'What binds me has been slain, and what surrounds me has been destroyed, and my desire has been brought to an end, and my ignorance has died. In a world, I was set loose from a world and in a type, from a type which is above, and [from] the chain of forgetfulness that exists in time. From now on, for the rest of the course of the [due] measure of the time of the age, I will rest i[n] silence.'"

When Mary said these things, she fell silent, since it was up to this point that the Savior had spoken to her.

10. Andrew sai[d, "B]rothers, what is your opinion of what was just said? I for one don't believe that the S[a]vior said these things, be[cause] these opinions seem to be so different from h[is th]ought."

After reflecting on these ma[tt]ers, [Peter said], "Has the Sa[vior] spoken secretly to a wo[m]an and [not] openly so that [we] would all hear? [Surely] he did [not wish to indicate] that [she] is more worthy than we are?"

Then Mary wept and said to Peter, "Peter, my brother, what are you imagining about this? Do you think that I've made all this up secretly by myself or that I am telling lies about the Savior?"

Levi said to Peter, "Peter, you have a constant inclination to anger and you are always ready to give way to it. And even now you are doing exactly that by questioning the woman as if you're her adversary. If the Savior considered her to be worthy, who are you to disregard her? For he knew her completely [and] loved her devotedly.

"Instead, we should be ashamed and, once we clothe ourselves with perfect humanity, we should do what we were commanded. We should announce the good news as the Savior ordered, and not be laying down any rules or making laws."

After he said these things, Levi left [and] began to announce the good news.

Source: Gnostic Gospel of Mary, from *The Complete Gospels.*

EARLY STATEMENTS OF FAITH

BAPTISM, PRAYER, AND THE EUCHARIST: *DIDACHE*

Discovered in 1873, the Didache *is a manual of early Church doctrine from the Syrian Church of Antioch. Eusibius, a fourth-century bishop, notes the high value placed on the* Didache *by early churches. Although the original date of the work is disputed, scholars believe that some parts are of first-century origin and contemporaneous with the Gospels. The brief work can be divided into four parts. The opening lists a series of moral injunctions culled from various parts of the Bible. Instructions concerning baptism, fasting, and prayer ritual follow. Next, instructions are given on receiving new prophets, apostles, and Christians. Finally, a warning is given concerning the return of Jesus. Following are the instructions on ritual from the second division.*

7. *Concerning Baptism.* Concerning baptism, baptize in this way: Having first said everything in these Teachings, baptize in the name of the Father and of the Son, and of the Holy Spirit, in living water. If you have not living water, baptize in other water; and if you cannot in cold, in warm. If you do not have either, pour out water three times upon the head in the name of Father, Son and Holy Spirit. Before the baptism let the baptizer fast, as well as the baptized, and whoever else can. But you shall order the baptized to fast for one or two days before.
8. *Concerning Fasting and Prayer.* But do not let your fasts be like those of the hypocrites; for they fast on the Monday and Thursday; instead, you should fast on the Wednesday and Friday. Also do not pray as the hypocrites do. Instead, pray in this way as the Lord commanded in His Gospel: "Our Father who are in heaven blessed be your name. May your kingdom come. May your will be done, as in heaven, so on earth. Give us today our daily bread, and forgive our debt as we also forgive our debtors. And bring us not into temptation, but deliver us from the evil one. For yours is the power and the glory forever." Pray this way three times a day.
9. *The Thanksgiving (Eucharist).* Now concerning the thanksgiving, give thanks in this way. First, concerning the cup: "We thank you, our Father, for the holy vine of David your servant, which you made known to us through Jesus your servant; may you be glorified forever." And concerning the broken bread: "We thank you, our Father, for the life and knowledge which you made known to us though Jesus your servant; may you be glorified forever. Even as this broken bread was scattered over the hills, and was gathered together and became one, so let your Church be gathered together from the ends of the earth into your kingdom; for yours is the glory and the power through Jesus Christ forever." Let no one eat or drink of your Thanksgiving, except those who have been baptized to the name of the Lord; for concerning this also the Lord has said, do not give that which is holy to the dogs.
10. *Prayer after Communion.* But after you are filled, give thanks in this way: "We thank you, holy Father, for your holy name which you caused to dwell in our hearts, and for the knowledge and faith and immortality, which you made known to us through Jesus your Servant; may you be glorified forever. You, Master almighty, created all things for your name's sake; you gave food and drink to men for enjoyment, that they might give thanks to you. You freely gave to us spiritual food and drink and life eternal through your servant. Before all things we thank you, who are mighty. May you be exalted forever. Remember, Lord, your Church, to deliver it from all evil and to make

it perfect in your love, and gather it from the four winds, sanctified for your kingdom which you have prepared for it; may you be glorified forever. Let grace come, and let this world pass away. Hosanna to the God (Son) of David! If anyone is holy, let him come; if anyone is not so, let him repent. Maranatha. Amen."

Source: *Didache* 7–10, adapted from *Ante-Nicene Father* (Edinburgh: T. and T. Clark, 1867–1872), vol. 7.

APOSTLES' CREED

In the early Church, many controversies erupted over fine points of Christian theology. This often resulted in the creation of some creed that distinguished acceptable theological positions from unacceptable ones. Composed around 150 C.E.*, the Apostles' Creed is perhaps the first of these. The controversy was gnosticism, the view that we should free our spirits from the evil material world by acquiring special knowledge. Christian Gnostics believed that God was not really the creator of the world and that Jesus could not have suffered and died because he was a spiritual being. The Apostles' Creed opposes both of these contentions.*

I believe in God the Father Almighty, maker of heaven and earth. And in Jesus Christ his only Son our Lord, who was conceived by the Holy Spirit, born of the virgin Mary. He suffered under Pontius Pilate, was crucified, died, and was buried; He descended into hell. The third day He rose again from the dead. He ascended into heaven and is seated at the right hand of God the Father Almighty. From there He shall come to judge the living and the dead. I believe in the Holy Spirit, the holy catholic church, the communion of saints, the forgiveness of sins, the resurrection of the body, and the life everlasting. Amen.

Source: Apostles' Creed, from *The Book of Common Prayer* (London: Bagster, 1885).

NICENE CREED

The Nicene Creed emerged in response to the Arian controversy, a dispute involving the claims of a Christian priest named Arius (c. 250–336) that Christ was created by God and hence was not God himself. The Council of Nicaea was called in 325 to resolve the issue, which was decided against Arius. The Nicene Creed's exact date of origin is a matter of dispute, and at least some components of it were added in later centuries. Nevertheless, its content reflects the Council's decision against Arianism. At a minor Church council in 589, the sentence "I believe in the Holy Ghost . . . who proceeds from the father" was expanded to read "who proceeds from the father and the son (filioque).*" The issue involves whether the Holy Ghost originated from the father alone, or from both the father and the son. Known as the* filioque *clause, its inclusion provoked discord with the Eastern Orthodox churches and became their rallying cry in the Great Schism of 1054. The* filioque *clause was definitively added to the creed by the Catholics at the Second Council of Lyons in 1274. Today, the Nicene Creed remains the most popular confession of faith in Catholic, Orthodox, and most Protestant liturgies, although Orthodox churches omit the* filioque *clause.*

I believe in one God, the Father Almighty, Maker of heaven and earth, of all things visible and invisible. And in one Lord Jesus Christ, the only-begotten Son of God, begotten of His Father before all worlds, God of God, Light of Light, Very God of very God, begotten, not made, being of one substance with the Father; by whom all things were made; who for us and for our salvation came down from heaven, and was incarnate by the Holy Spirit of the virgin Mary, and was made man; and was crucified also for us under Pontius Pilate; He suffered and was buried, and the third day He rose again according to the Scriptures, and ascended into heaven, and is seated at the right hand of the Father; and He shall come again, with glory, to judge both the living and the dead; whose kingdom shall have no end. And I believe in the Holy Spirit, the Lord and giver of life, who proceeds from the Father and the Son; who with the Father and the Son together is worshipped and glorified; who spoke by the Prophets; and I believe one holy catholic and apostolic church; I acknowledge one baptism for the remission of sins; and I look for the resurrection of the dead, and the life of the world to come. Amen.

Source: Nicene Creed, from *Nicene and Post-Nicene Fathers* (New York: The Christian Literature Company, 1890–1900), series 2, vol. 7.

CHALCEDON CREED

In 451, the Council of Chalcedon was called to address two controversial theological positions. A position called Nestorianism *denied the unity of Christ's divinity and humanity; in this view, Christ had two distinct personas. A contrasting position called* Monophysitism *held that Christ in fact had one nature, part of which was divine and the other part human. Against both of these positions, the Chalcedon council held that Christ has one substance but two natures: He is both fully human and fully God. This official view is reflected in the Chalcedon Creed.*

Following, then, the holy fathers, we unite in teaching all men to confess the one and only Son, our Lord Jesus Christ. This selfsame one is perfect both in deity and in humanness; this selfsame one is also actually God and actually man, with a rational soul and a body. He is of the same reality as God as far as his deity is concerned and of the same reality as we ourselves as far as his humanness is concerned; thus like us in all respects, sin only excepted. Before time began he was begotten of the Father, in respect of his deity, and now in these "last days," for us and on behalf of our salvation, this selfsame one was born of Mary the virgin, who is God-bearer in respect of his humanness.

We also teach that we apprehend this one and only Christ-Son, Lord, only-begotten—in two natures; and we do this without confusing the two natures, without transmuting one nature into the other, without dividing them into two separate categories, without contrasting them according to area or function. The distinctiveness of each nature is not nullified by the union. Instead, the "properties" of each nature are conserved and both natures concur in one "person" and in one reality. They are not divided or cut into two persons, but are together the one and only and only-begotten Word of God, the Lord Jesus Christ. Thus have the prophets of old testified; thus the Lord Jesus Christ himself taught us; thus the Symbol of Fathers has handed down to us.

Source: Chalcedon Creed, from *Nicene and Post-Nicene Fathers*, series 2, vol. 7.

CHURCH FATHERS, SAINTS, AND MYSTICS

THE MARTYRDOM OF POLYCARP

During the first three centuries C.E., *several Roman rulers systematically persecuted Christians. Some victims were outspoken leaders, and others became conspicuous for not participating in pagan religious rituals. In either case they were barbarically executed, as were Jesus and the Apostles before them. Stories of religious martyrs became an important part of early Christian writing, both to commemorate the tragic events and to instill a sense of religious bravery in those who might experience a similar fate. The most popular of all early stories of martyrs is that of Polycarp (c. 69–c. 155), bishop of Smyrna, who was arrested during a pagan festival for failing to participate. He was burnt to death after refusing to renounce his faith.*

9. As Polycarp was entering the stadium, there came to him a voice from heaven, saying, "Be strong, and show yourself a man, O Polycarp!" No one saw who it was that spoke to him; but those of our brethren who were present heard the voice. And as he was brought forward, the tumult became great when they heard that Polycarp was taken. When he came near, the proconsul asked him whether he was Polycarp. On his confessing that he was, [the proconsul] sought to persuade him to deny [Christ], saying, "Have respect for your old age," and similar things, according to their custom, [such as], "Swear by the fortune of Caesar; repent, and say, Away with the Atheists." But Polycarp, gazing with a stern countenance on all the multitude of the wicked heathen then in the stadium, and waving his hand towards them, while with groans he looked up to heaven, said, "Away with the Atheists." Then the proconsul urged him, saying, "Swear, and I will set you at liberty; reproach Christ." Polycarp declared, "Eighty and six years I have served Him, and He never did me any injury. How then can I blaspheme my King and my Savior?" . . .
12. While he spoke these and many other like things, he was filled with confidence and joy. His countenance was full of grace, so that not merely did it not fall as if troubled by the things said to him, but, on

the contrary, the proconsul was astonished. He sent his herald to proclaim in the middle of the stadium three times, "Polycarp has confessed that he is a Christian." This proclamation having been made by the herald, the whole multitude—both of the heathen and Jews who dwelt at Smyrna—cried out with uncontrollable fury, and in a loud voice, "This is the teacher of Asia, the father of the Christians, and the overthrower of our gods, he who has been teaching many not to sacrifice, or to worship the gods." Speaking this, they cried out, and besought Philip the Asiarch to let loose a lion upon Polycarp. But Philip answered that it was not lawful for him to do since the shows of wild beasts were already finished. Then it seemed good to them to cry out with one consent, that Polycarp should be burnt alive. . . .

13. This, then, was carried into effect with greater speed than it was spoken. The multitudes immediately gathering together wood and fagots out of the shops and baths; the Jews especially, according to custom, eagerly assisting them in it. . . .
15. When he had pronounced this *amen,* and finished his prayer, those who were appointed for the purpose kindled the fire. As the flame blazed in great fury, we, to whom it was given to witness it, saw a great miracle, and have been preserved that we might report to others what took place. For the fire, shaping itself into the form of an arch, like the sail of a ship when filled with the wind, encompassed the body of the martyr like a circle. And he appeared within not like flesh which is burnt, but as bread that is baked, or as gold and silver glowing in a furnace. Moreover, we perceived a sweet odor [coming from the pile], as if frankincense or some such precious spices had been smoking there.
16. Eventually, when those wicked men perceived that his body could not be consumed by the fire, they commanded an executioner to go near and pierce him through with a dagger. And on his doing this, there came forth a dove, and a great quantity of blood, so that the fire was extinguished; and all the people wondered that there should be such a difference between the unbelievers and the elect, of whom this most admirable Polycarp was one, having in our own times been an apostolic and prophetic teacher, and bishop of the Catholic Church which is in Smyrna. For every word that went out of his mouth either has been or shall yet be accomplished.

Source: *The Martyrdom of Polycarp,* adapted from *Ante-Nicene Fathers,* vol. 1.

TERTULLIAN ON HERETICS

Early Christians were forced to defend their faith against attacks by both Jewish and Roman critics. Christianity was new and comparatively distinct from more ancient religious traditions and was thus frequently ridiculed by outsiders. Even within Christianity, theological disputes erupted between factions, resulting in defenses on both sides of the issue. One of early Christianity's most influential defenders was Tertullian (c. 160–c. 225), who emphasized the importance of nonrational faith when confronting the more perplexing doctrines of Christianity, such as the divine incarnation and the crucifixion of Jesus. In the selections here we find Tertullian's most famous anti-intellectual expressions: "What indeed has Athens to do with Jerusalem?" and "It is by all means to be believed, because it is absurd."

These [pagan philosophies] are "the doctrines" of men and "of demons" produced for itching ears of the spirit of this world's wisdom. This the Lord called "foolishness," and "chose the foolish things of the world" to confound even philosophy itself. For (philosophy) it is which is the material of the world's wisdom, the rash interpreter of the nature and the dispensation of God. Indeed heresies are themselves instigated by philosophy. . . . Whence spring those "fables and endless genealogies," and "unprofitable question," and "words which spread like a cancer?" From all these, when the apostle would restrain us, he expressly names philosophy as that which he would have us be on our guard against. Writing to the Colossians, he says, "See that no one beguile you through philosophy and vain deceit, after the tradition of men, and contrary to the wisdom of the Holy Ghost." He had been at Athens, and had in his interviews (with us philosophers) become acquainted with that human wisdom which pretends to know the truth, while it only corrupts it, and is itself divided into its own manifold heresies, by the variety of its mutually repugnant sects. What indeed has Athens to do with Jerusalem? What concord is there between the Academy and the Church? What between heretics and Christians? Our instruction comes from "the porch of Solomon," who had himself taught that "the Lord should be sought in simplicity of heart." Away with all attempts to produce a mottled Christianity of Stoic, Platonic, and dialectic composition! We want no curious disputation after possessing Christ Jesus, no inquisition after enjoying the gospel! With our faith, we desire no further belief. For this is our palmary faith, that there is nothing which we ought to believe besides.

Source: Tertullian, *The Prescription Against Heretics*, ch. 7, adapted from *Ante-Nicene Fathers*, vol. 3.

There are, to be sure, other things also quite as foolish [as the birth of Christ], which have reference to the humiliations and sufferings of God. Or else, let them call a crucified God "wisdom." But Marcion will apply the knife to this doctrine [of the crucifixion] also, and even with greater reason. For which is more unworthy of God, which is more likely to raise a blush of shame, that God should be born, or that He should die? that He should bear the flesh, or the cross? Be circumcised, or be crucified? be cradled, or be coffined? be laid in a manger, or in a tomb? Talk of "wisdom!" You will be more arbitrary if you refuse to believe this also. But, after all, you will not be "wise" unless you become a "fool" to the world, by believing "the foolish things of God." Have you, then, cut away all sufferings from Christ, on the ground that, as a mere phantom, He was incapable of experiencing them? . . . The Son of God was crucified; I am not ashamed because men are ashamed of it. And the Son of God died; it is by all means to be believed, because it is absurd. And He was buried, and rose again; the fact is certain, because it is impossible. But how will all this be true in Him, if He was not Himself true—if He really had not in Himself that which might be crucified, might die, might be buried, and might rise again?

Source: Tertullian, *On the Flesh of Christ,* ch. 5, adapted from *Ante-Nicene Fathers,* vol. 3.

JEROME'S PREFACE TO THE VULGATE

During the first few centuries, disorganized and conflicting Latin versions of the Christian scriptures circulated among churches. Hoping to finally put the matter in order, near the close of the fourth century Pope Damasus commissioned a scholar from Italy named Jerome (c. 342–420) to compile a definitive Latin text of the Old and New Testaments. The project took some time, but Jerome succeeded in translating most of it. His work became the foundation for the Latin Vulgate, the authoritative text of the Bible in the Roman Catholic world. The following is his Preface to the four Gospels, which was addressed to Pope Damasus in 383 C.E. *The issues Jerome raises here are precisely those that modern translators of the Bible must also face.*

You urge me to revise the old Latin version, and, as it were, to sit in judgement on the copies of the Scriptures which are now scattered throughout the whole world; and, inasmuch as they differ from one another, you would have me decide which of them agree with the Greek original. The labor is one of love, but at the same time both perilous and presumptuous; for in judging others I must be content to be judged by all. And how can I dare to change the language of the world in its hoary old age, and carry it back to the early days of its infancy? Is there a man, learned or unlearned, who will not, when he takes the volume into his hands, and perceives that what he reads does not suit his settled tastes, break out immediately into violent language, and call me a forger and a profane person for having the audacity to add anything to the ancient books, or to make any changes or corrections therein? Now there are two consoling reflections which enable me to bear the odium. First, the command is given by you who are supreme bishop; and secondly, even on the showing of those who revile, readings at variance with the early copies cannot be right. For if we are to pin our faith to the Latin texts, it is for our opponents to tell us *which;* for there are almost as many forms of texts as there are copies. If, on the other hand, we are to glean the truth from a comparison of *many,* why not go back to the original Greek and correct the mistakes introduced by inaccurate translators, and the blundering alterations of confident but ignorant critics, and, further, all that has been inserted or changed by copyists more asleep than awake? I am not discussing the Old Testament, which was turned into Greek by the Seventy elders, and has reached us by a descent of three steps. . . . I therefore promise in this short Preface the four Gospels only, which are to be taken in the following order, Matthew, Mark, Luke, John, as they have been revised by a comparison of the Greek manuscripts. Only early ones have been used. But to avoid any great divergences from the Latin which we are accustomed to read, I have used my pen with some restraint, and while I have corrected only such passages as seemed to convey a different meaning, I have allowed the rest to remain as they are.

Source: Jerome, Preface to the Four Gospels, adapted from *Nicene and Post-Nicene Fathers,* series 2, vol. 6.

AUGUSTINE'S CONFESSIONS

Perhaps the most important theologian in the history of Christianity is Augustine (354–430), bishop of the North African city of Hippo. Like Tertullian, Augustine defended Christianity against attacks by Roman pagans and Christian heretics alike. He wrote on a range of issues of Christian doctrine, and his views helped shape the direction of the religion. His most famous work is his autobiography, the Confessions, *which describes his struggle to find spiritual contentment through hedonism, through the Manichean religious cult, and finally through Christianity.*

Book 2. . . . I will now call to mind my past foulness, and the carnal corruptions of my soul, not because I love them, but that I may love you, O my God. . . . I had a desire to commit robbery, and did so. I was compelled neither by hunger, nor poverty, but through a distaste for doing right, and a desire for wickedness. For I stole things that I already had, and much better. Nor did I desire to enjoy what I stole, but only the theft and sin itself. There was pear tree close to our vineyard, heavily loaded with fruit, which was tempting neither for its color nor its flavor. Late one night, a few of us shameless young folk went to shake and rob it, having, according to our disgraceful habit, prolonged our games in the streets until then. We carried away great loads, not to eat ourselves, but to fling to pigs, having only eaten some of them. This pleased us all the more because it was not permitted. . . .

Book 3. I came to Carthage, where a cauldron of unholy loves bubbled up all around me. . . . I contaminated the spring of friendship with the filth of sensuality, and I dimmed its luster with the hell of lustfulness. Foul and dishonorable as I was, through an excess of vanity, I nevertheless craved to be thought elegant and urbane. I fell rashly, then, into the love in which I longed to be ensnared. . . . [In time] I directed my mind to the Holy Scriptures, so that I might see what they were . . . [but] my inflated pride rejected their style, nor could the sharpness of my wit pierce their inner meaning. . . . I then fell among [Manichean] men proudly raving, very carnal, and voluble, in whose mouths were the snares of the devil—the lure being composed of a mixture of the syllables of your name, and of our Lord Jesus Christ, and of the Intercessor, the Holy Ghost, the Comforter. . . .

Book 5. . . . For nearly the whole of those nine years during which, with unstable mind, I had followed the Manicheans, I had been looking forward with great eagerness for the arrival of [the Manichean teacher] Faustus. The other members of the sect whom I had chanced to encounter, when unable to answer the questions I raised, always directed me to look forward to his coming. By discoursing with him, these, and greater difficulties if I had them, would be most easily and amply cleared away. When at last he arrived, I found him to be a man of pleasant speech, who spoke of the very same things as they themselves did, although more fluently, and in better language. But of what profit to me was the elegance of my cup-bearer, since he failed to offer me the more precious draught for which I thirsted? . . . When it became plain to me that he was ignorant of those arts [of rhetoric] in which I had believed him to excel, I began to despair of his clearing up and explaining all the perplexities that harassed me.

I came to Milan and went to Ambrose the bishop, known to the whole world as among the best of men. . . . I studiously listened to him preaching to the people, not with the proper motive, but, as it were, trying to discover whether his eloquence matched his reputation. . . . And while I opened my heart to admit how *skillfully* he spoke, there also gradually entered with it how *truly* he spoke! These things also began to appear to me to be defensible. The Catholic faith, for which I had felt nothing could be said against the attacks of the Manichaeans, I now conceived might be maintained without presumption. . . . And so I earnestly bent my mind to see if I could possibly prove the Manichaeans guilty of falsehood. . . . Because these philosophers were without the saving name of Christ, I utterly refused to have them cure my fainting soul. I resolved, therefore, to be a catechumen in the Catholic Church, which my parents had commended to me, until something settled should manifest itself to me towards which I might steer my course.

Book 6. . . . When I had disclosed to my mother that I was now no longer a Manichaean, though not yet a Catholic Christian, she did not leap for joy. . . . She replied to me that she believed in Christ, that before she departed this life, she would see me a Catholic believer. . . . Active efforts were made to get me a wife. I wooed, I was engaged, my mother taking the greatest pains in the matter, that when I was once married, the health-giving baptism might cleanse me. . . . A maiden came forward who was two years under the marriageable age, but, as she was pleasing, I waited for her. . . . Meanwhile my sins were multiplying. My mistress was torn from my side as an impediment to my marriage, and my heart, which clung to her, was racked, and wounded, and bleeding. She went back to Africa, making a vow to you to never know another man, and leaving with me my natural son by her. But I unhappily could not imitate her and, impatient of delay, I took another mistress—since it would be two years until I was to marry my betrothed, and I was not so much a lover of marriage as a slave to lust. . . .

Book 8. The very toys of toys, and vanities of vanities, my old mistresses, still enthralled me. . . . But when a profound reflection had, from the secret depths of my soul, drawn together and heaped up all my misery before the sight of my heart, there arose a mighty storm, accompanied by as mighty a shower of tears. So that I might pour forth fully with natural expressions, I left [my friend] Alypius; for it seemed to me that solitude was fitter for the business of weeping. So I retired to such a distance that even his presence could not be oppressive to me. . . . I flung myself down, how, I do not know, under a certain fig-tree, giving free course to my tears, and the streams of my eyes gushed out, an acceptable sacrifice to you. And, not indeed in these words, yet to this effect, I spoke to you: "But you, O Lord, how long? How long, Lord? Will you be angry forever?". . .

I was saying these things and weeping in the most bitter contrition of my heart, when suddenly I heard the voice, sounding like a boy or girl—I don't know which—coming from a neighboring house, chanting, and repeating, "Take up and read; take up and read." Immediately my expression changed, and I earnestly considered whether it was usual for children in any kind of game to sing these words. Nor could I remember ever to have heard the like. So, restraining the torrent of my tears, I rose up, interpreting it no other way than as a command to me from heaven to open the book, and to read the first chapter I should light upon. For I had heard that Anthony, accidentally coming in while the gospel was being read, received the admonition as if what was read were addressed to him: "Go and sell what you have, and give to the poor, and you shall have treasure in heaven, and come and follow me." And by this oracle he was immediately converted to you. I quickly returned to the place where Alypius was sitting; for there had I put down the volume of the apostles, when I rose from there. I grasped, opened, and in silence read that paragraph on which my eyes first fell: "Not in rioting and drunkenness, not in chambering and wantonness, not in strife and envying; but put on the Lord Jesus Christ, and make no provision for the flesh, to fulfill the lusts there of." I did not read any further, nor did I need to; for instantly, as the sentence ended—by a light of security, so to speak, infused into my heart—all the gloom of doubt vanished away.

Source: Augustine, *Confessions,* adapted from *Nicene and Post-Nicene Fathers* (New York: The Christian Literature Co., 1886–1890), series 1, vol. 1.

THE RULE OF SAINT BENEDICT

Benedict of Nursia (480–547), an Italian monk within the Roman Catholic Church, is most remembered for the Rule, or list of precepts, that he created for a monastic community that he founded in southern Italy. Hailed for its balance and moderation, his Rule was adopted by monasteries throughout Western Europe, resulting in Benedict's designation as "the Father of Western Monasticism." The Rule consists of seventy-three sections; the three presented below deal with the varieties of monastic life, vows of silence, and vows of poverty.

Concerning the kinds of monks and their manner of living. It is evident that there are four kinds of monks. The cenobites are the first kind; that is, those living in a monastery, serving under a rule of an abbot. Then the second kind is that of the anchorites; that is, the hermits, —those who, not by the new fervor of a conversion but by the long probation of life in a monastery, have learned to fight against the devil, having already been taught by the solace of many. They, having been well prepared, in the army of brothers for the solitary fight of the hermit, being secure now without the consolation of another, are able, God helping them, to fight with their own hand or arm against the vices of the flesh or of their thoughts.

But a third very bad kind of monks are the sarabaites, approved by no rule, experience being their teacher, as with the gold which is tried in the furnace. But, softened after the manner of lead, keeping faith with the world by their works, they are known through their tonsure to lie to God. These being shut up by twos or threes, or, indeed, alone, without a shepherd, not in the Lord's but in their own sheep-folds,—their law is the satisfaction of their desires. For whatever they think good or choice, this they call holy; and what they do not wish, this they consider unlawful. But the fourth kind of monks is the kind which is called gyratory. During their whole life they are guests, for three or four days at a time, in the cells of the different monasteries, throughout the various provinces. They are always wandering and never stationary, given over to the service of their own pleasures and the joys of the palate, and in every way worse than the sarabaites. Concerning the most wretched way of living of all of such monks it is better to be silent than to speak. These things therefore being omitted, let us proceed, with the aid of God, to treat of the best kind, the cenobites.

Concerning silence. Let us do as the prophet says: "I said, I will take heed to my ways that I sin not with my tongue, I have kept my mouth with a bridle: I was dumb with silence, I held my peace even from good; and my sorrow was stirred." Here the prophet shows that if one ought at times, for the sake of silence, to refrain from good sayings; how much more, as a punishment for sin, ought one to cease from evil words. And therefore, if anything is to be asked of the prior, let it be asked with all humility and subjection of reverence, lest one seem to speak more than is fitting. Scurrilities, however, or idle words and those exciting laughter, we condemn in all places with a lasting prohibition: nor do we permit a disciple to open his mouth for such sayings.

Whether the monks should have anything of their own. More than anything else is this special vice to be cut off root and branch from the monastery, that one should presume to give or receive anything without the order of the abbot, or should have anything of his own. He should have absolutely nothing—neither a book, nor tablets, nor a pen—nothing at all. For indeed it is not allowed to the monks to have their own bodies or wills in their own power. But all things necessary they must not expect from the Father of the monastery; nor is it allowable to have anything which the abbot did not give or permit. All things shall be common to all, as it is written: "Let not any man presume or call anything his own." But if any one shall have been discovered delighting in this most evil vice, being warned once and again, if he does not amend, let him be subjected to punishment.

Source: The Rule of Saint Benedict, Sects. 1, 6, 33, tr. Ernest F. Henderson.

AQUINAS ON FAITH AND REASON

During the Middle Ages, one of the chief theological issues was the relation between faith and reason. Tertullian addressed this issue with his famous rhetorical question "What does Athens have to do with Jerusalem?" implying that reason plays no role in matters of faith. Thomas Aquinas (1225–1274) argued to the contrary that reason can go a long way in establishing religious truths, such as the existence and nature of God. However, he argued, faith in divine revelation still is required for establishing the more particular truths of Christianity. In the selection below, Aquinas explains the dual paths toward knowledge of God, the need for faith in addition to reason, and the compatibility of faith and reason.

3. *The Truths which we Confess concerning God Fall under two Categories.* The truths that we confess concerning God fall under two categories. Some things that are true of God are beyond all the competence of human reason, such as that God is three and one. There are other things to which even human reason can attain, such as the existence and unity of God, which philosophers have proved to a demonstration under the guidance of the light of natural reason. It is clear that there are points of absolute intelligibility in God that are altogether beyond the compass of human reason. . . . Human understanding cannot go so far with its natural power as to grasp God's substance, since, under the conditions of the present life, knowledge and understanding begin with the senses. Therefore, objects beyond the senses cannot be grasped by human understanding except so far as knowledge is gathered of them through the senses. But things of sense cannot lead our understanding to discover in them the essence of the divine substance, since they are effects inadequate to the power that caused them. Nevertheless our understanding is thereby led to some knowledge of God, namely, of his existence and of other attributes that must necessarily be attributed to the first cause. There are, therefore, some points of intelligibility in God, accessible to human reason, and other points that altogether transcend the power of human reason. . . .
4. *It is an Advantage for the Truths of God, known by Natural Reason, to be Proposed to Humans to be Believed on Faith.* If a truth of this nature were left to the sole inquiry of reason, three disadvantages would follow.

One is that the knowledge of God would be confined to few. The discovery of truth is the fruit of studious inquiry, and very many people are hindered from this. . . . Another disadvantage is that those who did arrive at the knowledge or discovery of the aforesaid truth would take a long time to gain it, because of the profundity of such truth and the many prerequisites to the study. . . . A third disadvantage is that, because of the infirmity of our judgment and the disquieting force of imagination, there is some mixture of error in most of the investigations of human reason. . . .

7. *The Truth of Reason is not Contrary to the Truth of Christian Faith.* The natural dictates of reason must certainly be quite true: it is impossible to think of their being otherwise. Nor again is it permissible to believe that the tenets of faith are false, being so evidently confirmed by God. Since therefore falsehood alone is contrary to truth, it is impossible for the truth of faith to be contrary to principles known by natural reason. Whatever is put into the disciple's mind by the teacher is contained in the knowledge of the teacher, unless the teacher is teaching dishonestly, which would be a wicked thing to say about God. But the knowledge of principles naturally known is put into us by God, since God himself is the author of our nature. Therefore these principles also are contained in the divine wisdom. Whatever therefore is contrary to these principles is contrary to divine wisdom, and cannot be of God. . . .
8. *The Relation of Human Reason to the first Truth of Faith.* Things of the senses, from which human reason takes its beginning towards knowledge, retain in themselves some trace of imitation of God, insofar as they exist and are good. Yet this trace is so imperfect that it proves wholly insufficient to declare the substance of God himself.

Source: Thomas Aquinas, *Summa Contra Gentiles,* Book 1, chs. 3, 4, 7, 8. Adapted from *Of God and His Creatures,* tr. Joseph Ricaby (London: Burnes and Oates: 1905).

THE COUNCIL OF TRENT

Held between the years 1545 and 1563, the Council of Trent was the nineteenth ecumenical council recognized by the Catholic Church, and was initiated at the insistence of Holy Roman Emperor Charles V to help bridge the gap between Catholics and Protestants. While Protestant representatives attended some of the sessions, the end result of the Council was the reaffirmation of Catholicism's doctrines that had spawned the Protestant Reformation to begin with. The Council of Trent marks the beginning of a period of Church history known as the Counter-Reformation during which time the Catholic Church combated the Protestant doctrine and the advance of Protestantism in Europe and elsewhere. The selections below address several of the most central issues that divide Catholicism from Protestantism, namely, transubstantiation, purgatory, religious images, and indulgences.

On Transubstantiation. Because Christ, our Redeemer, declared that which He offered under the species of bread to be truly His own body, therefore has it ever been a firm belief in the Church of God, and this holy Synod does now declare it anew, that, by the consecration of the bread and of the wine, a conversion is made of the whole substance of the bread into the substance of the body of Christ our Lord, and of the whole substance of the wine into the substance of His blood. This conversion is, by the holy Catholic Church, suitably and properly called Transubstantiation.

On Purgatory. The Catholic Church, instructed by the Holy Ghost, has, from the sacred writings and the ancient tradition of the Fathers, taught, in sacred councils, and very recently in this ecumenical Synod, that there is a Purgatory, and that the souls there detained are helped by the prayers of the faithful, but principally by the acceptable sacrifice of the altar. Accordingly, the holy Synod commands to bishops that they diligently endeavor that the sound doctrine concerning Purgatory, transmitted by the holy Fathers and sacred councils, be believed, maintained, taught, and everywhere proclaimed by the faithful of Christ. But let the more difficult and subtle questions, which tend not to edification, and from which for the most part there is no increase of piety, be excluded from popular discourses before the uneducated multitude. In like manner, such things as are uncertain, or which labor under an appearance of error, let them not allow to be made public and so treated. While those things which tend to a certain kind of curiosity or superstition, or which savor of filthy lucre, let them prohibit as scandals and stumbling-blocks of the faithful. But let the bishops take care that the prayers of the faithful who are living, that is, the sacrifices of masses, prayers, alms, and other works of piety, which have been customarily performed by the faithful for the other faithful departed, be piously and devoutly performed, in accordance with the institutes of the church. Whatever is due on their behalf, from the endowments of testators, or in other ways, shall be discharged, not in a thoughtless manner, but diligently and accurately, by the priests and ministers of the church, and others who are bound to render this service.

On Sacred Images. The images of Christ, of the Virgin Mother of God, and of the other saints, are to be had and retained particularly in temples. Due honor and veneration are to be given them, not that any divinity or virtue is believed to be in them on account of which they are to be worshipped; or that anything is to be asked of them; or, that trust is to be reposed in images, as was of old done by the Gentiles who placed their hope in idols. But [honor and veneration are given to them] because the honor which is shown them is referred to the prototypes which those images represent. Accordingly, by the images which we kiss, and before which we uncover the head, and prostrate ourselves, we adore Christ. And we venerate the saints, whose likeness they bear, as, by the decrees of Councils, and especially of the second Synod of Nicaea, has been defined against the opponents of images.

On Indulgences. The power of conferring Indulgences was granted by Christ to the Church, and she has, even in the most ancient times, used that power, delivered to her by God. The sacred Holy Synod teaches, and commands, that the use of Indulgences, for the Christian people most salutary, and approved of by the authority of sacred Councils, is to be retained in the Church. It condemns with anathema those who either assert that they are useless, or who deny that there is in the Church the power of granting them. In granting them, however, it desires that, in accordance with the ancient and approved custom in the Church, moderation be observed to help prevent ecclesiastical discipline from being weakened by excessive practice. And being desirous that the abuses which have crept therein, and by occasion of which this honorable name of Indulgences is blasphemed by heretics, be amended and corrected, it ordains generally by this decree, that all evil gains for the obtaining thereof (from which source a most prolific cause of abuses amongst the Christian people has been derived) be wholly abolished. But as regards the other abuses which have proceeded from superstition, ignorance, irreverence, or from whatever other source, since, by reason of the manifold corruptions in the places and provinces where the said abuses are committed, they cannot conveniently be specially prohibited. It commands all bishops, diligently to collect, each in his own church, all abuses of this nature, and to report them in the first provincial Synod, that, after having been reviewed by the opinions of the other bishops also, they may forthwith be referred to the Sovereign Roman Pontiff, by whose authority and prudence that which may be expedient for the universal Church will be ordained; that this the gift of holy Indulgences may be dispensed to all the faithful, piously, holily, and incorruptly.

Source: Council of Trent, Sessions 13, 25, tr. J. Waterworth.

TERESA OF AVILA ON THE PRAYER OF UNION

Teresa of Avila (1515–1582), a sixteenth-century Spanish mystic, entered a Carmelite convent at age 19. With St. John of the Cross she established the Discalced (barefoot) order, which was stricter and wore only sandals. She had visions and raptures; in her most memorable vision, an angel pierced her heart with a flaming arrow, which, when removed, left her with a love for God. Teresa's most systematic work, Interior Castle *(1577), uses the metaphor of seven series of mansions to represent various stages of spiritual development. The mystic enters the castle door through prayer and then roams the mansions' millions of rooms at will. She describes the fifth series of mansions as the Prayer of Union, by which the mystic's soul is possessed by God. In the following selection, she explains the effects of this union using the analogy of a silkworm. The silkworm starts from a tiny egg that feeds on mulberry leaves, spins a cocoon, and emerges as a butterfly. The silkworm represents the soul, its nourishment is the Church, the silk house is Christ, and the spinning of the cocoon is the prayer of union. Thus, the union experience, which does not last even a half hour, transforms the mystic, and the new "butterfly" feels like a stranger in its new world.*

You will have heard of the wonderful way in which silk is made—a way which no one could invent but God—and how it comes from a kind of seed which looks like tiny peppercorns. (I have never seen this, but only heard of it, so if it is incorrect in any way the fault is not mine.) When the warm weather comes, and the mulberry-trees begin to show leaf, this seed starts to take life; until it has this sustenance, on which it feeds, it is as dead. The silkworms feed on the mulberry-leaves until they are full-grown, when people put down twigs, upon which, with their tiny mouths, they start spinning silk, making themselves very tight little cocoons, in which they bury themselves. Then, finally, the worm, which was large and ugly, comes right out of the cocoon a beautiful white butterfly. . . .

The silkworm is like the soul which takes life when, through the heat which comes from the Holy Spirit, it begins to utilize the general help which God gives to us all, and to make use of the remedies which He left in His Church—such as frequent confessions, good books and sermons, for these are the remedies for a soul dead in negligences and sins and frequently plunged into temptation. The soul begins to live and nourishes itself on this food, and on good meditations, until it is full grown—and this is what concerns me now: the rest is of little importance.

When it is full-grown, then, as I wrote at the beginning, it starts to spin its silk and to build the house in which it is to die. This house may be understood here to mean Christ. I think I read or heard somewhere that our life is hid in Christ, or in God (for that is the same thing), or that our life is Christ. (The exact form of this is little to my purpose.)

Here, then, daughters, you see what we can do, with God's favor. May His Majesty Himself be our Mansion as He is in this Prayer of Union which, as it were, we ourselves spin. When I say He will be our Mansion, and we can construct it for ourselves and hide ourselves in it, I seem to be suggesting that we can subtract from God, or add to Him. But of course we cannot possibly do that! We can neither subtract from, nor add to, God but we can subtract from, and add to, ourselves, just as these little silkworms do. And, before we have finished doing all that we can in that respect, God will take this tiny achievement of ours, which is nothing at all, unite it with His greatness and give it such worth that its reward will be the Lord Himself. And as it is He Whom it has cost the most, so His Majesty will unite our small trials with the great trials which He suffered, and make both of them into one.

On, then, my daughters. Let us hasten to perform this task and spin this cocoon. Let us renounce our self-love and self-will, and our attachment to earthly things. Let us practice penance, prayer, mortification, obedience, and all the other good works that you know of. Let us do what we have been taught; and we have been instructed about what our duty is. Let the silkworm die—let it die, as in fact it does when it has completed the work which it was created to do. Then we shall see God and shall ourselves be as completely hidden in His greatness as is this little worm in its cocoon. Note that, when I speak of seeing God, I am referring to the way in which, as I have said, He allows Himself to be apprehended in this kind of union.

And now let us see what becomes of this silkworm, for all that I have been saying about it is leading up to this. When it is in this state of prayer, and quite dead to the world, it comes out a little white butterfly. Oh, greatness of God, that a soul should come out like this after being hidden in the greatness of God, and closely united with Him, for so short a time—never, I think, for as long as half an hour! I tell you truly, the very soul does not know itself. For think of the difference between an ugly worm and a white butterfly, it is just the same here. The soul cannot think how it can have merited such a blessing—whence such a blessing could have come to it, I meant to say, for it knows quite well that it has not merited it at all. It finds itself so anxious to praise the Lord that it would gladly be consumed and die a thousand deaths for His sake. Then it finds itself longing to suffer great trials and unable to do otherwise. It has the most vehement desires for penance, for solitude, and for all to know God. And hence, when it sees God being offended, it becomes greatly distressed. In the following Mansion we shall treat of these things further and in detail, for, although the experiences of this Mansion and of the next are almost identical, their effects come to have much greater power, for, as I have said, if after God comes to a soul here on earth it strives to progress still more, it will experience great things.

Source: Teresa of Avila, *Interior Castle,* Fifth Mansion, ch. 2, from *Interior Castle,* tr. E. Allison Peers (Garden City, NY: Doubleday, 1961). Reprinted by permission.

PROTESTANT STATEMENTS OF FAITH

LUTHERANS: AUGSBURG CONFESSION

As Protestant Christian Churches throughout Europe took issue with the Roman Catholic Church, they created confessions of faith that defined their principal theological tenets. Among the first of these was the Augsburg Confession, *written in part by Martin Luther (1483–1546) in 1530. Even today it is a foundational statement for most Lutheran denominations, and Lutheran clergy take an oath by it upon ordination. In spite of Luther's harsh attacks on core Catholic doctrine, the original twenty-one articles of the Augsburg Confession highlight the similarities between Lutheran Protestants and Catholics, rather than the differences. Seven articles added later discuss Catholic abuses. The selected articles have a distinctively Lutheran tone.*

Article 4. Of Justification. [Our Churches] . . . teach that men cannot be justified before God by their own strength, merits, or works, but are freely justified for Christ's sake, through faith, when they believe that they are received into favor, and that their sins are forgiven for Christ's sake, who, by His death, has made satisfaction for our sins. This faith God imputes for righteousness in His sight. Rom. 3 and 4.

Article 7. Of the Church. Also they teach that one holy Church is to continue forever. The Church is the congregation of saints, in which the Gospel is rightly taught and the Sacraments are rightly administered.

And to the true unity of the Church it is enough to agree concerning the doctrine of the Gospel and the administration of the Sacraments. Nor is it necessary that human traditions, that is, rites or ceremonies, instituted by men, should be everywhere alike. As Paul says: One faith, one Baptism, one God and Father of all, etc. Eph. 4, 5, 6.

Article 10. Of the Lord's Supper. Of the Supper of the Lord they teach that the Body and Blood of Christ are truly present, and are distributed to those who eat the Supper of the Lord; and they reject those that teach otherwise.

Article 11. Of Confession. Of Confession they teach that Private Absolution ought to be retained in the churches, although in confession an enumeration of all sins is not necessary. For it is impossible according to the Psalm: Who can understand his errors? Ps. 19, 12.

Article 21. Of the Worship of the Saints. Of the Worship of Saints they teach that the memory of saints may be set before us, that we may follow their faith and good works, according to our calling, as the Emperor may follow the example of David in making war to drive away the Turk from his country. For both are kings. But the Scripture teaches not the invocation of saints or to ask help of saints, since it sets before us the one Christ as the Mediator, Propitiation, High Priest, and Intercessor. He is to be prayed to, and has promised that He will hear our prayer; and this worship He approves above all, to wit, that in all afflictions He be called upon, 1 John 2, 1: If any man sin, we have an Advocate with the Father, etc.

Article 23. Of the Marriage of Priests. There has been common complaint concerning the examples of priests who were not chaste. For that reason also Pope Pius is reported to have said that there were certain causes why marriage was taken away from priests, but that there were far weightier ones why it ought to be given back; for so Platina writes. Since, therefore, our priests were desirous to avoid these open scandals, they married wives, and taught that it was lawful for them to contract matrimony. . . .

Source: Augsburg Confession, in *Triglot Concordia: The Symbolical Books of the Evangelical Lutheran Church* (St. Louis: Concordia Publishing House, 1921).

ANGLICANS: THIRTY-NINE ARTICLES OF RELIGION

Between 1534 and 1563—a particularly volatile period of British history—the Church of England moved toward Protestantism. In 1571, during the reign of Queen Elizabeth, Parliament enacted Thirty-Nine Articles of Religion, which, influenced by Calvinist theology, defined the new denomination. Clergy today in the Church of England are required to assent to the Thirty-Nine Articles, and the Articles of Religion in other Anglican churches—such as the Episcopalian Church in the United States—are based on these. Since 1784, Methodist churches have followed Twenty-Four Articles of Religion taken from these. The selections here reflect

Anglican views of Church hierarchy, rejecting the papacy and establishing the British monarch as the Church's head.

Article 19: Of the Church. The visible Church of Christ is a congregation of faithful men, in which the pure word of God is preached and the sacraments be duly ministered according to Christ's ordinance in all those things that of necessity are requisite to the same. As the Church of Jerusalem, Alexandria, and Antioch have erred: so also the Church of Rome hath erred, not only in their living and manner of ceremonies, but also in matters of faith.

Article 23: Of Ministering in the Congregation. It is not lawful for any man to take upon him the office of public preaching or ministering the sacraments in the congregation, before he be lawfully called and sent to execute the same. And those we ought to judge lawfully called and sent, which be chosen and called to this work by men who have public authority given unto them in the congregation to call and send ministers into the Lord's vineyard.

Article 37: Of the Civil Magistrates. The Queen's Majesty hath the chief power in this realm of England and other her dominions, unto whom the chief government of all estates of this realm, whether they be ecclesiastical or civil, in all causes doth appertain, and is not nor ought to be subject to any foreign jurisdiction.

Where we attribute to the Queen's Majesty the chief government, by which titles we understand the minds of some slanderous folks to be offended, we give not to our princes the ministering either of God's word or of sacraments, the which thing the Injunctions also lately set forth by Elizabeth our Queen doth most plainly testify: but only that prerogative which we see to have been given always to all godly princes in Holy Scriptures by God himself, that is, that they should rule all estates and degrees committed to their charge by God, whether they be temporal, and restrain with the civil sword the stubborn and evil-doers.

The Bishop of Rome hath no jurisdiction in this realm of England. The Laws of the realm may punish Christian men with death for heinous and grievous offences.

It is lawful for Christian men at the commandment of the Magistrate to wear weapons and serve in the wars.

Source: "Articles of Religion," from *The Book of Common Prayer* (London: Bagster, 1855).

PRESBYTERIANS: WESTMINSTER CONFESSION

At the beckoning of the British Parliament, the Westminster Confession was created in 1646 by churches in England that followed the reformed theology of John Calvin (1509–1546). Although the Anglican Church abandoned it shortly afterward, the Confession was adopted by the Scottish Parliament in 1649, making it a cornerstone of

Presbyterianism. The Confession also was adopted in modified form by other Protestant denominations throughout Europe and America. The chapters presented here reflect the distinctively Calvinistic points of the Confession.

Chapter 6. Of the Fall of Man, of Sin, and of the Punishment Thereof. 1. Our first parents, being seduced by the subtlety and temptation of Satan, sinned in eating the forbidden fruit. This their sin God was pleased, according to his wise and holy counsel, to permit, having purposed to order it to his own glory. 2. By this sin they fell from their original righteousness, and communion with God, and so became dead in sin, and wholly defiled in all the faculties and parts of soul and body. 3. They being the root of all mankind, the guilt of this sin was imputed, and the same death in sin and corrupted nature conveyed to all their posterity, descending from them by ordinary generation. 4. From this original corruption, whereby we are utterly indisposed, disabled, and made opposite to all good, and wholly inclined to all evil, do proceed all actual transgressions. 5. This corruption of nature, during this life, doth remain in those that are regenerated: and although it be through Christ pardoned and mortified, yet both itself, and all the motions thereof, are truly and properly sin. 6. Every sin, both original and actual, being a transgression of the righteous law of God, and contrary thereunto, doth, in its own nature, bring guilt upon the sinner, whereby he is bound over to the wrath of God, and curse of the law, and so made subject to death, with all miseries spiritual, temporal, and eternal. . . .

Chapter 10. Of Effectual Calling. 1. All those whom God hath predestinated unto life, and those only, he is pleased, in his appointed and accepted time, effectually to call, by his Word and Spirit, out of that state of sin and death, in which they are by nature, to grace and salvation by Jesus Christ; enlightening their minds spiritually and savingly, to understand the things of God; taking away their heart of stone, and giving unto them a heart of flesh; renewing their wills, and by his almighty power determining them to that which is good, and effectually drawing them to Jesus Christ, yet so as they come most freely, being made willing by his grace. 2. This effectual call is of God's free and special grace alone, not from any thing at all foreseen in man, who is altogether passive therein, until, being quickened and renewed by the Holy Spirit, he is thereby enabled to answer this call, and to embrace the grace offered and conveyed in it. 3. Elect infants, dying in infancy, are regenerated and saved by Christ through the Spirit, who worketh when, and where, and how he pleaseth. So also are all other elect persons, who are incapable of being outwardly called by the ministry of the Word. 4. Others, not elected, although they may be called by the ministry of the Word, and may have some common operations of the Spirit, yet they never truly come to Christ, and therefore cannot be saved; much less can men, not professing the Christian religion, be saved in any other way whatsoever than by Christ, be they never so diligent to frame their lives according to the light of nature, and the law of that religion they do profess; and to assert and maintain that they may is without warrant of the World of God. . . .

Chapter 17. Of the Perseverance of the Saints. 1. They whom God hath accepted in his Beloved, effectually called and sanctified by his Spirit, can neither totally nor finally fall away from the state of grace; but shall certainly persevere therein to the end, and be eternally saved. 2. This perseverance of the saints depends, not upon their own free will, but upon the immutability of the decree of election, flowing from the free and unchangeable love of God the Father; upon the efficacy of the merit and intercession of Jesus Christ; the abiding of the Spirit and of the seed of God within them; and the nature of the covenant of grace: from all which ariseth also the certainty and infallibility thereof. 3. Nevertheless they may, through the temptations of Satan and of the world, the prevalency of corruption remaining in them, and the neglect of the means of their preservation, fall into grievous sins; and for a time continue therein: whereby they incur God's displeasure, and grieve his Holy Spirit; come to be deprived of some measure of their graces and comforts; have their hearts hardened, and their consciences wounded; hurt and scandalize others, and bring temporal judgments upon themselves.

Source: *The Westminster Confession of Faith* (Edinburgh: T. and T. Clark, 1882).

BAPTISTS: FIRST LONDON BAPTIST CONFESSION OF FAITH

In sixteenth-century England, a group of independent churches emerged based on the conviction that local congregations should be free from the authority of larger governing bodies. By their very nature, these congregations were diverse, formulating their own practices and theology. In 1608, former Anglican minister John Smyth (1554–1612) founded the first Baptist church in Amsterdam. Smyth and his followers moved back to England, establishing Baptist churches there. After his untimely death from tuberculosis, Baptists split into two groups: General Baptists, who believed that Christ died for all people, and Particular Baptists, who held that he died only for the elect. In 1643, Particular Baptists in London created a confession of faith. Unlike later Baptist confessions, which were modifications of the Westminster Confession, this one has a distinct content. The following selections, taken from the 1646 edition of this Confession, highlight key points of Baptist theology, and article 21 specifically articulates the position of the Particular Baptists.

21. Jesus Christ by His death did purchase salvation for the elect that God gave unto Him: These only have interest in Him, and fellowship with Him, for whom He makes intercession to His Father in their behalf, and to them alone doth God by His Spirit apply this redemption; as also the free gift of eternal life is given to them, and none else. . . .
25. The preaching of the gospel to the conversion of sinners, is absolutely free; no way requiring as absolutely necessary, any qualifications, preparations, or terrors of the law, or preceding ministry of the law, but only and alone the naked soul, a sinner and ungodly, to receive

Christ crucified, dead and buried, and risen again; who is made a prince and a Savior for such sinners as through the gospel shall be brought to believe on Him. . . .

36. Being thus joined, every [local] church hath power given them from Christ, for their well-being, to choose among themselves persons for elders and deacons, being qualified according to the word, as those which Christ hath appointed in His testament, for the feeding, governing, serving, and building up of His Church; and that none have any power to impose on them either these or any other. . . .
39. Baptism is an ordinance of the New Testament, given by Christ, to be dispensed upon persons professing faith, or that are made disciples; who upon profession of faith, ought to be baptized, and after to partake of the Lord's Supper. . . .
42. Christ hath likewise given power to His Church to receive in, and cast out, any member that deserves it; and this power is given to every congregation, and not to one particular person, either member or officer, but in relation to the whole body, in reference to their faith and fellowship.

Source: *Confession of Faith of Seven Congregations or Churches of Christ in London* (London: 1646).

CONGREGATIONALISTS: SAVOY *DECLARATION OF FAITH AND ORDER*

In addition to the Baptists, another group of independent churches in England was the Congregationalists. In 1658, representatives from about 120 of these churches met in Savoy Palace in an effort to unify their congregations. Modifying the Westminster Confession, they created the Savoy Declaration of Faith and Order. *The selection here is one of their two principal additions to the Westminster Confession, which asserts the right of a congregation to govern itself.*

The Institution of Churches, and the Order Appointed in Them by Jesus Christ. 1. By the appointment of the Father all power for the calling, institution, order, or government of the Church, is invested in a supreme and sovereign manner in the Lord Jesus Christ, as King and Head thereof. 2. In the execution of this power wherewith he is so entrusted, the Lord Jesus calleth out of the world unto communion with himself, those that are given unto him by his Father, that they may walk before him in all the ways of obedience, which he prescribeth to them in Word. 3. Those thus called (through the ministry of the Word by his Spirit) he commandeth to walk together in particular societies or churches, for their mutual edification, and the due performance of that public worship, which he requireth of them in this world. 4. To each of these churches thus gathered, according to his mind declared in his Word, he hath given all that power and authority, which is any way needful for their carrying on that order in worship and discipline, which he hath instituted for them to observe, with commands and rules for the due and right exerting and executing of that power. 5. These particular churches thus appointed by the authority of Christ, and entrusted with power from him for the ends before expressed, are each of them as unto those ends, the seat of that power which he is pleased to communicate to his saints or subjects in this world, so that as such they receive it immediately from himself. 6. Besides these particular churches, there is not instituted by Christ any church more extensive or catholic entrusted with power for the administration of his ordinances, or the execution of any authority in his name. 7. A particular church gathered and completed according to the mind of Christ, consists of officers and members. The Lord Christ having given to his called ones (united according to his appointment in church-order) liberty and power to choose persons fitted by the Holy Ghost for that purpose, to be over them, and to minister to them in the Lord. . . .

Source: *Declaration of Faith and Order* (London: J. P., 1659).

ASSEMBLIES OF GOD: STATEMENT OF FUNDAMENTAL TRUTHS

The Pentecostal movement began around 1900 through the ministry of Charles Parham (1873–1929), who emphasized baptism of the Holy Spirit and speaking in tongues. In 1974, several independent Pentecostal congregations formed the Assemblies of God denomination. Pentecostals initially resisted creeds, but theological disputes prompted the General Council of the Assemblies of God to create a Statement of Fundamental Truths in 1916. Of the seventeen statements, the more uniquely Pentecostal ones are presented here.

5. *The Promise of the Father.* All believers are entitled to, and should ardently expect, and earnestly seek the promise of the Father, the baptism in the Holy Ghost and fire, according to the command of the lord Jesus Christ. This was the normal experience of all in the early Christian church. With it comes the enduement of power for life and service. The bestowment of the gifts and their uses in the work of the ministry. Luke 24:49; Acts 1:4, 1:8; 1 Cor. 12:1–31.
6. *The Full Consummation of the Baptism in the Holy Ghost.* The full consummation of the baptism of believers in the Holy Ghost and fire, is indicated by the initial sign of speaking in tongues, as the spirit of God gives utterance. Acts 2:4. This wonderful experience is distinct from and subsequent to the experience of the new birth. Acts 10:44–46; 15:8,9.
12. *Divine Healing.* Deliverance from sickness is provided for in the atonement, and is the privilege of all believers. Isa. 53:4,5; Matth. 8:16,17.
14. *The Blessed Hope.* The Resurrection of those who have fallen asleep in Christ. The rapture of believers, which are alive and remain, and the translation of the true church, this is the blessed hope set before all believers. 1 Thess. 4:16–17; Rom. 8:23; Tit. 2:13.

15. *The Imminent Coming and Millennial Reign of Jesus.* The premillennial and imminent coming of the Lord to gather his people unto himself, and to judge the world in righteousness while reigning on the earth for a thousand years is the expectation of the true church of Christ.
16. *The Lake of Fire.* The devil and his angles, the beast and false prophet, and whosoever is not found written in the book of Life, the fearful and unbelieving, and abominable, and murderers and whoremongers, and sorcerers, and idolators and all liars shall be consigned to everlasting punishment in the lake which burneth with fire and brimstone, which is the second death.
17. *The New Heavens and New Earth.* We look for new heaven and a new earth wherein dwelleth righteousness. 2 Pet. 3:13; Rev. 1 and 22.

Source: "A Statement of Fundamental Truths," General Council of the Assemblies of God, October 2–7, 1916.

RECENT SECTARIAN MOVEMENTS

UNITARIANISM: WILLIAM ELLERY CHANNING

Denominations emerging from the Protestant Reformation initially shared basic theological assumptions with the older Catholic and Orthodox traditions. Foremost among these were the notion of the Trinity and the idea that the Bible was the unique word of God. Growing political freedom in Europe and America permitted some Christian groups to step outside these traditional theological boundaries. One of the first such groups was the Unitarians, who, as their name implies, denied the Trinity in favor of a unified conception of God. Jesus, in their view, was a divinely appointed prophet and teacher, but not God himself. In America, Unitarianism became more formally organized through the efforts of William Ellery Channing (1780–1842), a former Congregationalist pastor. Though denying the Trinity, Channing remained committed to other tenets of Christianity. Some later Unitarians departed not only from Christian theology, but from all traditional religion, adopting instead a scientific humanism. The following selections are from Channing's seminal sermon Unitarian Christianity, *delivered in 1819 at an ordination ceremony in Baltimore, Maryland.*

I. We regard the Scriptures as the records of God's successive revelations to mankind, and particularly of the last and most perfect revelation of his will by Jesus Christ. Whatever doctrines seem to us to be clearly taught in the Scriptures, we receive without reserve or exception. We do not, however, attach equal importance to all the books in this collection. Our religion, we believe, lies chiefly in the New Testament. The dispensation of Moses, compared with that of Jesus, we consider as adapted to the childhood of the human race, a preparation for a nobler system, and chiefly useful now as serving to confirm and illustrate the Christian Scriptures. Jesus Christ is the only master of Christians, and whatever he taught, either during his personal ministry, or by his inspired Apostles, we regard as of divine authority, and profess to make the rule of our lives.

This authority, which we give to the Scriptures, is a reason, we conceive, for studying them with peculiar care, and for inquiring anxiously into the principles of interpretation, by which their true meaning may be ascertained. The principles adopted by the class of Christians in whose name I speak, need to be explained, because they are often misunderstood. We are particularly accused of making an unwarrantable use of reason in the interpretation of Scripture. We are said to exalt reason above revelation, to prefer our own wisdom to God's. Loose and undefined charges of this kind are circulated so freely, that we think it due to ourselves, and to the cause of truth, to express our views with some particularity.

Our leading principle in interpreting Scripture is this, that the Bible is a book written for men, in the language of men, and that its meaning is to be sought in the same manner as that of other books. We believe that God, when he speaks to the human race, conforms, if we may also say, to the established rules of speaking and writing. How else would the Scriptures avail us more, than if communicated in an unknown tongue? . . .

II. Having thus stated the principles according to which we interpret Scripture, I now proceed to the second great head of this discourse, which is, to state some of the views which we derive from that sacred book, particularly those which distinguish us from other Christians.

1. In the first place, we believe in the doctrine of God's *unity*, or that there is one God, and one only. To this truth we give infinite importance, and we feel ourselves bound to take heed, lest any man spoil us of it by vain philosophy. The proposition, that there is one God, seems to us exceedingly plain. We understand by it, that there is one being, one mind, one person, one intelligent agent, and one only, to whom underived and infinite perfection and dominion belong. We conceive, that these words could have conveyed no other meaning to the simple and uncultivated people who were set apart to be the depositaries of this great truth, and who were utterly incapable of understanding those hair-breadth distinctions between being and person, which the sagacity of later ages has discovered. We find to intimation, that this language was to be taken in an unusual sense, or that God's unity was a quite different thing from the oneness of other intelligent beings.

We object to the doctrine of the Trinity, that, whilst acknowledging in words, it subverts in effect, the unity of God. According to this doctrine, there are three infinite and equal persons, possessing supreme divinity, called the Father, Son, and Holy Ghost. Each of these persons, as described by theologians, has his own particular consciousness, will, and perceptions. They love each other, converse with each other, and delight in each other's society. They perform different parts in man's redemption, each having his appropriate office, and neither doing the work of the other. The Son is mediator and not the Father. The Father sends the Son, and is not himself sent; nor is he conscious, like the Son, of taking flesh. Here, then, we have three intelligent agents, possessed of different consciousness, different wills, and different perceptions, performing different acts, and sustaining different relations; and if these things do not imply and constitute three minds or beings, we are utterly at a loss to know how minds or beings are to be formed. It is difference of properties, and acts, and consciousness, which leads us to the belief of different intelligent beings, and, if this mark fails us, our whole knowledge fall; we have no proof, that all the agents and persons in the universe are not one and the same mind. When we attempt to conceive of three Gods, we can do nothing more than represent to ourselves three agents, distinguished from each other by similar marks and peculiarities to those which separate the persons of the Trinity; and when common Christians hear these persons spoken of as conversing with each other, loving each other, and performing different acts, how can they help regarding them as different beings, different minds? . . .

Source: William Ellery Channing, *Unitarian Christianity*, in *The Works of William E. Channing* (Boston: American Unitarian Association, 1882).

MORMONISM: JOSEPH SMITH

Mormonism encompasses a few historically related denominations, the largest of which is the Church of Jesus Christ of Latter-Day Saints. Mormon belief is founded on the work of Joseph Smith (1805–1844), who maintained that an angelic vision revealed to him the location of gold plates buried during a previous age. Smith's translation of these plates comprises the Book of Mormon, *first published in 1830. The work chronicles the history and religious practices of a band of Israelites who migrated to America in 600 B.C.E. Under two leaders, two distinct conflicting cultures emerged: the civilized Nephites, and the nomadic and warring Lamanites. Ostensibly the forefathers of the native Americans, the Lamanites exterminated the Nephites. Anticipating their demise, Moroni, a Nephite chronicler, buried a golden copy of the* Book of Mormon *to preserve their story. A twenty-page section of the* Book of Mormon *describes how Jesus visited the Nephites and gave them Christian doctrine, much of which is paraphrased from the Gospels. Selections from this are given below.*

11. . . . And it came to pass, as they understood they cast their eyes up again towards heaven; and behold, they saw a Man descending out of heaven; and he was clothed in a white robe; and he came down and stood in the midst of them; and the eyes of the whole multitude were turned upon him, and they durst not open their mouths, even one to another and wist not what it meant, for they thought it was an angel that had appeared unto them. And it came to pass that he stretched forth his hand and spake unto the people, saying:

Behold, I am Jesus Christ, whom the prophets testified shall come into the world. . . .

Behold, verily, verily, I say unto you, I will declare unto you my doctrine. And this is my doctrine, and it is the doctrine which the Father hath given unto me; and I bear record of the Father, and the Father beareth record of me, and the Holy Ghost beareth record of the Father and me; and I bear record that the Father commandeth all men, everywhere, to repent and believe in me. And whoso believeth in me, and is baptized, the same shall be saved; and they are they who shall inherit the kingdom of God. And whoso believeth not in me, and is not baptized, shall be damned.

Verily, verily, I say unto you, that this is my doctrine, and I bear record of it from the Father; and whoso believeth in me believeth in the Father also; and unto him will the Father bear record of me, for he will visit him with fire and with the Holy Ghost. And thus will the Father bear record of me, and the Holy Ghost will bear record unto him of the Father and me; for the Father, and I, and the Holy Ghost are one.

And again I say unto you, ye must repent, and become as a little child, and be baptized in my name, or ye can in nowise receive these things. And again I say unto you, ye must repent, and be baptized in my name, and become as a little child, or ye can in nowise inherit the kingdom of God. Verily, verily, I say unto you, that this is my doctrine, and whoso buildeth upon this buildeth upon my rock, and the gates of hell shall not prevail against them. And whoso shall declare more or less than this, and establish it for my doctrine, the same cometh of evil, and is not built upon my rock; but he buildeth upon a sandy foundation, and the gates of hell stand open to receive such when the floods come and the winds beat upon them. Therefore, go forth unto this people, and declare the words which I have spoken, unto the ends of the earth. . . .

17. Behold, now it came to pass that when Jesus had spoken these words he looked round about again on the multitude, and he said unto them: Behold, my time is at hand. I perceive that ye are weak, that ye cannot understand all my words which I am commanded of the Father to speak unto you at this time. Therefore, go ye unto your homes, and ponder upon the things which I have said, and ask of the Father, in my name, that ye may understand, and prepare your minds for the morrow, and I come unto you again. But now I go unto the Father, and also to show myself unto the lost tribes of Israel, for they are not lost unto the Father, for he knoweth whither he hath taken them.

And it came to pass that when Jesus had thus spoken, he cast his eyes round about again on the multitude, and beheld they were in tears, and did look steadfastly upon him as if they would ask him to tarry a little longer with them. And he said unto them: Behold my bowels are filled with compassion towards you. Have ye any that are sick among you? Bring them hither. Have ye any that are lame, or blind, or halt, or maimed, or leprous, or that are withered, or that are deaf, or that are afflicted in any manner? Bring them hither and I will heal them, for I have compassion upon you; my bowels are filled with mercy. . . .

18. . . . Therefore, keep these sayings which I have commanded you that ye come not under condemnation; for woe unto him whom the Father condemneth. And I give you these commandments because of the

disputations which have been among you. And blessed are ye if ye have no disputations among you. And now I go unto the Father, because it is expedient that I should go unto the Father for your sakes.

And it came to pass that when Jesus had made an end of these sayings, he touched with his hand the disciples whom he had chosen, one by one, even until he had touched them all, and spake unto them as he touched them. And the multitude heard not the words which he spake, therefore they did not bear record; but the disciples bare record that he gave them power to give the Holy Ghost. And I will show unto you hereafter that this record is true. And it came to pass that when Jesus had touched them all, there came a cloud and overshadowed the multitude that they could not see Jesus. And while they were overshadowed he departed from them, and ascended into heaven. And the disciples saw and did bear record that he ascended again into heaven.

Source: *Book of Mormon,* Third Nephi 11:8–10, 31–41; 17:1–7; 18:33–39.

JEHOVAH'S WITNESSES: CHARLES TAZE RUSSELL

The Jehovah's Witnesses denomination is based on the views of Charles Taze Russell (1852–1916), who, though not ordained, spent his life preaching about the second coming of Jesus. Russell believed that the Bible provided clues for the end times, and based on this belief he made an unsuccessful prediction of Jesus' return. Attracting many followers, he formed an independent church in 1878 and the following year founded a periodical called The Watchtower, *which became a major outlet for his theological views. Since 1931, the movement he started has gone by the name Jehovah's Witnesses. In this selection, Russell emphasizes Jesus' messianic role and the ability of the church to partake in the divine nature.*

The word Christ or *Kristos* is a Greek word, introduced into our English language, but not *translated* into it. Its translation is, ANOINTED.

"Unto us a child is born," etc., and "they shall call his name Jesus." The name Jesus means Deliverer or Savior, and the child was named in view of a work he was to do; for we are told, "he *shall* save his people from their sins." Jesus was always his name, but from the time of his baptism, when the Holy Ghost descended upon him and *anointed* him as the High Priest, preparatory to his making "the sin offering" on the cross, and thus accomplishing what is indicated by his *name,* his *title* has been "The Anointed,"—Jesus "the *Christ* (anointed) of God."—Lu 9:20. Jesus was frequently called by this *title* instead of by his name; as English people oftenest speak of their sovereign as "the Queen," instead of calling her by her name—*Victoria.*

But, as Jesus was in God's plan as the *anointed one,* before the foundation of the world, so too THE CHURCH of Christ, was recognized in the same plan; that is, God purposed to take out of the world a "little flock," whom he purposed raising above the condition of the *perfect human* nature, to make them "partakers of the *Divine nature.*" The relationship of Jesus toward these, is that of "*Head* overall, God blessed forever," "for he hath given him to head over *the church* (of the first-born) which is his body." As Jesus was foreordained to be *the anointed one,* so we, also, were chosen to the same anointing of the Spirit, as members in his body and under him as our head. And so we read (Eph 1:3:) "God hath blessed us with all spiritual blessings *in Christ* according as he hath chosen us *in him* before the foundation of the world, that we should be holy and without blame before him in love; having predestinated us unto the adoption of children by Jesus Christ to himself . . . wherein he hath made us accepted *in the beloved.*" (See also *vs. 20–23.*) Again, (Ro 8:29) "Whom he did foreknow he also did predestinate to be conformed to the image of his Son, that he (head and body) might be the *first-born* (heir) among many brethren."

God's plan of saving *the world* by a "restitution of all things," waits until first, this bride of Jesus—these members of the Spirit-anointed body, shall be gathered out from the world according to his purpose. . . .

Source: Charles Taze Russell, "The Christ of God," *Food for Thinking Christians,* part 5, in *Zion's Watchtower,* 1881.

CHRISTIAN SCIENCE: MARY BAKER EDDY

The Christian Science movement was founded by Mary Baker Eddy (1821–1910), who believed that the central message of Christianity is healing. In her most influential work, Science and Health *(1875), she argues that the material world and all illness associated with it are unreal and illusory. Healing comes after prayer when God simply removes the afflicted person's false belief in the illusion.*

Chapter 2. *Healing Primary.* First in the list of Christian duties, he [i.e., Jesus] taught his followers the healing power of Truth and Love. He attached no importance to dead ceremonies. It is the living Christ, the practical Truth, which makes Jesus "the resurrection and the life" to all who follow him in deed. Obeying his precious precepts—following his demonstration so far as we apprehend it—we drink of his cup, partake of his bread, are baptized with his purity; and at last we shall rest, sit down with him, in a full understanding of the divine Principle which triumphs over death. For what says Paul? "As often as ye eat this bread, and drink this cup, ye do show the Lord's death till he come."

Healing Early Lost. The proofs of Truth, Life, and Love, which Jesus gave by casting out error and healing the sick, completed his earthly mission; but in the Christian Church this demonstration of healing was early lost, about three centuries after the crucifixion. No ancient school of philosophy, *materia media,* or scholastic theology ever taught or demonstrated the divine healing of absolute Science.

Chapter 4. *Real and Unreal Identity.* The divine Mind maintains all identities, from a blade of grass to a star, as distinct and eternal. The questions are: What are God's identities? What is Soul? Does life or soul exist in the thing formed? Nothing is real and eternal—nothing is Spirit—but

God and His idea. Evil has no reality. It is neither person, place, nor thing, but is simply a belief, an illusion of material sense.

The identity, or idea, of all reality continues forever; but Spirit, or the divine Principle of all, is not in Spirit's formations. Soul is synonymous with Spirit, God, the creative, governing, infinite Principle outside of finite form, which forms only reflect.

Real Life Is God. When being is understood, Life will be recognized as neither material nor finite, but as infinite—as God, universal good; and the belief that life, or mind, was ever in a finite form, or good in evil, will be destroyed. Then it will be understood that Spirit never entered matter and was therefore never raised from matter. When advanced to spiritual being and the understanding of God, man can no longer commune with matter; neither can he return to it, any more than a tree can return to its seed. Neither will man seem to be corporeal, but he will be an individual consciousness, characterized by the divine Spirit as idea, not matter. Suffering, sinning, dying beliefs are unreal. When divine Science is universally understood, they will have no power over man, for man is immortal and lives by divine authority.

Chapter 6. *Christian Science Discovered.* In the year 1866, I discovered the Christ Science or divine laws of Life, Truth, and Love, and named my discovery Christian Science. God had been graciously preparing me during many years for the reception of this final revelation of the absolute divine Principle of scientific mental healing.

Causation Mental. Christian Science explains all cause and effect as mental, not physical. It lifts the veil of mystery from Soul and body. It shows the Scientific relation of man to God, disentangles the interlaced ambiguities of being, and sets free the imprisoned thought. In divine Science, the universe, including man, is spiritual, harmonious, and eternal. Science shows that what is termed *matter* is but the subjective state of what is termed by the author *mortal mind.*

Mind the Only Healer. Science not only reveals the origin of all disease as mental, but it also declares that all disease is cured by divine Mind. There can be no healing except by this Mind, however much we trust a drug or any other means towards which human faith or endeavor is directed. It is mortal mind, not matter, which brings to the sick whatever good they may seem to receive from materiality. But the sick are never really healed except by means of the divine power. Only the action of Truth, Life, and Love can give harmony.

Source: Mary Baker Eddy, *Science and Health*, from chs. 2, 4, and 6 (Boston: Christian Science Publishing Company, 1875).

NEW AGE CHRISTIANITY: LEVI H. DOWLING

The New Age religious movement is based on the astrological concept that the current Piscean age is closing and will be followed by a new age of Aquarius. With the coming of this new age, a new conception of the world and religious truth will also take hold, emphasizing the unity of all things, individual freedom, and the relativity of truth. New Age religion intentionally lacks the formal institutional and doctrinal structure of the major world religions and draws liberally from many religious sources—including astrology, Wicca, and paganism, as well as the major religions themselves. Among the influential New Age writings distinctly in the Christian tradition is the Aquarian Gospel of Jesus the Christ, *which first appeared in 1907. Its author, Levi H. Dowling (1844–1911), was a pastor and physician who claimed to have transcribed this book from the universal Akashic records. The work amplifies the account of Jesus' life and teachings in the New Testament, describing Jesus' childhood and trips to the Far East. Like the New Age movement itself, the religious views expressed here are highly eclectic, influenced particularly by Hinduism, Buddhism, Taoism, Gnosticism, and Zoroastrianism. The New Testament book of Matthew states that Joseph fled to Egypt with Mary and the infant Jesus, thereby avoiding Herod's efforts to kill the newborn king of the Jews. Developing this plot, Dowling describes Jesus' early childhood in Egypt under the tutelage of Elihu and Salome. Although the Elihu character does not appear in the New Testament, the book of Mark mentions a woman named Salome who was present at Jesus' crucifixion. In the selection below, Elihu lectures Mary and Jesus about the unity of all things, the higher and lower human selves, and the nature of God.*

Chapter 8. Again Elihu met his pupils in the sacred grove and said, No man lives unto himself; for every living thing is bound by cords to every other living thing. Blest are the pure in heart; for they will love and not demand love in return. They will not do to other men what they would not have other men do unto them. There are two selfs; the higher and the lower self. The higher self is human spirit clothed with soul, made in the form of God. The lower self, the carnal self, the body of desires, is a reflection of the higher self, distorted by the murky ethers of the flesh. The lower self is an illusion, and will pass away; the higher self is God in man, and will not pass away. The higher self is the embodiment of truth; the lower self is truth reversed, and so is falsehood manifest. The higher self is justice, mercy, love and right; the lower self is what the higher self is not. The lower self breeds hatred, slander, lewdness, murders, theft, and everything that harms; the higher self is mother of the virtues and the harmonies of life. The lower self is rich in promises, but poor in blessedness and peace; it offers pleasure, joy and satisfying gains, but gives unrest and misery and death. It gives men apples that are lovely to the eye and pleasant to the smell; their cores are full of bitterness and gall. If you would ask me what to study I would say, your selfs; and when you well had studied them, and then would ask me what to study next, I would reply, your selfs. He who knows well his lower self, knows the illusions of the world, knows of the things that pass away; and he who knows his higher self, knows God; knows well the things that cannot pass away. Thrice blessed is the man who has made purity and love his very own; he has been ransomed from the perils of the lower self and is himself his higher self. Men seek salvation from an evil that they deem a living monster of the nether world; and they have gods that are but demons in disguise; all powerful, yet full of jealousy and hate and lust; whose favors must be bought with costly sacrifice of fruits, and of the lives of birds, and animals, and human kind. And yet these gods possess no ears to hear, no eyes to see, no heart to sympathize, no power to save. This evil is myth; these gods are made of air, and clothed with shadows of a thought. The only devil from which men must be redeemed is self, the lower self. If man would find his devil he must look within; his name is self. If man would find his savior he must look within; and when the demon self has been dethroned the savior, Love, will be exulted to the throne of power. The David of the light is Purity, who slays the strong Goliath of the dark, and seats the savior, Love, upon the throne.

Source: Levi H. Dowling, *The Aquarian Gospel of Jesus the Christ,* ch. 8 (Los Angeles: Cazenove, 1908).

CPSIA information can be obtained
at www.ICGtesting.com
Printed in the USA
FFOW03n1309290813
1675FF

MGH000013694